S0-ARP-633

*James G. Simmons* is President of Cambrian Financial Corporation. A retired banker and 20-year veteran of commercial and industrial financing and leasing, he has been extensively involved in thousands of commercial loans, leases, and contracts.

# CREATIVE

How to Make Your Best Deal

# BUSINESS FINANCING

## When Negotiating Equipment Leases and Business Loans

JAMES G. SIMMONS

Prentice-Hall, Inc., Englewood Cliffs, New Jersey 07632

*Library of Congress Cataloging in Publication Data*

SIMMONS, JAMES G.
Creative business financing.

"A Spectrum Book."
Includes index.
1. Loans–Handbooks, manuals, etc.
2. Industrial equipment leases–Handbooks, manuals, etc. 3. Accounts receivable loans–Handbooks, manuals, etc. I. Title.
HG3751.S57 1982 658.1'5242 82-11250
ISBN 0-13-189159-6
ISBN 0-13-189142-1 (pbk.)

*Creative Business Financing: How to Make Your Best Deal When Negotiating Equipment Leases and Business Loans* by James G. Simmons


A SPECTRUM BOOK. Printed in the United States of America.

10 9 8 7 6 5 4 3 2 1

ISBN 0-13-189142-1 {PBK.}

ISBN 0-13-189159-6

Editorial/production supervision by Louise Marcewicz and Carol Smith
Cover design by Jeannette Jacobs
Manufacturing buyer: Barbara A. Frick



Prentice-Hall International, Inc., *London*
Prentice-Hall of Australia Pty. Limited, *Sydney*
Prentice-Hall Canada Inc., *Toronto*
Prentice-Hall of India Private Limited, *New Delhi*
Prentice-Hall of Japan, Inc., *Tokyo*
Prentice-Hall of Southeast Asia Pte. Ltd., *Singapore*
Whitehall Books Limited, *Wellington, New Zealand*

# CONTENTS

## 3

## THE MATHEMATICS OF FINANCING MADE EASY 70



## 4

## HOW TO NEGOTIATE YOUR BEST DEAL 120



## 5

## YOUR CREDIT AND FINANCIAL STATEMENTS 144



## 6

## GAMES LENDERS PLAY 200



## 7

## THE INSIDE SCOOP ON LEASING 225

# PREFACE

This book was written to assist business owners and their managers in making decisions when borrowing or arranging equipment financing. Students will find "real world" information and examples not ordinarily found in their textbooks. Those persons contemplating acquiring an established business or hoping to start their own will find this book an invaluable guide.

The field of commercial financing and leasing is a multifaceted, often-confusing segment of today's business world. There is a limited amount of reference material available on negotiating, contract fine print, accounts receivable financing, and obtaining financing using an effective presentation.

On the other hand, the accounting, financial statement, credit-collection, and paperwork aspects of business management suffer from a glut of information. Much of this reference material is presented in detailed, technical language not readily absorbed or put to practical use by busy owners or managers unskilled in financial management. The Uniform Commercial Code, for instance, runs to several volumes. We have segregated those parts that are relevant to business borrowers.

Persons who run their own businesses or managers who are responsible for the financing and accounting functions need to understand credit analysis and financial statements and their ratios. There are legal ramifications and tax implications peculiar to commercial financing and leasing. The book focuses on each of these areas by isolating problems commonly encountered by businesses when arranging financing.

Lenders are often secretive about their methods of making credit decisions and determinations of rate of interest. They are vague in communicating their expectations or requirements to "get the job done." There are other lender "secrets" they would just as soon leave a mystery to borrowers. Unhappy surprises are hidden away in the fine print. Verbal agreements or promises fail to appear in the final documents Borrowers find themselves too far into lending arrangements to change their minds or try elsewhere. Only then, with documents in front of them for final signature, do they learn of added collateral taken, restrictive covenants imposed, prepayment penalties, and a host of lender "safeguards" and boiler-plate legal requirements.

*Creative Business Financing* sifts through a plethora of detail and technical jargon to inform in an easy-to-read format. The reader can readily absorb new information and gain useful insight by reading the narrative, which is free of technical distraction. The charts and forms for specific technical applications are located at the end of each related chapter. They are available for ready reference whenever needed for resolving financing or leasing questions.

# 1

# KNOWLEDGE IS POWER

Borrowers often fear the banks and finance companies. Fear has its foundation in the lack of financial knowledge. To overcome fear of being turned down, of making mistakes, or of being taken advantage of, borrowers need to become more savvy to the ways of the lenders. There is a tendency on the part of the borrower to avoid that which appears complicated. The lenders sometimes instill fear by appearing mysterious, remote, and complex. The purpose of this book is simply to uncomplicate the basic elements, piece by piece, enabling borrowers to approach the lenders with knowledge and greater confidence.

The once simple world of commercial financing and business borrowing has become complicated. Loans are more difficult to obtain. If financing is located, the interest rate is horrendous. The major banks' latest prevailing prime rate is front-page news. Business people are making decisions on the basis of inflationary expectations.

The prime rate's fluctuations makes projecting money costs a guessing game, confounding the economists and frustrating business people. Banks seem more difficult to do business with. They pursue larger businesses, shunting smaller businesses aside more and more frequently. They demand more from smaller businesses: more information, more projections and planning, more detailed financial statements—and, yes, also more interest!

Gone are the days when equipment financing was a simple matter of a few references and a good down payment. Finance companies used to ask, "Do you pay promptly? Good, just sign here for 36 easy payments!" Remember how the banker once said, "Just come down and sign our note. Drop off a copy of your latest financial statement. We'll put the money in your account immediately"?

Those were the good old days, when the bank's prime rate was 6¾%. Most business people didn't think much about the prime rate. They just knew the banker would tack on a point or two to whatever their best rate was and it would be OK. Business people would say, "What's to worry? I'll pay about 8 or 9%, take an interest expense tax deduction, and end up paying an effective 4% or so."

Whatever happened to those good old days? Well, friends, they ended on August 22, 1977! On that day, the prime rate started a relentless upward march, never to see 6¾% again! The year 1978 saw 5% added to the prime, reaching 11¾%. Everyone thought it was terrible but strictly temporary. And 1979 wasn't much better, adding another 3½%, ending at 15¼%. Then came December 1980, when the prime rate hit 21½%—another 5¼% on top of the 1978 and 1979 increases. What is happening here? The economists and even the bankers kept saying, "It's only temporary, we've seen the top, things will get back to normal soon." In three years, the prime rate had more than tripled! An uncomplicated business finance world had suddenly become complex. Borrowing for working capital or to finance machinery and equipment became painfully expensive.

The prime rate of interest—the interest banks claim to charge their most credit-worthy customers—had reached astronomical levels many never even dreamt about three or four years earlier. To make matters even more unsettling, this once respected guideline rate has been fluctuating with disturbing frequency. In one four-month period in 1980, the rate went from 20% to 10¾%—a 9¼% swing! A few months later, it was up to 21½%. Not since the Civil War has the money market been so volatile, so disrupted.

Smaller businesses have become painfully aware of the prime rate. Once a mundane matter, a percentage number buried in the financial pages, it had become page one information. There are reports that this rate is no longer "law." It does not mean the same as it did just a few years ago. Some banks admit to loaning to select customers at rates below their prime rate. Here and there a maverick bank will go against the big banks' dictates and charge less than the prevailing prime rate. Like their customers, some banks were finding weekly ¼% to ½% up-and-down changes very disruptive.

For businesses, the average interest expense of loans has risen from approximately 14% of net profits, before taxes, to an attention-getting 45%! Incredible? That figure is right out of our government's statistics. Business loans obtained from banks are nearly all tied to the prime rate. With smaller businesses generally paying 1% to 4% over prime, it's no wonder they have learned the importance of the prime rate!

Interest rate fluctuations and high money costs are only part of business's feelings of consternation. Machinery and equipment have doubled and tripled in cost. Businesses need a computer to manage their accounting and inventories properly. Computers themselves represent a new and costly investment—not to mention additional complexity in getting them financed.

Machine tools have advanced from manual controls to numerical controls to computerized numerical controls. The lathe or milling machine that once cost about twice as much as a good automobile now costs more than the average home! Bulldozers and other construction equipment are in the same price class, many of them costing $150,000 to $250,000. Diesel truck tractors for highway hauling used to cost about $30,000. Try to find a new one today for twice that! High equipment costs complicate financing, especially when their costs accelerate so rapidly that product or services pricing cannot be proportionately adjusted. On top of much higher equipment costs, interest costs have tripled.

All of which brings us to another complication in today's business financing arena. How does the smaller business finance these greatly increased costs in equipment, machinery, and business machines? How do they cope with lagging receivables or borrow for working capital and other needs such as inventory? For many, if not all, businesses, failure to modernize and update plant and equipment results not just in stagnation but in failure altogether. The answer may be creative financing, much like in today's real estate market.

We are seeing down payment requirements decrease. Terms have been steadily increased in length. Tailor-made repayment plans were once mainly finance company talking points. Once in the while they materialized in the form of skip payments for winter downtime months. Now, even the usually staid banks are trying to innovate with special finance programs.

Equipment leasing is playing an increasing role in business's search for a means to acquire needed equipment while conserving cash. Leasing adds yet another complication to the decision process in light of today's high money cost and inflation mentality. There are some amazing things happening in the leasing business today, with the big money lenders taking some risks on future equipment values. Even some usually conservative lenders are providing "medium ticket" ($25,000-$250,000 cost range) equipment leasing with very little advance cash paid in. You should investigate this financing alternative. Even with tax gimmicks, varying tax considerations and differences in "lingo," leasing is not as complicated as you may think. Some advance knowledge in any finance situation goes a long way—but in leasing, a grasp of the fundamentals is essential. *Creative Business Financing* is going to provide you with those fundamentals.

## A LITTLE KNOWLEDGE GOES A LONG WAY

Knowledge is your best weapon in dealing with any lender—bank, finance company, or leasing company. After twenty-one years in the lending business, I have yet to see any miracle answers or secret finance sources that are of practical use to business people. And, particularly, no such answers or avenues have appeared that are available to smaller companies. Nothing beats simple awareness, preparedness, and advance planning. Nothing. For all practical purposes, your best avenue to obtain suitable financing is through better use of the conventional lending channels. You can perform your own miracles, using practical knowledge with these lenders, be they a bank or finance company or a private investor seeking a tax shelter or an opportunity to place money for profit.

A little knowledge is your best insurance against being overcharged or even ripped off by the lenders. A little knowledge goes a long way toward smoothly obtaining suitable financing for your business needs. Being able to borrow all of the money you need at the most attractive rates available is vital to your success. One objective of this book is to assist you in obtaining suitable financing at the proper price.

Let me emphasize my intentional use of the word *little*. It is accurate. It does not take extensive financial or mathematical knowledge to defend yourself in dealing with lenders. What it does take is preparedness. It takes knowing a little more about your business from an accounting and financial statement standpoint. And it takes knowing a little more about the lender's side of the fence.

Many of you are less successful in dealing with lenders than you could be. Uncertainty about borrowing money, not knowing how lenders think and how banks work, even fear of the bank results in decreased effectiveness and lost opportunities.

Look, no one wants to pay too much in interest or finance charges for a commercial loan or for business equipment acquired on a contract or lease. But many do, every business day. Everyone wants to feel he or she obtained fair and reasonably equal treatment from the scores of lenders businesses must turn to for their money. But they don't. Every single day, business people place their signature by that X, innocently agreeing to improper or unsuitable terms, conditions, and interest rates.

I know, because for over twenty years, as the lender's representative, I stood there and said, "Yes, just sign by the X—and here, and here—and don't forget to initial here and here. Yes, I'm sorry, there is a lot of fine print, but you know, it's all standard. No problem, really."

I know, because my record of volume production—loans, leases, and contracts—add up to some $125 million! There were over three thousand individual transactions requiring signatures by that X. I did a few jumbo deals in my time. But most of my kind of finance business involved small manufacturers, contractors, truckers, doctors, dentists, farmers, retail shop owners, restaurant operators, and just about every imaginable smaller business.

I make no pretense of having been lily-white. There *were* problems in that fine print. Although I would not rate-gouge, many of my loans, leases, or contracts could have been written at lower interest rates. Had my customers been more knowledgeable, more demanding they could have obtained better terms and conditions from my lender or elsewhere. Sometimes I still shudder, thinking about the hundreds of times my documents were signed in haste—never read or checked by my customers. Often the most penetrating question asked was, "What did you say my payments would be? Oh, yes, they came out close. Where do I sign?"

Believe me, business people, my customers should not have been so easy, even in the days of much lower interest costs. Today, and in the foreseeable future, with high inflation and double-digit interest rates, none of you can afford the luxury of such a casual approach to borrowing.

To familiarize you with the world of business financing, I am going to take you down my memory lane of those three thousand transaction experiences. In the least technical words and phrases possible, still maintaining textbook accuracy, *Creative Business Financing* will simplify and explain the financing business. We shall endeavor to uncomplicate the seemingly complicated.

In any business for profit, a great deal of knowing and doing precedes the actual sale. Selling money is no different. To understand obtaining financing and making your best deal, it will help you to understand financial knowing and doing. Money is a nice product—everyone wants it. The lenders have money stored on their shelves like cans of beans. The trick is deciding who qualifies as a money buyer and who doesn't. The sale is anticlimactic. Lenders have another advantage—they can sell their "beans" at all different prices. And they never have to run a special sale.

## WHY DO 400,000 BUSINESSES CLOSE THEIR DOORS EACH YEAR?

Business statistics reveal that only about 20% of all businesses started will survive! Over 400,000 businesses close their doors every year. That's the present shocking failure rate, with the number of actual bankruptcies accelerating with each passing year.

The primary reason given for business failure is undercapitalization. *Creative Business Financing* cannot do anything about those who plunge in undercapitalized. The sad truth is, many of those failures would have occurred anyway, even with more start-up capital. That is why undercapitalization is a catch-all term.

The truth of the matter lies somewhere in these paradoxical questions: Why do some businesses succeed even when they were started on a shoestring? Why do so many more businesses fail, after dumping in what should have been enough money?

The answers to these questions help substantiate our belief that undercapitalization is a catch-all explanation. Business success or failure is determined by numerous interrelated factors which defy a single, easy explanation.

The absence of financial planning would have to top the list of contributing factors. Failure to establish a business plan, with goals and objectives, is a common shortcoming of smaller businesses. Even the most elementary planning, such as income and expense projections, will help the lightly capitalized business survive. The simple act of putting your financial data on paper, where it can be reviewed and revised as needed, helps to avoid mistakes and decreases procrastination in decision making.

The problem with playing it by ear, especially with those who are less experienced and working with minimal capital, is in trying to convince the lenders you know where you're heading. Conversation is not only cheap, it is unconvincing unless you have a track record to talk about. If you don't have a track record, you need a believable written plan.

It is in recognition of these contributing factors that this book was put together, with the emphasis on increasing your financial knowledge and helping you to run your business more efficiently. Saving money by reducing interest expense is a benefit that should naturally follow.

It doesn't matter how severe the money or credit crunch is now or becomes in the future, *every* business must get its house in better order, just to survive in the computerized, tougher competition of the 1980s.

## MONEY CRUNCH EQUALS CREDIT CRUNCH

It doesn't matter if there is a credit crunch or if money is plentiful, running your business with greater efficiency is a continuing and evolutionary process. Making sound money-saving decisions—including preparing to obtain the money, negotiating for the money, making sure the terms and conditions are as right as you can make them—goes on, credit crunch or no credit crunch.

A credit crunch (selectivity as to who gets the money) starts with a shortage of lendable funds—a money crunch. In the immediate forseeable future, the emphasis is on getting the money, even though it is costly. Minimizing the cost, always desirable, must take a back seat to avoiding being eliminated from credit consideration and becoming a credit crunch casualty.

Professional financial counselors, people who make their living by arranging loans and financing, claim money is always available for well-run businesses. In their opinion, the most important element in financing is the availability of money. Structuring the financing is second. The cost of the money, the interest rate, is in third place. In our opinion, if money is extremely scarce, structuring and money costs are academic. The order of these elements is of little importance. Assuming availability of money, the financing arrangement consists of a blending of suitable terms, conditions, and interest costs. The way it works out, each of these elements will be arrived at by lender measurements of a business's stature, stability, and ability to repay. "Get the money at any price" can be carried too far.

These are the times when the lenders start separating the men from the boys—or the women from the girls, if you will! Marginal credits start getting turned down or pushed into even higher-cost loans, contracts, or lease arrangements. These are the times when the less knowledgeable, less efficient businesses are shunted onto sidetracks. The banks accelerate their quest for the larger, safer risks, where they can lend their restricted available funds.

These are the times when it is especially appropriate to tighten up your business operation. Reexamine your accounting, billing, and collection systems. Read and analyze your financial statements more thoroughly. If you must borrow money or buy equipment requiring financing, spend more time in planning and preparation. Give yourself more lead time prior to actual need. With money tight and costly, you cannot afford to approach the lenders ill-prepared.

## ASKING SIGNIFICANT QUESTIONS

The mark of an effective manager is one who is well prepared. To be an effective manager, you should master the art of asking significant questions. How can you possibly ask significant questions in a field like financing and leasing if you are not knowledgeable in those subjects? And how can you be knowledgeable when you spend 90% or more of your time just trying to keep your business running?

Now, let's take the topic another step. The art of negotiating requires you to put the adversary on the defensive. The way you do that is to ask questions—to which you know the answers—while the adversary doesn't even suspect you know the right questions!

Use questions that create discomfort. The most upsetting questions you can put to the lenders are those that surprise them. Remember, many lenders have already pegged you as just another dumb business person who is always "flying by the seat of your pants." Why not surprise them with your knowledge?

Use questions that will increase the lender's feelings of respect for you. Overcome the attitude prevalent among lenders, particularly bankers, that business people are generally deficient in financial knowhow. Many of these bankers and other lender representatives are firmly convinced that the bulk of their smaller business clients survive only by hard work, long hours, and sheer determination. Their commonly held belief is, you're great at widget making (or whatever your business does), but you know nothing about finance or accounting. Their thinly disguised disrespect can translate into higher interest costs unless you take steps to counter their preconceived notions.

Unfortunately, business people are often their own worst enemies when it comes to borrowing money or financing equipment. Poorly prepared financial statements are tossed in a file drawer after a cursory glance. Too many business people run their business out of their checkbook and their heads. Sure, that banker or lender representative takes you out to lunch and picks up the tab. But behind that smile you might find a leer. Can you hear them saying, "You are going to pay plenty for this lunch. You are going to pay for all the trouble you've put me through, piecing this loan together, with your inadequate financial statements and pie-in-the-sky projections. When I slide that extra ½% in, you'll never even know it!"

To illustrate the art of asking significant questions which will garner a little more respect and put the lender on the defensive for a change, I've selected some case histories. Sprinkled through these stories of circumstances and questions are tips you might employ. By using the technical data in this book, you can formulate your own significant questions to fit the circumstances.

### Floating Rate Loan

CIRCUMSTANCES The borrower has negotiated a five-year commercial loan for $100,000. He was quoted 2%, floating over the bank's prime rate, repayable monthly, principal and interest, on the balance.

The prevailing prime rate is defined as a bank's lowest interest rate being quoted to their best customers. At the time of this case history, the prevailing prime rate was 15%.

QUESTIONS The borrower is speaking to the commercial loan officer, who has returned to the borrower's place of business, to close the loan transaction. (The borrower has properly insisted on having the loan documents completely prepared and left for his review.)

"I have reviewed the loan documents, and I notice you have inserted a floor to the interest rate. That floor has been set at 13%. That seems to be a very comfortable minimum for your protection. It means I never pay less than 15%.

"I will get back to that. But first, answer this question: Where is my ceiling? How can you insert a floor and not offer me a ceiling? Do you have the authority to change that floor, which is too high, and insert a ceiling? If you do, we can settle this now. I will sign your loan documents. If you do not have the authority, can you reach your superior on the telephone to request his permission and approval of my suggestions?

"Bear in mind, friend banker, I am fully aware of the fact we keep an average balance of $20,000 on free deposit in our checking account. I know that this balance is worth money to you. Now your loan agreement calls for a checking balance of not less than 20% of any outstanding loan balances, exclusive of float.

"Now you are not talking about an *average* balance; not when you adjust for the float. For all practical purposes, you're talking about a *minimum* balance. Correct? You're going to loan me $100,000, but I get the use of about $80,000, correct? According to my calculations, with the prime at 15%, me floating at 2%, and adding about 4½% for that free deposit balance you can reinvest, I'm paying 21½%, not 17%. I also notice that your bank is using a 360 day year. When you figure interest on that basis, I'm paying almost ¼% additional interest, true?*

"So here is my proposal. I stay with your bank. You keep the historical average of $20,000 as your compensating balance. I will agree to reasonably maintain that average. How's that?

"You decrease your floor from 13% to 10%—that's in excess of your average money cost anyway. You insert a ceiling of 19%, OK? Now, friend banker, if you'll just put your initials right here and here, agreeing to these minor adjustments, you'll still have me as a nice commercial depositor."

## Lease

CIRCUMSTANCES Getting ready to acquire new shop equipment, you have decided to investigate leasing, to minimize cash outlay. Other than your car lease, you have not had experience with this financing alternative. For comparison, you have obtained four lease quotations.

The quotes are confusing, even though it is a simple matter to multiply the payments out and then add the purchase option to arrive at the gross cost. However, each quote involved a different number of advance rentals, two had oddball terms of 66 and 69 months, and two proposed a true lease. One of these required that the lessor retain the investment tax credit; the other would pass it through to you.

You decide to investigate the lease quote that permits you to retain the ITC. The investment tax credit can be as much as 10% of the equipment's purchase price. At tax time you can deduct the ITC from your tax obligation. This deduction is treated in more detail in chapter seven, "The Inside Scoop on Leasing."

QUESTIONS The bank leasing representative who provided the quote comes to your office for a second round of discussions. These are the questions you should ask:

"Your quote has outlined the rental payments and other cost factors; but you end up stating that the quote is "subject to credit approval." When we first met, you were provided three year-end financial statements, our bank and other credit references, and my personal financial statement. What else do you require to provide a firm

***Our business owner obtained the 4½% free deposit percentage from our chart titled "Compensating Balances and Equivalent Yields" at the end of chapter four. The comment about a 360-day year's adding interest was derived from Figure 1-1 at the end of this chapter.**

approval? I want to know now. I want prior approval now, so I know what I have, if I agree to your terms."

The reply is: "We first want to know if you will go ahead with our lease, if we do approve it. Saves us wasting our time."

"You have things turned around. My time is valuable, too, and as your potential customer, I am entitled to your commitment in exchange for my commitment. Doesn't that seem fair to you?"

The reply is: "We get lots of companies like yours. After we break our necks and make a firm commitment, you shop our rate.

"Isn't that my prerogative? How else can I make valid comparisons? I don't intend to split hairs, I appreciate your efforts, but I expect you to treat me like I do my customers. I make my quotes as competitive as possible, to get the business and make a profit. They know once I've quoted I will deliver at that price. There's no 'subject to' or 'maybe.' Why not do what I do? I commit for sixty days but require confirmation agreement within fifteen days.

"While you are here, let's resolve my other questions, to save us both time. You call this a 'true' lease. I want an exact copy of the investment tax credit pass-through form you provide. Do you have one with you?

"You have stated that at lease termination I may purchase the equipment for fair market value. I want a copy of the exact terminology you provide. Is the purchase option clause in the lease document, or is it on a separate page? Do you have the option clause with you?

"You said you were able to provide a low monthly payment because your bank is utilizing the depreciation. I have present-valued the accelerated depreciation allowances that I would normally have with a financed purchase. Then I factored in the 10% security deposit, and I ran a yield calculation. It appears to me that your 'lower' rental payment is not returning to me the benefits I am losing with this 'true' lease. Are you prepared now, or when you return, to show me in black and white my actual trade-off benefits and your interest earnings?

When you were here the first time, you said the lease would contain renewal options. There is no mention of this in your quote. When you come back, I am requiring you to provide these renewal options, giving their explicit conditions and annual percentages.

"And before you leave, please provide me with an exact copy of every document you will require. In the event we get together, I want to be able to examine them beforehand, without any pressure."

## Skip-Payment Loan

CIRCUMSTANCES In order to produce several close-tolerance component parts, in fairly small repetitive batches, you have decided to purchase a $265,000 CNC machining center. This machine will reduce setup time, minimize inspection procedure, and may be operated by less costly employees.

You are not worried about the machine's paying for itself. You're concerned with making provisions for handling the payments out of normal cash flow. Because the processing and shipping time of the parts is running forty-five days, followed by thirty to forty days before payment is received, the money turnaround time is averaging seventy-five days.

Your bank has declined the financing, feeling it was "too big an investment" in relation to your net worth. They were also unwilling to provide the special terms and longer repayment time you requested. Convinced the machine is a wise investment, you have called in two commercial finance companies to see what they could offer. We relate below an abbreviated line of questioning, centering only on rate and terms.

QUESTIONS "Your advertisements in the trade journals boast how flexible you can be in fitting terms to circumstances. Can you offer skip payments on a machine tool like you do on bulldozers when they are idle in the winter months?

"After I put 20% cash down, I need three skip months for the start-up time. Then I will need annual skips in August and September, to cover the slow cash flow months caused by vacations. You see, I half shut down in July to concentrate the vacations over about five weeks. It shows up in the cash flow in August and September.

"Can you offer this kind of special repayment plan? I have never dealt with a finance company before, so you tell me how you go about calculating something like this. Also, what is your desired yield—your total interest rate—for seven-year financing?

"Oh, by the way, have you ever heard of a book called *Creative Business Financing*? They offer a skip-payment calculator formula for my guidance. When you make your payment quotation, remember I'll be checking you out."

## LOSING BY INTIMIDATION

Our significant question examples incorporated a couple of recommended negotiating elements, surprise and discomfort—using the power of knowledge to put your adversary on the defensive and to gain respect.

The underlying premise is that even though the lender has the money you want and need, *you* must conduct the interview. Ask the right questions. Voluntarily provide the lender with answers and information he will require anyway. Stay ahead and stay more in control. Do not allow the lender's questions to intimidate you. Give him fewer questions to ask by anticipating them. It is not easy for the lender to put you on the defensive if you are prepared and use previously acquired knowledge on him.

Bankers make a big deal out of taking a risk, lending their depositors' money, to earn their money markup. True enough, but you are the one giving them that profit opportunity. You are paying the lender back, not with someone's deposit or spare venture money but with money you must earn by your sweat and risk.

Sometimes when you are in the negotiating stages the lender goes into that old "we're doing you a favor" routine. There is a tendency for you to fall into line and momentarily forget about your long pay-back obligation. If you do, your negotiating aggressiveness has been dulled by intimidation. The result can be that you pay a little more or agree to unwarranted restrictive terms and conditions.

Constantly bear in mind that you are the business person who will be doing the paying back, including a profit for the lender. The lenders make a big deal about "living with" a loan or lease for those *l-o-n-g* contract years. Don't lose by intimidation; don't forget you'll be living with it too. You owe it to yourself to negotiate every loan, lease, or contract to the best of your ability and to your best possible advantage.

## YOUR INTEREST RATES: "BY GUESS AND BY GOLLY"

The interest or finance charge rates being offered to commercial and industrial businesses has historically been less regulated and less formalized than any other lending market. Automobile finance rates are frequently advertised and are subject to truth-in-lending and consumer protection laws. The annual percentage rate (APR) must be disclosed. Housing mortgage or trust deed interest rates are clearly stated by sellers and lenders. Not so with commercial and industrial loans and equipment financing. Except for the much talked about prevailing prime rate, business people have little to guide them as to the going rate.

The major national finance companies have a "street rate," which is often exactly the same from one company to another. But just try calling them on the telephone for a best-rate quotation! They might "ball-park" a quote. More likely they will hedge and try to qualify you through a myriad of questions. If they like your answers, they will want to send out a field representative.

If you call your bankers, unless he or she knows you well and has previously loaned you money, you will be asked to stop in to discuss your needs. Rarely will the banker quote a rate flat out. "Let's see what we can work out. I'll try to get you a point or two over prime rate." If you call another bank, where you are not a depositor, you will probably get a qualifying routine and, perhaps, a ball-park rate quote. If your needs are big enough in dollars, the banker may want to come visit you. If not, you'll be invited to drop around. "We'll work something out. We'd like to have you for a customer." Why not? Interest isn't usually paid on commercial checking accounts.

The point is, you can't shop interest rates on the telephone. You must first deal with a contact person—a bank loan officer, finance company field representative, account manager, or any of a dozen other titles used to describe the person with whom you must first negotiate. Whether you recognize it or not, this is the beginning of your problem—dealing with the lender's contact person. But instead of a problem, consider it a challenge and an opportunity.

Nearly everyone must pay a money markup. The prime rate is "reserved for the bank's best customers"—but even *they* pay a money markup. They're simply buying their money at the bank's lowest retail price. Because they represent minimal risk and are big depositors, some banks admit to loaning to them at below their prevailing prime rate.

All the rest of us "buck privates" pay a "spread" over the prime rate. Being much riskier than those best customers, we pay a higher retail price. And, as the risk increases—in the lenders' opinion—they are obliged to increase the spread. "Risk is a major element of rate determination," the lenders are fond of saying, but believe me, the determination of risk versus rate is a very inexact science!

"By guess and by golly" enters into determining how much money markup will be charged. The difference between 1% over prime rate and 3% over prime can be influenced by emotions, prejudices, temperament, favoritism versus dislike of a particular person or type of business, the degree of competence of a loan officer—a host of interpersonal differences or conflicts. There is even intragroup conflict—satisfying the real or imagined needs of the lender's top management. Line managers are told, "My department gets top rates. We have no losses. When quoting a rate, always start a little high; you can always come down."

These human elements insert themselves into virtually all commercial lending. They can vitally affect your borrowing costs. Remarkably similar businesses, with virtually the same financial statements and profit pictures, end up paying entirely different rates. This may occur with the same lending institution or from one bank to another down the street, or within the same finance or leasing company or from one to another down the street.

Aside from the human elements at work in the lender world of business financing, lenders have definite problems with measurement standards and rate determination. We're not saying lenders lack measuring tools. But after they have spread your financial statements, they are not always sure what the answers really mean. Good ratios are an obvious plus. Poor ratios are clearly a negative. However, businesses are extremely diverse, and the black-and-white, arithmetical answers are sometimes insufficient for decision making. The numbers are history, out of the past. They are an important reflection of track record, but they cannot reveal for sure the future—such as new management's plans for a turnaround, new products, better controls, or other positives just then taking place. Few lenders have credit analysts or loan committees who know every type of business.

To get a reading on a particular business, they must depend to some degree on their customer-contact person. If they are not highly motivated, poorly trained or ill-informed, *you* are likely to suffer. Your lender contact person has latitude in deciding what to tell you and what to quote as a rate. You are very dependent on this person to carry your story to the lender's credit management. You must provide this person with the unwritten story that does not appear in your financial statements. It is to your ultimate benefit to supply this person with whatever is needed. Do this promptly and in sufficient detail, so that he or she can "do a number" on the credit numbers people!

The next chapter, "How to Make a Good Presentation," will help you work effectively with the lender's contact person. A complete presentation can make the difference between a credit approval and a denial. It can vitally affect the rate you end up paying.

## HUMAN FACTORS: BORROWERS VERSUS LENDERS

Business financing, by its very diversity, defies formularization. There is a much wider range of possible interest rate charges for businesses, all of which may be acceptable credit risks. Automobile financing is set up with a very narrow range of rates and acceptable down payments. Collateral decisions are made with the help of an accepted guidebook of values. The credit risk is measured by a series of "scores" derived from the borrower's credit references and indications of stability. The questions are predictable: Homeowner? How long lived there? How long on the job? Bad score? No car from *us*! Go see some other company!

The credit manager or loan officer performing this scoring task doesn't need credit judgment, he or she just needs to know what numbers to insert and which box to check and to be able to add a column of numbers. This is not so with business financing.

On the other side of the coin are the very human business people. They are not protected by consumer truth-in-lending and rate-disclosure laws. When you and your human factors are pitted against the lender's, and you throw in all the types of businesses, the array of kinds of equipment being used, and set the pot boiling with your financial statements—which too often range from barely adequate to just plain awful—you may begin to see how unscientific the "rate and risk" process really is!

*C'est la guerre*? It can't be helped? Many business people accept these problems of doing battle with the lenders as inevitable, part of the business borrowing game. We would like to encourage business people to minimize those negative "*C'est la vie*" feelings. Business borrowing does not have to be antagonistic or uncomfortable. Those austere and sometimes difficult-to-approach bankers are only human beings. Like yourself, they have their own set of problems to live with each day.

### Threatening Is Not Negotiating

If our series of circumstances and questions was not directly applicable to your business and negotiating problems, we hope you were able to read between the lines enough to see how adaptable the inferences might be to your situation. Rather than utilizing the purely technical approach, we are trying to put across a number of messages through a story-type approach. Here are two messages we want to convey: Threatening is *not* negotiating, and being a nice guy (or gal) can—but doesn't necessarily—produce results.

Let's look at threatening as a substitute for negotiating. Even though you may be an important bank customer or a major repeat borrower with a finance or leasing company, do not waste your leverage or clout using threats. "I'll yank my account!" . . . "That's the last deal I'll ever do with you people!" . . . "I'll sign *this* time, but never again!"

You may have scared hell out of the branch manager or someone in the sales end of banking or finance, but you probably lost the war. You might feel better after venting your wrath, but you made a deal you basically didn't like. You yelled and they won. If you have clout, use it like a velvet glove around the manager's neck. Have your alternative moves firmly arranged, just in case! Idle threats are a waste of time and effort. Like the boy who cried "wolf!" too often, the lenders get to know who you are. They laugh when you leave the premises or get off the telephone knowing you'll be back for more.

Threatening can also backfire and cost you even more money. Up jump those human factors. You need the support of that bank manager or other lender contact person to carry the ball to those credit managers. (They're the ones with the combination to the safe!) Even though you are totally upset with the manager and his lending institution, your objective is to *motivate* that person to work on those who have the final say. You want to get that contact person to request a lower rate, better terms—preferably in the first place, and certainly in any renegotiation or future financing situation.

Here's why pure threat can work against you: the person you are dealing with can have literally a score of negative positions or attitudes. To name a few, your lender contact person may:

- be ready to quit anway, so doesn't care;
- be ready for promotion and doesn't care (This person may even remember and get you from that new position of authority);
- be virtually powerless to change things, so they strike back at you for causing them embarrassment, frustration, or trouble;
- be able to change things, but your threatening causes negative instead of positive responses;
- chalk it up to bad mood or any number of possible personal problems; your threats fall on a closed mind and you end up ninety-ninth on the officer's care list. No motivation was possible.

The list of human factors is endless, but it boils down to this: Avoid character assassination or attacking the person. Deal in facts, not outraged verbiage. Ask knowledgeable, factual questions that continually require agreement; seek positive action, not negative or defensive answers. Go for accomplishment of your objectives by garnering respect rather than winning by fear. Definitely use your clout or leverage, but only while striving to enlist the support of the person addressed.

### Nice Guys Can Produce Results

It's nice to be nice. But there is a difference between being a "real nice guy," all soft and pliable, and one who nicely insists on fairness and best efforts from the lenders. I am in total disagreement with those who advocate winning by being an S.O.B. Suggestions that require domination, fear, threats, and miserableness are not suitable ways of operating for smaller businesses. Few small businesses have the leverage or clout to successfully carry off a power approach with lenders.

On the other hand, there is a definite danger in being purely a nice, pleasant person in dealing with lenders. The reason is simple: lenders count on finding enough "easy marks" to make up for all those hard negotiators who through knowledge and preparedness insist on the best possible rate and terms. Nice guys finish last if nice is all they are.

Lenders also count on the vast number of business people who are psyched into being just plain grateful that the lender condescends to loan them anything. Within this same group are those who rationalize their negotiating weaknesses. They minimize the impact of extra interest costs on their bottom line with excuses such as "It's tax-deductible anyway" or "Live and let live" or "It doesn't amount to that much anyway. I'll just tack it onto my product or service charges."

There are two other nice-guy types who most consistently pay more and get less from the lenders: the I'll-throw-myself-on-the-mercy-of-the-court type and the bootlicker soft-soap type.

The show-me-mercy type is perpetually unprepared. Lacking knowledge, he lives in constant awe of simple mathematics, accounting, and lenders in general. This nonnegotiator type is the one most frequently brushed aside by the banks for their lower-cost loans and leases, ending up in the clutches of some high-binder loan or lease company that really shows no mercy. They make this nice guy pay for being led by the hand. The sad part of this story is that many such business people do not belong in the high binder's clutches, if they would just take the time and make the effort to strengthen their negotiating armaments.

The show-me-mercy types that do manage to borrow from the banks pay top rates. They persist in starting out every negotiation with the plaintive attitude "I don't know anything about financing (or leasing), but I know you'll be fair with me because I'm a real nice guy."

The boot-licker or soft-soaper thinks that if he is super nice to the lenders and bows and scrapes often enough, the lender will return his nice-guy overtures by giving him the lowest rate, the fairest deal he could ever have obtained by the minor discomfort of negotiating. "Fred is such a nice guy, I couldn't possibly overcharge him!" Oh, no?

This nonnegotiator type thinks that by buddying up to the bank manager or finance or leasing company representative there is no necessity of actually working out loan or lease details or the interest rate. Having ingratiated himself with friend lender, a "good enough" deal will automatically be forthcoming.

This nice guy or gal thinks all he or she needs to do is toss together some financial statements and make a generalized request. Lender friend will do all the rest. Some friendly conversation, a cocktail or two, supposedly does wonders in smoothing over poorly prepared statements, a loosely run business operation, and any number of shortcomings. Just have faith, be nice, and it will all work out for the best.

Unquestionably, a friendly relationship with any lender representative is invaluable in obtaining financing. If your relationship is long-standing and the lender is kept well informed and supplied with updated financial data, being a nice person is highly commendable. This solid, respect-producing customer status often results in the lender friend's offering his or her very best, without being leaned on at all.

Sometimes, because you have been straight and decent, though vulnerable, your lender friend will piece together a loan or lease simply because you are a friend. However, this type of relationship is becoming increasingly rare because of the demands placed on lender representatives by their bank or loan company management. The ever-present system of checks and balances imposed on bank officers or other lender representatives makes it impossible to help an otherwise unprepared friend.

The truth about the nice-guy glad-hander who is not in a well-established position with the lender or does not have a hard-working lender ally is that he only incurs lender disdain. He'll pay a price for whatever he gets. The same holds true for the nice guy who is too easy, too trusting, even if he is well qualified as a commercial borrower or lessee.

Like the person who buys a car from a close relative or uses the services of a neighbor who is a lawyer, very often, these close-relationship deals are not the best you could have obtained from a perfect stranger—and that's putting it mildly!

The major instances in which the pure and simple nice guy loses out occur under the following general circumstances:

- The lender friend, knowing his man and sure that he will not be challenged, charges nice-guy customer as much as or more than the harder, more businesslike negotiator. In fact, relying on a number of these nice-guy relationships, he will consistently make up for the skinny deals with the nice guy deals.
- The lender representative, outwardly all smiles, is gritting his teeth, anxious for revenge upon the soft-soaper for making him

work so hard, piecing together inadequate data into a doable loan or lease. Mr. Nice Guy will pay in the end!

- The lender friend is fired, promoted, transferred, or retired. The nice guy abruptly learns that being a nice guy doesn't mean a thing to the new manager.
- The nice guy's latest request exceeds the lender friend's credit limit. And, brother, those hard-nosed credit managers downtown in the ivory tower could hardly care less about Mr. Nice Guy—they go by the numbers. And sometimes, if the lender friend manager dares to say, "This is my friend, Mr. Nice Guy. Take care of him," the results are *worse*!

So, be honest with yourself. If you have had show-me-mercy, glad-hander or easy-and-trusting tendencies, think about what can happen to you if you have come to rely upon the nice-guy routines. They're not a substitute for being a good business person—a negotiator to be reckoned with. It is entirely possible to be a well-liked, respected business person and still achieve acceptable results. But in today's ever-changing world, with often short-lived friendships and cold, hard facts, don't expect nice conversation to consistently carry the day.

### How Borrowers Do It to Themselves

Being a nice, trusting person—easily pushed around by the lenders—is just one way borrowers do it to themselves. It's been almost an American tradition for business people to accept with a shrug whatever the lenders dish out. The problem has become that ready acceptance of "that's how it is" is now an expensive attitude to take. Even if you are in the 50% tax bracket, paying 25% simple interest still costs about an effective 12½%, after expensing money cost. You know interest expense is eating into your profits at such high percentages.

It's inescapable: if we must borrow or finance equipment these days, all must pay the higher rates. But wandering into poorly structured loans and leases at excessive rates because you "hate to haggle" or believe too much in "live and let live" is becoming an expensive as well as dumb excuse. Those attitudes must join "It's tax deductible anyway" as a weak rationale.

If we could peek into the lenders' customer files, we would find untold thousands of loans on a "floating with prime" basis. Although there are no public statistics, my personal records indicate that many of these transactions involved no ceiling on the interest rate. True, from 1977 through late 1979, with the prevailing prime rate ranging from 6½% to 12¾%, the wisdom of asking for a ceiling of 15% or so may not have been apparent. When you add that oversight to the usual lackadaisical borrower acceptance of a 2% to 4% float percentage when by simply asking or through a little negotiating the float percentage could have been ½% to 2%, we can see how we may have done it to ourselves. Just a few months after September 7, 1979, the rate skyrocketed to

20%! Shocked business people who found negotiating distasteful started receiving interest-payable notices of 24%!

After twenty years of negotiating and closing loans, leases, and contracts with a cross-section of small to medium-sized businesses, I developed a summary of recurring mistakes or negotiating weaknesses commonly encountered. I hope you will accept my list in the constructive spirit in which it is offered—even if you see yourself mirrored somewhere in my words.

*Don't count on or expect too much from unmotivated lender people.* Even those who are motivated (or would like to be) are enmeshed in the rules, regulations, and general red tape of huge bank or finance company bureaucracies. Be willing to lead them by the hand and help them rather than hurting yourself by complaining when they "don't do their job."

*Don't be stubborn, hard-nosed, or antagonistic.* "If they want something, let 'em ask" only costs you time and money in the end. Be cooperative and businesslike, and expect the same from the lender people.

Blustering, overly pushy business people who uniformly try to win by threat and fear may be astounded to learn they are uniformly paying more because every lender representative has some latitude to set the rate. Unless you have real clout at the bank or finance company, being overbearing will backfire more often than it succeeds.

*Don't get taken in by low-ball or approximate quotes.* It happens to everyone somewhere along the way, but the damage occurs when your ego gets in the way and you refuse to admit you were had or that due to your carelessness you fail to detect how expensive those raised-up "approximates" turned out.

*Manage your time; set priorities.* When you are sitting down to negotiate, focus completely on the matter at hand. Forget the phone bill you want to reduce, shop problems that may need solving, and all other distractions.

Don't permit interruptions or outside interference. Devote all the time and attention the negotiating may require—within reason and on *your* time schedule, not necessarily the lender's.

Don't talk when you should be listening.

*Always take notes; don't rely on your memory.* If you are requesting finance or lease quotes from several lenders, make notes of each conversation or telephone call. Head each page with the company name, contact person's name, and phone number. Even if you are dealing with only one or two lenders, jot down the essentials.

Situations arise in which the lender representative makes promises that are legal commitments. It's easier to enforce them if you kept careful written notes. Equally important are those situations in which the contact person purposely "low-balls" the rate or the monthly payments. They are counting on being able to add fractional percentage amounts or a few dollars to each monthly payment to reach an acceptable yield for the lender—or to increase his or her own commission!

When the completed documents are placed in front of you, compare all rate, term, and payment aspects to your notes. Don't sign if you feel there are unexplained deviations.

Your notes are also useful for reconsideration and calculations after the contact person leaves. Use your notes in discussions with partners, department managers, or your accountant.

## BANK MONEY COSTS

Banks do not have the same money costs. Their borrowing costs depend in part on the size of their checking and savings account base. Large banks have huge sums of internally generated monies to lend out. They have a much larger float of lendable funds flowing through daily. Of course, banks must maintain required reserve levels to back up demand deposits and to cover those loans that become uncollectable. When you read about the New York Federal Reserve Bank's discount rate—the rate the "Fed" charges member banks when they borrow—and you see a rate only fractionally below the existing prime rate, don't feel sorry for those banks. Many banks rarely, if ever, use the Fed as a source of wholesale money. Also, do not confuse the federal discount rate with federal funds. The discount rate is the federal reserve's charge on loans made to member banks. National banks are members of the federal reserve system. State banks may join if they wish.

The funds most used by banks are the federal funds. These are reserve monies, in sums of $1 million or more, traded among commercial banks for overnight use on a bid basis. Banks needing these monies paid record-breaking interest rates exceeding 20% for brief periods in 1980-81. It's hard to make a profit, paying wholesale prices as high as the prime rate! The banks are more accustomed to 2% to 4% markups from federal fund monies (to their prime rate). Then, of course, for all those borrowers "floating" 1% to 3% over prime, their money cost becomes prime plus 3% to 7%.

After blending available free checking account balances, lower-interest passbook savings accounts, and interest-bearing checking accounts, banks usually have base average money costs of something like 7%. Unfortunately, many savings accounts have left the banks in search of higher earnings. Still, the banks have huge savings deposits to work with, at lower interest rates and massive interest-free or low-interest checking accounts. In recent times, bank money costs have been pushed steadily upwards by higher-yielding Certificates of Deposit and other similar types of long-term savings instruments, issued in large denominations. When all sources of lendable funds are averaged together—from what are now high-priced discount rates and federal funds to free commercial checking account monies (which they have constantly for no more than the cost of the people and machinery needed to handle them)—the banks obviously still enjoy ample profits.

## DEALING WITH THE BANKS

The biggest banks, despite their lower money costs and their ability to attract more lendable funds, are not necessarily the best places for small or medium-sized business owners to go money-shopping. Nor do they necessarily offer the lowest rates. Because of their size, many are inflexible, making negotiating a lower rate less possible. Here are the disadvantages of dealing with many of the big banks and their far-flung branch systems:

- Customer-oriented money-gathering outposts—Managers are running a three-ring circus, force-focused upon checking accounts and auto and home improvement loans and riding herd on tellers.
- Inadequate branch manager credit limits—This forces extensive, heavily detailed loan request writeups, which take time and effort and cause managers to give up.
- Long, highly structured lines of authority—Many confirming signatures are required on every loan, with too many in and out baskets along the way.
- Unresponsive local managers—The distance between the lowly branch and top management makes it easy for branch managers to escape being held accountable for evasiveness or inordinate time consumed in loan processing. It is difficult for top management to know what's really going on in the branches, and if they ask questions, the branch can make up excuses that are hard to verify.
- Rate structuring by formula—Big bank organizations tend to cast rate guidelines in concrete. Managers work with manuals a foot thick and must "go by the book."
- Managers lack business-type expertise—Branch managers tend to be jacks of all trades, with little business-analysis experience. They lack loan-structuring expertise and are inclined toward playing it safe and just running the store.
- Your clout is lost; you're just a number—The bigger the pool, the smaller the fish.

We realize you may have little choice but to deal with a big bank. When you look around, all you see are more big banks—and a bank is a bank is a bank. If you are forced to deal with a big bank, we have some suggestions that will assist you in coping with their managers.

Big-bank branches are woefully ill-equipped to handle efficiently many of your business financing requirements. This is particularly true when it comes to equipment financing and leasing. It is also true with regard to the many other specialized forms of business-type financing, such as inventory loans, accounts receivable financing, rediscounting, and floor-plan financing.

When shopping for a bank offering any of these particular services, you must not only determine availability—you also need to know the bank's guidelines to qualify for those services. Some large banks tend to favor big businesses when it comes to inventory loans, receivable financing, and equipment financing. For instance, it is futile to select a bank because it offers receivable financing only to learn they require $100,000 per month of pledged invoices and your sales are only half that amount.

If possible, go directly to the manager or bank officer in charge of the particular specialized department or departments you need. Find out what their policies and guidelines are, and relate them to your business. Don't waste your time on a bank that cannot get down to your requirement or size level. If your balance sheet or sales volume don't measure up to the guidelines, go elsewhere—don't fight it!

Unfortunately, most big-bank systems require that you start your discussions and negotiations with your branch manager. Even more unfortunately and too frequently, this manager is not knowledgeable enough and is torn in too many different directions to be really effective or positively helpful. And this includes the many managers who are well-intentioned, as well as the unqualified buffoons masquerading as bankers. They are caught up in the "big system," just like you are.

For these reasons, you will save time and money if you resolve yourself to come to the bank manager fully prepared and willing to lead *him* by the hand to obtain what you want!

## Yes, You Can Negotiate with Your Banker!

When it comes to your interest rate, remember, even with the big banks (and their monolithic interest rate guidelines), your initial contact with their loan officer or manager is important. Here are considerations to bear in mind:

Most bank officers have some latitude in what they may charge as your interest rate. This latitude also extends to what they are willing (or unwilling) to write up and recommend to a credit officer or committee.

Knowing this, rate negotiation should be preceded by an adequate verbal and written presentation of vital facts and financial data.

You must do a selling job on the loan officer.

The time for rate negotiation is immediately after the presentation and selling job but *before* the loan officer writes a single word for loan committee review.

If the loan officer requests time to review everything, which they often do, specifically request that you meet again to discuss your requirements before he writes it up. This is the time to correct any errors or misconceptions about your company's financial status. This is the time to be certain the financing is structured to your business needs and cash flow.

It is a mistake to postpone rate of interest discussions until after the loan officer has completed the write-up. Once a bank officer has written a recommendation down, he or she starts to believe it is cast in stone.

It is an even bigger mistake to allow the write-up to be completed, sent to credit review, returned as approved, and then start rate negotiating. The loan officer becomes personally committed to his or her recommendation. The credit manager or committee has locked into the rate as an integral part of the rate-and-risk consideration. Very few loan officers have the authority or the desire to lower a credit-approved rate.

Unless you have previously established what is a "going and satisfactory" rate for your loan requests, never let the loan officer proceed with the write-up without knowing what he or she is going to insert in the write-up.

Never underrate the importance of simply asking for a rate of interest lower than the suggested rate first offered. (Figures 1–2 through 1–6 at the end of this chapter demonstrate how rewarding small rate reductions can be.) Like the young salesman who could not understand his mediocre performance until the "old pro" sales manager asked him, "Are you asking for the order or expecting volunteers?" Never be afraid to ask for a lower rate than the loan officer first volunteers!

## What Do You Want from Your Bank, Convenience or Expertise?

If your business requires strong bank services in special areas—accounts receivable financing, real estate, vendor financing or rediscounting (placing your product sales into some form of credit line for long-term contract financing or leasing), inventory or flooring-type loans, machinery financing or leasing—it's unwise to open an account at a bank that is merely convenient.

If you are fortunate enough to locate a bank that fulfills your business needs (even if you must grow into the bank's services while starting with a commercial finance company), don't give away what little clout you may have for the sake of convenience. Locating a bank with expertise can take some shopping around—but it's worth trying to find such a bank or individual banker. One of the major reasons for changing banks among established businesses is the search for expertise in their particular business needs.

If you have found expertise and rapport with a bank or bank manager, treasure and nurture it. But don't forget to keep them on their toes with your knowledge. Question their quoted rates and other decisions from time to time. Do an occasional dry run, obtaining competitive bids from their competitor banks, just to reassure yourself that they are not taking you for granted. Try to be prepared for that unpleasant day when your bank friend is no longer there to fight your financing battles.

## How to Pick the Right Bank

If your business is located in a community where you have a choice of several big banks or one of the smaller independent banks, here are some recommendations:

Check out the smaller banks in search of the expertise and rapport that are complementary to your particular business needs.

Sometimes these small banks are staffed by experienced management—perhaps old-timers who became disenchanted with big-bank red tape, politics, or ivory-tower thinking. These officers can give you valuable business counseling.

You may find that the small bank is not so wrapped up in the usual consumer loans and checking-account money chase. They may take the time to understand your business and your money needs.

You will have more opportunities to talk and negotiate on a one-to-one basis, without concern for a distant, perhaps disinterested credit committee.

The disadvantages are that the smaller banks are often restricted in their lending limits. They may be ultraconservative because they cannot stand loan losses or much delinquency in their loan portfolio. Or, infected with that big-bank bugaboo, they're in banking to serve the consumer and make that higher rate in small loans and through credit-card participation.

Smaller banks always have higher money costs than big banks. This may be partially offset by lower overhead costs.

Check out the big banks by going behind the scene.

The larger banks all offer virtually identical checking-account services, with drive-in and walk-up windows and other service gimmicks like automatic tellers. These are all very nice, but how does that bank fit with your real business needs?

Find out about their business banking services. Listed below are the important services which may not be visible when you visit their branch offices. Only you can choose those services which may prove most useful to your business now or in the future, as your business grows.

- *Accounts receivable financing*—Do they have a separate department to handle receivable financing? Find out what their requirements are. How is it handled? Where are the decisions made? How much expertise do they seem to have in your types of receivables?

- *Equipment financing or leasing*—Do they have a department that specializes in heavy equipment? What are their requirements in dollar amounts, down payments, and terms? Where are the decisions made? Who put the loans or leases together? (It can be an advantage *not* to have the branch manager involved in these specialized needs.)

  Helpful hint: Many banks have established holding companies to facilitate offering specialized financing services. These "outside" operations can prove helpful to business owners. The reasons are several. Less attention is paid to balance sheet ratios and more reliance is placed on equipment or collateral values. Many holding company operations are more or less autonomous from the regular banking system.

  They have found it wise and expedient to staff these outside companies with managers and representatives who know equipment and secured-type lending. Before you select one big bank over another, find out which banks have such operations. Those that do might speak your language more fluently than a regular branch banker. If you're a good checking-account and loan customer, it can help in obtaining equipment financing or leasing, with less hassle and time spent on your part. The bank already has your records on hand.

- *Inventory loans, rediscounting, floor-plan–type loans*—If any of these specialized financing forms are of major importance to your business, check out the way the big bank handles these particular loan functions, the same as with receivables or equipment financing.
- *Corporate banking services and "heavy-duty" commercial loan departments*—Big banks often maintain entirely separate departments so their larger customers can deal direct rather than through a branch manager. Unfortunately, many small to medium-sized businesses do not have large enough requirements to qualify or even interest these "big-time operators."

  However, there is considerable variation from one big bank to another in this banking service. If you are large enough, or heading in that direction, get behind the branch scene by investigating the big bank's guidelines. The capability of the commercial loan officer and the amount of interest he or she takes in your business are very important. Get acquainted with the officer who would be in charge of your account.

- *National or international business needs*—Some businesses rely on a bank that can provide meaningful out-of-state or out-of-country services. Letters of credit, knowledgeable and functional export-import officers, good correspondent bank relations (located where you need them) can be the main reason for your selection of a particular big bank.

These are some of the criteria to take into account in intelligently selecting one big bank over another big bank. Notice that how late the drive-up window stays open is not one of them!

## FINANCE COMPANY MONEY COSTS

The larger finance companies have almost identical, low money costs. Their costs are fractionally lower than some slightly smaller finance companies who can only qualify to borrow in the dealer commercial paper market. The major finance companies have significantly lower borrowing costs than the smaller finance companies, who obtain their funds almost exclusively from banks.

These lower borrowing costs make the major commercial finance companies generally the best place for smaller businesses to money-shop. You will find the lowest rates with these majors, but there are problems inherent in dealing with them, somewhat similar to borrowing from the big banks.

When the banks are unable (or unwilling) to provide you with the business-type financing you need, the most logical place to start is with the *major* finance companies. These financial "giants," many whose names have almost become household words, are:

Aetna Business Credit Inc.
Associates Commercial Corporation
Avco Financial Services
Bankamerilease Group
C.I.T. Corporation
Citicorp Leasing Inc.
Commercial Credit Corp.
Equico Lessors Inc.
Equilease Corporation
Ford Motor Credit Company
General Electric Credit Company
Greyhound Leasing & Financial Corp.
Walter E. Heller Inc.
ITT Industrial Credit Company
International Paper Credit
Litton Industries Credit Corporation
Manufacturers Hanover Leasing Corporation
Westinghouse Credit Corporation.

These are the biggest and best known of the nearly one hundred names to be found in large-city Yellow Pages. Some of them are part of a major bank or manufacturing company. These companies sometimes rely on the parent company for money supply or as a borrowing entity.

The others, using their well-rated promissory notes—sometimes aided by the added clout of the parent company—borrow in the short-term commercial paper money market. These borrowings are for periods of 30 to 270 days. They do not use a dealer; they borrow direct from huge companies having temporary excess cash. For long-term money, they float a variety of stock issues (often preferred stock), bonds, and debentures. These issues, very solid risks, are at low yields or money costs comparable to the highest-grade issues of any Fortune 500 company.

The major finance companies also have sizable lines of credit available through banks all over the country. These credit lines carry interest rates at or below the prime rate. Just like banks that do not use Federal Reserve money, though available, the major finance companies seldom use bank money unless less costly money becomes unavailable—and they do not use this money for any extended period of time. The reasons are the same: Fed money is expensive to the banks, so bank money is expensive to the large commercial finance companies.

Without low-interest-rate checking accounts and savings deposits, the finance companies have never had it so good as banks. But with the commercial paper market hitting historical highs, all of the finance companies were caught in the high purchase cost of lendable funds. Their plight was much worse than that of the major banks; many of them are still in the position of having much lower-cost funds derived from their asset (deposit) base. Of course, many banks, large and small, also had to "purchase" their money at record-high costs, compelling them to raise their rates.

The commercial finance companies generally mark up their money 4% to 7% over their average money cost. They continually raise their "retail" rates to maintain this spread. Only exceptionally strong and creditworthy businesses can qualify for floating rates of 1% to 4% over the prevailing prime rate money cost. Finance company street rates rose to unprecedented levels of over 12% "add-on." Even 12% add-on provides "only" 20.3% A.P.R. (annual percentage rate) yield on a 60-month, equal-payment contract or loan.

Smaller finance companies, including those just barely out of the "major" category, often utilize a combination of expensive bank money and commercial paper from dealers. Dealer commercial paper, with fees added, is always more expensive than prime commercial paper which the majors borrow direct, without dealer fees. Smaller finance company rates reached such astronomical levels in 1979–81 that it is difficult to understand how their customers could afford to pay the rate and still stay in business.

## DEALING WITH FINANCE OR LEASING COMPANIES

There are similarities between working with a bank loan officer and a finance or leasing company field representative. Both are responsible for preparation of the financing package, which they submit for credit approval. Like the banker, the representative has some latitude as to the interest or lease rate he or she will present or request, along with recommendations and your financial data. Like the branch bank loan officer, these representatives seldom have sufficient credit limits for today's high-priced machinery or equipment. In fact, very few finance or lease representatives have any credit authority.

Our negotiating suggestions apply equally to the finance or lease representatives. Establish your rate and terms before he or she submits your financing request. These representatives get locked into an approved rate, as do bank loan officers. After the credit approval comes back, which always confirms or sets the rate, it is often too late to start negotiating. Terms and conditions likewise can become locked.

Although bankers do make house calls, they prefer that you come to them to negotiate on their own turf. Finance and lease people prefer to come to you. Being more collateral-oriented, they want to see your equipment and business operation in addition to just looking at your financial statement numbers.

Financing and leasing representatives are generally more positive-thinking and sales-minded than their banker counterparts. This can work to your advantage in obtaining needed financing, because they often will work hard to sell their credit management your package. Bear in mind that most major financing and leasing companies are now paying some form of bonus or commission to their outside contact people. It is at least in part based upon the A.P.R. you end up paying. However, on an overall basis, their bonuses do not depend entirely on sticking you with a high rate but on making a quota of volume, combined with rates that are satisfactory to their management.

Leasing company representatives are more likely to be in a commission program tied directly to lease rate yields. In some cases their rewards go up in direct proportion to how much excess rate they can get you to accept. If you have ever dealt with a leasing sales person, you know they are the strongest in sales push, compared to the finance company rep or banker. Most bank officers are not paid any form of commission, but they may have performance quotas or an annual bonus program that considers solicitation calls made, volume of loans, and A.P.R. averaged.

## SUMMARY OF TIPS IN DEALING WITH ALL LENDERS

Here is a round-up of tips and clues in dealing knowledgeably with any of the lenders.

BE HONEST WITH YOURSELF Hate to haggle? Do not confuse haggling with determined, carefully planned negotiating. Haggling is for the Persian marketplace or a shop in Mexico. You cannot negotiate from a position of weakness, and lack of knowledge is where weakness starts.

It doesn't matter if your business is small and only nominally profitable; you will fare much better if you at least appear to know what you are talking about.

Know your financial statement numbers. Be able to recite from memory the more critical ratios, your cash flow, your inventory and receivable turnover. Know what you want, how you can service the debt, and how your business plan will take you from point A to point B. Avoid flat statements like "Just give me the money, I'll get there" or "I know what I can afford." Even if you are right, tell the lender why you know you are right.

Don't pretend to know all the answers, but try hard to know the right questions. You lose lender respect by appearing naive, compliant, or unquestioning.

HESITANT, MYSTIFIED, INTIMIDATED? Hesitant in even asking for a loan? Mystified or intimidated by financial or leasing jargon? A little afraid because you are not a mathematical whiz kid or not accounting-oriented? Ever try to negotiate a loan or lease, only to be overwhelmed by fast talk or put down by a domineering banker or lender representative?

Each of these roadblocks can be removed or eased by increasing your knowledge, giving you more self-confidence and helping you to be better prepared. Remember taking tests in school or making that first talk in front of your classmates? You knew you would fail when you did not prepare. You felt success was certain when you knew the material and felt ready. Succeeding with the lenders requires virtually the same preparedness—self-confidence and knowledge!

KEEP YOUR LENDER CLUED IN; MAINTAIN YOUR CREDIBILITY In any continuing lender relationship, particularly with your bank, let them know your future plans well in advance. A good banker, especially one who has gone to bat for you, likes to feel that he or she is important to your operation. Such bankers take pride in their customers' progress and successes. But they hate surprises and panicked cries for help when confronted with a sudden problem they didn't know existed. If you are having problems, it's often better to talk them over with your lender than to conceal them and hope they'll go away.

Keep your promises to the lenders. If you promised to render quarterly financial statements and send them a copy, mark it on your calendar and send it promptly. Avoid making them call you for promised reports of any kind. Failure to keep your promises damages credibility.

THE BANK YOU LOVE TO HATE Having an adversary relationship with your bank is a losing battle. As difficult, pessimistic, and closed-minded as the bank may appear to be, you need it as an ally. A banker that is good for your company feels that your success is also his or her success.

Reexamine your previous contacts with bankers or other lenders to see if your clashes and conflicts were not partially or entirely of your own doing. Did you create adversity by your arbitrary or demanding nature? Was there an unproductive personality conflict? Did you fail to come through with information they requested reasonably?

Stay away from the "I hate 'em but know I need 'em" dilemma by sticking to well-prepared facts. Give them what they need voluntarily and what they ask for promptly.

CURB YOUR EGO; AVOID BEING FLAMBOYANT Most bankers do not have the guts or "street smarts" to be in private business. By nature, they're not risk takers. They proceed cautiously and are usually pessimists. Yet they are convinced their grasp of financial theory, planning, and accounting surpasses your "learn-by-doing" and "college of hard knocks" approach.

Many business people succeed through perseverance, a willingness to work long, hard hours, and making the best use of their skills or creative talents. Often, they succeed despite weaknesses in the paperwork, administrative, or accounting aspects of their business.

Unfortunately, the bankers have witnessed or been told about the numerous business failures precipitated by these weaknesses. They may have a case, but they persist in applying their theories and yardsticks to everyone. They are weak in discerning exceptions to the rule.

Instead of rubbing your successes and profits in their salaried noses, suppress those desires and the idea of dazzling them with verbal footwork. If you have big plans, hopes, or dreams of even more and bigger profits, reduce them to a factual presentation. Avoid the wheeler-dealer, "I am the greatest" approach.

You would be shocked and amazed at what goes on in the heads of those credit administrators! They often have only barely concealed power complexes because of their control of the purse strings of a bank or other financial institution. If you come on too strong with the "self-made man" approach or display other traits of being pushy, these keepers of the vault can be small-minded and vindictive. They will kill loans, stall them, become arbitrary and extra demanding, simply to display their power.

This, of course, is not a blanket indictment of all credit people. Some of them are courageous and open-minded. But deal makers are few and far between in most loan departments. And then there are credit people who are actually frightened and draw back when confronted with an achiever or highly successful self-made man or woman.

Discretion is the better part of valor, when dealing with these credit authorities. Better to win the war than a few skirmishes.

**STRIVE TO AVOID BEING REJECTED** This is not a simplistic or trite statement. It is very damaging to your creditibility to apply for credit when unprepared or to use a poor presentation and get turned down. You may not know it, but each time you apply, an inquiry will show up on your credit bureau report. Although it is not conclusive evidence you are being turned down, if you were lender number three or four being approached, what would you think of those inquiries over the previous thirty days, leading to no new loans? In this same connection, through credit interchange, lenders can learn about declines in some detail. This occurs between lenders and in some cases through commercial credit bureaus.

## WHAT TO DO IF CREDIT IS REJECTED

"Rejected" is a difficult word to swallow. Some lenders are more polite. They say "declined," "turned down," or "Sorry, but you do not qualify." It doesn't make much difference—you're not going to get the money.

Sometimes the lenders are clever with their declines. They give you an approval they're sure you will not be able to live with. You're forced into turning the lender down, instead of vice versa.

The reasons for lender declines are endless. Sometimes their explanations are more evasively polite than factual. Other times they offer logical-sounding reasons that mask their true feelings or concerns. Occasionally a concerned lender will provide constructive comments along with a well-defined turndown. This is what every applicant is entitled to receive. Unfortunately, such concern is not often in evidence.

Usually you get the word coldly and hurriedly by an embarrassed, disappointed branch manager or other lender contact person. Often the deniers are not in agreement with their credit people. Just as often they do not fully understand the reasoning behind the credit decline. This lack of understanding doesn't help you, because the contact person is unable to communicate the credit thinking properly. Usually the credit analyst or manager will have spent considerable time in analyzing your company's financial statements, projections, and pay habits. Even though the approach may be mistaken or pessimistic, a negative credit decision is not generally a snap judgment.

Whenever you are declined for credit or receive an approval that contains unlivable terms and conditions, do not walk away angry and uninformed. Learn something from the bad experience. Try to reverse the decision, with that lender if at all possible. Here are some suggestions for your guidance in the event of a credit application rejection.

BE SURE TO OBTAIN A COMPREHENSIVE EXPLANATION OF THE REASONING BEHIND THE DECLINE Usually a credit manager's or credit committee's decision is transmitted by your original lender contact person. You must be fully satisfied with that person's explanation.

Never accept a hasty, telephoned decline. Even though the turndown was not an unexpected decision, you owe it to yourself to learn from an adverse credit determination. As a minimum, sit down and discuss the outcome personally with your lender contact.

LOOK FOR ERRORS IN THE LENDER'S CREDIT DETERMINATION This is one paramount reason for insisting on an understandable, detailed explanation. You must dig beneath the often superficial explanation provided by the lender contact. Get all the facts out in the open.

Credit decisions are often made by credit management based on a list of positives and negatives. These abbreviated pluses and minuses are derived from an analysis of your financial statements, personal and business credit reports, and certain objective and subjective findings or opinions of the credit analyst or manager. Surprisingly, the decline may be the result of a series of small negatives that to the credit manager add up to an insurmountable big negative. You must get in a position to examine each negative carefully for discrepancies. These can range from erroneous credit reports to misprints or errors in your financial statements.

If you fail to dig, you will never learn that a credit report really belonged to some other person or company with a similar name. Or you may be shocked to learn that the company giving you special open account terms of 90 days is reporting you as slow-paying! Those are just two instances of the importance of examining every negative finding.

Credit managers make errors too, just like us mortals. Under pressure of spreading dozens of financial reports for analysis, they may have made simple arithmetical errors affecting your ratios and a host of other financial measurements.

ASK TO READ THE LENDER CONTACT PERSON'S ORIGINAL WRITE-UP OR CREDIT REQUEST APPLICATION FORMS In actual practice, particularly when you are involved in a large, important financing request, you should have at least read this write-up before submission to the credit department. Many astute borrowers make it a practice to actually assist the lender contact person in writing the credit request! Others, taking no chances, prepare a detailed presentation, relieving the contact person of much preparation in completing the lender's application format.

Again, look for errors in the credit request write-up. Make sure your story was accurately told. If the credit department does not receive correct, adequate information, it is hampered or prevented from making a positive decision.

Look for subtle differences between your intentions and the actual write-up. For instance, were you really inflexible on the down payment, terms of repayment, or other structuring aspects, or did an erroneous write-up give the credit department that impression? Too often, there is faulty communication between yourself and the lender contact or between that person and the credit people. Credit people have been known to decline simply because they thought the submission represented an inflexible, one-way street.

## FIND OUT HOW THE CREDIT DECISION MIGHT BE REVERSED

The most obvious way to reverse a negative decision is to see if revisions to the basics will make the application acceptable. These may include: increasing the down payment, if it is a purchase-money loan or contract; decreasing the amount of loan requested, if you can live with a smaller loan advance; shortening or revising the repayment term; agreeing to personal or corporate guaranties not originally offered; offering additional security for the loan or contract with real estate or personal property; or supporting the loan or contract with one or more co-signers or recourse (endorsement) by the seller, if obtainable.

Less obvious ways to reverse the decision may take time and, perhaps require unpalatable measures. These might include: taking a variety of corrective actions to improve your balance sheet ratios, such as controlling costs to shape up your income statement; proving your projections by actual performance over a designated period; bringing in a partner, stockholder, or one or more investors to improve ratios and/or insure adequate cash flow to service new debt; or selling off unneeded assets such as stagnant inventories or idle equipment to improve cash position.

When seeking to reverse a credit decision through changes in the requirements, first find out what specifics the credit department may demand. Then try for their firm commitment to proceed if you perform. Also, try for an express time span to assure ultimate approval, based on completion of promised performance.

Constructive, business-oriented credit people will accompany their declines with alternatives which will automatically reverse their decision if you agree to and can perform to their suggestions. In the finance business, these credit people are called deal makers. Competent loan officers or other lender contact persons should also be adept at structuring your loan requests and then working out acceptable alternatives in the event of a rejection.

Unfortunately, there are not enough deal makers for the number of borrowers who need them! Don't count on finding them—turning a reject around is usually your problem to resolve.

GET SATISFACTORY EXPLANATIONS OR GO DIRECTLY TO THE CREDIT PEOPLE There are variations in pursuing this route, dictated by circumstances too numerous to cover. Basically, either after exhausting discussions of the turndown with the lender contact or upon determining that that person is incompetent or incapable of acting as intermediary with the credit people, you should, with or without this contact's permission, make an appointment with the credit person who declined your application. Even though a credit committee rendered the final decision, very often a credit analyst or manager gave them the facts and a recommendation for their adverse determination. Once again, in direct discussions with this credit person, go through our suggested procedure—checking for errors and misunderstandings—and try for alternative means of approval.

Come to this meeting prepared with facts, including new ones, if possible. If positive and negative columns were made, obtain the list if at all possible. Prepare the best rebuttal you can muster, point by point.

Sometimes it is impossible to arrange a meeting with the credit people. However, if you persist, few lenders will deny you a telephone discussion.

GET THE CREDIT MANAGER OR OTHER CREDIT AUTHORITY TO VISIT YOUR BUSINESS LOCATION Some lenders, particularly banks, prefer to keep the credit people away from the borrowers. They fear emotional involvement or distraction from cold-blooded numbers analysis, even bribery—perhaps not payoffs so much as inducement through entertainment or "favors." They do not want their credit people out of the office, away from their analysis duties. Lender reluctance is understandable, particularly concerning smaller loans or marginal, less profitable customers.

Finance companies are less restrictive about credit people visiting the borrower's place of business. In part, this is because they are secured lenders and they take more interest in the actual machinery and their values. They also look more at the operation's potential and how profits are earned, rather than at balance sheets and income statements.

No matter who your lender is, there are circumstances under which credit people can be induced to visit your operation. If it is a bank, a credit administrator who is on the credit committee might come out, along with your local branch manager.

The advantages of a personal visit should be obvious. The credit people can see for themselves all of the things that did not make it to your financial statements. They can see potential, recent changes or improvements, management teamwork and capabilities. They can be made more comfortable with the credit risk.

Having the credit people out to see your operation is also a good ploy *before* you make a formal credit request. Not only is this more palatable to a loan contact person, but it also assists in completing the loan application and can turn a potential decline into an approval.

IN SHORT, FIGHT BACK AGAINST A CREDIT REJECTION If you can't reverse it, learn from it. If you decide to try elsewhere, don't repeat the mistakes made in your original approach. If there are errors in credit bureau reports, get them corrected. If your suppliers are incorrectly reporting your paying habits, straighten them out. If your financial statements were found lacking in details or contained errors, correct them! If you were turned down for specific operational or financial shortcomings, take steps to change them.

Realize that credit turndowns are entered on your credit reports in some way. They make your next request that much more difficult. Credit negatives have a way of accumulating–they won't go away by themselves. If you are declined by your bank and you are convinced they erred, find another bank by using our suggested methods. If your loan request is patently unsuitable for bank financing, locate a major finance company. Make your presentation to them better by learning from the bank's decline reasoning.

Many of you lack the clout to use arm-twisting persuasion on the lenders. Don't use threats, use facts. Some of you have the clout but are not using it properly–or you are unwilling to be hard enough to at least try. Some of you think it just doesn't make any difference, no matter what you know or how hard you try. You are wrong. The lenders are strong and in the power position, but they need knowledgeable borrowers to stay in business and make a profit.

Insight adds to knowledge. Knowledge is the great equalizer, if properly applied. Nothing can so consistently succeed as the practical application of knowledge. Francis Bacon had it right when he said, "Knowledge is power."

FIGURE 1-1

# HOW BANKS GET YOU FOR *MORE INTEREST*

We all know that most years have 365 days . . . except Leap Year, which has 366 days . . . but the lenders, especially many BANKS, count FUNNY. They have always treasured their OWN YEAR, which contains ONLY 360 days! This *Special Year* doesn't exist, except in their *"interest-gathering" heads*, of course.

A 360 day year makes it a little more profitable for lenders when they compute loan interest because it "creates" a higher daily interest earnings rate than dividing the annual rate by that "awkward" 365-366 day year. HOW MUCH DIFFERENCE?

Well, at a 10% quoted (or "stated") rate, you're paying over 1/8th% per annum more . . . 10.1389%, to be exact. If you're borrowing at a "stated" rate of 18%, it becomes a FULL ¼% more . . . 18.25%. Nothing dramatic, but certainly IRKSOME . . . an UNNECESSARY COST TO YOU . . . more PROFITS for them.

The provisions of the Truth-In-Lending Act requires full "Disclosure" of the Annual Percentage Rate ("A.P.R."), on certain Commercial Loans. So, when they HAVE TO . . . they write the NOTE at a STATED RATE of say, 15% . . . but CHARGE INTEREST AT 15.2083% . . . and "disclose" this in the text. Many banks and other lenders charge interest for actual days . . . BUT CALCULATE INTEREST ON 360 DAYS. So, YOUR BEST DEAL has provided a handy CONVERSION CHART. You might want to agitate them by inserting . . *"interest rate to be based on a 365 day year . . 15% = 15% . . . 'cepting Leap Year, which has 366 days"*.

## CONVERSION of "STATED" INTEREST to ANNUAL PERCENTAGE RATE

- **This TABLE indicates EXACT ANNUAL PERCENTAGE RATE that banks or other lending institutions EARN when they charge loan interest at a stated rate on the ACTUAL DAYS, but calculate interest on a 360 DAY BASIS.**

| Loan Made at | Annual Percentage Rate | Loan Made at | Annual Percentage Rate | Loan Made at | Annual Percentage Rate |
|---|---|---|---|---|---|
| 8 1/2 | 8.6181 | 12 | 12.1667 | 15 1/2 | 15.7153 |
| 8 3/4 | 8.8715 | 12 1/4 | 12.4201 | 15 3/4 | 15.9688 |
| 9 | 9.1250 | 12 1/2 | 12.6736 | 16 | 16.2222 |
| 9 1/4 | 9.3785 | 12 3/4 | 12.9271 | 16 1/4 | 16.4757 |
| 9 1/2 | 9.6319 | 13 | 13.1806 | 16 1/2 | 16.7292 |
| 9 3/4 | 9.8854 | 13 1/4 | 13.4340 | 16 3/4 | 16.9826 |
| 10 | 10.1389 | 13 1/2 | 13.6875 | 17 | 17.2361 |
| 10 1/4 | 10.3924 | 13 3/4 | 13.9410 | 17 1/4 | 17.4896 |
| 10 1/2 | 10.6458 | 14 | 14.1944 | 17 1/2 | 17.7431 |
| 10 3/4 | 10.8993 | 14 1/4 | 14.4479 | 17 3/4 | 17.9965 |
| 11 | 11.1528 | 14 1/2 | 14.7014 | 18 | 18.2500 |
| 11 1/4 | 11.4063 | 14 3/4 | 14.9594 | 18 1/4 | 18.5035 |
| 11 1/2 | 11.6597 | 15 | 15.2083 | 18 1/2 | 18.7569 |
| 11 3/4 | 11.9132 | 15 1/4 | 15.4618 | 18 3/4 | 19.0104 |
| | | | | 19 | 19.2639 |

To determine effective rate for loans made at rates not shown on tables, multiply stated rate by 1.013889.

FIGURE 1-2

# INTEREST and FINANCE CHARGE . . .

## "SAVINGS-AT-A-GLANCE"

It is easy to LOSE SIGHT of Interest, Finance or Lease Charge SAVINGS that are possible when you FIRST LOOK at the "Stated Rate". When you think about "CUTTING-IT-BACK" a ½%, or so, MOST PEOPLE FAIL to comprehend the ACCUMULATIVE EFFECT of even fractional reductions.

It's also easy to "WAVE-OFF" the SAVINGS difference as TAX-DEDUCTIBLE . . . so "Why Bother"? Little, innocent-appearing fractional point differences REALLY ADD-UP for LENDERS . . . who pick-up a ¼% here, ½% there . . . here a POINT, there a POINT . . . ALL FROM BORROWERS or LESSEES who only occasionally require financing.

The shame of it is . . . many creditworthy business owners "GIVE-AWAY" too much RATE MARK-UP, to already PROSPEROUS LENDERS. Very often, they pay the higher-rate because they did not WANT TO ASK for a LOWER RATE . . . or, they simply didn't realize HOW MUCH they were giving away. Others MISTAKENLY THINK that RATE QUOTATIONS ARE ENGRAVED IN GRANITE and IMMUNE FROM NEGOTIATION.

YOUR BEST DEAL has put together three groups of charts to ACCENTUATE and DRAMATIZE how QUICKLY WORTHWHILE SAVINGS can be made by minor RATE DECREASES.

These charts cover Simple Interest, "Add-On" Finance Charges and Lease Finance Charges. We present "SAVINGS-AT-A-GLANCE" in each of these categories . . . using TYPICAL EQUIPMENT COSTS or LOAN BALANCES . . . TYPICAL TERMS OF REPAYMENT . . . and the INCREMENTAL SAVINGS THAT ARE POSSIBLE.

It is not possible to give ALL ENCOMPASSING CHARTS for these savings . . . nor are the charts intended to replace more exacting calculations you can make when utilizing our RATE CHARTS and other FORMULAS and CALCULATORS.

Each of these charts are expandable by simple interpolation and substitution of your own LOAN BALANCE or EQUIPMENT COSTS. The MAIN PURPOSE of the charts, however, is to BRING THE SAVINGS POSSIBILITIES TO YOUR ATTENTION. It is entirely possible . . . with proper UNDERSTANDING and TIMING . . . to SAVE YOURSELF several hundred or thousand DOLLARS . . . in ONE SIMPLE SENTENCE . . . ASK!!

FIGURE 1-3

## REDUCE THE RATE ½ of 1% Simple Interest -- (14½% Versus 15%)

### YOUR INTEREST SAVINGS at VARYING TERMS

| LOAN BALANCE | 36 Months | 60 Months | 84 Months | 120 Months |
|---|---|---|---|---|
| $ 25,000.00 | $ 219.96 | $ 392.40 | $ 588.00 | $ 914.40 |
| 50,000.00 | 439.92 | 784.80 | 1,173.48 | 1,828.80 |
| 75,000.00 | 637.92 | 1,177.20 | 1,760.64 | 2,743.20 |
| 100,000.00 | 879.84 | 1,570.20 | 2,346.96 | 3,657.60 |
| 250,000.00 | 2,199.60 | 3.925.20 | 5,867.40 | 9,144.00 |

## REDUCE THE RATE 1% Simple Interest -- (14% Versus 15%)

### YOUR INTEREST SAVINGS at VARYING TERMS

| LOAN BALANCE | 36 Months | 60 Months | 84 Months | 120 Months |
|---|---|---|---|---|
| $ 25,000.00 | $ 438.84 | $ 782.40 | $1,168.44 | $1,820.40 |
| 50,000.00 | 877.32 | 1,564.80 | 2,337.72 | 3,640.80 |
| 75,000.00 | 1,317.60 | 2,347.80 | 3,507.00 | 5,462.40 |
| 100,000.00 | 1,755.72 | 3,130.20 | 4.676.28 | 7,281.60 |
| 250,000.00 | 4,388.76 | 7,825.20 | 11,690.28 | 18,204.00 |

## REDUCE THE RATE 2% Simple Interest -- (13% Versus 15%)

### YOUR INTEREST SAVINGS at VARYING TERMS

| LOAN BALANCE | 36 Months | 60 Months | 84 Months | 120 Months |
|---|---|---|---|---|
| $ 25,000.00 | $ 874.44 | $1,555.20 | $2,320.08 | $3,607.20 |
| 50,000.00 | 1,748.16 | 3.110.40 | 4,640.16 | 7,214.40 |
| 75,000.00 | 2,622.60 | 4,665.60 | 6,960.24 | 12,021.60 |
| 100,000.00 | 3,497.04 | 6,221.40 | 9,280.32 | 14,428.80 |
| 250,000.00 | 8,742.24 | 15,553.20 | 23,200.80 | 36,072.00 |

Note: These INTEREST SAVINGS amounts interpolate readily and with reasonable accuracy. For instance; you can divide the $50,000. interest savings by 1/5th to obtain incremental savings of $10,000., etc.

FIGURE 1-4

## REDUCE THE RATE ½% "ADD-ON" -- (8½% "A.O." Versus 9% "A.O.")

### YOUR FINANCE RATE SAVINGS at VARYING TERMS

| CONTRACT BALANCE | 36 Months | 60 Months | 84 Months | 120 Months |
|---|---|---|---|---|
| $ 25,000.00 | $ 375.00 | $ 625.00 | $ 875.00 | $ 1,250.00 |
| 40,000.00 | 600.00 | 1,000.00 | 1,400.00 | 2,000.00 |
| 65,000.00 | 975.00 | 1,625.00 | 2.275.00 | 3,250.00 |
| 125,000.00 | 1,875.00 | 3,125.00 | 4,375.00 | 6,250.00 |
| 200,000.00 | 3,000.00 | 5,000.00 | 7,000.00 | 10,000.00 |

## REDUCE THE RATE 1% "ADD-ON" -- (8% "A.O." Versus 9% "A.O.")

### YOUR FINANCE RATE SAVINGS at VARYING TERMS

| CONTRACT BALANCE | 36 Months | 60 Months | 84 Months | 120 Months |
|---|---|---|---|---|
| $ 25,000.00 | $ 750.00 | $1,250.00 | $1,750.00 | $ 2,500.00 |
| 40,000.00 | 1,200.00 | 2,000.00 | 2,800.00 | 4,000.00 |
| 65,000.00 | 1,950.00 | 3,250.00 | 4,550.00 | 6,500.00 |
| 125,000.00 | 3,750.00 | 6,250.00 | 8,750.00 | 12,500.00 |
| 200,000.00 | 6,000.00 | 10,000.00 | 14,000.00 | 20,000.00 |

Note: We have included the ½% and 1% Add-On Rate SAVINGS to accentuate the amounts saved . . . and they are DIRECTLY PROPORTIONATE. You can tell AT-A-GLANCE what your SAVINGS will be . . and it's obvious you save EXACTLY TWICE as MUCH, from ½% to 1%.

Therefore, you can determine what a ¼% SAVINGS would be . . . OR ANY INCREMENTAL CHANGE. You can also obtain the SAVINGS for different CONTRACT BALANCES . . . by DIRECT INTERPOLATION.

FIGURE 1-5

# LEASE FINANCE CHARGE . . .

## "SAVINGS-AT-A-GLANCE"

Our charts on LEASE RATE SAVINGS are presented differently than the Interest or Finance Charge "SAVINGS-AT-A-GLANCE", because Lease Payments are CALCULATED DIFFERENTLY.

Lease Payments are USUALLY calculated by using rates expressed in "Dollars Per Hundred or Per Thousand, Per Month or Per Quarter" . . . this "Factor" is then MULTIPLIED times the EQUIPMENT COST to arrive at the monthly lease payment. For instance . . . a Rate Per Thousand of $20.1143, with 84 Monthly Lease Payments, one Monthly Rental in Advance and a 10% Purchase Option due at the end of the lease . . . would COST YOU 18% Simple Interest . . . (thus, YIELDING 18% to the LESSOR).

Our CHART PRESENTATION is therefore based on REDUCING THE RATE PER THOUSAND DOLLARS, PER MONTH, by 25¢. 50¢, 75¢ and $1.00. We projected these REDUCTIONS to GRAPHICALLY PRESENT THE NET SAVINGS YOU MIGHT NEGOTIATE . . by shaving 25¢, or more, off the QUOTED RATE. Of course, ANY reduction in the Rate Per Thousand, reduces the LESSOR'S YIELD and YOUR NET INTEREST COSTS. We are dealing with a CONSTANT REDUCTION, that is PRO-RATA APPLICABLE to ANY YIELD, TERM or RATE PER THOUSAND.

You should . . . (and probably do) . . . compare the monthly or quarterly payments RESULTING from RATE PER THOUSAND quotations. The PROBLEMS ARISE when the Lease Rate is rapidly quoted and negotiated, while the LESSOR introduces the many VARIABLE FACTORS peculiar to LEASING . . . which make it difficult to compare APPLES and APPLES.

LESSEES tend to LOSE-THE-RATE and YIELD IMPLICATIONS in the LEASE STRUCTURING complexities . . . such as, Purchase or Renewal Options . . . Advance Payments or Deposits . . . Tax (?) Benefits . . . ITC "Pass-Through" or Retention . . . "Expense-it-Off" fictions . . . and other variations that OBSCURE the TRUE YIELD to the LESSOR.

Our LEASE FINANCE CHARGE "SAVINGS-AT-A-GLANCE" charts simply ACCENTUATE your POTENTIAL SAVINGS . . . or . . . conversely, how RAPIDLY the Lessor's YIELD INCREASES . . . if they successfully ADD even a FEW PENNIES to the RATE PER THOUSAND.

FIGURE 1-6

# YOUR LEASE FINANCE CHARGE SAVINGS at VARYING TERMS

## RATE PER THOUSAND REDUCTIONS

| EQUIPMENT COST | 25¢ | 50¢ | 75¢ | $1.00 | LEASE TERM |
|---|---|---|---|---|---|
| $30,000.00 | $ 270.00 | $ 540.00 | $ 810.00 | $ 1,080.00 | 36 Months |
| | 450.00 | 900.00 | 1,350.00 | 1,800.00 | 60 Months |
| | 630.00 | 1,260.00 | 1,890.00 | 2,520.00 | 84 Months |
| | 900.00 | 1,800.00 | 2,700.00 | 3,600.00 | 120 Months |
| $75,000.00 | $ 675.00 | $ 1,350.00 | $ 2,025.00 | $ 2,700.00 | 36 Months |
| | 1,125.00 | 2,250.00 | 3,375.00 | 4,500.00 | 60 Months |
| | 1,575.00 | 3,150.00 | 4,725.00 | 6,300.00 | 84 Months |
| | 2,250.00 | 4,500.00 | 6,750.00 | 9,000.00 | 120 Months |
| $200,000.00 | $ 1,800.00 | $ 3,600.00 | $ 5,400.00 | $ 7,200.00 | 36 Months |
| | 3,000.00 | 6,000.00 | 9,000.00 | 12,000.00 | 60 Months |
| | 4,200.00 | 8,400.00 | 12,600.00 | 16,800.00 | 84 Months |
| | 6,000.00 | 12,000.00 | 18,000.00 | 24,000.00 | 120 Months |
| $500,000.00 | $ 4,500.00 | $ 9,000.00 | $13,500.00 | $18,000.00 | 36 Months |
| | 7,500.00 | 15,000.00 | 22,500.00 | 30,000.00 | 60 Months |
| | 10,500.00 | 21,000.00 | 31,500.00 | 42,000.00 | 84 Months |
| | 15,000.00 | 30,000.00 | 45,000.00 | 60,000.00 | 120 Months |

The LEASE RATE SAVINGS shown above are symmetrical because we are dealing with the CONSTANTS of reducing a RATE PER THOUSAND, PER MONTH, by 25¢ to $1.00, Per Thousand, Per Month, (of Equipment Cost). We have provided a wide-range of possible savings to make VISUAL IMPACT.

For instance, take the $75,000.00, 84 Month Lease Term example. Suppose you were to negotiate a lease with a Rate Per Thousand of $20.1143, with one Advance Rental and a 10% Purchase Option. This rate would YIELD the LESSOR 18%. Your Lease Payments would be $1,508.57. Your Lease Finance Charges would total $59,219.88. You would REPAY $134,219.88.

If you NEGOTIATE a RATE DECREASE of only 75¢ Per Thousand, Per Month, DOWN to $19.3643 . . . your Lease Payment DROPS to $1,452.32. The $56.25 monthly REDUCTION results in a $4,725.00, SAVINGS TO YOU. That's an 8% SAVINGS on the original Lease Finance Charge. You have reduced the LESSOR'S YIELD from 18% to 16.9%.

The Lessor makes ONLY $54,494.88, on his $75,000.00, investment, over the 84 month term . . . rather than $59,219.88. THEY CAN PROBABLY AFFORD IT MORE THAN YOU CAN . . . the SAVINGS are ATTAINABLE . . . WORTHWHILE . . . and usually, JUSTIFIABLE. Give yourself a RAISE . . . or, take your wife or secretary out for dinner 84 times and spend $56.25, each time you do! If the SAVINGS are not that consequential to YOU . . . maybe you can THINK of a more WORTHY CAUSE than the LESSOR'S POCKET!

# 2

# HOW TO MAKE A GOOD PRESENTATION

Presentation! Presentation! I wish I could write it in 3-D, full color on a wide screen. If you want to get the money your way, on terms, conditions, and interest costs most satisfactory to you, make a *good* presentation! Without question, an adequate presentation is an essential aspect of obtaining suitable financing, at the lowest possible cost and in the shortest conceivable time. Even the most routine, readily acquired financing deserves certain minimal preparation and should have adequate content commensurate with the borrowing situation.

A presentation should tell your story. It should clearly communicate the reason for your money requirement. It should contain the facts that will enable a lender's credit department to make a prompt decision. If you are unable to talk directly to those who need to understand your money needs, how else can you communicate, except by the written word? How many of you get the opportunity to discuss your financial situation with the credit manager or analyst? Can you have a face-to-face meeting with the credit committee? They are the decision makers in the vast majority of your loan or lease applications. They are the people with the power of *yes* or *no*.

Your line of communication is usually through a bank loan officer, a finance company representative, or a leasing sales contact person. These people seldom have credit authority. All they can do is draft a write-up and make a recommendation. You depend upon them to transmit your story and explain your money request. You hope they will put your package together to get the job done. How many times have those you counted on done an inadequate or even miserable job of communicating your needs to the decision makers? Can you afford to take the chance they might not devote the time and energy to adequately prepare your financing request? Can you afford the wasted time or stand the aggravation of being bounced around by the credit people if your contact person is inept, poorly motivated, or "too busy"?

In addition to failing to recognize the value of making a good presentation, too many borrowers persist in making a game out of providing lenders with as little information as possible. Some carry the game to ridiculous lengths by acting surprised, injured, or annoyed by the lender's requests for business or personal statements or tax returns. Others play the game of "ask and ye shall receive"—but if you fail to ask, we volunteer nothing! Sounds ridiculous, doesn't it? In the end, it is terribly wasteful of your time, and often self-defeating.

We mention the extremes to emphasize the importance of embracing our constructive suggestions. After all my years in the finance business, despite the increasing awareness and sophistication of business people, the majority of the presentations I review are still inadequate or must be pieced together. Earlier in this book I estimated completing some three thousand transactions. How many more did I review and return as impossibly difficult or unworthy of submission to the credit department? Probably another three thousand! Believe me when I say that half of those approved required extreme efforts to put together a presentation that stood a chance with the credit decision makers. Of those that failed to make the grade, many simply fell apart for lack of facts and the borrower's making it too difficult to obtain data for me to prepare a believable write-up. Let me assure you, I am on your side; I'm not a propaganda agent of the lenders. The purpose of this presentation guide is to make favorable results easier for you, not to ease the work of the lenders!

The norm of everyday presentations isn't borrower reluctance or game playing. The norm is inadequate, untimely preparation. There is uncertainty of what is required. There is an inability to organize that which is necessary. The norm is reaching into files for copies of whatever the lender representative asks for; perhaps not finding all that is required. The norm is hastily assembled information, more like an afterthought or an interruption of more important business matters. There is a strong tendency to lean upon the lender contact person. This dependency too often results in disappointments and failure to achieve your objective. The lender leads you by the nose; you are not in control, they are.

## THE BENEFITS OF A GOOD PRESENTATION

A good presentation

- *Assists in reducing interest costs or finance or lease charges*—Your good presentation can earn some respect from lenders.

You will find the quotations that come back from lenders or lessors tend to be lower in cost. In many cases, the first quote you receive will be their very best, without the need for you to quibble or arbitrate.

- *Shortens the time to obtain credit approval*—Your good presentation got their attention! A complete, comprehensive presentation reduces or removes the need for the lender to ask more questions. Instead of several time-consuming meetings or lengthy telephone calls, avoid it all with one good meeting, one good presentation. If the credit decision maker can go from front to back in one easy-reading session of your presentation, you will see a fast decision. Even if it is a fast, polite no, you are better off than if you had endured days or weeks of questioning with the same result.
- *Makes approval of your credit request more probable*—Your good presentation offered convincing facts. Even though your company is small, barely profitable, or just getting underway, if your presentation convinces the credit manager you know what you are talking about, approval is more likely. If the credit people are forced to dig and dig for necessary facts and figures, even stronger companies can be shunted aside, turned down, or offered less than they requested. Your presentation should supplement and bolster the write-up of the lender contact person. If you are obliged to approach the lenders by mail, without the assistance of a contact person, can it stand on its own merits? Does it tell your story and support your request with the necessary facts?
- *Definitely helps in obtaining funds that are normally difficult to locate*—New ventures and unusual collateral such as high-technology, custom-built, or low-resale-value equipment need the support of a strong presentation.

All forms of specialized financing require a presentation: accounts receivable financing, borrowing against your existing equipment, refinancing existing loans, as in debt consolidation, using real estate as additional security, or any loan proposal to raise cash or working capital. In terms of raising capital from outside investors, bringing in new partners or officer stockholders to be active in a closely held corporation, or in selling your business, where would you be without a comprehensive presentation in these situations? Communicating with these outsiders is very much like communicating with a credit manager. They all want to analyze the risk before they invest their money, just as the credit manager does before investing his company's money.

## THE ELEMENTS OF A GOOD PRESENTATION

The basic elements of a good presentation are appearance, organization, clarity, comprehensive content, and accuracy. We will take these elementary considerations one at a time. These seemingly picayune details are important. If your presentation ignores enough of these basics, it will suffer accordingly.

APPEARANCE Your presentation is *you.* Those pieces of paper you offer are all the credit decision makers are likely to see of you. Copies must be clearly legible. They must not appear as though you have made a hasty distribution to dozens of lenders. Do not use coated copy-paper duplicates. They are hard to thumb through, detract from prestige appearance, do not duplicate as clearly, are hard to write on, and cost twice as much per page as plain bond copies. Always use plain bond copies.

Do not use unusual size paper. Stick with 8½″ X 11″ copies. Eliminate or minimize fold-outs or the use of legal-size paper. If it is necessary to present facts, charts, or statements which you originally had on fold-outs or legal-size paper, have them photo-reduced to 8½″ X 11″. Many copy centers have copy size reduction capabilities.

If covers seem appropriate, avoid outsized or heavy covers. Simple 9″ X 12″ covers are best.

ORGANIZATION AND CLARITY A good presentation "reads easy." It is arranged in logical sequence. We offer a suggested sequence at the end of this chapter.

The objectives of your proposal must be made immediately apparent. Avoid technical or scientific terminology. Stay away from abbreviations or buzzwords familiar only to you or those in your industry. Most credit people are strictly lay persons, and they tend to resent being snowed with unfamiliar language.

COMPREHENSIVE CONTENT AND ACCURACY Your presentation must be easily comprehended. Critical parts must not be omitted. If they are, credit approval is unnecessarily delayed.

Accuracy and completeness aid in comprehension and avoid those "twenty questions" phone calls from the lender. Inaccurate numbers and statements seriously detract from your credibility.

Do not omit schedules or explanations that help support your claims or financial reports. For instance, don't strip your financial statements down to just a balance sheet and income statement; include all of the supporting schedules supplied by your accountant. Do not provide income tax returns with related schedules missing. Give the lender copies of the entire tax return; the same as provided the IRS. When providing references, give phone numbers including area codes and addresses with zip codes.

Provide your correct, personal *legal name*, your residence address including zip code, and your social security number. Avoid using your first initials only or giving a nickname.

Provide the *exact legal name* of your company or corporation. If you are a registered proprietorship or partnership with a DBA ("doing business as" trading name), take the name directly from the registration, license, or county- or state-filed papers. If incorporated, refer directly to your incorporation documents. Or read your name off of the outer ring of your corporate seal. (If the denomination "Corporation," "Inc.," or "Incorporated" does not appear in the outer ring, it is *not* part of your legal corporate name.) If your seal is different than your charter indicates, the seal was made incorrectly.

### Don't Overwhelm Them

A comprehensive presentation does not imply that you should come on with a dressed-up, gaudy, or overextensive presentation. The presentation must be appropriate to the circumstances and objectives of the financing sought. An overly dressed encyclopedic proposal that is too slick can spell "No" to the lenders. Don't make them wary with too much sell and not enough facts that tell your financial situation. Avoid overkill—elaborate presentations are not necessary for credit analysis and can even cause confusion.

### Don't "Underwhelm" Them Either!

Underestimating the extent of your proposal's content usually happens because you are overconfident or unaware of changes that took place since your last borrowing request. Even though you are going back to the same old lender, there are many circumstances requiring a full presentation. Take a few minutes to assess the situation. Miscalculating and striking out, especially when time is short, can be damaging.

- Will your borrowing request exceed a previously established limit? If so, you are almost starting over and should gear your presentation accordingly.
- Has your friendly loan officer or finance manager moved on? Who will push your new request?
- Are you an old customer or a new borrower? If you have not approached your lender for a year or so, you will probably have to at least update the lender's credit file. Might as well do it right, with a good thorough presentation.
- While you were out of the borrowing market, has your lender changed his criteria? Has management changed? Is your lender averse to certain kinds of equipment borrowing? Some banks and finance companies would prefer not to finance computers or other high-technology equipment.
- Are you an old customer who needs new services? Many lenders, banks included, have different departments using differing credit criteria. If you should require lease financing, an accounts receivable loan, inventory financing, or some other specialized type of lending, be ready to present your case as if you had gone to a new lender!

We recommend that you prepare a good presentation in each of the above or similar situations. Although the lenders all interchange and work with your old file information, reactions can be very slow. You are relying on possibly disinterested parties to reassemble a profile of you or your company. A completely new, comprehensive package will expedite and decrease the possibility of a decline. And if your lender has become complacent or you are dissatisfied with his decision, you are ready to look elsewhere.

## THE COMPONENT PARTS OF A GOOD PRESENTATION

We are providing you with a complete list of all the component parts of a good presentation. Each of these components has our comments and suggestions to assist you in its proper use. Naturally, some of the components will not be necessary for your particular proposal and presentation. We have divided the list into two parts: the basic components, usual to almost all new financing requests, and special components, to be used according to the dictates of your particular presentation. The elements of a good presentation should be consistently applied to any component parts chosen for a presentation.

### Basic Components

APPLICATION We recommend advance preparation of an application form containing all the routine historical and identifying credit data lenders universally require.

Even though you are returning to your regular lender, who has your history on file, complete a new application in advance. (If you call them with a new loan request, don't they almost invariably start over with a dozen basic questions, "just in case some of your data has changed"?)

If you are planning to shop around among several lenders, an application form, neatly typed and containing all the basic details, does more than just save time. It helps you maintain control of the situation—it is part of staying in the driver's seat.

Our application forms at the end of this chapter will assist you in organizing the information most lenders require. We have included both a finance (Fig. 2-1) and a leasing (Fig. 2-2) application form because of the different requirements in explaining your needs for these types of financing. Either form can be adapted in applying for a loan.

Many commercial finance companies and banks prefer not to distribute a standard form for larger financing requests. Indeed, many of them do not have a form beyond the format used by their contact people. They want to come to you and obtain answers. In many cases, this is only part of the "take charge" psychology which they hope will isolate you while the contact people ingratiate themselves with their "service."

A completed form enables you to avoid entrapping meetings with the contact person interviewing you. Instead of spending most or all of your meeting answering mundane questions like "What is your bank account number?", hand them your presentation and start asking your own questions. *You* conduct the interview!

A good application form capsulizes all of your historical credit data on one page and also provides space to list your financing needs on the reverse side.

Indicate your equipment choice, desired terms, planned down payment, or proposed advance lease payments. You will note that our form provides space to put all vital transaction data on a single sheet. This way, you are telling the lender specifically what you want in organized, typewritten format. This preparation prevents being quizzed on routine matters that may divert you from actual negotiating.

PROPOSAL LETTER In the event your requirements are more complex, such as applying for a working capital loan or for some specialized form of borrowing, such as accounts receivable financing, use a proposal letter.

You may either use our application form to provide the historical data or incorporate this data in your proposal contents.

This proposal should be the first thing the lender reads in your presentation. If you also use an application or information form, it should be the second item in the package.

Address each proposal letter as you would any business letter to each lender you plan to contact. This can sometimes be reduced to a simple cover letter which refers to the application or to a business plan. The proposal letter should briefly but thoroughly outline the following particulars:

- *How much money is required* for the loan or for the equipment to be leased or purchased on a time-sale contract.
- *How the money is to be used.* If it is for a purchase-money loan, describe what equipment you will buy, what the equipment will do, and how it will help your business.

Under some circumstances, it helps to provide some detail as to money to be saved by reduced labor or profits to be earned from increased production.

If the money is for working capital, it is better to explain the reason for the need and how it will be employed than to just say "needed for working capital." For instance, if you have a new contract requiring more labor and supplies than you can handle, before the receivables convert to cash, provide some details concerning the contract. If you have a long-run manufacturing job, with few or no progress payments, give the details. Explain whatever caused the working capital need.

If the funds are to be used for multiple purposes, such as new plant and equipment, debt consolidation, remodeling or expansion, real estate purchase, or other business needs, it is better to make only a brief reference in the proposal letter. Attach more detailed schedules, plans, cost estimates, and other specifics, or incorporate the requirements in your business plan.

- *When the money will be required.* Some businessmen hesitate in letting the lender know the funds won't be needed for six or more months. They rightfully fear that the proposal will be pigeonholed and sidetracked until there is an urgency; meanwhile, the lender handles loan requests with a shorter fuse.

The solution is to require a lender commitment. Place a reasonable time limit on the date this commitment must be in your hands, in writing. Put this time limit date in your original proposal letter. If your presentation package is as complete as this book recommends, there is no reason this time limit should be longer than fifteen business days. For less complex proposals, ten business days is entirely reasonable.

Note: If your proposal letter requests not only a credit commitment but a rate commitment as well, you should expect to allow the lender to "hedge his bet" by stating that the commitment will remain good if your financial condition does not change. Also, the rate remains good, subject to prime rate changes.

This time aspect is the reason we recommend being prepared. Don't wait until you need the money yesterday. Lenders, particularly banks, are notorious for foot dragging while they build their file and deliberate.

The fact is, the slowness often starts with you, which only encourages the banker or lender manager you first talk with. If you give your lender contact completely adequate information, he or she has no reason to delay the write-up and recommendation.

Most credit requests, of any size, require two or more approval signatures. Many lenders have credit committees that meet periodically—some every day, some twice a week, some only occasionally each month. Under the best circumstances, days go by just getting *two* people to review and approve.

This is why your presentation should facilitate the write-up and recommendation. And why you should insert a time limit for the commitment—to motivate your lender, especially your contact bank officer, who has to start the ball rolling. Don't let him or her relax!

The time limit commitment gives you time to plan. It gives you negotiating room. Don't hesitate to work competing lenders over. Competition helps keep them on their toes.

YOUR BUSINESS FINANCIAL STATEMENTS *Creative Business Financing* covers your financial statements from every working, practical angle. We hope that you will utilize our suggestions. Your statements, with needed improvements, will be clear, concise, and properly detailed.

We suggest that you attach your last two year-end balance sheets and income statements, as a minimum. If your reports were drawn up with the latest fiscal year and the previous year columned next to each other, your two most recent statements will automatically provide three year-end reports. If your documents do not contain previous-year comparisons, we suggest you provide each lender with three year-end financial statements.

If more than six months have transpired since your year-end report, we urge you to provide the latest possible interim financial statement; that is, the last quarterly or semiannual statement prepared by your accountant.

If you prepare internal monthly statements, either manually or from your computer, attach a copy of each since the end of the last financial year. If the monthly report indicates year-to-date and present month, attach only the latest available month.

It is not essential for you to update your balance sheet on a monthly basis. It is better for lender analysis if your quarterly or semiannual financial statements also include an adjusted balance sheet. Major financing requests should include a late interim financial report in almost the same detail as your year-end financial statements.

If your financial statements are prepared within your company, by computer or your own accounting staff, it can help if they are signed and dated by the president, treasurer, financial officer, or controller. If your internally prepared statements are not footnoted and explained as they would be by a CPA or public accountant, we suggest attaching a cover letter to the statements, explaining any unusual entries, or using footnote explanations, as an accountant normally would.

YOUR PERSONAL FINANCIAL STATEMENTS This component part will be covered in considerable detail. However, when it comes to voluntarily inserting personal financial statements in an initial proposal or presentation, we know there is room for argument and disagreement by many business people.

Individuals of substantial personal worth hesitate to include their personal statements because of concern that lenders will assume their personal guaranties will also be automatically available.

Some businessmen want their corporation to stand on "it's own worth." Others do not want their personal worth floating around among several lenders, for many eyes to see. Sometimes the principals own widely differing percentages of stock and understandably dislike putting up their personal worth when they only hold 10% or 15% of the shares. Therefore, using this component part is your personal decision.

To make that decision, consider how the lenders think and the criteria that result from that thinking. If the borrower's business is a proprietorship or partnership, lenders know they have achieved personal responsibility when the documents are signed. Yet each individual's personal worth serves as a secondary source of repayment.

The lender cannot make a valid determination of the worth of this secondary source without a complete personal financial statement. They do not have insight into the individual's personal progress or how they handle themselves personally.

They do not have a clear picture of the individual's personal assets with just the document signatures, especially in the community property state, so lenders much prefer to have personal financial statements signed by husband and wife. In addition, they usually want the spouse to sign a separate personal guaranty.

Those persons who own small to medium-sized proprietorships and partnerships might just as well include personal financial statements in the original presentation. The lenders will insist on them anyway. Don't let them lay your proposal aside while you provide the facts they invariably need to make a favorable decision.

Unincorporated businesses with ten or more years of history, substantial net worth, and continuing profits may decide to forego personal statements in their initial package. They can await final negotiations to see if the lender will go ahead purely on the company track record and obvious financial strength.

If you are borrowing as a corporation, the lender criteria for requiring personal financial statements are fairly clear-cut.

Except for the older and obviously strong corporations, all major principals in closely held corporations and sub-Chapter S corporations will be asked to provide personal financial statements.

Unless the corporation is a public company, with shares traded over-the-counter or offered on one of the stock exchanges, the lenders want to see personal statements. They may not also automatically require personal guaranties, but they certainly want to look at the personal assets and liabilities of the principals. Most lenders will use the personal statement information to investigate each officer's paying habits. They look for evidence of poor debt management or tendencies to overspend.

If the lender asks for personal guaranties, they are often obtained to create a feeling of moral obligation. They want the principals to put their best efforts into the corporation, not hide behind it. However, if a corporation fails or defaults and the lender is unable to recover sums owed from repossessed equipment or other asset liquidations, they will then look to the personal assets of the officer guarantors. Nevertheless, many lenders hesitate to rely on recoveries from personal guaranties. They know recovery from individuals, if not voluntarily given, can be slow in legal process. Lenders are often unsuccessful in the courts when taking action against individuals involving personal guaranties.

Presentations are often used to search for willing lenders at the best possible rate and terms. If you send your financing proposal to two or more lenders, we believe it is most advantageous to immediately take your best shot. Don't hold back, hoping to be able to add to your presentation once a lender shows initial interest. You may never get the opportunity. Lenders who find proposals lacking in critical data will either quickly decline or pigeonhole your request. Include all of your business and personal financial strengths in the initial presentation. Get the lenders' attention and make them want you. Even if your personal financial statement signals to the lenders that your guaranty will also be obtainable, you may still negotiate its terms or dissuade them from requiring it.

After all, your objectives are to get the money on the best terms, at the lowest rate, and with the fewest limiting conditions or covenants. Remember, too, when the lender says, "The rate charged is derived from the extent of risk involved," to tell them, "If my personal guaranty reduces your risk, reduce my interest rate!"

In summary, the basic components of your presentation are:

- Application or information form
- Proposal letter
- Business financial statements
- Personal financial statements

These basic components, if properly prepared and done so in adequate detail, are generally sufficient for most routine equipment finance or lease "shopping" purposes. By providing the lenders with just these components, using neat, legible copies, you will get a better reception than you might with the usual haphazard approach.

By having copies organized and readily available in advance, you are free to use meeting time to communicate and negotiate. If you hand your presentation to the contact person, it will facilitate an accurate write-up. If you decide to mail it to selected lenders, you will also get better receptions. The lenders can swiftly analyze your proposal and financial qualifications. If questions develop, they will be fewer in number.

Many financing proposals fall apart or are sidetracked because they are incomplete or inadequate in relation to your requirements. If you decide to do without a presentation and depend on going through lender interviews and meetings, you run the risk of becoming the victim of lender ineptitudes.

If you offer a poor presentation that barely creates lender interest, the "we need" questions will start. "You show $375,000 in equipment assets but no list of equipment. What equipment do you have? What kind of expenses do you anticipate in your new operation? How long before it becomes self-supporting? When do you turn the corner? We need an interim financial statement. We need a cash forecast. We need—we need!" Don't invite endless questions. Don't risk being put on the bottom of the pile of loan requests.

If you are approaching three or four lenders, your problems multiply because the questions multiply. It just isn't worth shopping without a good presentation. Even if you spend a month in preparation and several hundred extra dollars in time and effort on those important borrowing or financing proposals, shape up that presentation! You'll get it back in lower rates, the right terms and conditions, and a valuable fast answer. Often you get an unexpected bonus when preparing a good presentation: you learn more about the financial aspects of your business! It also becomes a lesson in planning.

Finally, don't count on finding a lending officer or finance representative who is aggressive and truly interested in your needs. When you and your presentation go away, the lender person still has a secure job—and you're still looking for money! There aren't many deal-maker loan officers out in lender world—especially if your loan proposal needs a lot of work before credit approval presentation. A good presentation helps you lead them by the hand.

## Special Component Parts

Outlined below are the special component parts you should consider including when making a complete presentation. We will cover most of the possibilities, with comments that may prove helpful. It is your decision as to which parts are necessary to strengthen your particular proposal.

BUSINESS AND PERSONAL REFERENCES Sometimes the typical application form has inadequate space for references, or you may have chosen to omit this form. Rather than clutter up your proposal letter, make up a separate 8½" × 11" page listing your most important references. Do them in the order listed below:

*Bank references:* First indicate your business checking account, including number, branch name or location, telephone number, and officer to contact (if there is an individual who knows you and your account record). Indicate what types of accounts you have at this bank: checking, savings, loans, payroll account, etc.

Second, indicate any other banks you are presently dealing with. Repeat the detailed information suggested above. Consider including significant "closed" bank loan accounts—but not if over two years old.

*Finance or lease companies:* Account numbers and where lender should make reference contact is very important when listing these outside lenders. Quite often your account records are in a central file or computer in a distant headquarters. The local office where you set up the loan or lease may not have your current balance or full payment history on hand. Provide phone numbers to make it easy for lenders to obtain your payment performance.

*Nonbank savings accounts and mortage or trust deed loan accounts:* These are often with savings and loan associations. Most need to be checked by the lender, by mail. Many require your prior permission to release the savings balance or loan payment information.

If your savings accounts or mortgage payment records are sizable and significant in building a strong presentation, consider obtaining in advance a signed "statement of account," with dates and a rating from each account location. Why? First, you can attach these "proofs" to each proposal letter. Second, it can save a lot of time. Many S & Ls and mortgage holders take two to three weeks to reply. By the time your lender obtains your authorization, sends out an inquiry, and receives the rating, your loan request file is gathering dust.

*Supplier references:* Start with major suppliers with whom you know you're in good standing. Provide full data on account number (if any), whom to call, phone number and extension.

Consider indicating what type of supplier (if not self-evident from the name) and your average balance or credit limit. Indicate also if you are paying on special terms or by special agreement. Remember, suppliers may be reporting you as a "slow 60" or "slow 120" when you are really paying promptly under a special agreement with the supplier!

We don't think it is worthwhile to list oil company accounts (unless they're a major supplier, such as with truckers). Also, forget small-balance occasional suppliers. Of course, if you are a small business and have few open accounts, list anywhere your credit is established.

A complete, updated reference list is always useful to businesses, large or small; it is a timesaver that shortens those long lender interviews. It is ready to mail or use on the phone. You will find yourself using it for smaller loans or financing not requiring a full presentation. Keep the list up-to-date and extra copies on hand.

For individuals requesting a loan or lease for business purposes, you can prepare a similar reference list. It is usually best to attach personal references to your personal financial statement.

This personal reference list can also be used over and over, if prepared separately, even when you are not using a personal statement. The list saves you the time and effort required to insert in on the personal statement form or on an inadequate application form. A good reference list stops lender calls—"You show $9,975 in the bank. Which bank?" "You indicate a $90,000 equity in property with a $30,000 balance owing—to whom? Where can we call to verify?"

*Special references:* Indicate the name of your accountant and his phone number. If you have a CPA firm, their statements usually do not indicate the individual most familiar with your statements and business operation. Many accounting services omit the preparer's name or how to reach this person. If you prepare your own statements and/or someone in your company is responsible for accounting and statement preparation, it is expedient to provide this individual's name and phone number so that lenders can obtain answers without disturbing you. (If you prefer to provide the answers, simply request that lenders speak only to you or to a specific individual you authorize to handle this.)

You may also wish to list outside business consultants, equipment or real estate appraisers, or any other individuals or companies who are well acquainted with you or your company and its operation.

INCOME TAX RETURNS It is difficult to forecast or recommend when tax returns should be included or omitted from your presentations. Normally, we would prefer to see only well-prepared business and personal financial statements in the initial presentation.

Tax returns have always carried the connotation of being a private matter between an individual or company and the IRS. Aside from a certain "invasion of privacy" feeling, tax returns generally do not have financial data in sufficient detail for credit analysis. However, there has been an increasing trend among lenders to request tax returns, both business and personal, which they use to compare and confirm entries made in your financial statements. Under some circumstances, many lenders, particularly leasing companies, make tax returns a mandatory initial requirement.

The intent of a good presentation is to convince a lender or lessor to provide financing and to persuade him as completely as possible in the initial approach. If your income tax returns will contribute to your credibility and aid in winning credit approval, include the prior two years' statements immediately after the applicable financial statement.

There are occasions when inclusion of tax returns is helpful. Sometimes your income tax returns, prepared by a professional tax service, look better than your internally prepared financial statements. If you are borrowing money for a new venture and you are making the acquisition as an individual, your prior year tax returns may be your most convincing proof of earning capability or financial strength.

If you do include tax returns, provide them complete with all schedules and attachments. Go back two or three years so that the lender can see trends, progress, and stability. Always have several copies made before sending originals to the IRS. Keep good bond copies on file, ready for those lenders who require them.

EQUIPMENT APPRAISALS These can be expensive and are unnecessary if used in routine loan requests. We do not urge appraisals on our readers. Sometimes, however, you already have them from some recent loan or insurance requirement. Or, you may want to obtain an appraisal for your own future use. If so, it doesn't hurt to include a qualified appraisal or an appraisal letter that confirms your present or appraised value columns.

If your loan request is sizable in relation to your net worth and the loan is dependent in whole or in part upon equipment equities, an appraisal may very well be worth the cost. In many cases, without an appraisal, the lenders won't even consider the loan.

Quite often your balance sheet equipment asset account, after depreciation, is a very poor indicator of true value on today's market, especially if you have utilized accelerated depreciation. Some lenders, when they see equipment depreciated down, may assume it is old and not worth much in terms of loan security. In truth, due to inflation, using rapid depreciation methods and today's replacement costs, many items of well-maintained equipment have held their value, or actually increased. (Some machine tools are an excellent example of this phenomenon.) If this is your situation, you should strongly consider an appraisal.

Many lenders lack the expertise to look past the depreciated asset values with any degree of certainty. Lender analysts often have insufficient knowledge of current equipment values to properly adjust depreciated asset values. Those who may possess the necessary expertise still have difficulty convincing the credit committee. An appraisal can resolve this problem. Here are our suggestions concerning appraisals.

Don't get sold on an elaborate, expensive appraisal if your requirements do not warrant the cost and time involved.

Some appraisals are oversold by the professionals and are unnecessarily detailed. Unless you are going after an equipment loan between one half and several million dollars, you don't really need an appraisal that provides two or three remarketing values (such as auction value, fair market value, and quick-sale). These costly appraisals also may include an item-by-item condition inspection and condition opinion, painstaking reverification of model and serial numbers, a reinventory of every attachment or accessory, and even studies as to where equipment might be resold in the event of default.

These appraisals can take two or three weeks and require your time (or your manager's) to assist the appraisers. Although you may be presented a book-bound volume and a "certified" opinion, you might have done just as well—for less money—with a straightforward appraisal such as the following:

Locate a well-known auctioneer in your immediate area who is experienced in your type of equipment. Although some auctioneers conduct sales of several equipment types, your best choice is an auctioneer who specializes in your major asset items—trucks and trailers, construction equipment, machine tools, electronic and test equipment, etc. Auctioneers who do appraisals usually have standardized costs based on time spent, number of items, travel-time expense, and, perhaps, a flat cost tied to the amount of money involved. Determine these costs in advance and get at least an estimate of expected total cost.

Obtain a written agreement or a letter of agreement from the auctioneer, outlining when the appraisal will be started, when the completed written appraisal will be presented to you, what the appraisal will cover and in what detail, and how much the appraisal will cost.

In addition to providing a conservative value on each item, some auctioneers will provide a guaranteed total sales value. They will sometimes offer to buy the equipment prior to the auction at their appraised value, take all that does not sell, and make other assurances.

Owners seeking to borrow often have thoughts of selling out if they can't obtain desired loans or refinancing. Sometimes they decide to auction or privately sell only a portion of unneeded equipment to raise all or part of the funds needed to stay in business or expand—or do whatever they originally sought the funds for. The guaranty by the auctioneer is also a reinforcement of the actual appraisal. Borrowers frequently show this guaranted buy-out to the lender(s), to convince them the appraisal is not wishful thinking or padded.

Another suggestion would be to locate a used equipment dealer in your area, specializing in your types of equipment. Some dealers are experienced in preparing a valid appraisal. They know current values from years of buying at private and auction sales and their own sales experiences. Even if this dealer is not able to render a "certified" appraisal, if he has been in business for a number of years, his professional opinion is meaningful to the lenders.

Dealers usually have access to used equipment guidebooks and auction sale reports, and they also know how to quickly confirm special or unusual equipment values with other dealers or through market research. A dealer may prove the most reasonable in cost. Take care to choose one with a good reputation whom the lenders will accept as an authority. Work out an agreement in advance, as suggested for auctioneer appraisals.

You will get better results, at less cost in money and time, if you provide the appraiser with a well-organized, detailed equipment list. He should be spending his time setting values, not searching for equipment and accessories.

Some lenders have appraisers on their staff or regularly use outside firms or individuals. Inquire with them, but realize that these appraisers will have the lender's best interests in mind, rather than yours. As a result, many staff appraisers, especially those with banks, are ultraconservative. They also lack expertise in many equipment fields and are slow to react and to complete the task. You can, however, negotiate low-cost appraisals with lenders and sometimes obtain a refund of costs if you borrow from that lender.

If the loan is sizable and critical to your company's survival, future progress, or expansion, call in a recognized appraiser who belongs to the American Society of Appraisers. Three such appraisers are American Appraisal Co., Inc., General Appraisal Company, and Tait Appraisal Company.

There are also many excellent local companies that belong to the society. For these, and appraisers who specialize in particular types of equipment, consult your Yellow Pages, under Appraisers.

Their appraisals are generally more costly. They are thorough and usually respected by lenders. Be sure to have a good list ready and assist them to expedite completion.

REAL ESTATE APPRAISALS If you are going to use land or buildings to help secure an equipment loan, or the values and equities are a critical part of your net worth (company or personal), your presentation could include an appraisal or realtor's opinion.

If you use a real estate broker to help substantiate your values and equities, we suggest that you have them include recent comparative sales of similar local property. Find a respected broker who knows your type of property.

If you are going into an extensive real property appraisal, be sure the appraiser is a current member of the American Institute of Real Estate Appraisers or the American Society of Real Estate Counselors. You will find these appraisers in the telephone directory Yellow Pages designated as accredited M.A.I. (Member of Appraisal Institute) or as C.R.E. (Counselor of Real Estate). Lenders accept their opinions and appraisal valuations, knowing they are accredited and the most qualified.

Sometimes, the only way to obtain financing is to provide positive proof of real estate values. Many equipment lenders are not equipped to provide this service but may require appraisals before loaning money. Banks will sometimes provide this service, but they may prove slow and ultraconservative. Often, they do only reverifications and residential-type appraisals.

ACCOUNTS RECEIVABLE AGING This subject is covered in chapter eight. Figure 8-1 at the end of that chapter, provides a suggested A/R aging form.

There are occasions when an aging is not needed in your presentation. This is particularly true in essentially cash-type businesses with only minor monthly receivables, in contract work concentrated in one or two major receivables, or when the receivables are obviously turning very well and not an analysis factor.

For most other businesses, your A/R and how you handle them is a definite concern to all lenders. Whenever your loan, lease, or purchase request is sizable, the lenders always analyze your receivable turnover in relation to monthly or annual sales. If there is any indication of "slow turn," unusual returns and allowances, heavier-than-usual discounts, or excessive bad debt write-offs, then questions will start.

Anticipate their questions by including your most current aging in neat, legible form. If your A/R are a key issue, it is sometimes impressive and helpful to include the prior three or six end-of-month agings so they can see a pattern.

If your A/R consist of hundreds of accounts of smaller balances, a customer list is impractical. Instead, present an analysis of A/R aging by dollar amount totals and the number of accounts in each age category—current, 31 to 60 days, 61 to 90 days, and 91 days and over. An exception to this category treatment might be a computer printout of all customers, dollars owed, and age.

Although accounts receivables are often the guts of the typical business, maintaining a well-kept aging is sadly neglected by numerous business people. If your A/R are in good shape, you should proudly offer the aging as a display of strength. If they are not in good shape, it is quite useless to avoid the issue by omitting the list. The lender will come after it anyway. After all, your slow collections may be the very reason you are borrowing or trying to conserve cash with lease financing. You'll do much better with the lenders by being "up front" and at least demonstrating that you recognize and are handling your receivables problems.

If you are seeking accounts receivable financing, you have wasted your time if you omit a detailed aging.

If you are concerned about revealing your customers' identities in an initial presentation, replace the names with account numbers. Or substitute an aging by category. It is usually nonsense to worry that lender of stature and reputation for confidentiality might reveal your customers' names to your competition.

If your customer list consists of strong, easily recognized names who have a reputation for prompt payment, your A/R list will enhance your presentation. When you include an aging in your presentation, place it immediately after your most recent financial statements.

ACCOUNTS PAYABLE AGING OR RECAP If your A/P are apparently under control and not a significant factor in total current liabilities, an aging can be omitted. If your payables are close to one-to-one with your receivables, it might be reassuring to the lenders to see an aging, so they can analyze your handling of them.

If you are seeking a debt consolidation loan which would involve paying some or all of the open accounts, an aging or recap is mandatory.

DEBT CONSOLIDATION If your loan request involves debt consolidation, it is important to list the obligations you wish to pay off.

If you wish to prepay any contracts, loans, leases, or accounts payable, provide a complete list of who is owed and where the payables are located, amounts due, account numbers, and phone numbers (if possible). The idea is to expedite "how paid" verifications and to ascertain correct amounts actually due.

If you are paying off contracts with precomputed finance charges, there will be refunds of unearned charges in most cases. Sometimes these refunds are sizable and will affect the amount to be borrowed. Obtain closeouts from the lenders in advance, so that you can project the net balance due and schedule that amount in your consolidation loan request. You may also calculate your own closeouts and determine the proper refund of unearned finance charges.

By using our refund charts, you can guard against being short changed on refunds by the lenders' quoting balances due. We treat the entire matter of proper refund computations in chapter six, including an explanation of the "Rule of 78ths." Figures 6-1 and 6-2 at the end of that chapter provide refund charts and explanations. You will find these charts useful in preplanning and also in checking the final results of balances due to be refinanced in the consolidation loan. The new lender will verify all loan balances due, after refunds, and they usually send closeout proceeds to all lenders being paid off.

Protect yourself against improper or inaccurate computations of all closeouts by rechecking them. Be aware that your new lender may simply accept whatever the other lenders say is due to close out old loan balances.

If your loan request is for multiple purposes, including extensive debt consolidation and, perhaps, money for equipment acquisitions, real estate, remodeling and expansion, or other uses, be sure to include a summary identifying each part of your requirements. This list will help the lender to understand your needs and expedite their consideration. An organized summary of a multipurpose loan is businesslike and useful to the borrower and the lenders, to whom a presentation is sent or offered in personal meetings.

INVENTORY, WORK IN PROCESS, AND WORK IN PROGRESS REPORTS Whenever your inventories are heavy or make up an important part of your assets, it is a good idea to anticipate lender questions with an inventory recap.

Describe and value finished goods, partially completed products, raw materials, and, possibly, their salability. If your inventories consist of materials tied up in long-run construction or in manufacturing custom machinery, it is often helpful to provide customer names (or job numbers for confidentiality) in addition to the inventory dollars tied up in each job.

- *Work in process:* When significant, such work should be broken down by customer name or job number, dollars involved, and percentage completed or expected completion dates.

  If computerized inventory or work in process printouts are available, attach them to your presentation. Reduce these printouts to 8½" × 11" recaps.
- *Work in progress:* When you have extensive construction work

in various stages of completion, you also have labor, materials, and other running expenses—money tied up.

Provide the lenders with a good breakdown by customer or contract name, location, dollars involved, percent completed, and dates of expected completion.

In either of these cases, if you hold deposits or advances or if there will be retentions for future release, such data should be included in your recap.

If possible, include copies of production contracts, work agreements, bid proposals, or construction awards to substantiate your future cash flow. Contractors involved with bonding companies should provide copies of their bonding qualifications and supporting data.

REMODELING, EXPANSION, AND NEW BUILDING PLANS If your loan request is for any of these purposes, summarize the use of funds. Be careful not to oversimplify your outline by saying too little. Don't just say, "Need money to remodel. We plan to buy another building." Provide the lender with preliminary or completed drawings, bids, and cost details. Color snapshots or drawings are particularly effective visual aids for credit managers. Always explain, in at least some detail, what the changes or additions will do for your business.

EQUIPMENT DATA Brochures, photographs, and equipment specifications are great visual aids and help the credit analyst understand what he or she is considering financing. Credit people are notoriously short on imagination, and they are often "tied to the desk." What is common and ordinary to a borrowing contractor, production shop owner, food processor-packer, doctor, or dentist can be a whole new experience to a credit manager working on the twenty-ninth floor of an office building.

It is usually easy to obtain color brochures from the vendor of new equipment. If you are borrowing against your existing equipment, take your own pictures. Just good color snapshots, mounted on an 8″ X 11″ sheet of heavy paper and properly captioned, can give your proposal graphic meaning. Include as many pictorial and visual aids as possible throughout the presentation.

PRO FORMA FINANCIAL STATEMENTS AND PROJECTIONS
Whenever you are trying to borrow or finance equipment for a new venture to materially expand an existing business, adding equipment that is costly in relation to your net worth, you need to provide pro forma financial statements and/or projections to demonstrate what should happen when the capital is injected or the equipment added.

The most difficult pro formas are those for a completely new venture. No matter how carefully you construct these statements, with extensive projections, credit analysts are inclined to place little reliance on your crystal ball unless supported by historical facts. Your projected balance sheet and income statements, of necessity, are filled with "if" numbers. If any of the "if" numbers fail to materialize, the other numbers may not hold together.

The solution is to make the pro forma statements as real as possible. The starting point is to substantiate your capital investment—and any investment monies to come in during future months. Then plug in the proposed borrowed funds and the ensuing projected payback on the desired terms. If you are borrowing to finance equipment, project potential sales and profits the equipment will realistically produce.

There are many other financial statement numbers that you can substantiate from precedents and historical data derived from similar circumstances. You can project, with reasonable accuracy, the salaries and wages to be paid, taxes, insurance, telephone and postal costs, interest expenses, and payments to be made on loans and equipment. Be realistic, not overoptimistic. Cite similar cases whenever possible.

The difficult number to project is anticipated sales. This estimate should be on the conservative side. But just saying it is conservative and easy to attain is not sufficient. Provide backup proof such as:

- *Income statements from your previous business*, if similar in operation. If buying an existing business, present prior year income statements and provide explicit examples and reasoning for claims of improvements in sales and profits.
- *Comparable income statements derived from similar businesses and circumstances.* Cite comparisons based on number of employees, square footage of production areas, number of machines, or units of construction equipment in production.
- *Actual records of other shops, distributorships, or sales outlets.* Franchise operations are a good example of readily available statistical income statement data. Many other businesses have industry average sales statistics on record. At the public library, check U.S. government reports and books specifically about your business or industry.

As an alternative, or to reinforce pro forma financial statements, use projections. These can consist of:

- Projected sales
- Projected production
- Income and expense projections
- Cash-flow projections
- Projected contract completions
- Projected incoming capital

Present projections on a month-by-month basis for the first

year. Perhaps you might add annual year-end totals for one or more additional years. Back your numbers with historical precedents whenever possible.

It's virtually impossible to obtain financing for new ventures, mergers, acquisitions, or major refinancing without well-prepared pro forma statements and/or projections. If you are going after bigger bucks than you are accustomed to seeking, consider using the assistance of an outside accountant or business consultant.

Don't sell yourself short on working up a presentation. You probably know more about the business you are in or are seeking to acquire than any outsiders. Your input and savvy, properly organized and aided by technical advice, will be the backbone of a good presentation. Draw upon the talents of people in your company. Start early, plan carefully, and put your know-how into a winning presentation!

BUSINESS PLANS A good business plan combines pro forma statements and projections with the following possible additional data:

- Company history
- Experience and personal history of principals
- Company goals, objectives, and accomplishments
- Pictures, charts, and graphs
- Projections or budgets with variables: Plug numbers into these forecasts on the basis of "what if" hypotheses. For example: What if we borrow X dollars? What if we lease instead of borrow? What if we inject capital and also borrow? What if we add three machines instead of one? What happens at differing sales volumes?
- Capital equipment acquisition plans and budgets
- Departmental budgets
- Direct labor-hour analysis
- Management decision analysis (How we came to our decisions or conclusions)
- Results of simulated models
- Scheduled or projected plant openings and expansions
- Timetables of forecasts or future events

An all-inclusive list isn't possible, but we hope our suggestions have stimulated your imagination. The objective of a business plan is to provide the lender's credit management with maximum reassurances they are making a good decision. The soundness of your plan must convince a credit manager or committee to recommend your financing request. Give the lender the ammunition to say yes. Unless you are borrowing directly from a wealthy investor, all credit people are employees entrusted with company money. They all need positive reinforcement and your help to convince themselves that their yes was wise and will prove ultimately profitable.

## YOUR PRESENTATION DOESN'T HAVE TO BE A WORK OF ART

A business plan could combine all of our suggested basic component parts and those special components that lend themselves to an effective presentation. The business plan, therefore, could be your entire proposal, except for the details of your money requirements.

Normally, however, a business plan is itself a special component part. It is a crucial part when seeking special situation financing. Its main purpose is to set forth an organized picture of your future plans and how you propose to achieve your goals with the lender's assistance.

Your presentation doesn't have to be a work of art to be an effective tool in achieving the best deal. In its simplest form, all that is really necessary is that you take care in providing a presentation incorporating the basic elements of appearance, organization, and clarity, with accurate and complete contents.

Staple together each of the basic component parts and mail them to your selected lender with a cover letter outlining your requirements. Or, call the lenders and arrange appointments with their contact people.

No matter which approach you take, your well-prepared presentation helps keep you in the driver's seat. Instead of being on the defensive, answering the lenders' questions and scrambling to fulfill their "we needs," you are in a position to launch a bit of an offensive—to negotiate.

You can take your presentation to any length or depth the situation seems to require to accomplish your borrowing objective. For your important borrowings your presentation will likely be in greater depth. Put the financial statements in covers with titles appearing on labels or in slotted openings. Additional data with special component parts could be in additional 9" X 12" covers, organized and identified with titles.

An extensive presentation could be put together in a loose-leaf binder, complete with a table of contents and divider tabs. Many copy centers now offer inexpensive plastic-ring or pressed plastic-strip bindings. Without overdoing it, try to provide the lender with a neat, well-organized package that is not bulky and is easy to review. If overdone and too flashy in appearance, it could spell "con" to the credit analyst; if too much technical or extraneous material is included, it could cause confusion.

Your presentation is an investment of time, effort, and money that should pay dividends. It should help you avoid going after the money on a piecemeal basis. The objective is to eliminate or minimize hassles with the lenders that end up taking up more of your time than you would spend on advance preparation of a comprehensive presentation. A good presentation helps keep you in a position of control yet allows you time to do what you do best—run your business!

## CHECKLIST FOR YOUR PRESENTATION

Here is a summary of the basic and special component parts that you may utilize in your presentation:

- Proposal letter
- Application or information form
- Business financial statements
- Personal financial statements
- Business or personal references
- Income tax returns
- Equipment lists
- Equipment appraisals
- Real estate appraisals
- Accounts receivable aging
- Accounts payable aging or recap
- Debt consolidation
- Inventory, work in process, and work in progress reports
- Remodeling, expansion, and new building plans
- Equipment data
- Pro forma financial statements and projections
- Business plans

FIGURE 2-1

# FINANCE APPLICATION

A COMPLETE APPLICATION WILL EXPEDITE OUR ANSWER

Company Name ________ Date ________

Address ________
Street

City ________ State ________ Zip ________

Nature of Business ________

Person to Contact ________
Title

Telephone Number ________
Area Code & No. Extension

**Form of Organization**

☐ Corporation (Complete 1A, Below)

State of Incorporation ________

☐ Proprietorship (Complete 1B, Below)

☐ Partnership (Complete 1C, Below)

When Business Organized ________
Date or Year

1A.
Officers: President ________ Vice President ________ Treasurer ________

Controller, or, Vice President-Finance ________ Secretary ________ Other Authorized Agent ________

1B. (Residence and Personal Data)
Name of Owner ________ Res. Phone ________ Spouse' First Name ________
Street Address ________ City ________ State ________ Zip ________
Bank and Branch (Personal Account) ________ Contact: ________

1C. (Residence and Personal Data)
Name of Partner ________ Res. Phone ________ Spouse' First Name ________
Street Address ________ City ________ State ________ Zip ________
Bank and Branch (Personal Account) ________ Contact: ________

1C. (Residence and Personal Data)
Name of Partner ________ Res. Phone ________ Spouse' First Name ________
Street Address ________ City ________ State ________ Zip ________
Bank and Branch (Personal Account) ________ Contact: ________

1C. (Residence and Personal Data)
Name of Partner ________ Res. Phone ________ Spouse' First Name ________
Street Address ________ City ________ State ________ Zip ________
Bank and Branch (Personal Account) ________ Contact ________

**Credit Information**

Banking Connections (Business)

1. Bank ________
Branch Address ________
Street
________
City Zone State

Person to Contact ________

2. Bank ________
Branch Address ________
Street
________
City Zone State

Person to Contact ________

over

(APPLICANT – LEAVE THIS SECTION BLANK)

| Type of Account | Loans Outstanding | How Secured | Average Balances | Rating |
|---|---|---|---|---|
| | | | | |

FIGURE 2-1 (continued)

FINANCE APPLICATION (Continued)

Trade References (Provide Telephone Number or Full Address)

1. Name Street City State Zip

2. Name Street City State Zip

3. Name Street City State Zip

Other Lease or Contract Obligations (Provide Phone Number or Full Address)

1. Name Street City State Zip

2. Name Street City State Zip

3. Name Street City State Zip

Description of Equipment

New ☐ Used ☐ Reconditioned ☐

| Quantity | Type | Manufacturer | Model/Serial Number | Itemized Cost |
|---|---|---|---|---|
| | | | | |
| | | | | |
| | | | | |
| | | | | |
| | | | | |
| | | | | |
| | | | | |
| | | | | |

(If Space Insufficient, Attach Description Lists)

If equipment purchased may become affixed to realty, provide the following information:

Landlord Name ______ Term of Lease ______

Address ______ Renewal ______

Mortgagee Name ______ Monthly Rent ______
(or, Monthly mortgage payments)

Address ______

Seller ______

Address ______
Street

City State Zip Phone No.

Salesman ______ Phone No. ______

Approximate Delivery Date ______
(Enter Date Buyer will Receive Equipment)

Terms Desired ______
(Enter No. of Months or Years)

Preferred Date in Month for payments ______
(Enter 5th, 10th, 15th, 20th, 25th)

Payments to be made: Monthly ______ Quarterly ______ Special ______

Special Terms Desired ______
(Enter Seasonal Skips or other Terms)

Freight ______
Installation ______
Other ______
Total Price ______
State & Local Sales Tax ______
Special Tax ______
Total Sales Price ______
Down Payment ______
Balance Financed ______

All Statements Contained in this Application For Credit A Warranted to be True and Accurate

Company Name ______

Signature of Applicant ______

Title ______ Date ______

FIGURE 2-2

# LEASE APPLICATION

A COMPLETE APPLICATION WILL EXPEDITE OUR ANSWER

Company Name ______ Date ______

Address ______
Street

City ______ State ______ Zip ______

Nature of Business ______

Person to Contact ______
Title

Telephone Number ______
Area Code & No. Extension

Form of Organization

☐ Corporation (Complete 1A, Below)

State of Incorporation ______

☐ Proprietorship (Complete 1B, Below)

☐ Partnership (Complete 1C, Below)

When Business Organized ______ Date or Year

1A.

Officers: President ______ Vice President ______ Treasurer ______

Controller, or, Vice President-Finance ______ Secretary ______ Other Authorized Agent ______

1B. (Residence and Personal Data)

Name of Owner ______ Res. Phone ______ Spouse' First Name ______

Street Address ______ City ______ State ______ Zip ______

Bank and Branch ______ Contact: ______

(Personal Account)

1C. (Residence and Personal Data)

Name of Partner ______ Res. Phone ______ Spouse' First Name ______

Street Address ______ City ______ State ______ Zip ______

Bank and Branch ______ Contact: ______

(Personal Account)

1C. (Residence and Personal Data)

Name of Partner ______ Res. Phone ______ Spouse' First Name ______

Street Address ______ City ______ State ______ Zip ______

Bank and Branch ______ Contact: ______

(Personal Account)

1C. (Residence and Personal Data)

Name of Partner ______ Res. Phone ______ Spouse' First Name ______

Street Address ______ City ______ State ______ Zip ______

Bank and Branch ______ Contact ______

(Personal Account)

## Credit Information

Banking Connections (Business)

1. Bank ______

Branch Address ______
Street

______
City Zone State

Person to Contact ______

2. Bank ______

Branch Address ______
Street

______
City Zone State

Person to Contact ______

(APPLICANT – LEAVE THIS SECTION BLANK)

| Type of Account | Loans Outstanding | How Secured | Average Balances | Rating |
|---|---|---|---|---|
| | | | | |

over

FIGURE 2-2 (continued)

LEASE APPLICATION (Continued)

Trade References (Provide Telephone Number or Full Address)

1. ____ Name ____ Address or Phone ____ City ____ State ____ Zip

2. ____ Name ____ Address or Phone ____ City ____ State ____ Zip

3. ____ Name ____ Address or Phone ____ City ____ State ____ Zip

Other Lease or Contract Obligations (Provide Phone Number or Full Address)

1. ____ Name ____ Address or Phone ____ City ____ State ____ Zip

2. ____ Name ____ Address or Phone ____ City ____ State ____ Zip

3. ____ Name ____ Address or Phone ____ City ____ State ____ Zip

Description of Equipment

New ☐ Used ☐ Reconditioned ☐

| Quantity | Type | Manufacturer | Model/Serial Number | Itemized Cost |
|---|---|---|---|---|
| | | | | |
| | | | | |
| | | | | |
| | | | | |
| | | | | |
| | | | | |
| | | | | |

(If Space Insufficient, Attach Description Lists)

If equipment to be leased may become affixed to realty, provide the following information:

Landlord Name ____ Term of Lease ____

Address ____ Renewal ____

Mortgagee Name ____ Monthly Rent ____ (or, monthly mortgage payments)

Address ____

Vendor ____

Address ____ Street

____ City ____ State ____ Zip ____ Phone No.

Representative ____ Phone No. ____

Approx. Delivery Date ____ (Enter Date Lessee Will Receive Equipment) Term of Lease Desired ____ (Enter No. of Months or years)

Date Lease to Commence ____ Payments: Monthly ☐ Quarterly ☐

Equipment Location ____ (Give Complete Address)

F.O.B. ____ VIA: ____ Prepaid ☐ Collect ☐

*State and city sales tax varies. In some jurisdictions tax may be imposed on total invoice on the monthly lease payment (use tax).

Freight ____
Installation ____
Total ____
Federal Excise Tax ____
Sales Tax* ____
Total Invoice Cost ____
Multiply By Lease Rate ____
Monthly Lease Payment ____
Advance Lease Payment ____

All Statements Contained in this Application For Credit Are Warranted to be True and Accurate

____ Company Name

____ Signature of Applicant

____ Title ____ Date

# 3

# THE MATHEMATICS OF FINANCING MADE EASY

The mathematics employed to determine payment schedules for commercial and industrial financing is relatively simple. Various rate factors have been developed to shortcut the calculations necessary to arrive at monthly, quarterly, semiannual, or annual repayment schedules. These rate factors are equivalent to an annual interest rate, which is in turn directly related to the agreed term of repayment.

Use of a rate factor simplifies arriving at the total finance charge for a given term of an unpaid loan or contract balance. The rate factor eliminates the need to prepare an interest-principal amortization schedule for each finance transaction. The factors can be quickly and accurately used by sales people as well as trained bank or finance company personnel.

All rate factors relate to an actuarial annual interest rate. This actuarial rate expresses the true return on an investment. By the same token, the equivalent interest rate also represents your true cost of financing. To the lenders and lessors, the true interest rate represents their gross "yield" in a given finance transaction. From this gross yield they must deduct their own "wholesale" money costs and all monies expended in locating borrowers or lessees, booking the transaction, and collecting the payments.

Whenever a lease or finance rate factor is used to determine finance charges and a repayment schedule, you will have a "fixed-rate" transaction. That is, the finance costs are a predetermined amount. The equivalent simple interest rate will prevail for the duration of the loan, lease, or contract. The repayment schedule, whether it be monthly or at some other calendar interval, is calculated to return the lender or lessor's investment plus the desired yield or interest rate.

The rate factors used in fixed-rate financing are:

1. Add-on rates
2. Discount rates
3. Lease rates

Each of these rate factors has been reduced to rate charts, broken down to varying repayment periods and the equivalent simple interest rate. In the case of lease rate factors, the rate charts also take into consideration many of the common variations that occur because of differing advance rentals, deposits, and purchase options. Business people who are frequently involved in loans or equipment financing or leasing or in making budgets and projections involving the attendant payment schedules should consider purchasing these charts. They are relatively inexpensive and easy to use. Two major sources for these publications are listed at the end of this chapter.

For those infrequently involved in interest rate and payment determinations, the charts provided in this book should prove adequate for most situations. All business people will benefit from having a basic understanding of rate factors and how they are used by the lenders and lessors. A grasp of the fundamentals will assist you in dealing more knowledgeably with all money sources. The same knowledge will simplify and expedite your planning and budgeting, minimizing size-of-payment and interest rate guesswork in forecastings.

## ADD-ON RATES

Finance companies often talk in terms of a rate or charge called an add-on rate. They call it that because the resultant finance charge is added to your unpaid balance, either after a down payment on a purchase or on the total amount they loan to you.

It is a very simple calculation. If the add-on rate is, for example, 10% and your contract will run for 3 years, in 36 equal monthly payments, just multiply 3 (years) times 10% (add-on), which equals a "factor" of 30%, or .30.

Your unpaid contract balance or loan amount is then multiplied by .30 to arrive at the finance charge. This finance charge is added to your unpaid balance or loan amount and then divided by the number of months (in this case, 36) to arrive at your monthly payment.

Similarly, if your contract or loan balance will run 2 years, repayable in 24 equal monthly payments, or 4 years, in 48 equal monthly payments, or 5 years, in 60 equal monthly payments, simply multiply the number of years times the desired add-on rate, times your unpaid balance or loan amount.

Thus, 10% add-on times 2 years becomes 20%, or a .20 factor;

4 years at 10% add-on times 4 years gives a .40 factor; and 5 years at 10% add-on times 5 years results in a .50 factor.

Are you therefore paying 10% interest, or 20% interest for 2 years, 30% for 3 years, etc.? The answer is no; it is not interest you are paying.

What you are paying is a finance charge or credit service charge that is added to the entire original balance. It is a simple means of calculation, long employed by sales finance companies. When quoted as an annual rate, such as 10% "A.O.," it doesn't sound so high as the equivalent actuarial simple interest rate, which on a 3-year basis would be 17.92%.

In addition to simplifying the calculations, depending upon your state laws, an add-on rate can circumvent usury laws limiting interest rates expressed as "simple interest." It isn't interest per se but a finance charge, time-balance credit charge. (See Fig. 3-1 at the end of this chapter.)

The add-on rate discussed above requires a series of consecutive, equal monthly payments, without any skip-payment months or variation in amount. By utilizing formulas or rate charts, the add-on rate can be used to determine the finance charge and payment schedule for quarterly, semiannual, annual, or skip-payment transactions. You will be able to calculate unusual payment schedules by working with our skip-payment format. For those who are constantly working with seasonal or crop payments, quarterly, semiannual, or annual payments, it might be worthwhile to obtain rate charts covering such schedules. They will shortcut the more lengthy calculations required in our formula for "skips," presented later in this chapter. On the other hand, just as the basic add-on rates depend on consecutive, equal monthly payments, the regular quarterly, semiannual, and annual charts depend on consecutive and equal payments on the period basis. Our skip-payment formula permits calculation of all manner of intermittent skip months.

RULE OF 78THS The add-on method of calculation permits the lender to use a formula for refunding unearned finance charges, if you repay early, called the "rule of 78ths." This is also called the "78ths method" or the "sum-of-the-digits method." All three names are correct; they mean the same. Simply put, this formula enables the lender to determine how much of the precalculated finance charge has been earned and how much should be rebated, at the point of early payout. For an explanation, see Figure 6-1.

It is interesting to note that if a consumer borrows on a fixed-rate basis, the lender will report annually to the borrower how much in finance charges they took into earnings. The consumer borrower then knows how much "interest" is deductible on that year's income tax return. Not so with business borrowings. Most businesses must determine independently how much was paid in finance charge interest on commercial loans, contracts, or leases. Generally speaking, you can simplify this calculation by reversing the percentages in our refund charts (Figs. 6-1 and 6-2). That is, if the percentage indicated for a given elapsed number of months tells you how much rebate would be forthcoming (if you paid off the loan), then the opposite percentage is the amount the lender earned during the same elapsed months. Just as with your home mortgage payments, the interest costs are at their highest levels when the loan starts, gradually descending as each payment is applied. Check with your accountant; but you should be able to expense the finance charges at the same rate the lender is taking these charges into earnings. I have seen many business people, particularly those doing their own tax returns, simply divide the number of months of the contract term into the original finance charge. They then deduct or expense an equal amount of finance charge for each year of the loan. This is not the way the lender is earning interest on the investment.

The rule of 78ths method is covered in chapter six "How to Calculate Your Own Closeout Refund." If you do not know the simple interest equivalent charged on your loans or contracts—or if you would prefer not going through a simple interest amortization calculation to determine finance charges paid in your tax year—use our rule of 78ths charts.

In recent years, with many commercial finance companies on computerized accounting, they are either voluntarily advising their customers or will advise, on request, how much interest was earned. Ask them, if you are doing your own accounting and tax reporting; it will save you considerable time. And with interest costs at extremely high levels, you should expense all you can to reduce your tax obligation. As an illustration, on a sixty-month equal-payment contract, calculated at a fixed add-on rate, in the first year the lender will have earned at least 35.74% of the total original finance charge!

In summary, the add-on rate is the charge, per $100 of original balance per year, applied for the full term. The actuarial interest rate on funds actually in use used to be something less than double the stated rate of charge. Using this as a rule of thumb was never very accurate. Yet, as recently as 1976, business people would hear an add-on rate of, say, 6% and say to the lender, "Oh, yes, 6% add-on is about 12% simple interest." It was a poor rule of thumb then and it is useless now. If you use it with a lender today, it is a sure tip-off that your understanding of finance rates is limited.

For instance, at today's higher interest rates, an add-on rate of 11.13 (per hundred per year), on a sixty-month repayment term, equals 19% simple interest. Years ago, with interest at the 9 to 10% level, the rule of thumb was closer to valid, but hardly an accurate way to determine your true interest cost.

## DISCOUNT RATE

Another standard finance rate is the discount rate factor. It is not used as frequently as the add-on rate. In fact, it is not employed by as many banks and finance companies as was common practice prior to about 1965. Sometimes bankers will call a fixed-rate factor a "discount rate" when they really mean an add-on rate.

The main use of a discount rate factor is for commercial loans other than equipment finance contracts. Simply put, the discount finance charge is deducted from the loan proceeds in advance. Thus, if you borrow $50,000 and the lender employs a discount rate, your loan proceeds are reduced by the entire finance charge. You repay the full $50,000, but the lender has received his interest charge "in front."

Of course, if you need a net of $50,000 in loan proceeds, it is necessary to borrow more so that the lender could "discount the loan." In use, the discount rate factor works very much like an add-on rate. The same simple arithmetic is employed. Our example below demonstrates a discount-rate loan transaction and at the same time illustrates the size loan necessary to net $50,000 at 19% simple interest equivalent. The example loan is for three years, repayable in 36 equal monthly payments.

### Example of Discount Rate Calculations

The discount rate factor that will provide a simple interest equivalent of 19% on a 36-month, equal-payment contract is 8.07. (This rate factor can be found by referring to our Discount Rate Chart, Fig. 3-3, at the end of this chapter.)

| | | |
|---|---|---|
| Discount rate factor: | 8.07 | |
| Three-year term | X 3 | (36 monthly payments) |
| | 24.21 | |

Desired loan amount: $50,000.00

Amount required to net $50,000.00 is approx. $66,000.00.

| | |
|---|---|
| $66,000.00 | |
| X .2421 | Rate for three-year term |
| $15,978.60 | Finance charge |
| $66,000.00 | Amount borrowed |
| −15,978.60 | Finance charge |
| $50,021.40 | Net loan to borrower |

Payment calculation:

$66,000.00 ÷ 36 (months) = $1,833.33 per month

Commercial bank loans are still made on this basis in certain parts of the country, particularly the South and the Southeast. The discount rate factor is not useful in sales contract financing, because the unpaid balance is generally the amount the lender pays to the seller of the product. The add-on finance charge is applied to this unpaid balance. There is a psychological advantage to quoting a discount rate of "8.07 discount per year"—it doesn't sound as high as 19% simple interest per annum, which it really equals.

## LEASE RATES

The third fixed-rate factor in general use is the lease rate factor. Lease rate factors are easy to use because by simple multiplication you can arrive at a monthly payment. The only thing difficult about figuring a lease payment is the large number of possible variables. Basically, the variances are caused by how many advance rentals or security deposits are paid "up front" and how much of the purchase option will be paid, if any, at the end of the lease term. The advance rentals or security deposits paid to the lender or lessor immediately decreases the size of his investment. The lessor, generally a bank or finance company or one of their leasing subsidiaries, pays a vendor or distributor for the product being leased. Any front money from you, the lessee, decreases his out-of-pocket investment. The purchase option amount, generally paid after the lease has run the agreed term, also contributes to the lessor's earnings. Once again, there is considerable variance in just how much value this option has to a lessor, how it is determined when the option is exercised, and the manner in which that future value is calculated into the monthly lease payment.

Just as with add-on and discount rates, the more commonly used lease rates have been reduced to Lease Rate Charts. (See Fig. 3-4). These charts commonly cover the usual number of years that leases are extended. In addition, the charts are broken down to cover the usual number of advance rentals or security deposits and several different purchase option percentages. The Lease Rate Charts at the end of this chapter cover a range of simple interest equivalents and are all based on equal monthly lease payment terms. As with add-on and discount rates, quarterly, semiannual, and annual fixed lease payment charts are available. Most leases are structured with payments in advance. All of our charts are based on advance rentals or security deposits.

We will confine ourselves here to explaining the basics of working with lease rate factors. Chapter Seven, "The Inside Scoop on Leasing," covers the leasing variables in more depth, including pertinent terminology and peculiarities.

Unlike add-on or discount rate calculations, the fixed lease finance charges are not readily apparent. They are not a separately stated amount. The finance costs are seldom stated because lease payments are supposedly "rental" payments. Nevertheless, each lease payment contains a portion of the lessor's interest earnings.

It is safe to say that the majority of leases being written today are not really "true" leases, but a financing arrangement structured to appear as a lease. Even the more complex true leases involving an unstated "fair market value" purchase option amount will include interest earnings to the lessor. For explanatory purposes, we will outline a typical finance lease arrangement. At the end of the example, we illustrate a simple way to extract finance charges contained in the "rental payments" and/or fixed purchase option.

Most lessors who treat the lease as financing will not depreciate the equipment purchased, even though they purchase with their own dollars. By the same token, they will bring the lease finance charges into income based generally on the rule of 78ths. Properly, then, as lessee, you can determine annual lease finance charges in the same manner as an add-on or discount rate finance charge.

## Fundamentals of Lease Payment Calculations

Most lease rate factors are expressed as a cost per hundred dollars or per thousand dollars of total equipment being purchased for the lease. The stated lease factor is directly related to the terms of repayment. Charts utilizing lease rate factors stated in cost per hundred or per thousand dollars per month (or other regular calendar interval) are available, just as for add-on or discount rates.

For illustration, we have selected a lease rate cost factor from our Lease Rate Chart (Fig. 3-4). By following our list of assumptions, you will readily locate this factor and be able to follow the arithmetic necessary to arrive at the monthly lease rentals. Our charts are all based on equal monthly lease payments and are expressed in equipment cost per thousand dollars per month.

*Assumptions*

1. Simple interest equivalent inherent in lease = 20% per annum.
2. Lease term = 5 years, with 60 equal monthly lease payments.
3. Advance rentals or security deposits = one month, payable in advance.
4. Purchase option = 10% of total original equipment cost.
5. Equipment cost = $10,000.00, in this case including sales tax, freight, and installation.

Follow these steps to see how our Lease Rate Chart can be used to quickly determine monthly lease payments. Steps five and six show how easily you can extract the actual finance charges on this type of lease.

1. Find the chart headed "20% Actuarial Yield" in Figure 3-5.
2. Locate the section headed "10% Purchase Option."
3. Locate rate factors for zero security deposits in the 10% Purchase Option section. Since the lease is for sixty months, read across to the column headed "5-Yrs." and find the rate per thousand: 25.09.

*Note:* You have used the zero line because no additional security deposits are required, which means that only the first monthly rental is paid in advance.

4. To arrive at the monthly rental payment:

| | |
|---|---|
| Equipment cost | $10,000.00 |
| Example rate factor | X .2509 |
| Rental payment per month | $ 250.90 |

5. To determine gross lease cost:

| | |
|---|---|
| Monthly rental payment | $250.90 |
| 5 years in 60 payments | X 60 |
| Total rental payments | $15,054.00 |
| Add: 10% purchase option | 1,000.00 |
| Gross lease cost | $16,054.00 |

6. To determine lease finance charges:

| | |
|---|---|
| Total payments and purchase option | $16,054.00 |
| Original total equipment cost | -10,000.00 |
| Lease finance charges | $ 6,054.00 |

Most finance leases are just that easy to calculate. If you know the yield (the simple interest equivalent) you wish to pay or forecast for a projection, you can assume the other variables suitable to your situation. You can then come up with an accurate monthly lease payment schedule. Or, if you wish to check out a lessor's quotation, find out what they are trying to yield. Be careful to include the lessor's variables as to advance rentals and purchase option amount, if stated. In the case of a $1.00 option lease, use the 0% Purchase Option section. Read the section "Any Variation Changes the Yield" in chapter seven.

## VARIATIONS ON THE THEME

We have covered the three basic rate factors in use today by banks, finance companies, leasing companies, and other commercial lenders which will result in a fixed, predeterminable interest or finance charge cost. Common to each of them is the interest rate or yield, which remains constant throughout the repayment term. When you enter into a lease, loan, or time-sale contract using these rate factors, you have, in most cases, "locked" the rate. That means that the interest rate equivalent will prevail throughout the term of repayment. I suppose there have been some ingenious exceptions negotiated by borrowers or invented by lenders, but they are rare. They would have to entail a special provision which would trigger recalculation, such as when the prevailing prime rate drops below a certain point. In most cases, the only way to escape from a fixed-rate transaction is to prepay the required close-out. Then it might be possible to renegotiate a new loan at the lower prevailing interest rate.

## Accelerated Payment Plans

There are numerous variations on fixed-rate, equal-payment structures which predominantly utilize add-on rate factors. These include a variety of accelerated payment plans which feature higher payments in the first twelve months and descending in regular increments in succeeding years. Basically the finance charges are less because the lender earns his desired yield due to the accelerated return of his investment.

Commercial finance companies and some banks offer fixed-rate, accelerated-payment terms under such names as "Pay As You Depreciate" (P.A.Y.D.) or "Earned Depreciation Plan" (E.D.P.). As the terms imply, payments are similar to sum-of-the-digits or declining balance depreciation schedules which are highest in the first year, descending each year thereafter. These plans accordingly may specify (on a five year contract) 30% payback in the first twelve monthly payments, 25% in the next twelve, then 20%, 15%, and 10%, respectively in the remaining twelve-month payment periods. These percentages of payback may vary according to the lender's policies or credit criteria to achieve desired equity.

Because there is such a wide variety of possibilities and payback plans being offered, we shall confine ourselves to a general explanation. There are two primary reasons businesses consider an accelerated payment plan. First, it reduces the gross finance charges from a comparable term of repayment on equal monthly payments. For instance, if the going rate for equal payments is 11% add-on per year, the accelerated-payment add-on rate might be only 7¾% add-on per year. Thus, on a five-year financing, the add-on multiplier would be 55.00 (11.00 X 5 years) on equal monthly payback and only 38.75 (7.75 X 5 years) on an accelerated schedule. On a $100,000 unpaid balance, the finance charges would be $55,000 versus $38,750 on the accelerated-payment schedule.

The second reason for using an accelerated-payment schedule is to achieve a credit approval when the lender is reluctant to approve equipment financing with equal monthly payments. Perhaps the equipment is custom-made or of questionable resale value. Or, the down payment was small and the lender is more comfortable about achieving a better equity through high early payments. In some cases, a borrower's prior credit record is not strong enough but the lender can be convinced future cash flow will support the accelerated payments.

If you have the cash flow to handle a more rapid payback schedule, inquire about these variations with your lender. The accelerated payments will reduce the finance charge dollars on a given transaction, but not the true interest cost in relation to the present value of your accelerated outgoing dollars.

## Skip Payments

This variation on the theme is very important to many types of businesses. Without the relief of skip payments, there would be a lot less logging, construction, and farm equipment sold. These businesses in particular experience two to five months every year when income stops or is greatly reduced. When cash flow stops, even well-established and adequately capitalized companies need the relief of skip payments. Smaller businesses often simply cannot handle large, equal monthly payments on equipment idled by winter snow or rainy seasons.

Skip payments are useful to all manner of seasonal or intermittent-income businesses. However, the use of skip payments is not restricted to only those types of operations. Businesses with cyclical high- and low-income months can utilize variations on the skip-payment format. For instance, some shops close down totally or partially for one or more months for vacations. Others may produce heavily for eight or nine months and reduce operations substantially in the other months. Certain businesses, offering long invoice terms, have months of high receivable collections and virtually none in others. Skip payments have also been programmed for businesses who know they will close down for remodeling or expansion.

Business people should be aware of the possibilities and usefulness of skip payments. Many of the commercial finance companies traditionally offer skip payments to loggers, farmers, construction contractors, and others with uneven income months. They will also listen to reasonable proposals from less typical businesses. In some cases, equipment may be slow coming on line to maximum productivity, due to "learning curve" problems, "getting the bugs out," or a long turnaround time from production to collection of receivables. In these cases, it is possible to negotiate two- or three-month "front-end" skips to alleviate strain on available cash.

For those who have a need to forecast payment schedules on any skip-payment basis, we have developed a Skip Payment Calculator similar to those used by commercial finance companies (see Figs. 3-5 and 3-6). You will find them extremely flexible and easy to use. Take them line by line and follow our instructions and supplementary explanations. Use them to check out the finance charges and payments quoted by finance companies on your equipment financings. Or, develop your own skip-payment plan and propose it to your bank or finance company if they do not ordinarily offer such a payment plan.

## SIMPLE INTEREST FINANCING

We have discussed the most frequently used fixed-rate factors which produce predetermined finance charges. Another rate factor which might be thought of as "fixed" is the familiar simple interest percentage per annum. However, except for the fact that simple interest percentage usually remains constant, use of the percentage does not produce a predetermined finance charge.

Whenever a loan is negotiated using simple interest as the cost of financing, we naturally think of payments containing a principal amount to reduce the loan. Added to the reducing principal balance is the agreed interest charge.

Most of us relate to this because of home mortgages. The repayment plan, typically over twenty-five or thirty years, will have an amortization schedule. The payment, generally monthly, is usually a fixed amount; this setup is referred to as level payments. The agreed interest rate is collected each month, along with some principal reduction. The amortization schedule is calculated so that the level payment will be the same amount in the first month as it is in the last month, twenty-five or thirty years later. However, if you have ever looked at an amortization schedule, you will see that the principal reduction in the first month is very small while the interest makes up most of that first level, equal payment. The last payment is mostly principal and only pennies or a few dollars in interest.

## Calculating a Simple Interest Loan

In commercial financing, particularly when dealing with the banks, the majority of loans and time-sale contracts are simple interest-type transactions. However, many of these loans require payments of principal plus interest that are different each month. That is, the typical principal payment is determined by first dividing the original loan by the number of months in the agreed term. This calculation provides the principal amount to be repaid each month. The agreed interest is calculated on the reduced loan balance outstanding each month (or other payment period interval).

*Example*

| | | |
|---|---|---|
| Assumptions: | Interest rate: | 18% simple per annum |
| | Term of loan: | 60 months, repayable monthly |
| | Amount of loan: | $100,000.00 |
| | First payment due: | 30 days after loan funded |
| Calculations: | Principal calculation: | $100,000.00 ÷ 60 (mos.) = $1,667.67 (P) |
| | Interest calculation: | .18 (18%) ÷ 12 (mos.) = .015 (I, per mo.) |
| | First month's interest: | $100,000.00 X .015 = $1,500.00 (I) |
| | First month's payment: | $1,666.67 (P) + $1,500.00 (I) = $3,166.67 |
| | Loan balance calculation: | $100,000.00 + $1,500.00 (I) = $101,500.00<br>$101,500.00 – $3,166.67 (P+I) = $98,333.33 |
| | Second month's interest: | $98,333.33 X .015 = $1,475.00 (I) |
| | Second month's payment: | $1,667.67 (P) + $1,475.00 (I) = $3,142.67 |

Loan balance calculation: $98,333.33 + $1,475.00 (I) = $99,808.33
$99,803.33 - $3,142.67 (P+I) = $96,665.66

This process is repeated each month, with interest first applied to the outstanding loan balance from the prior period. The interest then due is paid, together with the required principal reduction. It is important to understand that interest begins to accumulate from the first day after the lender funds the loan.

Most commercial loans, either for working capital or to purchase equipment, are for much shorter periods than home mortgage or other real estate-type financings. First there are the short-term loans for temporary business needs, to buy goods to convert to a product, crop loans, quick "in and out" receivable loans, money for payroll, and tax obligation loans. These loans run from thirty to perhaps 360 days. Sometimes they may be extended for longer periods by partial principal reduction or simply "renewed" by payment of accrued interest.

Other loans, particularly those secured by equipment or to buy equipment, carry terms of two to seven years. The vast majority require monthly principal reduction.

## Floating Over Prime Rate

With banks, most short- or long-term loans are made on the basis of some percentage over their prime rate. The prime rate is extended to their largest and best customers. All others are required to pay a simple interest rate, marked up from the prevailing prime rate. Typically this ranges from ½% to 3%. This arrangement is called "floating over prime," "floating with prime," or "prime rate plus."

In recent years the commercial finance companies have increasingly been offering floating-over-prime loans or security agreements to fund equipment purchases. Because finance companies do not have their own prime rate, they utilize some formula to establish a prime rate. Some finance companies simply use the prime rate of their own bank. Others will select a major bank in New York, Chicago, Los Angeles, or San Francisco. Others develop a formula which requires an average of three major banks' prime rates.

## How Floating Over Prime Works

When a floating-rate loan is negotiated, the lender quotes a percentage amount over the prevailing prime rate. If the lender is a bank, it uses its own prime rate. If it is a finance company, it uses one of the formulas mentioned above. Traditionally, the finance companies used to quote a higher percentage amount over prime than the banks did. In recent years this gap has narrowed or disappeared, except as explained in the variations described below.

An illustration will show how most floating-over-prime-rate loans are set up and calculated:

| Assumptions: | Prevailing prime rate: | 16% |
|---|---|---|
| | Negotiated % over prime: | 2% |
| | Rate of interest on loan: | 18% |
| | Amount of loan: | $100,000.00 |
| | Principal payment: | $1,667.67 per month over 60 months |

Let's assume the prime rate changes twice during the thirty days after the loan is funded. Going in, as indicated above, the interest was 18% simple per annum. For fifteen days, the prime rate remains at 16%, so the borrower at 2% over prime pays 18% for those fifteen days. The daily interest rate is generally based on a 360-day year.

| | |
|---|---|
| To obtain daily rate: | .18 (18%) ÷ 360 (days) = .0005 per day |
| Interest charges for 15 days: | .0005 X $100,000.00 X 15 = $750.00 |

Assume prime rate decreases to 15½% for the next fifteen days:

| | |
|---|---|
| Floating rate correction: | .1550 (15½%) + .02 (2%) = .175 (17½%) (new interest charge) |
| To obtain daily rate: | .175 (17½%) ÷ 360 (days) = .00048611 |
| Interest charges for 15 days: | .00048611 X $100,000.00 X 15 = $729.17 |
| Total interest charges for first 30 days: | $750.00 + 729.17 = $1,479.17 |

When the first payment comes due, the loan balance is $100,000 + $1,479.17 = $101,479.17. Assuming a principal payment of $1,666.67, the first payment, the amount due and next loan balance would be: $1,667.67 (P) + $1,479.17 (I) = $3,146.84.

Loan balance reduction: $101,479.17 - $3,146.84 = $98,332.33, new loan balance at the beginning of the second month.

This process is continued throughout the term of the loan, with interest calculations based on fluctuations in the prime rate.

### Variations on Floating Over Prime

The commercial finance companies have developed several variations on the basic principle of floating over prime. Leasing companies have also developed plans which tie their lease rate factors to changes in the prime. They have devised these variations for several reasons:

1. to be more competitive with the banks
2. to simplify their billing and accounting procedures
3. to provide customers with principal-interest loans that are easier to understand, pay, and forecast
4. to protect themselves against extreme prime-rate fluctuations or against a preponderance of fixed-rate financing when the prime rate is rising

We shall cover the three most frequently used methods of calculating variations on standard prime-rate-plus plans.

LEVEL-PAYMENT PLANS The finance companies have devised a payment plan which floats with prime but still offers equal monthly payments. Some banks also offer the same plan, particularly when providing equipment financing. The premise is quite simple: provide the customer with equal monthly payments, and adjust the fluctuating interest costs quarterly, semiannually, or annually. Some plans even provide for a settlement at the end of the payment term.

From the lender's viewpoint, the level payments must not be too low, or the borrower will not achieve adequate and progressive equity in the equipment. Or, in the case of a loan, there might be inadequate principal reduction to retire the loan within the agreed term. Obviously, a strong-credit-risk borrower financing highly resalable equipment can qualify for lower level payments than a lesser-credit borrower financing rapidly depreciating equipment or that which runs the risk of early obsolescence. In some cases, the borrower is expected to make up for a lag in principal reduction.

Here is the essence of most level-payment plans that float with prime:

1. The loan balance is divided by the number of months in the term to obtain the minimum principal payment.
2. Based on the prime rate effective at the time the loan is funded, the agreed "plus" percentage is added to that, and an amortization schedule is computed. It is calculated as if the prime rate will remain at that same percentage throughout the term.
3. The level payment is then set forth to achieve full payout, the same as with a home mortgage with a fixed interest rate.
4. The borrower makes the agreed equal monthly payments. The lender keeps track of all fluctuations in the prime rate (to which the agreed "plus" percentage is added).

   Each quarter or other agreed interval, the lender advises the borrower if additional interest is payable or if a "credit" is forthcoming. (It is possible, of course, that if there is a drop in the prime rate, the level payments are larger than would have been necessary to amortize the loan over the fixed term.)

Note: There are a number of variations in the way lenders approach establishing the level payments. Depending on the credit risk involved, the equipment being financed, or anticipated large drops in the prime rate, the lender may offer even lower than a calculated, amortizing level-payment schedule.

They may provide a formula for "pickup payments" to cover shortfalls in desired principal reduction. They may also work out level payments that are higher (but equal) in the first twelve months, descending each twelve months thereafter—yet even the first year the payments would be less than on a straight principal-plus-interest loan schedule such as the one illustrated under "How Floating Over Prime Works." In that example, note that the first monthly payment is $3,146.84, but the last payment would be only a few dollars over the principal amount of $1,667.67.

PERCENTAGE OF PRIME RATE METHOD This plan involves working out a percentage factor of the prime rate which remains constant—such as 120% or 130% (of the prevailing prime rate). In actual practice, the lender devises a percentage which provides his desired markup; 121.675%, for example.

This percentage factor is multiplied by the existing prime rate to arrive at your interest cost on the outstanding balance. Every time the prime rate changes, the percentage rate provides a ready-to-use multiplier to determine the new equivalent simple interest charge.

Here is how the percentage factor works:

1. You negotiate or the lender offers a percentage of, say, 121.675%. The prime rate at the time is 15% per annum.

   Your rate would be 1.21675 X .15 = .1825, or 18¼%.

2. The lender will use the percentage factor or 121.675% (of prime rate) each time an interest calculation is needed. If there are no changes in the prime rate, obviously they will just charge 18¼% simple interest on the outstanding loan balance.

In this example, the lender apparently wanted to start at least 3¼% over the prevailing prime rate. As a borrower, you were apparently satisfied with a floating rate of that percentage. But watch out for the "percentage of prime" formula as the prime rate moves up!

For instance, if the prime rate increased to 19%, you would pay 1.21675 X .19 = 23.12%, or 4.12% over prime rate. Conversely, if your crystal ball is working better than the lender's, look how a drop to 11% prime rate decreases the percent over prime: 1.21675 X .11 = 13.38%, or 2.38% over prime.

GRADUATED PRIME RATE PLANS This is a relatively new variation on the standard floating-with-prime plan. It was conceived by the finance companies to protect themselves in the event the prime rate drops rapidly and their money costs cannot be adjusted as quickly. This plan is also called variable floating rate.

Here is a typical version of a graduated or variable floating rate plan:

1. As in the standard floating rate plan, a percentage over the prime rate is agreed upon. For illustration, assume a prime rate of 18% and the floating percentage is set at 2%; your effective interest cost is 20% simple interest per annum.
2. The finance company stipulates a "variable point," or percentage level of the prevailing prime rate below which the agreed floating rate percentage will change fractionally. When the prime rate goes below this preset level, preagreed fractional additions are made to the float percentage. For instance, the lender may arbitrarily set 14% as the variable point. If the prime rate drops to 13½%, the contract or promissory note may provide that for each ½% the prime rate falls below 14%, they will add ¼% to the originally agreed 2% float percentage.
3. In most of these plans, the lender arbitrarily establishes a ceiling and a floor above and below which the interest rate—including the agreed float percentage, together with adjustments—will not change. In this example, if the ceiling is set at 23% and the prime rate reaches 22%, even with the 2% float over prime, the borrower pays a maximum ceiling rate of 23% interest. At the other end, the floor may be set at, say, 10% (prevailing prime rate). That means, with the variable point at 14%, if the prime rate drops to 10%, the lender will not adjust the agreed float percentage any further. No matter how far the prime rate may drop below 10%, the borrower still must pay the 2% floating over prime rate, plus the ¼% adjustments for each ½% below 14% the prime rate may fall. Thus, in our example, if the prime rate decreases to 10%, the borrower will be paying the original 2% floating over prime, plus eight ¼% adjustments. The floating over prime rate will have become 4%. The borrower pays 10% prevailing prime rate, plus 4% floating rate, or 14%. Because of the floor, no matter how low the prime rate may go below 10%, the borrower continues to pay a minimum of 14% simple interest on the unpaid loan balance.

## Summary of Simple Interest, Floating Rate Financing

Simple interest, floating rate financing is becoming the predominant means of determining finance costs. Just as 25- or 30-year, fixed simple-interest-rate financing is disappearing in home mortgage loans, so it is with shorter-term equipment financing and commercial lending. More and more, commercial finance companies are tending toward floating rate financing, rather than fixed rates such as add-on or discount rates. Although the banks have long used their prime rate as a base for determining the interest rate they will charge various customers of differing risk levels, in general they have not been flexible or innovative. With the onset of soaring interest costs, highly volatile rate swings up and down, and longer repayment terms providing the impetus, all lenders have been obliged to protect themselves.

We have outlined the major variations to the standard simple interest, floating rate financing historically offered by banks and joined later by commercial lenders and lessors. They are an important, integral part of today's mathematics of financing. Bear in mind that each of the plans outlined offers many opportunities for negotiation. The elements of any one of them can be tailored to your individual needs.

Whenever finance plans contain so many variables, the way is open for the lenders to be arbitrary or highhanded in their structuring of the parameters. As a potential borrower, perhaps involved for the first time in some of these complexities, it is essential to know the possible variations available. More important, be aware that what the lender offers originally may be altered. Lenders always structure the promissory note or contract in terms most favorable to themselves.

From the floating-with-prime percentage amount to the floor, ceiling, and variable point to any other adjustable part of these individually quoted plans, nothing is cast in stone. This does not mean that the lender will readily alter the structure originally offered. As borrower, you must first read the terms carefully. You must counteroffer something reasonable you can live with. Horse-trading may be necessary. High interest costs, coupled with numerous variables, demand that you, as borrower, get into some hard negotiating.

## NEGOTIATING YOUR BEST FLOATING-WITH-PRIME DEAL

All of the floating-with-prime loans and contracts will provide you with a determinable principal and interest schedule. Many lenders are now providing borrowers with a computerized printout showing the descending loan balance, interest charged, and principal payment applied. If they do not, they are at least providing monthly or quarterly reports of that period's chargeable interest and new loan balance. For the most part, loans or contracts based on the prime rate, plus some percentage over that fluctuating rate, are more clear-cut than fixed-rate add-on financing. Your accounting is simplified as to interest expense and outstanding loan balance. The rule of 78ths is not used to determine early closeouts. You have therefore avoided those hard-to-detect prepayment penalties some lenders charge by short rebates.

But beware! Most finance companies are *not* interested in short-term loans. They do not like going through the time and expense of making a five-year loan that is repaid in a few months. They particularly do not want borrowers who will close out early because they find a lower interest rate elsewhere. To eliminate taking on short-term and unprofitable borrowers, they will usually require early payment penalties. Sometimes this penalty clause is buried in the fine print of the promissory note or contract. The lender may not voluntarily discuss this clause. You must find it! Here is what to look for:

1. The penalty clause is generally inserted in the promissory note or contact form as a percentage of the unpaid loan balance applicable to the timing of the early closeout.
2. For instance, it may require a penalty of 3% of the unpaid principal loan balance during the first twelve months. This may descend to 2% during the second year of the term and 1% during the third year. Sometimes, on a four- or five-year loan, there are no penalties in the final years.
3. Sometimes the lender will spell out how much in additional principal payments are acceptable in a given period of time. Woven into this wording you may find there is a charge for paying all or more than an acceptable part of the loan balance. This charge can run a consistent 1% to 3% of the loan balance all the way through the loan term.
4. The prepayment penalties imposed are widely variable and usually negotiable. Just because the lender types or prints the percentages on the note does not necessarily mean they can't be changed.

### Where There's a Floor, There Should Be a Ceiling

We have touched on this before, but it's so important to all who borrow on any floating-rate basis that we are going to define and explain again. Untold thousands of borrowers have blithely signed promissory notes containing a floor, generally high so as to favor the lender, but no ceiling. Or, in some cases, the ceiling inserted was set so high, it meant nothing. In recent years, with the prime rate skyrocketing from 8% in 1978 to over 20% in 1980-81, many borrowers were shocked to learn they had signed no-ceiling notes. Those who were wise enough to insist on a reasonable ceiling rate avoided paying the 21% to 27% interest no-ceiling note holders had to face.

A floor means a bottom rate the lender will charge, regardless of how low the prime rate may go. The lender strives to place this floor as high as possible. You should negotiate the lowest floor you can obtain.

For example, assume you agree to a 10% floor. First, there may be differences as to what is meant by "floor." Some notes refer to the prevailing prime rate. If the prime rate reaches the stated 10%, you will pay 10% interest plus your agreed percentage float over prime. If the prime rate goes below 10%, you will still pay 10% plus the agreed float percentage.

Some notes may refer to the lowest rate you will pay, "but not less than," say, 10%. Still pegged to the prime rate, this wording says that your agreed floating percentage plus the prevailing prime rate cannot add up to less than 10%. Check the wording carefully, to be sure your floor is where you think it should be.

A ceiling is simply the highest amount of interest the lender may charge you. Again, depending on the wording, if pegged to the prime rate, you may pay the highest prevailing prime rate set forth plus the agreed floating-with-prime percentage. Or, "not more than" a given percentage, adding prevailing prime rate and floating percentage together.

Negotiate the ceiling as low as possible. Who knows how high the prevailing prime rate will go five to seven years from when you negotiate your loan? Read your promissory note carefully. Many banks and finance companies will intentionally present a note for signature without inserting a ceiling. Or they will insert unreasonably high floor percentages and a ridiculously high ceiling.

### Location of the Lender Can Be Important!

Another consideration when negotiating a "prime-plus" loan is the location of the finance company headquarters where your payments are sent. Watch out for the distant accounting center, because it can cost you significant lost time and interest!

If your balance is quite large, a few days lost each month in posting your payments adds up to greater interest costs. Some finance companies will blame slow posting on poor mail service. Be it slow mail or poor office procedures, you will find you are paying interest for two to ten "float days" on the old outstanding balance!

No matter what the reason for the delay, you are a victim of the old "float trick." Your money is quickly deposited to the finance company account, but your loan balance is credited later—perhaps several days later.

The cure isn't simple, but try certified mail, return receipt requested, to establish the actual arrival date. Or, bank-transfer your payment from your account to their account, then calculate interest. What could be more fair or accurate?

If possible, borrow from a local company or a national company with localized accounting. If you have a large loan balance, bearing high interest, make it your business to know the posting procedures of your payments. Keep watch over how long posting takes. Those lost float days can add hundreds, even thousands of dollars to your interest costs.

### How Much "Plus" Should You Pay?

This question can only be resolved by obtaining at least two or three rate quotations from banks or finance companies. If you can qualify to borrow or finance equipment through your bank, it is probable other banks will also be interested in providing a credit approval and rate quotation. Assuming you want to use bank financing—the length of repayment is satisfactory and you can live with the sometimes more stringent down-payment requirements—you will probably find their "plus" percentage over prime at ½% to 3%.

With the prime rate at extremely high levels, many banks have lowered somewhat their nearly consistent 1½% to 2% over-prime float. The banks place considerable weight on your value as a commercial depositor. Your general credit standing and financial statement strengths also influence their decision as to how much over prime they will quote on a loan or contract. The very strong and important customer may borrow even below the existing prime rate. If you approach other banks for a quotation, many will expect you to move your checking account and other business over to their bank. Sometimes other banks will reach out and quote fairly low in the hope of eventually bringing you in as a regular customer. However, many banks will not go after an individual loan or financing if they can't "control their account"—meaning no checking account, no quotation.

This selectivity by other banks versus your bank may oblige you to seek out a commercial finance company as a competitive bidder for your loan business. We suggest that you obtain one or more finance company quotations to use as leverage against your bank, which may be complacent or overconfident that you will not stray from the fold. Assuming you are basically happy with your bank and its loan terms and conditions, work them over with the finance company quotes in hand. Press the bank to reduce the plus percentage and lower the floor and ceiling originally quoted. The bank may not budge, but you owe it to yourself and your business to at least try.

The major finance companies will usually quote the same prime-plus percentages—just as several banks will offer very similar or even identical quotes. Prior to the extreme highs in the prevailing prime rate, the commercial finance companies traditionally quoted 2% to 5% floating over prime. These markups were reduced to 1% to 2½% in 1980-81. However, many companies have felt obliged to protect themselves with early payment penalties or variable prime-rate plans in case the prime rate drops rapidly.

In short, those of you who have been compelled to borrow or finance equipment in times of very high prime rates must do your best to cut the best deal you can—while protecting yourself against paying too much on the down side. In addition, looking to the future, you must also protect yourself against the return of high interest costs. Let's face facts: entering into a five- to seven-year loan or contract today probably means facing a new cycle of higher interest costs during that period. That is why the ceiling negotiated today may be so very important two to seven years from now.

## Lock the Rate—or Float It?

Interest-bearing, prime-plus loans can be a gamble, especially when the economic indicators point toward rising money costs. If you are about to enter into a five- to seven-year loan or equipment financing, you must at least consider where you are in the interest-rate cycle. Recently we have seen many short-run predictions off their mark. Yet historically the prime rate rises, falls back, and rises again, always notching up to a somewhat higher "low point." At the beginning of your financing, with the balance high, interest expense has a heavy impact on your monthly cash flow. If your loan is tied to a rapidly falling prime rate, the interest savings can be significant.

To get your best deal, weigh prime plus carefully against using an add-on or discount fixed rate. First, convert the rate factor to its simple interest equivalent, for a direct comparison. Use our rate charts at the end of this chapter for easy conversion. Remember, the add-on or discount rate fixes your finance costs for the term. Compare the simple interest equivalent of the fixed rate to the total interest percentage of the prime rate plus your agreed floating percentage. Forecast, by your best estimate, if the prime rate and your floating percentage rate will average out lower than the fixed simple-interest equivalent of the add-on or discount rate.

After all, the fixed rate locks the rate for the entire contract term. Your payments are a known amount, which you can put into your planning or budget. Floating-rate loans, even on a level-payment basis, may require large interest payment adjustments if the prime rate rises. Or, the interest cost plus principal payment on a straight floating basis may be difficult to handle out of cash flow in the early months of the loan.

If you negotiate your best deal down to the lowest possible fixed rate, you might be better off than gambling against the prime rate's cycling back up to the new historic highs three to seven years hence. The likelihood of ever-increasing higher interest-rate levels is the reason fixed-rate financing is becoming less available these days.

FIGURE 3-1

# FINANCE RATE CHARTS

## HOW TO USE FINANCE RATE CHARTS

CHART FUNDAMENTALS:

On the next four pages, you will find CHARTS designed for EASY-TO-READ conversion from ANNUAL ACTUARIAL INTEREST to ADD-ON and DISCOUNT RATES.

Annual Actuarial Interest is the RATE charged . . . usually applied monthly . . . on outstanding declining balances, which permits a loan to be paid-off during a given term . . . with the same monthly payment.

These actuarial interest rates indicate the CORRECT "A.P.R." . . . ANNUAL PERCENTAGE RATE. You can translate the equivalent add-on or discount rate back to the appropriate annual actuarial interest column and have the "A.P.R."

Many finance companies use ADD-ON RATES. Some banks and finance companies quote DISCOUNT RATES . . . especially when extending a loan . . . when they "discount" . . . taking out their interest in front . . . so your actual loan proceeds are after deduction of discount rate charge.

USING ADD-ON RATE CHARTS:

- Column 1 indicates the Annual Actuarial Interest Rate, starting with 6% and increasing in ¼% increments until reaching 10%; then in ½% increments . . . to a 25% ANNUAL ACTUARIAL INTEREST RATE.
- Vertical Month Columns are graduated from a 3 month term . . . (of a loan or contract) . . . through 144 months . . . permitting calculations up to a 12 year loan or contract.
- The numbers appearing horizontally . . . on line with the equivalent ANNUAL ACTUARIAL RATE . . . are the EQUIVALENT ADD-ON RATES . . . which MUST BE CORRECTLY "CONVERTED" TO ARRIVE AT ACTUAL FINANCE CHARGES . . . (in DOLLARS) . . . as demonstrated below in our EXAMPLE.

FIGURE 3-1 (continued)

- You must understand the ADD-ON RATES are the ANNUALIZED RATE. Therefore, the only rate that CAN BE APPLIED DIRECTLY is the "12 mo." column. In this column . . . 3.28% ADD-ON RATE equals 6% ANNUAL ACTUARIAL INTEREST or A.P.R. The add-on rate can be applied directly to the unpaid contract or loan balance to DETERMINE FINANCE CHARGES TO BE ADDED. This PRODUCT is added to the loan . . . you divide by twelve (12) . . . and you have the EQUAL MONTHLY PAYMENT.

  Here is an additional EXAMPLE . . . to assist you in TRANSLATION and USE of these CHARTS:

ASSUMPTIONS:

- Loan or Contract Balance $10,000.
- Annual Interest Rate 16%
- Term of Loan or Contract 30 mos.

STEPS:

1) In Column 1 . . . locate 16% rate.
2) Going across . . . horizontally to "30 mos." . . . locate ADD-ON RATE EQUIVALENT of 8.79.
3) 8.79 is the ANNUALIZED ADD-ON EQUIVALENT of 16% ANNUAL ACTUAL INTEREST . . . ON A 30 MONTH TERM . . . WITH AN EQUAL MONTHLY PAYMENT.
4) Since 30 months is 2½ years . . . you can multiply 8.79 x 2½ to arrive at 21.975 the "factor" used to multiply times the unpaid balance . . . to arrive at the CORRECT FINANCE CHARGE . . . as indicated below:

| | |
|---|---|
| $ 10,000. | Unpaid Balance |
| x 21.975 | Factor |
| $2,197.50 | Finance Charge |

5) To arrive at monthly payment:

   $10,000. + $2,197.50 = $12,197.50 ÷ 30(mos) = $409.58

FIGURE 3-1 (continued)

6) You can see by this example . . . the necessity of converting the ADD-ON RATE to a "factor" relating to the corrected annualized amount.

Of course . . . for three years . . . you could multiply the given ADD-ON RATE X THE UNPAID BALANCE X THREE (YEARS) . . . and obtain the same answer . . . which you then divide the total product by 36(mos), to arrive at the MONTHLY PAYMENT.

INTERPOLATION

INTERPOLATION BETWEEN MONTHS FOR EQUIVALENT ADD-ON RATES FOR OTHER TERMS THAN ARE STATED . . . WILL PRODUCE REASONABLY ACCURATE RESULTS . . . by simply working with the graduating rates that occur by the month. INTERPOLATION BETWEEN ANNUAL ACTUARIAL INTEREST RATES can also be accomplished with close results . . . by observing the graduations that occur between stated rates.

USING DISCOUNT RATE CHARTS:

These CHARTS are set-up in the same manner as the ADD-ON CHARTS.

- Just as with ADD-ON RATES . . . all DISCOUNT RATES are the ANNUALIZED DISCOUNT RATE EQUIVALENTS of the stated ANNUAL INTEREST RATE.
- To obtain the DISCOUNT RATE "FACTOR" . . . take the stated rate and multiply by the years in the loan or contract term.

Here is an EXAMPLE to assist you in use of these CHARTS.

ASSUMPTIONS:

- Loan Requested $72,000.
- Annual Interest Rate 15%
- Term of Loan 24 months

FIGURE 3-1 (continued)

STEPS:

1) In Column 1 . . . locate 15% Annual Actuarial Rate.

2) Going across . . . horizontally to "24 mos." . . . locate DISCOUNT RATE EQUIVALENT OF 7.03.

3) "24 mos." = 2 years . . . so, multiply 2 x 7.03 = 14.06.

4) Multiply DISCOUNT FACTOR of 14.06 times loan "request" of $72,000.

5) 14.06 X $72,000. = $10,123.20.

   $72,000. MINUS $10,123.20 = $61,876.80, LOAN ADVANCE.

6) You must repay the Gross Loan Amount. To determine the monthly payment:

   $72,000. DIVIDED BY 24 (mos.) = $2,578.20, per month.

FIGURE 3-2

# ACTUARIAL INTEREST TO ADD-ON RATE

| Annual Actuarial Rate | TERM - months | | | | | | | | | | |
|---|---|---|---|---|---|---|---|---|---|---|---|
| | 3 mo. | 6 mo. | 9 mo. | 12 mo. | 15 mo. | 18 mo. | 24 mo. | 30 mo. | 36 mo. | 42 mo. | 48 mo. |
| 6.00 | 4.01 | 3.51 | 3.36 | 3.28 | 3.24 | 3.21 | 3.18 | 3.17 | 3.17 | 3.18 | 3.18 |
| 6.25 | 4.17 | 3.66 | 3.50 | 3.42 | 3.37 | 3.35 | 3.32 | 3.31 | 3.31 | 3.31 | 3.32 |
| 6.50 | 4.34 | 3.81 | 3.64 | 3.56 | 3.51 | 3.48 | 3.46 | 3.45 | 3.45 | 3.45 | 3.46 |
| 6.75 | 4.51 | 3.96 | 3.78 | 3.69 | 3.65 | 3.62 | 3.59 | 3.58 | 3.58 | 3.59 | 3.60 |
| 7.00 | 4.68 | 4.10 | 3.92 | 3.83 | 3.78 | 3.76 | 3.73 | 3.72 | 3.72 | 3.73 | 3.74 |
| 7.25 | 4.84 | 4.25 | 4.06 | 3.97 | 3.92 | 3.89 | 3.86 | 3.85 | 3.86 | 3.86 | 3.87 |
| 7.50 | 5.01 | 4.40 | 4.20 | 4.11 | 4.06 | 4.03 | 4.00 | 3.99 | 3.99 | 4.00 | 4.01 |
| 7.75 | 5.18 | 4.55 | 4.34 | 4.25 | 4.20 | 4.16 | 4.14 | 4.13 | 4.13 | 4.14 | 4.15 |
| 8.00 | 5.35 | 4.69 | 4.48 | 4.39 | 4.33 | 4.30 | 4.27 | 4.27 | 4.27 | 4.28 | 4.30 |
| 8.25 | 5.51 | 4.84 | 4.63 | 4.52 | 4.47 | 4.44 | 4.41 | 4.40 | 4.41 | 4.42 | 4.44 |
| 8.50 | 5.68 | 4.99 | 4.77 | 4.66 | 4.61 | 4.58 | 4.55 | 4.54 | 4.55 | 4.56 | 4.58 |
| 8.75 | 5.85 | 5.14 | 4.91 | 4.80 | 4.75 | 4.71 | 4.68 | 4.68 | 4.69 | 4.70 | 4.72 |
| 9.00 | 6.01 | 5.28 | 5.05 | 4.94 | 4.88 | 4.85 | 4.82 | 4.82 | 4.83 | 4.84 | 4.86 |
| 9.25 | 6.18 | 5.43 | 5.19 | 5.08 | 5.02 | 4.99 | 4.96 | 4.96 | 4.97 | 4.98 | 5.00 |
| 9.50 | 6.35 | 5.58 | 5.33 | 5.22 | 5.16 | 5.13 | 5.10 | 5.10 | 5.11 | 5.12 | 5.15 |
| 9.75 | 6.52 | 5.73 | 5.48 | 5.36 | 5.30 | 5.26 | 5.24 | 5.23 | 5.25 | 5.27 | 5.29 |
| 10.00 | 6.69 | 5.87 | 5.62 | 5.50 | 5.44 | 5.40 | 5.37 | 5.37 | 5.39 | 5.41 | 5.44 |
| 10.50 | 7.02 | 6.17 | 5.90 | 5.78 | 5.71 | 5.68 | 5.65 | 5.65 | 5.67 | 5.69 | 5.72 |
| 11.00 | 7.36 | 6.47 | 6.19 | 6.06 | 5.99 | 5.96 | 5.93 | 5.93 | 5.95 | 5.98 | 6.01 |
| 11.50 | 7.69 | 6.76 | 6.47 | 6.34 | 6.27 | 6.23 | 6.21 | 6.22 | 6.24 | 6.27 | 6.31 |
| 12.00 | 8.03 | 7.06 | 6.76 | 6.62 | 6.55 | 6.51 | 6.49 | 6.50 | 6.52 | 6.56 | 6.60 |
| 12.50 | 8.36 | 7.35 | 7.04 | 6.90 | 6.83 | 6.79 | 6.77 | 6.78 | 6.81 | 6.85 | 6.90 |
| 13.00 | 8.70 | 7.65 | 7.33 | 7.18 | 7.11 | 7.07 | 7.05 | 7.07 | 7.10 | 7.14 | 7.19 |
| 13.50 | 9.03 | 7.95 | 7.61 | 7.46 | 7.39 | 7.35 | 7.33 | 7.35 | 7.39 | 7.44 | 7.49 |
| 14.00 | 9.37 | 8.25 | 7.90 | 7.74 | 7.67 | 7.63 | 7.62 | 7.64 | 7.68 | 7.73 | 7.79 |
| 14.50 | 9.71 | 8.54 | 8.18 | 8.03 | 7.95 | 7.91 | 7.90 | 7.93 | 7.97 | 8.03 | 8.09 |
| 15.00 | 10.04 | 8.84 | 8.47 | 8.31 | 8.23 | 8.20 | 8.18 | 8.21 | 8.27 | 8.33 | 8.40 |
| 15.50 | 10.38 | 9.14 | 8.76 | 8.59 | 8.51 | 8.48 | 8.47 | 8.50 | 8.56 | 8.63 | 8.70 |
| 16.00 | 10.71 | 9.44 | 9.05 | 8.88 | 8.80 | 8.76 | 8.76 | 8.79 | 8.86 | 8.93 | 9.01 |
| 16.50 | 11.05 | 9.73 | 9.33 | 9.16 | 9.08 | 9.04 | 9.04 | 9.09 | 9.15 | 9.23 | 9.32 |
| 17.00 | 11.39 | 10.03 | 9.62 | 9.45 | 9.36 | 9.33 | 9.33 | 9.38 | 9.45 | 9.53 | 9.63 |
| 17.50 | 11.72 | 10.33 | 9.91 | 9.73 | 9.65 | 9.61 | 9.62 | 9.67 | 9.75 | 9.84 | 9.94 |
| 18.00 | 12.06 | 10.63 | 10.20 | 10.02 | 9.93 | 9.90 | 9.91 | 9.97 | 10.05 | 10.15 | 10.25 |
| 18.50 | 12.40 | 10.93 | 10.49 | 10.30 | 10.22 | 10.19 | 10.20 | 10.26 | 10.35 | 10.45 | 10.56 |
| 19.00 | 12.73 | 11.23 | 10.78 | 10.59 | 10.50 | 10.47 | 10.49 | 10.56 | 10.65 | 10.76 | 10.88 |
| 19.50 | 13.07 | 11.53 | 11.07 | 10.87 | 10.79 | 10.76 | 10.78 | 10.86 | 10.96 | 11.07 | 11.20 |
| 20.00 | 13.41 | 11.83 | 11.36 | 11.16 | 11.08 | 11.05 | 11.07 | 11.16 | 11.26 | 11.39 | 11.52 |
| 20.50 | 13.74 | 12.13 | 11.65 | 11.45 | 11.37 | 11.34 | 11.37 | 11.46 | 11.57 | 11.70 | 11.84 |
| 21.00 | 14.08 | 12.43 | 11.94 | 11.74 | 11.65 | 11.63 | 11.66 | 11.76 | 11.88 | 12.01 | 12.16 |
| 21.50 | 14.42 | 12.73 | 12.23 | 12.02 | 11.94 | 11.92 | 11.96 | 12.06 | 12.19 | 12.33 | 12.48 |
| 22.00 | 14.76 | 13.03 | 12.52 | 12.31 | 12.23 | 12.21 | 12.25 | 12.36 | 12.50 | 12.65 | 12.81 |
| 23.00 | 15.43 | 13.63 | 13.10 | 12.89 | 12.81 | 12.79 | 12.85 | 12.97 | 13.12 | 13.29 | 13.46 |
| 24.00 | 16.11 | 14.23 | 13.69 | 13.47 | 13.39 | 13.38 | 13.45 | 13.58 | 13.75 | 13.93 | 14.12 |
| 25.00 | 16.78 | 14.83 | 14.27 | 14.05 | 13.97 | 13.96 | 14.05 | 14.20 | 14.38 | 14.58 | 14.79 |

FIGURE 3-2 (continued)

# ACTUARIAL INTEREST TO ADD-ON RATE

| Annual Actuarial Rate | TERM - months 54 mo. | 60 mo. | 66 mo. | 72 mo. | 78 mo. | 84 mo. | 96 mo. | 108 mo. | 120 mo. | 132 mo. | 144 mo. |
|---|---|---|---|---|---|---|---|---|---|---|---|
| 6.00 | 3.19 | 3.20 | 3.21 | 3.22 | 3.23 | 3.24 | 3.27 | 3.30 | 3.32 | 3.35 | 3.38 |
| 6.25 | 3.33 | 3.34 | 3.35 | 3.36 | 3.38 | 3.39 | 3.42 | 3.44 | 3.47 | 3.50 | 3.53 |
| 6.50 | 3.47 | 3.48 | 3.49 | 3.51 | 3.52 | 3.53 | 3.56 | 3.59 | 3.63 | 3.66 | 3.69 |
| 6.75 | 3.61 | 3.62 | 3.63 | 3.65 | 3.66 | 3.68 | 3.71 | 3.74 | 3.78 | 3.81 | 3.85 |
| 7.00 | 3.75 | 3.76 | 3.78 | 3.79 | 3.81 | 3.83 | 3.86 | 3.90 | 3.93 | 3.97 | 4.01 |
| 7.25 | 3.89 | 3.90 | 3.92 | 3.94 | 3.95 | 3.97 | 4.01 | 4.05 | 4.09 | 4.13 | 4.17 |
| 7.50 | 4.03 | 4.05 | 4.06 | 4.08 | 4.10 | 4.12 | 4.16 | 4.20 | 4.24 | 4.29 | 4.33 |
| 7.75 | 4.17 | 4.19 | 4.21 | 4.23 | 4.25 | 4.27 | 4.31 | 4.36 | 4.40 | 4.45 | 4.49 |
| 8.00 | 4.31 | 4.33 | 4.35 | 4.37 | 4.40 | 4.42 | 4.46 | 4.51 | 4.56 | 4.61 | 4.66 |
| 8.25 | 4.46 | 4.48 | 4.50 | 4.52 | 4.54 | 4.57 | 4.62 | 4.67 | 4.72 | 4.77 | 4.82 |
| 8.50 | 4.60 | 4.62 | 4.64 | 4.67 | 4.69 | 4.72 | 4.77 | 4.82 | 4.88 | 4.93 | 4.99 |
| 8.75 | 4.74 | 4.76 | 4.79 | 4.82 | 4.84 | 4.87 | 4.93 | 4.98 | 5.04 | 5.10 | 5.15 |
| 9.00 | 4.89 | 4.91 | 4.94 | 4.96 | 4.99 | 5.02 | 5.08 | 5.14 | 5.20 | 5.26 | 5.32 |
| 9.25 | 5.03 | 5.06 | 5.08 | 5.11 | 5.14 | 5.17 | 5.24 | 5.30 | 5.36 | 5.43 | 5.49 |
| 9.50 | 5.17 | 5.20 | 5.23 | 5.26 | 5.29 | 5.33 | 5.39 | 5.46 | 5.53 | 5.60 | 5.66 |
| 9.75 | 5.32 | 5.35 | 5.38 | 5.41 | 5.45 | 5.48 | 5.55 | 5.62 | 5.69 | 5.76 | 5.83 |
| 10.00 | 5.46 | 5.50 | 5.53 | 5.56 | 5.60 | 5.64 | 5.71 | 5.78 | 5.86 | 5.93 | 6.01 |
| 10.50 | 5.76 | 5.79 | 5.83 | 5.87 | 5.91 | 5.95 | 6.03 | 6.11 | 6.19 | 6.27 | 6.36 |
| 11.00 | 6.05 | 6.09 | 6.13 | 6.17 | 6.22 | 6.26 | 6.35 | 6.44 | 6.53 | 6.62 | 6.71 |
| 11.50 | 6.35 | 6.39 | 6.44 | 6.48 | 6.53 | 6.58 | 6.68 | 6.77 | 6.87 | 6.97 | 7.07 |
| 12.00 | 6.65 | 6.69 | 6.74 | 6.79 | 6.85 | 6.90 | 7.00 | 7.11 | 7.22 | 7.32 | 7.43 |
| 12.50 | 6.95 | 7.00 | 7.05 | 7.11 | 7.16 | 7.22 | 7.33 | 7.45 | 7.57 | 7.68 | 7.79 |
| 13.00 | 7.25 | 7.30 | 7.36 | 7.42 | 7.48 | 7.54 | 7.67 | 7.79 | 7.92 | 8.04 | 8.16 |
| 13.50 | 7.55 | 7.61 | 7.68 | 7.74 | 7.81 | 7.87 | 8.01 | 8.14 | 8.27 | 8.40 | 8.54 |
| 14.00 | 7.86 | 7.92 | 7.99 | 8.06 | 8.13 | 8.20 | 8.35 | 8.49 | 8.63 | 8.77 | 8.91 |
| 14.50 | 8.16 | 8.23 | 8.31 | 8.38 | 8.46 | 8.54 | 8.69 | 8.84 | 8.99 | 9.14 | 9.29 |
| 15.00 | 8.47 | 8.55 | 8.63 | 8.71 | 8.79 | 8.87 | 9.03 | 9.20 | 9.36 | 9.52 | 9.68 |
| 15.50 | 8.78 | 8.86 | 8.95 | 9.03 | 9.12 | 9.21 | 9.38 | 9.56 | 9.73 | 9.90 | 10.07 |
| 16.00 | 9.09 | 9.18 | 9.27 | 9.36 | 9.46 | 9.55 | 9.73 | 9.92 | 10.10 | 10.28 | 10.46 |
| 16.50 | 9.41 | 9.50 | 9.60 | 9.70 | 9.79 | 9.89 | 10.09 | 10.28 | 10.48 | 10.67 | 10.85 |
| 17.00 | 9.72 | 9.82 | 9.93 | 10.03 | 10.13 | 10.24 | 10.45 | 10.65 | 10.86 | 11.06 | 11.25 |
| 17.50 | 10.04 | 10.15 | 10.26 | 10.36 | 10.47 | 10.59 | 10.81 | 11.02 | 11.24 | 11.45 | 11.65 |
| 18.00 | 10.36 | 10.47 | 10.59 | 10.70 | 10.82 | 10.94 | 11.17 | 11.40 | 11.62 | 11.84 | 12.06 |
| 18.50 | 10.68 | 10.80 | 10.92 | 11.04 | 11.17 | 11.29 | 11.53 | 11.77 | 12.01 | 12.24 | 12.46 |
| 19.00 | 11.00 | 11.13 | 11.26 | 11.39 | 11.51 | 11.64 | 11.90 | 12.15 | 12.40 | 12.64 | 12.88 |
| 19.50 | 11.33 | 11.46 | 11.59 | 11.73 | 11.87 | 12.00 | 12.27 | 12.54 | 12.79 | 13.05 | 13.29 |
| 20.00 | 11.65 | 11.79 | 11.93 | 12.08 | 12.22 | 12.36 | 12.64 | 12.92 | 13.19 | 13.45 | 13.71 |
| 20.50 | 11.98 | 12.13 | 12.28 | 12.43 | 12.58 | 12.72 | 13.02 | 13.31 | 13.59 | 13.86 | 14.13 |
| 21.00 | 12.31 | 12.46 | 12.62 | 12.78 | 12.93 | 13.09 | 13.40 | 13.70 | 13.99 | 14.28 | 14.55 |
| 21.50 | 12.64 | 12.80 | 12.97 | 13.13 | 13.29 | 13.46 | 13.78 | 14.09 | 14.40 | 14.69 | 14.97 |
| 22.00 | 12.97 | 13.14 | 13.31 | 13.48 | 13.66 | 13.83 | 14.16 | 14.49 | 14.80 | 15.11 | 15.40 |
| 23.00 | 13.64 | 13.83 | 14.01 | 14.20 | 14.39 | 14.57 | 14.93 | 15.29 | 15.63 | 15.95 | 16.26 |
| 24.00 | 14.32 | 14.52 | 14.72 | 14.93 | 15.13 | 15.33 | 15.72 | 16.09 | 16.46 | 16.81 | 17.14 |
| 25.00 | 15.00 | 15.22 | 15.44 | 15.66 | 15.87 | 16.09 | 16.51 | 16.91 | 17.30 | 17.67 | 18.02 |

FIGURE 3-3

# ACTUARIAL INTEREST TO DISCOUNT RATE

| Annual Actuarial Rate | TERM - months 3 mo. | 6 mo. | 9 mo. | 12 mo. | 15 mo. | 18 mo. | 24 mo. | 30 mo. | 36 mo. | 42 mo. | 48 mo. |
|---|---|---|---|---|---|---|---|---|---|---|---|
| 6.00 | 3.97 | 3.45 | 3.27 | 3.18 | 3.11 | 3.06 | 2.99 | 2.94 | 2.90 | 2.86 | 2.82 |
| 6.25 | 4.13 | 3.60 | 3.41 | 3.30 | 3.24 | 3.19 | 3.11 | 3.06 | 3.01 | 2.97 | 2.93 |
| 6.50 | 4.29 | 3.74 | 3.54 | 3.43 | 3.36 | 3.31 | 3.23 | 3.17 | 3.12 | 3.08 | 3.04 |
| 6.75 | 4.46 | 3.88 | 3.67 | 3.56 | 3.49 | 3.43 | 3.35 | 3.29 | 3.23 | 3.19 | 3.14 |
| 7.00 | 4.62 | 4.02 | 3.81 | 3.69 | 3.61 | 3.56 | 3.47 | 3.40 | 3.35 | 3.30 | 3.25 |
| 7.25 | 4.79 | 4.16 | 3.94 | 3.82 | 3.74 | 3.68 | 3.59 | 3.52 | 3.46 | 3.40 | 3.35 |
| 7.50 | 4.95 | 4.30 | 4.07 | 3.95 | 3.86 | 3.80 | 3.70 | 3.63 | 3.57 | 3.51 | 3.46 |
| 7.75 | 5.11 | 4.44 | 4.21 | 4.07 | 3.99 | 3.92 | 3.82 | 3.74 | 3.68 | 3.62 | 3.56 |
| 8.00 | 5.27 | 4.58 | 4.34 | 4.20 | 4.11 | 4.04 | 3.94 | 3.85 | 3.79 | 3.72 | 3.67 |
| 8.25 | 5.44 | 4.73 | 4.47 | 4.33 | 4.23 | 4.16 | 4.05 | 3.97 | 3.89 | 3.83 | 3.77 |
| 8.50 | 5.60 | 4.87 | 4.60 | 4.46 | 4.36 | 4.28 | 4.17 | 4.08 | 4.00 | 3.93 | 3.87 |
| 8.75 | 5.76 | 5.01 | 4.73 | 4.58 | 4.48 | 4.40 | 4.28 | 4.19 | 4.11 | 4.04 | 3.97 |
| 9.00 | 5.93 | 5.15 | 4.87 | 4.71 | 4.60 | 4.52 | 4.40 | 4.30 | 4.22 | 4.14 | 4.07 |
| 9.25 | 6.09 | 5.29 | 5.00 | 4.84 | 4.73 | 4.64 | 4.51 | 4.41 | 4.32 | 4.24 | 4.17 |
| 9.50 | 6.25 | 5.43 | 5.13 | 4.96 | 4.85 | 4.76 | 4.63 | 4.52 | 4.43 | 4.35 | 4.27 |
| 9.75 | 6.41 | 5.57 | 5.26 | 5.09 | 4.97 | 4.88 | 4.74 | 4.63 | 4.53 | 4.45 | 4.37 |
| 10.00 | 6.58 | 5.71 | 5.39 | 5.21 | 5.09 | 5.00 | 4.85 | 4.74 | 4.64 | 4.55 | 4.46 |
| 10.50 | 6.90 | 5.98 | 5.65 | 5.46 | 5.33 | 5.23 | 5.08 | 4.95 | 4.85 | 4.75 | 4.66 |
| 11.00 | 7.22 | 6.26 | 5.91 | 5.71 | 5.57 | 5.47 | 5.30 | 5.17 | 5.05 | 4.95 | 4.85 |
| 11.50 | 7.55 | 6.54 | 6.17 | 5.96 | 5.81 | 5.70 | 5.52 | 5.38 | 5.25 | 5.14 | 5.04 |
| 12.00 | 7.87 | 6.82 | 6.43 | 6.21 | 6.05 | 5.93 | 5.74 | 5.59 | 5.46 | 5.33 | 5.22 |
| 12.50 | 8.19 | 7.09 | 6.69 | 6.45 | 6.29 | 6.16 | 5.96 | 5.80 | 5.66 | 5.53 | 5.41 |
| 13.00 | 8.51 | 7.37 | 6.94 | 6.70 | 6.53 | 6.39 | 6.18 | 6.01 | 5.85 | 5.71 | 5.59 |
| 13.50 | 8.83 | 7.64 | 7.20 | 6.94 | 6.76 | 6.62 | 6.39 | 6.21 | 6.05 | 5.90 | 5.76 |
| 14.00 | 9.15 | 7.92 | 7.46 | 7.19 | 7.00 | 6.85 | 6.61 | 6.41 | 6.24 | 6.09 | 5.94 |
| 14.50 | 9.48 | 8.19 | 7.71 | 7.43 | 7.23 | 7.07 | 6.82 | 6.61 | 6.43 | 6.27 | 6.11 |
| 15.00 | 9.80 | 8.47 | 7.97 | 7.67 | 7.46 | 7.30 | 7.03 | 6.81 | 6.62 | 6.45 | 6.29 |
| 15.50 | 10.12 | 8.74 | 8.22 | 7.91 | 7.70 | 7.52 | 7.24 | 7.01 | 6.81 | 6.63 | 6.46 |
| 16.00 | 10.43 | 9.01 | 8.47 | 8.15 | 7.93 | 7.74 | 7.45 | 7.21 | 7.00 | 6.80 | 6.62 |
| 16.50 | 10.75 | 9.28 | 8.72 | 8.39 | 8.15 | 7.96 | 7.66 | 7.40 | 7.18 | 6.98 | 6.79 |
| 17.00 | 11.07 | 9.55 | 8.97 | 8.63 | 8.38 | 8.18 | 7.86 | 7.60 | 7.36 | 7.15 | 6.95 |
| 17.50 | 11.39 | 9.82 | 9.22 | 8.87 | 8.61 | 8.40 | 8.07 | 7.79 | 7.54 | 7.32 | 7.11 |
| 18.00 | 11.71 | 10.09 | 9.47 | 9.10 | 8.84 | 8.62 | 8.27 | 7.98 | 7.72 | 7.49 | 7.27 |
| 18.50 | 12.02 | 10.36 | 9.72 | 9.34 | 9.06 | 8.84 | 8.47 | 8.17 | 7.90 | 7.65 | 7.43 |
| 19.00 | 12.34 | 10.63 | 9.97 | 9.57 | 9.29 | 9.05 | 8.67 | 8.35 | 8.07 | 7.82 | 7.58 |
| 19.50 | 12.66 | 10.90 | 10.22 | 9.81 | 9.51 | 9.27 | 8.87 | 8.54 | 8.25 | 7.98 | 7.73 |
| 20.00 | 12.97 | 11.17 | 10.46 | 10.04 | 9.73 | 9.48 | 9.07 | 8.72 | 8.42 | 8.14 | 7.88 |
| 20.50 | 13.29 | 11.43 | 10.71 | 10.27 | 9.95 | 9.69 | 9.26 | 8.90 | 8.59 | 8.30 | 8.03 |
| 21.00 | 13.60 | 11.70 | 10.96 | 10.50 | 10.17 | 9.90 | 9.46 | 9.09 | 8.76 | 8.46 | 8.18 |
| 21.50 | 13.92 | 11.97 | 11.20 | 10.73 | 10.39 | 10.11 | 9.65 | 9.26 | 8.92 | 8.61 | 8.33 |
| 22.00 | 14.23 | 12.23 | 11.44 | 10.96 | 10.61 | 10.32 | 9.84 | 9.44 | 9.09 | 8.77 | 8.47 |
| 23.00 | 14.86 | 12.76 | 11.93 | 11.42 | 11.04 | 10.73 | 10.22 | 9.79 | 9.41 | 9.07 | 8.75 |
| 24.00 | 15.48 | 13.29 | 12.41 | 11.87 | 11.47 | 11.14 | 10.60 | 10.14 | 9.73 | 9.36 | 9.02 |
| 25.00 | 16.11 | 13.81 | 12.89 | 12.32 | 11.90 | 11.55 | 10.97 | 10.48 | 10.05 | 9.65 | 9.29 |

FIGURE 3-3 (continued)

# ACTUARIAL INTEREST TO DISCOUNT RATE

| Annual Actuarial Rate | TERM - months | | | | | | | | | | |
|---|---|---|---|---|---|---|---|---|---|---|---|
| | 54 mo. | 60 mo. | 66 mo. | 72 mo. | 78 mo. | 84 mo. | 96 mo. | 108 mo. | 120 mo. | 132 mo. | 144 mo. |
| 6.00 | 2.79 | 2.76 | 2.73 | 2.70 | 2.67 | 2.64 | 2.59 | 2.54 | 2.49 | 2.45 | 2.40 |
| 6.25 | 2.90 | 2.86 | 2.83 | 2.80 | 2.77 | 2.74 | 2.68 | 2.63 | 2.58 | 2.53 | 2.48 |
| 6.50 | 3.00 | 2.96 | 2.93 | 2.90 | 2.86 | 2.83 | 2.77 | 2.72 | 2.66 | 2.61 | 2.56 |
| 6.75 | 3.10 | 3.07 | 3.03 | 2.99 | 2.96 | 2.93 | 2.86 | 2.80 | 2.74 | 2.69 | 2.63 |
| 7.00 | 3.21 | 3.17 | 3.13 | 3.09 | 3.05 | 3.02 | 2.95 | 2.88 | 2.82 | 2.76 | 2.71 |
| 7.25 | 3.31 | 3.27 | 3.22 | 3.18 | 3.15 | 3.11 | 3.04 | 2.97 | 2.90 | 2.84 | 2.78 |
| 7.50 | 3.41 | 3.36 | 3.32 | 3.28 | 3.24 | 3.20 | 3.12 | 3.05 | 2.98 | 2.91 | 2.85 |
| 7.75 | 3.51 | 3.46 | 3.42 | 3.37 | 3.33 | 3.29 | 3.21 | 3.13 | 3.06 | 2.99 | 2.92 |
| 8.00 | 3.61 | 3.56 | 3.51 | 3.46 | 3.42 | 3.37 | 3.29 | 3.21 | 3.13 | 3.06 | 2.99 |
| 8.25 | 3.71 | 3.66 | 3.61 | 3.56 | 3.51 | 3.46 | 3.37 | 3.29 | 3.21 | 3.13 | 3.05 |
| 8.50 | 3.81 | 3.75 | 3.70 | 3.65 | 3.60 | 3.55 | 3.45 | 3.36 | 3.28 | 3.20 | 3.12 |
| 8.75 | 3.91 | 3.85 | 3.79 | 3.74 | 3.68 | 3.63 | 3.53 | 3.44 | 3.35 | 3.27 | 3.18 |
| 9.00 | 4.00 | 3.94 | 3.88 | 3.82 | 3.77 | 3.72 | 3.61 | 3.51 | 3.42 | 3.33 | 3.25 |
| 9.25 | 4.10 | 4.04 | 3.97 | 3.91 | 3.85 | 3.80 | 3.69 | 3.59 | 3.49 | 3.40 | 3.31 |
| 9.50 | 4.20 | 4.13 | 4.06 | 4.00 | 3.94 | 3.88 | 3.77 | 3.66 | 3.56 | 3.46 | 3.37 |
| 9.75 | 4.29 | 4.22 | 4.15 | 4.09 | 4.02 | 3.96 | 3.84 | 3.73 | 3.63 | 3.53 | 3.43 |
| 10.00 | 4.39 | 4.31 | 4.24 | 4.17 | 4.11 | 4.04 | 3.92 | 3.80 | 3.69 | 3.59 | 3.49 |
| 10.50 | 4.57 | 4.49 | 4.41 | 4.34 | 4.27 | 4.20 | 4.07 | 3.94 | 3.82 | 3.71 | 3.61 |
| 11.00 | 4.76 | 4.67 | 4.59 | 4.51 | 4.43 | 4.35 | 4.21 | 4.08 | 3.95 | 3.83 | 3.72 |
| 11.50 | 4.94 | 4.84 | 4.75 | 4.67 | 4.58 | 4.50 | 4.35 | 4.21 | 4.07 | 3.94 | 3.82 |
| 12.00 | 5.12 | 5.01 | 4.92 | 4.83 | 4.74 | 4.65 | 4.49 | 4.34 | 4.19 | 4.06 | 3.93 |
| 12.50 | 5.29 | 5.18 | 5.08 | 4.98 | 4.89 | 4.80 | 4.62 | 4.46 | 4.31 | 4.16 | 4.03 |
| 13.00 | 5.46 | 5.35 | 5.24 | 5.14 | 5.03 | 4.94 | 4.75 | 4.58 | 4.42 | 4.27 | 4.12 |
| 13.50 | 5.64 | 5.51 | 5.40 | 5.29 | 5.18 | 5.08 | 4.88 | 4.70 | 4.53 | 4.37 | 4.22 |
| 14.00 | 5.80 | 5.67 | 5.55 | 5.43 | 5.32 | 5.21 | 5.00 | 4.81 | 4.63 | 4.46 | 4.31 |
| 14.50 | 5.97 | 5.83 | 5.70 | 5.58 | 5.46 | 5.34 | 5.13 | 4.92 | 4.74 | 4.56 | 4.39 |
| 15.00 | 6.13 | 5.99 | 5.85 | 5.72 | 5.59 | 5.47 | 5.24 | 5.03 | 4.83 | 4.65 | 4.48 |
| 15.50 | 6.29 | 6.14 | 6.00 | 5.86 | 5.73 | 5.60 | 5.36 | 5.14 | 4.93 | 4.74 | 4.56 |
| 16.00 | 6.45 | 6.29 | 6.14 | 6.00 | 5.86 | 5.72 | 5.47 | 5.24 | 5.03 | 4.82 | 4.64 |
| 16.50 | 6.61 | 6.44 | 6.28 | 6.13 | 5.98 | 5.84 | 5.58 | 5.34 | 5.12 | 4.91 | 4.71 |
| 17.00 | 6.76 | 6.59 | 6.42 | 6.26 | 6.11 | 5.96 | 5.69 | 5.44 | 5.21 | 4.99 | 4.79 |
| 17.50 | 6.92 | 6.73 | 6.56 | 6.39 | 6.23 | 6.08 | 5.80 | 5.53 | 5.29 | 5.07 | 4.86 |
| 18.00 | 7.07 | 6.87 | 6.69 | 6.52 | 6.35 | 6.19 | 5.90 | 5.63 | 5.38 | 5.14 | 4.93 |
| 18.50 | 7.21 | 7.01 | 6.82 | 6.64 | 6.47 | 6.31 | 6.00 | 5.72 | 5.46 | 5.22 | 4.99 |
| 19.00 | 7.36 | 7.15 | 6.95 | 6.76 | 6.59 | 6.42 | 6.10 | 5.80 | 5.54 | 5.29 | 5.06 |
| 19.50 | 7.50 | 7.29 | 7.08 | 6.88 | 6.70 | 6.52 | 6.19 | 5.89 | 5.61 | 5.36 | 5.12 |
| 20.00 | 7.64 | 7.42 | 7.21 | 7.00 | 6.81 | 6.63 | 6.29 | 5.97 | 5.69 | 5.42 | 5.18 |
| 20.50 | 7.78 | 7.55 | 7.33 | 7.12 | 6.92 | 6.73 | 6.38 | 6.06 | 5.76 | 5.49 | 5.24 |
| 21.00 | 7.92 | 7.68 | 7.45 | 7.23 | 7.03 | 6.83 | 6.47 | 6.13 | 5.83 | 5.55 | 5.30 |
| 21.50 | 8.06 | 7.81 | 7.57 | 7.34 | 7.13 | 6.93 | 6.55 | 6.21 | 5.90 | 5.62 | 5.35 |
| 22.00 | 8.19 | 7.93 | 7.69 | 7.45 | 7.23 | 7.03 | 6.64 | 6.29 | 5.97 | 5.68 | 5.41 |
| 23.00 | 8.45 | 8.18 | 7.91 | 7.67 | 7.43 | 7.21 | 6.80 | 6.43 | 6.10 | 5.79 | 5.51 |
| 24.00 | 8.71 | 8.41 | 8.14 | 7.87 | 7.63 | 7.39 | 6.96 | 6.57 | 6.22 | 5.90 | 5.61 |
| 25.00 | 8.96 | 8.64 | 8.35 | 8.07 | 7.81 | 7.57 | 7.11 | 6.71 | 6.34 | 6.00 | 5.70 |

FIGURE 3-4

# HOW TO USE
# LEASE RATE CHARTS

These tables provide LEASE YIELDS expressed in ACTUARIAL INTEREST RATES . . . from 12% to 30% . . . and the applicable MONTHLY RENTAL RATE FACTORS . . . PER THOUSAND DOLLARS OF EQUIPMENT COST.

Tables are based upon annual terms of 2 through 8 years, WITH EQUAL MONTHLY RENTAL PAYMENTS. Thus . . . 2 Years = 24 months, etc.

Purchase Options . . . as percentage of Original Equipment Cost . . . are provided for 0% . . . (used for $1.00 Purchase Option Leases), 5%, 10%, 15% and 20% Purchase Options.

Security Deposits range from "0", meaning THERE IS NO SECURITY DEPOSIT . . . (AND ONLY FIRST MONTH IN ADVANCE IS COLLECTED) . . . and 1 through 5 Security Deposits.

Monthly Rental Rate Factor can be read from the tables BY FOLLOWING THESE STEPS:

1) Turn to page with DESIRED YIELD . . . (top of page).
2) Determine Purchase Option of the equipment . . . find that percentage (%) section.
3) Select the desired TERM of LEASE . . . AND . . . the required NUMBER of Security Deposit(s) . . . READ ACROSS TO THE APPLICABLE RATE FACTOR.
4) Multiply the EQUIPMENT COST times the PER THOUSAND RATE indicated. The PRODUCT is the MONTHLY RENTAL PAYMENT . . . FOR THAT TERM. Payments are always EQUAL MONTHLY.

THESE TABLES ASSUME ALL PAYMENTS ARE PAYABLE IN ADVANCE. SECURITY DEPOSITS . . . One (1) through Five (5) . . . are HELD until LEASE TERMINATION and then refunded or APPLIED against any PURCHASE OPTION DUE the LESSOR.

There will be a very slight decrease in LESSOR'S YIELD if, instead of Security Deposits, they treat these deposits as ADVANCE RENTALS. Advance rentals, (other than the first month), are applied to the LAST months of the LEASE TERM. Thus, if your lease calls for 1st and LAST Month in Advance, you would select the line indicated for ONE SECURITY DEPOSIT.

## INTERPOLATION

To arrive at ¼% or ½% incremental interest rate . . . (such as 12¼, 12½, 12-3/4%) . . . DIRECT INTERPOLATION PRODUCES REASONABLE ACCURATE APPLICABLE RATE FACTORS.

FOR EXAMPLE: To arrive at 12½% Rate Factor . . . SUBTRACT 12% Rate from 13% Rate . . . Divide this differential by Two . . . and ADD the QUOTIENT to 12% Rate.

FIGURE 3-4 (continued)

## 12.00 % ACTUARIAL YIELD

0% PURCHASE OPTION

TERM OF LEASE

| No. of Security Deposits | 2 Yrs. | 3 Yrs. | 4 Yrs. | 5 Yrs. | 6 Yrs. | 7 Yrs. | 8 Yrs. |
|---|---|---|---|---|---|---|---|
| 0 | 46.61 | 32.89 | 26.07 | 22.02 | 19.36 | 17.48 | 16.10 |
| 1 | 46.15 | 32.56 | 25.82 | 21.81 | 19.17 | 17.30 | 15.93 |
| 2 | 45.70 | 32.25 | 25.57 | 21.60 | 18.98 | 17.13 | 15.78 |
| 3 | 45.26 | 31.94 | 25.32 | 21.39 | 18.80 | 16.97 | 15.63 |
| 4 | 44.83 | 31.63 | 25.08 | 21.19 | 18.62 | 16.82 | 15.48 |
| 5 | 44.41 | 31.33 | 24.84 | 20.99 | 18.44 | 16.66 | 15.34 |
| **5% PURCHASE OPTION** | | | | | | | |
| 0 | 44.77 | 31.74 | 25.26 | 21.42 | 18.88 | 17.10 | 15.78 |
| 1 | 44.33 | 31.43 | 25.02 | 21.21 | 18.70 | 16.93 | 15.63 |
| 2 | 43.90 | 31.12 | 24.77 | 21.00 | 18.52 | 16.77 | 15.48 |
| 3 | 43.48 | 30.82 | 24.54 | 20.80 | 18.34 | 16.61 | 15.33 |
| 4 | 43.07 | 30.53 | 24.30 | 20.60 | 18.16 | 16.46 | 15.19 |
| 5 | 42.66 | 30.24 | 24.07 | 20.41 | 17.99 | 16.31 | 15.05 |
| **10% PURCHASE OPTION** | | | | | | | |
| 0 | 42.94 | 30.59 | 24.46 | 20.81 | 18.41 | 16.72 | 15.47 |
| 1 | 42.52 | 30.29 | 24.22 | 20.61 | 18.23 | 16.56 | 15.32 |
| 2 | 42.10 | 29.99 | 23.98 | 20.41 | 18.05 | 16.40 | 15.18 |
| 3 | 41.70 | 29.70 | 23.75 | 20.21 | 17.88 | 16.25 | 15.03 |
| 4 | 41.30 | 29.42 | 23.52 | 20.02 | 17.71 | 16.10 | 14.89 |
| 5 | 40.91 | 29.14 | 23.30 | 19.83 | 17.54 | 15.95 | 14.76 |
| **15% PURCHASE OPTION** | | | | | | | |
| 0 | 41.10 | 29.44 | 23.65 | 20.21 | 17.94 | 16.34 | 15.16 |
| 1 | 40.70 | 29.15 | 23.42 | 20.01 | 17.76 | 16.18 | 15.02 |
| 2 | 40.30 | 28.87 | 23.19 | 19.81 | 17.59 | 16.03 | 14.87 |
| 3 | 39.92 | 28.59 | 22.97 | 19.62 | 17.42 | 15.88 | 14.73 |
| 4 | 39.54 | 28.32 | 22.75 | 19.44 | 17.25 | 15.73 | 14.59 |
| 5 | 39.16 | 28.05 | 22.53 | 19.25 | 17.09 | 15.59 | 14.45 |
| **20% PURCHASE OPTION** | | | | | | | |
| 0 | 39.27 | 28.29 | 22.84 | 19.60 | 17.47 | 15.96 | 14.86 |
| 1 | 38.88 | 28.01 | 22.61 | 19.41 | 17.29 | 15.81 | 14.71 |
| 2 | 38.50 | 27.74 | 22.40 | 19.22 | 17.13 | 15.66 | 14.57 |
| 3 | 38.13 | 27.47 | 22.18 | 19.03 | 16.96 | 15.51 | 14.43 |
| 4 | 37.77 | 27.21 | 21.97 | 18.85 | 16.80 | 15.37 | 14.30 |
| 5 | 37.41 | 26.95 | 21.76 | 18.68 | 16.64 | 15.23 | 14.17 |

FIGURE 3-4 (continued)

## 13.00 % ACTUARIAL YIELD

0% PURCHASE OPTION

TERM OF LEASE

| No. of Security Deposits | 2 Yrs. | 3 Yrs. | 4 Yrs. | 5 Yrs. | 6 Yrs. | 7 Yrs. | 8 Yrs. |
|---|---|---|---|---|---|---|---|
| 0 | 47.03 | 33.33 | 26.54 | 22.51 | 19.86 | 18.00 | 16.63 |
| 1 | 46.53 | 32.98 | 26.26 | 22.27 | 19.65 | 17.80 | 16.45 |
| 2 | 46.05 | 32.63 | 25.98 | 22.04 | 19.44 | 17.62 | 16.28 |
| 3 | 45.57 | 32.29 | 25.71 | 21.81 | 19.24 | 17.44 | 16.11 |
| 4 | 45.10 | 31.96 | 25.45 | 21.58 | 19.04 | 17.26 | 15.95 |
| 5 | 44.64 | 31.64 | 25.19 | 21.36 | 18.85 | 17.09 | 15.79 |

5% PURCHASE OPTION

| No. of Security Deposits | 2 Yrs. | 3 Yrs. | 4 Yrs. | 5 Yrs. | 6 Yrs. | 7 Yrs. | 8 Yrs. |
|---|---|---|---|---|---|---|---|
| 0 | 45.22 | 32.20 | 25.75 | 21.92 | 19.40 | 17.63 | 16.33 |
| 1 | 44.74 | 31.86 | 25.48 | 21.69 | 19.20 | 17.45 | 16.16 |
| 2 | 44.27 | 31.53 | 25.21 | 21.46 | 18.99 | 17.27 | 15.99 |
| 3 | 43.81 | 31.20 | 24.95 | 21.24 | 18.80 | 17.09 | 15.83 |
| 4 | 43.36 | 30.88 | 24.69 | 21.02 | 18.60 | 16.92 | 15.67 |
| 5 | 42.92 | 30.56 | 24.44 | 20.80 | 18.42 | 16.76 | 15.52 |

10% PURCHASE OPTION

| No. of Security Deposits | 2 Yrs. | 3 Yrs. | 4 Yrs. | 5 Yrs. | 6 Yrs. | 7 Yrs. | 8 Yrs. |
|---|---|---|---|---|---|---|---|
| 0 | 43.40 | 31.07 | 24.96 | 21.33 | 18.94 | 17.27 | 16.04 |
| 1 | 42.94 | 30.74 | 24.69 | 21.10 | 18.74 | 17.09 | 15.87 |
| 2 | 42.49 | 30.42 | 24.43 | 20.88 | 18.55 | 16.91 | 15.70 |
| 3 | 42.05 | 30.10 | 24.18 | 20.67 | 18.35 | 16.74 | 15.54 |
| 4 | 41.62 | 29.79 | 23.93 | 20.45 | 18.17 | 16.57 | 15.39 |
| 5 | 41.19 | 29.49 | 23.69 | 20.25 | 17.98 | 16.41 | 15.23 |

15% PURCHASE OPTION

| No. of Security Deposits | 2 Yrs. | 3 Yrs. | 4 Yrs. | 5 Yrs. | 6 Yrs. | 7 Yrs. | 8 Yrs. |
|---|---|---|---|---|---|---|---|
| 0 | 41.59 | 29.94 | 24.17 | 20.74 | 18.49 | 16.91 | 15.74 |
| 1 | 41.14 | 29.62 | 23.91 | 20.52 | 18.29 | 16.73 | 15.57 |
| 2 | 40.71 | 29.31 | 23.66 | 20.31 | 18.10 | 16.55 | 15.41 |
| 3 | 40.29 | 29.01 | 23.41 | 20.09 | 17.91 | 16.39 | 15.26 |
| 4 | 39.88 | 28.71 | 23.17 | 19.89 | 17.73 | 16.22 | 15.10 |
| 5 | 39.47 | 28.42 | 22.94 | 19.69 | 17.55 | 16.06 | 14.95 |

20% PURCHASE OPTION

| No. of Security Deposits | 2 Yrs. | 3 Yrs. | 4 Yrs. | 5 Yrs. | 6 Yrs. | 7 Yrs. | 8 Yrs. |
|---|---|---|---|---|---|---|---|
| 0 | 39.77 | 28.81 | 23.38 | 20.15 | 18.03 | 16.54 | 15.45 |
| 1 | 39.35 | 28.50 | 23.13 | 19.94 | 17.84 | 16.37 | 15.28 |
| 2 | 38.93 | 28.21 | 22.88 | 19.73 | 17.65 | 16.20 | 15.12 |
| 3 | 38.53 | 27.91 | 22.65 | 19.52 | 17.47 | 16.03 | 14.97 |
| 4 | 38.13 | 27.63 | 22.41 | 19.32 | 17.29 | 15.87 | 14.82 |
| 5 | 37.75 | 27.34 | 22.19 | 19.13 | 17.11 | 15.72 | 14.67 |

FIGURE 3-4 (continued)

## 14.00 % ACTUARIAL YIELD

**TERM OF LEASE**

| No. of Security Deposits | 2 Yrs. | 3 Yrs. | 4 Yrs. | 5 Yrs. | 6 Yrs. | 7 Yrs. | 8 Yrs. |
|---|---|---|---|---|---|---|---|
| **0% PURCHASE OPTION** | | | | | | | |
| 0 | 47.46 | 33.78 | 27.01 | 23.00 | 20.37 | 18.53 | 17.17 |
| 1 | 46.92 | 33.40 | 26.70 | 22.74 | 20.14 | 18.31 | 16.97 |
| 2 | 46.39 | 33.02 | 26.40 | 22.48 | 19.91 | 18.10 | 16.78 |
| 3 | 45.87 | 32.65 | 26.11 | 22.23 | 19.69 | 17.91 | 16.60 |
| 4 | 45.37 | 32.29 | 25.82 | 21.99 | 19.47 | 17.71 | 16.42 |
| 5 | 44.87 | 31.94 | 25.54 | 21.75 | 19.26 | 17.53 | 16.25 |
| **5% PURCHASE OPTION** | | | | | | | |
| 0 | 45.66 | 32.67 | 26.24 | 22.43 | 19.93 | 18.18 | 16.89 |
| 1 | 45.14 | 32.30 | 25.94 | 22.17 | 19.70 | 17.97 | 16.70 |
| 2 | 44.63 | 31.93 | 25.65 | 21.92 | 19.48 | 17.77 | 16.51 |
| 3 | 44.14 | 31.58 | 25.36 | 21.68 | 19.26 | 17.57 | 16.33 |
| 4 | 43.65 | 31.23 | 25.08 | 21.44 | 19.05 | 17.39 | 16.15 |
| 5 | 43.17 | 30.89 | 24.81 | 21.20 | 18.84 | 17.20 | 15.98 |
| **10% PURCHASE OPTION** | | | | | | | |
| 0 | 43.87 | 31.56 | 25.46 | 21.85 | 19.48 | 17.83 | 16.61 |
| 1 | 43.37 | 31.20 | 25.17 | 21.60 | 19.26 | 17.62 | 16.42 |
| 2 | 42.88 | 30.85 | 24.89 | 21.36 | 19.05 | 17.43 | 16.24 |
| 3 | 42.40 | 30.50 | 24.61 | 21.12 | 18.83 | 17.24 | 16.06 |
| 4 | 41.93 | 30.17 | 24.34 | 20.89 | 18.63 | 17.05 | 15.89 |
| 5 | 41.48 | 29.84 | 24.08 | 20.66 | 18.42 | 16.87 | 15.72 |
| **15% PURCHASE OPTION** | | | | | | | |
| 0 | 42.07 | 30.45 | 24.69 | 21.28 | 19.04 | 17.48 | 16.33 |
| 1 | 41.59 | 30.10 | 24.41 | 21.04 | 18.83 | 17.28 | 16.14 |
| 2 | 41.12 | 29.76 | 24.13 | 20.80 | 18.61 | 17.09 | 15.96 |
| 3 | 40.66 | 29.43 | 23.86 | 20.57 | 18.41 | 16.90 | 15.79 |
| 4 | 40.22 | 29.10 | 23.60 | 20.34 | 18.20 | 16.72 | 15.62 |
| 5 | 39.78 | 28.79 | 23.34 | 20.12 | 18.00 | 16.54 | 15.45 |
| **20% PURCHASE OPTION** | | | | | | | |
| 0 | 40.27 | 29.33 | 23.92 | 20.71 | 18.60 | 17.13 | 16.05 |
| 1 | 39.81 | 29.00 | 23.64 | 20.47 | 18.39 | 16.93 | 15.86 |
| 2 | 39.37 | 28.67 | 23.38 | 20.24 | 18.18 | 16.74 | 15.68 |
| 3 | 38.93 | 28.35 | 23.12 | 20.01 | 17.98 | 16.56 | 15.51 |
| 4 | 38.50 | 28.04 | 22.86 | 19.79 | 17.78 | 16.38 | 15.35 |
| 5 | 38.08 | 27.73 | 22.61 | 19.58 | 17.59 | 16.21 | 15.18 |

FIGURE 3-4 (continued)

## 15.00 % ACTUARIAL YIELD

0% PURCHASE OPTION

| No. of Security Deposits | 2 Yrs. | 3 Yrs. | 4 Yrs. | 5 Yrs. | 6 Yrs. | 7 Yrs. | 8 Yrs. |
|---|---|---|---|---|---|---|---|
| | **TERM OF LEASE** | | | | | | |
| 0 | 47.89 | 34.24 | 27.49 | 23.50 | 20.88 | 19.06 | 17.73 |
| 1 | 47.30 | 33.82 | 27.15 | 23.21 | 20.63 | 18.82 | 17.50 |
| 2 | 46.73 | 33.41 | 26.82 | 22.93 | 20.38 | 18.60 | 17.29 |
| 3 | 46.18 | 33.01 | 26.51 | 22.66 | 20.14 | 18.38 | 17.09 |
| 4 | 45.63 | 32.63 | 26.19 | 22.39 | 19.90 | 18.17 | 16.90 |
| 5 | 45.10 | 32.25 | 25.89 | 22.13 | 19.67 | 17.97 | 16.70 |
| **5% PURCHASE OPTION** | | | | | | | |
| 0 | 46.11 | 33.14 | 26.73 | 22.94 | 20.46 | 18.73 | 17.46 |
| 1 | 45.55 | 32.74 | 26.40 | 22.66 | 20.21 | 18.50 | 17.24 |
| 2 | 45.00 | 32.34 | 26.09 | 22.39 | 19.96 | 18.28 | 17.04 |
| 3 | 44.46 | 31.96 | 25.78 | 22.12 | 19.73 | 18.06 | 16.84 |
| 4 | 43.94 | 31.58 | 25.47 | 21.86 | 19.49 | 17.86 | 16.64 |
| 5 | 43.43 | 31.22 | 25.18 | 21.61 | 19.27 | 17.66 | 16.46 |
| **10% PURCHASE OPTION** | | | | | | | |
| 0 | 44.33 | 32.05 | 25.97 | 22.38 | 20.03 | 18.39 | 17.19 |
| 1 | 43.79 | 31.66 | 25.66 | 22.11 | 19.79 | 18.16 | 16.98 |
| 2 | 43.27 | 31.28 | 25.35 | 21.84 | 19.55 | 17.95 | 16.78 |
| 3 | 42.75 | 30.90 | 25.05 | 21.58 | 19.31 | 17.74 | 16.58 |
| 4 | 42.25 | 30.54 | 24.75 | 21.33 | 19.09 | 17.54 | 16.39 |
| 5 | 41.76 | 30.18 | 24.46 | 21.08 | 18.87 | 17.34 | 16.20 |
| **15% PURCHASE OPTION** | | | | | | | |
| 0 | 42.56 | 30.95 | 25.22 | 21.82 | 19.60 | 18.05 | 16.92 |
| 1 | 42.04 | 30.58 | 24.91 | 21.56 | 19.36 | 17.83 | 16.71 |
| 2 | 41.53 | 30.21 | 24.61 | 21.30 | 19.13 | 17.62 | 16.51 |
| 3 | 41.04 | 29.85 | 24.32 | 21.04 | 18.90 | 17.42 | 16.32 |
| 4 | 40.55 | 29.50 | 24.03 | 20.80 | 18.68 | 17.22 | 16.13 |
| 5 | 40.08 | 29.15 | 23.75 | 20.55 | 18.46 | 17.02 | 15.95 |
| **20% PURCHASE OPTION** | | | | | | | |
| 0 | 40.78 | 29.86 | 24.46 | 21.27 | 19.18 | 17.72 | 16.65 |
| 1 | 40.28 | 29.49 | 24.16 | 21.01 | 18.94 | 17.50 | 16.45 |
| 2 | 39.80 | 29.14 | 23.87 | 20.75 | 18.71 | 17.29 | 16.25 |
| 3 | 39.32 | 28.79 | 23.59 | 20.51 | 18.49 | 17.09 | 16.06 |
| 4 | 38.86 | 28.45 | 23.31 | 20.27 | 18.27 | 16.90 | 15.88 |
| 5 | 38.41 | 28.12 | 23.04 | 20.03 | 18.06 | 16.71 | 15.70 |

FIGURE 3-4 (continued)

## 16.00 % ACTUARIAL YIELD

0% PURCHASE OPTION

| No. of Security Deposits | TERM OF LEASE 2 Yrs. | 3 Yrs. | 4 Yrs. | 5 Yrs. | 6 Yrs. | 7 Yrs. | 8 Yrs. |
|---|---|---|---|---|---|---|---|
| 0 | 48.32 | 34.69 | 27.97 | 24.00 | 21.41 | 19.60 | 18.29 |
| 1 | 47.69 | 34.24 | 27.60 | 23.69 | 21.13 | 19.34 | 18.04 |
| 2 | 47.08 | 33.80 | 27.25 | 23.38 | 20.86 | 19.10 | 17.81 |
| 3 | 46.48 | 33.38 | 26.91 | 23.09 | 20.59 | 18.86 | 17.59 |
| 4 | 45.90 | 32.96 | 26.57 | 22.80 | 20.34 | 18.63 | 17.38 |
| 5 | 45.34 | 32.55 | 26.24 | 22.52 | 20.09 | 18.41 | 17.17 |

5% PURCHASE OPTION

| No. of Security Deposits | 2 Yrs. | 3 Yrs. | 4 Yrs. | 5 Yrs. | 6 Yrs. | 7 Yrs. | 8 Yrs. |
|---|---|---|---|---|---|---|---|
| 0 | 46.56 | 33.62 | 27.23 | 23.46 | 20.99 | 19.28 | 18.03 |
| 1 | 45.96 | 33.18 | 26.87 | 23.15 | 20.72 | 19.03 | 17.80 |
| 2 | 45.37 | 32.76 | 26.53 | 22.85 | 20.46 | 18.79 | 17.57 |
| 3 | 44.79 | 32.34 | 26.19 | 22.57 | 20.20 | 18.56 | 17.35 |
| 4 | 44.23 | 31.94 | 25.87 | 22.28 | 19.94 | 18.33 | 17.14 |
| 5 | 43.69 | 31.54 | 25.55 | 22.01 | 19.70 | 18.11 | 16.93 |

10% PURCHASE OPTION

| No. of Security Deposits | 2 Yrs. | 3 Yrs. | 4 Yrs. | 5 Yrs. | 6 Yrs. | 7 Yrs. | 8 Yrs. |
|---|---|---|---|---|---|---|---|
| 0 | 44.80 | 32.54 | 26.49 | 22.91 | 20.58 | 18.96 | 17.77 |
| 1 | 44.22 | 32.12 | 26.14 | 22.62 | 20.31 | 18.71 | 17.54 |
| 2 | 43.65 | 31.71 | 25.81 | 22.33 | 20.05 | 18.48 | 17.32 |
| 3 | 43.10 | 31.31 | 25.48 | 22.04 | 19.80 | 18.25 | 17.10 |
| 4 | 42.56 | 30.91 | 25.16 | 21.77 | 19.55 | 18.02 | 16.89 |
| 5 | 42.04 | 30.53 | 24.85 | 21.50 | 19.31 | 17.81 | 16.69 |

15% PURCHASE OPTION

| No. of Security Deposits | 2 Yrs. | 3 Yrs. | 4 Yrs. | 5 Yrs. | 6 Yrs. | 7 Yrs. | 8 Yrs. |
|---|---|---|---|---|---|---|---|
| 0 | 43.04 | 31.46 | 25.75 | 22.37 | 20.17 | 18.64 | 17.52 |
| 1 | 42.49 | 31.06 | 25.41 | 22.08 | 19.91 | 18.39 | 17.29 |
| 2 | 41.94 | 30.66 | 25.09 | 21.80 | 19.65 | 18.16 | 17.07 |
| 3 | 41.41 | 30.27 | 24.77 | 21.52 | 19.40 | 17.94 | 16.77 |
| 4 | 40.89 | 29.89 | 24.46 | 21.25 | 19.16 | 17.71 | 16.65 |
| 5 | 40.39 | 29.52 | 24.16 | 20.99 | 18.92 | 17.51 | 16.45 |

20% PURCHASE OPTION

| No. of Security Deposits | 2 Yrs. | 3 Yrs. | 4 Yrs. | 5 Yrs. | 6 Yrs. | 7 Yrs. | 8 Yrs. |
|---|---|---|---|---|---|---|---|
| 0 | 41.29 | 30.39 | 25.01 | 21.83 | 19.76 | 18.31 | 17.26 |
| 1 | 40.75 | 29.99 | 24.68 | 21.55 | 19.50 | 18.08 | 17.04 |
| 2 | 40.23 | 29.60 | 24.36 | 21.27 | 19.25 | 17.85 | 16.82 |
| 3 | 39.72 | 29.23 | 24.06 | 21.00 | 19.01 | 17.63 | 16.61 |
| 4 | 39.22 | 28.87 | 23.76 | 20.74 | 18.77 | 17.41 | 16.41 |
| 5 | 38.74 | 28.51 | 23.46 | 20.48 | 18.54 | 17.20 | 16.21 |

FIGURE 3-4 (continued)

## 17.00 % ACTUARIAL YIELD

**0% PURCHASE OPTION**

| No. of Security Deposits | TERM OF LEASE 2 Yrs. | 3 Yrs. | 4 Yrs. | 5 Yrs. | 6 Yrs. | 7 Yrs. | 8 Yrs. |
|---|---|---|---|---|---|---|---|
| 0 | 48.75 | 35.15 | 28.45 | 24.51 | 21.94 | 20.15 | 18.86 |
| 1 | 48.08 | 34.67 | 28.06 | 24.17 | 21.63 | 19.87 | 18.59 |
| 2 | 47.43 | 34.20 | 27.68 | 23.84 | 21.34 | 19.60 | 18.34 |
| 3 | 46.79 | 33.74 | 27.31 | 23.52 | 21.05 | 19.34 | 18.10 |
| 4 | 46.17 | 33.29 | 26.95 | 23.21 | 20.77 | 19.09 | 17.86 |
| 5 | 45.57 | 32.86 | 26.59 | 22.91 | 20.50 | 18.85 | 17.54 |

**5% PURCHASE OPTION**

| No. of Security Deposits | 2 Yrs. | 3 Yrs. | 4 Yrs. | 5 Yrs. | 6 Yrs. | 7 Yrs. | 8 Yrs. |
|---|---|---|---|---|---|---|---|
| 0 | 47.01 | 34.10 | 27.73 | 23.98 | 21.54 | 19.84 | 18.61 |
| 1 | 46.36 | 33.63 | 27.35 | 23.65 | 21.24 | 19.57 | 18.35 |
| 2 | 45.73 | 33.17 | 26.97 | 23.33 | 20.95 | 19.31 | 18.11 |
| 3 | 45.12 | 32.72 | 26.61 | 23.01 | 20.67 | 19.05 | 17.87 |
| 4 | 44.52 | 32.29 | 26.26 | 22.71 | 20.40 | 18.81 | 17.64 |
| 5 | 43.94 | 31.87 | 25.92 | 22.41 | 20.13 | 18.57 | 17.41 |

**10% PURCHASE OPTION**

| No. of Security Deposits | 2 Yrs. | 3 Yrs. | 4 Yrs. | 5 Yrs. | 6 Yrs. | 7 Yrs. | 8 Yrs. |
|---|---|---|---|---|---|---|---|
| 0 | 45.27 | 33.04 | 27.00 | 23.45 | 21.14 | 19.53 | 18.37 |
| 1 | 44.65 | 32.58 | 26.63 | 23.13 | 20.85 | 19.26 | 18.11 |
| 2 | 44.04 | 32.14 | 26.27 | 22.81 | 20.56 | 19.01 | 17.87 |
| 3 | 43.45 | 31.71 | 25.92 | 22.51 | 20.29 | 18.76 | 17.63 |
| 4 | 42.88 | 31.29 | 25.57 | 22.21 | 20.02 | 18.51 | 17.41 |
| 5 | 42.32 | 30.88 | 25.24 | 21.92 | 19.76 | 18.28 | 17.18 |

**15% PURCHASE OPTION**

| No. of Security Deposits | 2 Yrs. | 3 Yrs. | 4 Yrs. | 5 Yrs. | 6 Yrs. | 7 Yrs. | 8 Yrs. |
|---|---|---|---|---|---|---|---|
| 0 | 43.53 | 31.98 | 26.28 | 22.92 | 20.74 | 19.23 | 18.12 |
| 1 | 42.93 | 31.54 | 25.92 | 22.61 | 20.45 | 18.96 | 17.87 |
| 2 | 42.35 | 31.11 | 25.57 | 22.30 | 20.18 | 18.71 | 17.63 |
| 3 | 41.78 | 30.69 | 25.22 | 22.00 | 19.91 | 18.46 | 17.40 |
| 4 | 41.23 | 30.28 | 24.89 | 21.71 | 19.64 | 18.22 | 17.17 |
| 5 | 40.69 | 29.89 | 24.56 | 21.43 | 19.39 | 17.99 | 16.96 |

**20% PURCHASE OPTION**

| No. of Security Deposits | 2 Yrs. | 3 Yrs. | 4 Yrs. | 5 Yrs. | 6 Yrs. | 7 Yrs. | 8 Yrs. |
|---|---|---|---|---|---|---|---|
| 0 | 41.80 | 30.92 | 25.56 | 22.40 | 20.34 | 18.92 | 17.88 |
| 1 | 41.22 | 30.49 | 25.20 | 22.09 | 20.06 | 18.66 | 17.63 |
| 2 | 40.66 | 30.08 | 24.86 | 21.79 | 19.79 | 18.40 | 17.39 |
| 3 | 40.11 | 29.67 | 24.53 | 21.50 | 19.52 | 18.16 | 17.17 |
| 4 | 39.58 | 29.28 | 24.20 | 21.21 | 19.27 | 17.93 | 16.94 |
| 5 | 39.07 | 28.90 | 23.89 | 20.94 | 19.01 | 17.70 | 16.73 |

FIGURE 3-4 (continued)

## 18.00 % ACTUARIAL YIELD

0% PURCHASE OPTION

TERM OF LEASE

| No. of Security Deposits | 2 Yrs. | 3 Yrs. | 4 Yrs. | 5 Yrs. | 6 Yrs. | 7 Yrs. | 8 Yrs. |
|---|---|---|---|---|---|---|---|
| 0 | 49.19 | 35.62 | 28.94 | 25.02 | 22.47 | 20.71 | 19.43 |
| 1 | 48.47 | 35.10 | 28.52 | 24.65 | 22.14 | 20.40 | 19.15 |
| 2 | 47.77 | 34.60 | 28.11 | 24.30 | 21.83 | 20.11 | 18.87 |
| 3 | 47.10 | 34.11 | 27.71 | 23.96 | 21.52 | 19.83 | 18.61 |
| 4 | 46.44 | 33.63 | 27.33 | 23.62 | 21.22 | 19.56 | 18.36 |
| 5 | 45.80 | 33.17 | 26.95 | 23.30 | 20.92 | 19.30 | 18.11 |
| **5% PURCHASE OPTION** | | | | | | | |
| 0 | 47.47 | 34.58 | 28.23 | 24.51 | 22.09 | 20.41 | 19.20 |
| 1 | 46.77 | 34.07 | 27.82 | 24.15 | 21.76 | 20.12 | 18.92 |
| 2 | 46.10 | 33.58 | 27.42 | 23.80 | 21.45 | 19.83 | 18.65 |
| 3 | 45.45 | 33.11 | 27.03 | 23.47 | 21.15 | 19.55 | 18.39 |
| 4 | 44.82 | 32.65 | 26.66 | 23.14 | 20.85 | 19.29 | 18.14 |
| 5 | 44.20 | 32.20 | 26.29 | 22.82 | 20.57 | 19.03 | 17.90 |
| **10% PURCHASE OPTION** | | | | | | | |
| 0 | 45.75 | 33.53 | 27.52 | 23.99 | 21.70 | 20.12 | 18.97 |
| 1 | 45.08 | 33.05 | 27.12 | 23.64 | 21.39 | 19.82 | 18.69 |
| 2 | 44.43 | 32.57 | 26.73 | 23.31 | 21.08 | 19.54 | 18.43 |
| 3 | 43.80 | 32.11 | 26.36 | 22.98 | 20.78 | 19.27 | 18.17 |
| 4 | 43.19 | 31.66 | 25.99 | 22.65 | 20.49 | 19.01 | 17.92 |
| 5 | 42.60 | 31.23 | 25.63 | 22.34 | 20.21 | 18.75 | 17.68 |
| **15% PURCHASE OPTION** | | | | | | | |
| 0 | 44.03 | 32.49 | 26.82 | 23.48 | 21.32 | 19.82 | 18.74 |
| 1 | 43.38 | 32.02 | 26.43 | 23.14 | 21.01 | 19.53 | 18.46 |
| 2 | 42.76 | 31.56 | 26.05 | 22.81 | 20.70 | 19.25 | 18.20 |
| 3 | 42.16 | 31.11 | 25.68 | 22.49 | 20.41 | 18.99 | 17.95 |
| 4 | 41.57 | 30.68 | 25.32 | 22.17 | 20.13 | 18.73 | 17.70 |
| 5 | 41.00 | 30.26 | 24.97 | 21.87 | 19.85 | 18.48 | 17.46 |
| **20% PURCHASE OPTION** | | | | | | | |
| 0 | 42.30 | 31.45 | 26.11 | 22.97 | 20.93 | 19.52 | 18.50 |
| 1 | 41.69 | 30.99 | 25.73 | 22.64 | 20.63 | 19.24 | 18.23 |
| 2 | 41.09 | 30.55 | 25.36 | 22.31 | 20.33 | 18.98 | 17.97 |
| 3 | 40.51 | 30.12 | 25.00 | 22.00 | 20.04 | 18.70 | 17.72 |
| 4 | 39.94 | 29.69 | 24.65 | 21.69 | 19.76 | 18.45 | 17.48 |
| 5 | 39.39 | 29.29 | 24.31 | 21.39 | 19.49 | 18.20 | 17.25 |

FIGURE 3-4 (continued)

## 19.00 % ACTUARIAL YIELD

0% PURCHASE OPTION

| No. of Security Deposits | 2 Yrs. | 3 Yrs. | 4 Yrs. | 5 Yrs. | 6 Yrs. | 7 Yrs. | 8 Yrs. |
|---|---|---|---|---|---|---|---|
| | TERM OF LEASE | | | | | | |
| 0 | 49.62 | 36.08 | 29.43 | 25.54 | 23.01 | 21.27 | 20.02 |
| 1 | 48.85 | 35.52 | 28.97 | 25.14 | 22.65 | 20.94 | 19.71 |
| 2 | 48.17 | 35.01 | 28.55 | 24.77 | 22.32 | 20.63 | 19.41 |
| 3 | 47.52 | 34.52 | 28.14 | 24.41 | 21.99 | 20.33 | 19.13 |
| 4 | 46.87 | 34.05 | 27.75 | 24.05 | 21.68 | 20.03 | 18.85 |
| 5 | 46.22 | 33.61 | 27.38 | 23.73 | 21.38 | 19.75 | 18.58 |
| **10% PURCHASE OPTION** | | | | | | | |
| 0 | 46.22 | 34.04 | 28.05 | 24.54 | 22.27 | 20.70 | 19.57 |
| 1 | 45.53 | 33.52 | 27.62 | 24.17 | 21.93 | 20.39 | 19.27 |
| 2 | 44.89 | 33.04 | 27.22 | 23.81 | 21.60 | 20.08 | 18.99 |
| 3 | 44.29 | 32.58 | 26.83 | 23.47 | 21.29 | 19.79 | 18.71 |
| 4 | 43.73 | 32.14 | 26.46 | 23.14 | 20.99 | 19.50 | 18.44 |
| 5 | 43.21 | 31.72 | 26.10 | 22.82 | 20.69 | 19.23 | 18.18 |

## 20.00 % ACTUARIAL YIELD

0% PURCHASE OPTION

| No. of Security Deposits | 2 Yrs. | 3 Yrs. | 4 Yrs. | 5 Yrs. | 6 Yrs. | 7 Yrs. | 8 Yrs. |
|---|---|---|---|---|---|---|---|
| | TERM OF LEASE | | | | | | |
| 0 | 50.06 | 36.56 | 29.93 | 26.06 | 23.56 | 21.84 | 20.61 |
| 1 | 49.25 | 35.96 | 29.44 | 25.65 | 23.19 | 21.49 | 20.27 |
| 2 | 48.52 | 35.41 | 29.01 | 25.25 | 22.81 | 21.15 | 19.96 |
| 3 | 47.84 | 34.89 | 28.55 | 24.87 | 22.46 | 20.82 | 19.66 |
| 4 | 47.27 | 34.40 | 28.16 | 24.48 | 22.14 | 20.51 | 19.36 |
| 5 | 46.67 | 33.97 | 27.77 | 24.15 | 21.82 | 20.22 | 19.07 |
| **10% PURCHASE OPTION** | | | | | | | |
| 0 | 46.70 | 34.54 | 28.58 | 25.09 | 22.84 | 21.30 | 20.19 |
| 1 | 45.97 | 33.99 | 28.12 | 24.69 | 22.48 | 20.96 | 19.86 |
| 2 | 45.29 | 33.47 | 27.69 | 24.31 | 22.13 | 20.63 | 19.55 |
| 3 | 44.65 | 32.98 | 27.27 | 23.94 | 21.79 | 20.31 | 19.25 |
| 4 | 44.06 | 32.52 | 26.88 | 23.59 | 21.46 | 20.00 | 18.96 |
| 5 | 43.50 | 32.07 | 26.50 | 23.25 | 21.15 | 19.71 | 18.68 |

FIGURE 3-4 (continued)

## 21.00 % ACTUARIAL YIELD

0% PURCHASE OPTION

| No. of Security Deposits | TERM OF LEASE 2 Yrs. | 3 Yrs. | 4 Yrs. | 5 Yrs. | 6 Yrs. | 7 Yrs. | 8 Yrs. |
|---|---|---|---|---|---|---|---|
| 0 | 50.50 | 37.03 | 30.43 | 26.59 | 24.12 | 22.42 | 21.21 |
| 1 | 49.64 | 36.39 | 29.91 | 26.13 | 23.70 | 22.04 | 20.85 |
| 2 | 48.87 | 35.81 | 29.43 | 25.71 | 23.31 | 21.68 | 20.50 |
| 3 | 48.15 | 35.26 | 28.97 | 25.30 | 22.94 | 21.33 | 20.17 |
| 4 | 47.48 | 34.74 | 28.52 | 24.91 | 22.58 | 20.99 | 19.85 |
| 5 | 46.86 | 34.24 | 28.10 | 24.53 | 22.24 | 20.67 | 19.55 |

10% PURCHASE OPTION

| No. of Security Deposits | 2 Yrs. | 3 Yrs. | 4 Yrs. | 5 Yrs. | 6 Yrs. | 7 Yrs. | 8 Yrs. |
|---|---|---|---|---|---|---|---|
| 0 | 47.17 | 35.05 | 29.11 | 25.65 | 23.42 | 21.90 | 20.81 |
| 1 | 46.40 | 34.46 | 28.62 | 25.22 | 23.03 | 21.53 | 20.46 |
| 2 | 45.68 | 33.91 | 28.16 | 24.81 | 22.65 | 21.18 | 20.12 |
| 3 | 45.01 | 33.39 | 27.72 | 24.41 | 22.29 | 20.83 | 19.80 |
| 4 | 44.38 | 32.90 | 27.30 | 24.04 | 21.94 | 20.51 | 19.48 |
| 5 | 43.80 | 32.43 | 26.89 | 23.67 | 21.60 | 20.19 | 19.18 |

## 22.00 % ACTUARIAL YIELD

0% PURCHASE OPTION

| No. of Security Deposits | TERM OF LEASE 2 Yrs. | 3 Yrs. | 4 Yrs. | 5 Yrs. | 6 Yrs. | 7 Yrs. | 8 Yrs. |
|---|---|---|---|---|---|---|---|
| 0 | 50.95 | 37.50 | 30.94 | 27.12 | 24.67 | 23.00 | 21.82 |
| 1 | 50.04 | 36.83 | 30.39 | 26.64 | 24.23 | 22.59 | 21.43 |
| 2 | 49.23 | 36.22 | 29.87 | 26.18 | 23.82 | 22.21 | 21.06 |
| 3 | 48.47 | 35.64 | 29.38 | 25.75 | 23.42 | 21.83 | 20.70 |
| 4 | 47.77 | 35.08 | 28.91 | 25.33 | 23.04 | 21.47 | 20.36 |
| 5 | 47.11 | 34.56 | 28.47 | 24.93 | 22.67 | 21.13 | 20.03 |

10% PURCHASE OPTION

| No. of Security Deposits | 2 Yrs. | 3 Yrs. | 4 Yrs. | 5 Yrs. | 6 Yrs. | 7 Yrs. | 8 Yrs. |
|---|---|---|---|---|---|---|---|
| 0 | 47.65 | 35.55 | 29.65 | 26.21 | 24.01 | 22.51 | 21.44 |
| 1 | 46.84 | 34.94 | 29.13 | 25.75 | 23.59 | 22.11 | 21.06 |
| 2 | 46.08 | 34.35 | 28.63 | 25.31 | 23.18 | 21.73 | 20.69 |
| 3 | 45.37 | 33.80 | 28.16 | 24.89 | 22.79 | 21.36 | 20.35 |
| 4 | 44.71 | 33.28 | 27.72 | 24.49 | 22.42 | 21.01 | 20.01 |
| 5 | 44.09 | 32.78 | 27.29 | 24.10 | 22.06 | 20.67 | 19.68 |

FIGURE 3-4 (continued)

## 23.00 % ACTUARIAL YIELD

0% PURCHASE OPTION

| No. of Security Deposits | 2 Yrs. | 3 Yrs. | 4 Yrs. | 5 Yrs. | 6 Yrs. | 7 Yrs. | 8 Yrs. |
|---|---|---|---|---|---|---|---|
| | TERM OF LEASE | | | | | | |
| 0 | 51.39 | 37.98 | 31.45 | 27.66 | 25.24 | 23.60 | 22.43 |
| 1 | 50.44 | 37.28 | 30.86 | 27.15 | 24.77 | 23.16 | 22.02 |
| 2 | 49.58 | 36.63 | 30.32 | 26.66 | 24.33 | 22.74 | 21.62 |
| 3 | 48.79 | 36.01 | 29.80 | 26.20 | 23.90 | 22.34 | 21.24 |
| 4 | 48.05 | 35.43 | 29.30 | 25.76 | 23.50 | 21.96 | 20.87 |
| 5 | 47.36 | 34.88 | 28.83 | 25.34 | 23.10 | 21.59 | 20.52 |

10% PURCHASE OPTION

| No. of Security Deposits | 2 Yrs. | 3 Yrs. | 4 Yrs. | 5 Yrs. | 6 Yrs. | 7 Yrs. | 8 Yrs. |
|---|---|---|---|---|---|---|---|
| 0 | 48.13 | 36.07 | 30.19 | 26.78 | 24.60 | 23.12 | 22.07 |
| 1 | 47.27 | 35.41 | 29.63 | 26.29 | 24.14 | 22.69 | 21.66 |
| 2 | 46.47 | 34.79 | 29.11 | 25.82 | 23.71 | 22.28 | 21.27 |
| 3 | 45.72 | 34.21 | 28.61 | 25.37 | 23.30 | 21.89 | 20.90 |
| 4 | 45.03 | 33.66 | 28.14 | 24.94 | 22.90 | 21.52 | 20.54 |
| 5 | 44.38 | 33.14 | 27.68 | 24.53 | 22.52 | 21.16 | 20.19 |

## 24.00 % ACTUARIAL YIELD

0% PURCHASE OPTION

| No. of Security Deposits | 2 Yrs. | 3 Yrs. | 4 Yrs. | 5 Yrs. | 6 Yrs. | 7 Yrs. | 8 Yrs. |
|---|---|---|---|---|---|---|---|
| | TERM OF LEASE | | | | | | |
| 0 | 51.84 | 38.46 | 31.96 | 28.20 | 25.81 | 24.19 | 23.05 |
| 1 | 50.84 | 37.71 | 31.34 | 27.66 | 25.31 | 23.68 | 22.61 |
| 2 | 49.94 | 37.03 | 30.77 | 27.14 | 24.84 | 23.28 | 22.18 |
| 3 | 49.11 | 36.39 | 30.22 | 26.66 | 24.39 | 22.86 | 21.78 |
| 4 | 48.33 | 35.78 | 29.70 | 26.19 | 23.96 | 22.45 | 21.39 |
| 5 | 47.61 | 35.20 | 29.20 | 25.74 | 23.54 | 22.06 | 21.01 |

10% PURCHASE OPTION

| No. of Security Deposits | 2 Yrs. | 3 Yrs. | 4 Yrs. | 5 Yrs. | 6 Yrs. | 7 Yrs. | 8 Yrs. |
|---|---|---|---|---|---|---|---|
| 0 | 48.61 | 36.58 | 30.73 | 27.35 | 25.19 | 23.74 | 22.71 |
| 1 | 47.71 | 35.89 | 30.14 | 26.82 | 24.71 | 23.28 | 22.27 |
| 2 | 46.87 | 35.24 | 29.59 | 26.33 | 24.25 | 22.84 | 21.86 |
| 3 | 46.08 | 34.62 | 29.06 | 25.85 | 23.81 | 22.43 | 21.45 |
| 4 | 45.35 | 34.04 | 28.56 | 25.40 | 23.39 | 22.03 | 21.07 |
| 5 | 44.68 | 33.49 | 28.08 | 24.96 | 22.98 | 21.64 | 20.70 |

FIGURE 3-4 (continued)

## 25.00 % ACTUARIAL YIELD

0% PURCHASE OPTION

| No. of Security Deposits | TERM OF LEASE 2 Yrs. | 3 Yrs. | 4 Yrs. | 5 Yrs. | 6 Yrs. | 7 Yrs. | 8 Yrs. |
|---|---|---|---|---|---|---|---|
| 0 | 52.28 | 38.95 | 32.48 | 28.75 | 26.39 | 24.80 | 23.68 |
| 1 | 51.24 | 38.17 | 31.83 | 28.17 | 25.86 | 24.30 | 23.20 |
| 2 | 50.30 | 37.45 | 31.22 | 27.63 | 25.36 | 23.82 | 22.75 |
| 3 | 49.42 | 36.77 | 30.64 | 27.11 | 24.88 | 23.37 | 22.32 |
| 4 | 48.61 | 36.12 | 30.09 | 26.62 | 24.42 | 22.94 | 21.90 |
| 5 | 47.86 | 35.52 | 29.57 | 26.15 | 23.98 | 22.52 | 21.50 |

10% PURCHASE OPTION

| No. of Security Deposits | 2 Yrs. | 3 Yrs. | 4 Yrs. | 5 Yrs. | 6 Yrs. | 7 Yrs. | 8 Yrs. |
|---|---|---|---|---|---|---|---|
| 0 | 49.10 | 37.10 | 31.27 | 27.92 | 25.79 | 24.36 | 23.35 |
| 1 | 48.14 | 36.37 | 30.66 | 27.36 | 25.28 | 23.87 | 22.89 |
| 2 | 47.26 | 35.68 | 30.07 | 26.84 | 24.79 | 23.41 | 22.44 |
| 3 | 46.44 | 35.03 | 29.51 | 26.33 | 24.32 | 22.96 | 22.01 |
| 4 | 45.68 | 34.42 | 28.98 | 25.85 | 23.87 | 22.54 | 21.60 |
| 5 | 44.97 | 33.84 | 28.48 | 25.39 | 23.44 | 22.13 | 21.21 |

## 26.00 % ACTUARIAL YIELD

0% PURCHASE OPTION

| No. of Security Deposits | TERM OF LEASE 2 Yrs. | 3 Yrs. | 4 Yrs. | 5 Yrs. | 6 Yrs. | 7 Yrs. | 8 Yrs. |
|---|---|---|---|---|---|---|---|
| 0 | 52.70 | 39.42 | 32.99 | 29.30 | 26.96 | 25.40 | 24.31 |
| 1 | 51.64 | 38.61 | 32.31 | 28.69 | 26.41 | 24.87 | 23.81 |
| 2 | 50.66 | 37.86 | 31.67 | 28.12 | 25.88 | 24.37 | 23.33 |
| 3 | 49.74 | 37.14 | 31.06 | 27.57 | 25.37 | 23.89 | 22.86 |
| 4 | 48.89 | 36.47 | 30.48 | 27.05 | 24.88 | 23.43 | 22.42 |
| 5 | 48.11 | 35.84 | 29.93 | 26.55 | 24.42 | 22.99 | 22.00 |

10% PURCHASE OPTION

| No. of Security Deposits | 2 Yrs. | 3 Yrs. | 4 Yrs. | 5 Yrs. | 6 Yrs. | 7 Yrs. | 8 Yrs. |
|---|---|---|---|---|---|---|---|
| 0 | 49.58 | 37.61 | 31.82 | 28.50 | 26.39 | 24.99 | 24.00 |
| 1 | 48.58 | 36.85 | 31.17 | 27.91 | 25.82 | 24.47 | 23.51 |
| 2 | 47.66 | 36.12 | 30.55 | 27.35 | 25.33 | 23.97 | 23.03 |
| 3 | 46.80 | 35.44 | 29.96 | 26.82 | 24.83 | 23.50 | 22.58 |
| 4 | 46.00 | 34.80 | 29.41 | 26.31 | 24.36 | 23.05 | 22.14 |
| 5 | 45.26 | 34.20 | 28.87 | 25.83 | 23.90 | 22.62 | 21.72 |

FIGURE 3-4 (continued)

## 27.00 % ACTUARIAL YIELD

0% PURCHASE OPTION

| No. of Security Deposits | TERM OF LEASE 2 Yrs. | 3 Yrs. | 4 Yrs. | 5 Yrs. | 6 Yrs. | 7 Yrs. | 8 Yrs. |
|---|---|---|---|---|---|---|---|
| 0 | 53.15 | 39.91 | 33.52 | 29.86 | 27.55 | 26.01 | 24.95 |
| 1 | 52.04 | 39.07 | 32.80 | 29.22 | 26.96 | 25.46 | 24.41 |
| 2 | 51.02 | 38.27 | 32.13 | 28.61 | 26.40 | 24.92 | 23.90 |
| 3 | 50.06 | 37.52 | 31.49 | 28.04 | 25.86 | 24.42 | 23.41 |
| 4 | 49.18 | 36.82 | 30.88 | 27.49 | 25.35 | 23.93 | 22.95 |
| 5 | 48.36 | 36.16 | 30.32 | 26.96 | 24.86 | 23.47 | 22.50 |
| 10% PURCHASE OPTION | | | | | | | |
| 0 | 50.07 | 38.13 | 32.38 | 29.08 | 27.00 | 25.62 | 24.66 |
| 1 | 49.02 | 37.33 | 31.69 | 28.46 | 26.42 | 25.07 | 24.13 |
| 2 | 48.05 | 36.57 | 31.03 | 27.87 | 25.87 | 24.54 | 23.62 |
| 3 | 47.15 | 35.86 | 30.42 | 27.30 | 25.35 | 24.04 | 23.14 |
| 4 | 46.32 | 35.18 | 29.83 | 26.77 | 24.85 | 23.57 | 22.68 |
| 5 | 45.55 | 34.55 | 29.27 | 26.26 | 24.37 | 23.11 | 22.23 |

## 28.00 % ACTUARIAL YIELD

0% PURCHASE OPTION

| No. of Security Deposits | TERM OF LEASE 2 Yrs. | 3 Yrs. | 4 Yrs. | 5 Yrs. | 6 Yrs. | 7 Yrs. | 8 Yrs. |
|---|---|---|---|---|---|---|---|
| 0 | 53.51 | 40.40 | 35.05 | 30.42 | 28.14 | 26.64 | 25.59 |
| 1 | 52.85 | 39.52 | 33.30 | 29.75 | 27.52 | 26.04 | 25.03 |
| 2 | 51.38 | 38.69 | 32.59 | 29.11 | 26.93 | 25.48 | 24.48 |
| 3 | 50.38 | 37.90 | 31.91 | 28.50 | 26.36 | 24.94 | 23.96 |
| 4 | 49.46 | 37.17 | 31.28 | 27.92 | 25.82 | 24.43 | 23.47 |
| 5 | 48.61 | 36.48 | 30.67 | 27.37 | 25.31 | 23.94 | 23.00 |
| 10% PURCHASE OPTION | | | | | | | |
| 0 | 50.55 | 38.66 | 32.93 | 29.66 | 27.62 | 26.26 | 25.32 |
| 1 | 49.46 | 37.81 | 32.21 | 29.01 | 27.00 | 25.67 | 24.75 |
| 2 | 48.45 | 37.02 | 31.52 | 28.38 | 26.42 | 25.12 | 24.22 |
| 3 | 47.51 | 36.27 | 30.87 | 27.79 | 25.87 | 24.59 | 23.71 |
| 4 | 46.64 | 35.56 | 30.25 | 27.23 | 25.34 | 24.08 | 23.22 |
| 5 | 45.84 | 34.90 | 29.67 | 26.69 | 24.83 | 23.60 | 22.75 |

FIGURE 3-4 (continued)

## 29.00 % ACTUARIAL YIELD

0% PURCHASE OPTION

TERM OF LEASE

| No. of Security Deposits | 2 Yrs. | 3 Yrs. | 4 Yrs. | 5 Yrs. | 6 Yrs. | 7 Yrs. | 8 Yrs. |
|---|---|---|---|---|---|---|---|
| 0 | 54.06 | 40.90 | 34.58 | 30.99 | 28.74 | 27.26 | 26.25 |
| 1 | 52.85 | 39.97 | 33.79 | 30.28 | 28.08 | 26.63 | 25.64 |
| 2 | 51.74 | 39.10 | 33.05 | 29.60 | 27.46 | 26.04 | 25.07 |
| 3 | 50.70 | 38.29 | 32.34 | 28.97 | 26.86 | 25.47 | 24.52 |
| 4 | 49.74 | 37.52 | 31.68 | 28.36 | 26.29 | 24.93 | 24.00 |
| 5 | 48.86 | 36.80 | 31.04 | 27.78 | 25.75 | 24.41 | 23.50 |

10% PURCHASE OPTION

| No. of Security Deposits | 2 Yrs. | 3 Yrs. | 4 Yrs. | 5 Yrs. | 6 Yrs. | 7 Yrs. | 8 Yrs. |
|---|---|---|---|---|---|---|---|
| 0 | 51.04 | 39.18 | 33.49 | 30.25 | 28.23 | 26.90 | 25.98 |
| 1 | 49.09 | 38.30 | 32.73 | 29.56 | 27.59 | 26.28 | 25.39 |
| 2 | 48.85 | 37.46 | 32.01 | 28.90 | 26.97 | 25.69 | 24.82 |
| 3 | 47.87 | 36.68 | 31.32 | 28.28 | 26.38 | 25.13 | 24.27 |
| 4 | 46.96 | 35.95 | 30.68 | 27.69 | 25.83 | 24.60 | 23.76 |
| 5 | 46.13 | 35.25 | 30.07 | 27.13 | 25.30 | 24.09 | 23.26 |

## 30.00 % ACTUARIAL YIELD

0% PURCHASE OPTION

TERM OF LEASE

| No. of Security Deposits | 2 Yrs. | 3 Yrs. | 4 Yrs. | 5 Yrs. | 6 Yrs. | 7 Yrs. | 8 Yrs. |
|---|---|---|---|---|---|---|---|
| 0 | 54.52 | 41.40 | 35.12 | 31.56 | 29.35 | 27.89 | 26.90 |
| 1 | 53.26 | 40.43 | 34.29 | 30.81 | 28.65 | 27.23 | 26.26 |
| 2 | 52.10 | 39.52 | 33.51 | 30.10 | 27.99 | 26.60 | 25.65 |
| 3 | 51.02 | 38.67 | 32.77 | 29.44 | 27.36 | 26.00 | 25.08 |
| 4 | 50.03 | 37.87 | 32.08 | 28.80 | 26.77 | 25.43 | 24.52 |
| 5 | 49.10 | 37.12 | 31.42 | 28.20 | 26.20 | 24.89 | 24.00 |

10% PURCHASE OPTION

| No. of Security Deposits | 2 Yrs. | 3 Yrs. | 4 Yrs. | 5 Yrs. | 6 Yrs. | 7 Yrs. | 8 Yrs. |
|---|---|---|---|---|---|---|---|
| 0 | 51.53 | 39.71 | 34.05 | 30.85 | 28.85 | 27.55 | 26.65 |
| 1 | 50.34 | 38.78 | 33.25 | 30.12 | 28.17 | 26.89 | 26.02 |
| 2 | 49.24 | 37.91 | 32.50 | 29.43 | 27.52 | 26.27 | 25.42 |
| 3 | 48.23 | 37.10 | 31.78 | 28.77 | 26.91 | 25.68 | 24.84 |
| 4 | 47.29 | 36.33 | 31.11 | 28.15 | 26.32 | 25.12 | 24.30 |
| 5 | 46.42 | 35.61 | 30.47 | 27.55 | 25.76 | 24.58 | 23.78 |

FIGURE 3-5

# HOW TO CALCULATE SKIP PAYMENTS

EXPLANATION AND INSTRUCTIONS TO COMPLETE "SKIP PAYMENT CALCULATOR" - PART 1:

To "set-up" your calculations . . . enter the information about the loan transaction in the spaces provided on the SKIP PAYMENT CALCULATOR - PART 1. (We have inserted sample numbers to illustrate a typical transaction).

Amount of loan to be financed . . . "CASH BALANCE" . . . . . . . .$________
(This is the cash loan advance or cash balance, after down-pymt)

Date Contract will be signed . . . . . . . . . . . . . . . . . . . . . ________

Month first payment is scheduled for payment . . . . . . . . . . ________
(Enter your own estimated date if actual not known)

Which months are to be SKIPPED? Spell these out, by month's NAME. If different months, in succeeding years, enter month's names for EACH year there will be skips. Otherwise, enter (for instance), JAN., FEB., MAR., or whatever consistent months are skipped each year.

Enter the TOTAL CONTRACT TERM, (including skip months) . . . . . ________

Enter the TOTAL NUMBER OF PAYMENTS, (excluding skip months) . . ________

STEPS TO LAYOUT THE SKIP PAYMENTS - (Enter on SKIP PAYMENT CALCULATOR - PART 1)

Step No. 1: Enter the calendar year at the top of each YEAR COLUMN.

Step No. 2: Enter "D.S." next to the proper month, the "Date Signed" . . . or, when you PLAN TO SIGN. If the lender funds the loan or contract at that time, your 1st payment will usually "come-due" in 30 to 45 days. It is possible, of course, that the first month(s), after funding, SKIP MONTHS ARE SCHEDULED.

Step No. 3: Enter a - - (dash), next to the name of each month you PLAN to SKIP.

Step No. 4: Enter, in consecutive order, the numbers 1, 2, 3, 4, etc., for each open month of the contract term, counting each month as ONE . . . BUT BE SURE TO COUNT EACH SKIP MONTH AS "ONE", as you enter the addition numbers. That means, if the first month to be paid turns-out to be a SKIP MONTH, it is counted as ONE, etc. (Refer to our example).

Step No. 5: Add together the SUM of each year's columns, and enter in the "SUM-OF-THE-SERIES" Total. (Also, this answer is to be carried to Step No. 1, Part 2).

Step No. 6: COUNT the actual number of installments where a payment will be made, and ENTER in Step No. 2, Part 2. This is a simple addition count of each month where NO CASH appears).

FIGURE 3-5 (continued)

## SKIP PAYMENTS CALCULATOR -- PART 1

PURPOSE OF THESE CALCULATIONS: ____________________
(Enter here loan details or item(s) to be financed)

DATE CONTRACT TO BE SIGNED: __________ DOWN PAYMENT PLANNED $ __________

UNPAID CASH BALANCE $ __________ DATE OF 1st PAYMENT __________

NUMBER OF INSTALMENTS TO BE PAID ______ NAMES OF SKIP MONTHS __________

________________________________________

________________________________________

| YEAR | YEAR | YEAR | YEAR | YEAR | YEAR | YEAR | YEAR |
|---|---|---|---|---|---|---|---|
| ____ | ____ | ____ | ____ | ____ | ____ | ____ | ____ |
| JAN ____ | JAN ____ | JAN ____ | JAN ____ | JAN ____ | JAN ____ | JAN ____ | JAN ____ |
| FEB ____ | FEB ____ | FEB ____ | FEB ____ | FEB ____ | FEB ____ | FEB ____ | FEB ____ |
| MAR ____ | MAR ____ | MAR ____ | MAR ____ | MAR ____ | MAR ____ | MAR ____ | MAR ____ |
| APR ____ | APR ____ | APR ____ | APR ____ | APR ____ | APR ____ | APR ____ | APR ____ |
| MAY ____ | MAY ____ | MAY ____ | MAY ____ | MAY ____ | MAY ____ | MAY ____ | MAY ____ |
| JUN ____ | JUN ____ | JUN ____ | JUN ____ | JUN ____ | JUN ____ | JUN ____ | JUN ____ |
| JUL ____ | JUL ____ | JUL ____ | JUL ____ | JUL ____ | JUL ____ | JUL ____ | JUL ____ |
| AUG ____ | AUG ____ | AUG ____ | AUG ____ | AUG ____ | AUG ____ | AUG ____ | AUG ____ |
| SEP ____ | SEP ____ | SEP ____ | SEP ____ | SEP ____ | SEP ____ | SEP ____ | SEP ____ |
| OCT ____ | OCT ____ | OCT ____ | OCT ____ | OCT ____ | OCT ____ | OCT ____ | OCT ____ |
| NOV ____ | NOV ____ | NOV ____ | NOV ____ | NOV ____ | NOV ____ | NOV ____ | NOV ____ |
| DEC ____ | DEC ____ | DEC ____ | DEC ____ | DEC ____ | DEC ____ | DEC ____ | DEC ____ |
| TOTALS ==== | ==== | ==== | ==== | ==== | ==== | ==== | ==== |

Add together the amounts appearing in each of the TOTAL COLUMNS . . . the answer is the "SUM-OF-THE-SERIES" . . . ENTER TOTAL here and in Part 2, Step No. 1 . . . . . . . . . . . . . . . . . . . . . __________

Make an ACTUAL COUNT of INSTALMENTS to be PAID. Count each month as "ONE" to arrive at your answer - - DO NOT COUNT SKIP MONTHS. Enter TOTAL COUNT HERE and in Part 2, Step No. 2 . . . . . . . . . . __________

FIGURE 3-5 (continued)

## SKIP PAYMENT CALCULATOR -- PART 2

EXPLANATION AND TYPICAL TRANSACTION: (You MUST complete Part 1, to start these final calculations).

Step No. 1: Enter here the TOTAL of "SUM-OF-THE-SERIES" from Part 1 ________

Step No. 2: Enter here the ACTUAL NUMBER OF INSTALMENTS TO BE PAID, ________

Step No. 3: DIVIDE "Sum-of-the-series" BY "Number of Instalments to be Paid" . . . ENTER answer here . . . this provides the "AVERAGE MATURITY" . . . . . . . . . . . . . . . . ________

Step No. 4: Multiply "Average Maturity" by two (2), and SUBTRACT ONE (1), to get "RUNNING MONTHS", ENTER answer here . . ________

Step No. 5: Round-off "Running Months" to the NEAREST WHOLE NUMBER ________

Step No. 6: Multiply "Running Months" by "MONTHLY CHARGE", which is the ANNUAL "ADD-ON RATE", divided by Twelve (12), to obtain the "CHARGE PERCENTAGE". . . . . . . . . . . . . . ________

(NOTE: To HANDLE this calculation, we have included an explanation of Step No. 6, on the NEXT PAGE).

Step No. 7: Multiply "Cash Balance", (from top of Part 1 format), $ __________, by "Charge Percentage", from Step No. 6, to obtain "CHARGE AMOUNT" . . ENTER answer here . . . . $________

Step No. 8: ADD "Cash Balance" and "Charge Amount", to arrive at the "UNPAID TIME BALANCE" . . . . . . . . . . . . . . . . $________

Step No. 9: DIVIDE "Unpaid Time Balance", by "Number of Instalments to be Paid", (from Step No. 2, above), to obtain "AMOUNT OF EACH INSTALMENT" . . . . . . . . . . . . . . . $________

## EXPLANATION of STEP NO. 6:

The "Monthly Charge" refers to an Annual Add-on rate, divided by 12. Therefore, the formula is <u>not directly related</u> to a simple interest rate, such as 1½%, per month, or 18% simple-interest.

To "work" this Skip Payment Plan, it will be necessary for you to INSERT a <u>REALISTIC ANNUAL ADD-ON RATE</u>, which you DIVIDE by 12. We have included RATE CHARTS with which you can convert "ADD-ON" to "SIMPLE INTEREST".

We have structured our example to an ANNUAL ADD-ON RATE of 8.86% . . . the EQUIVALENT of 16% simple interest . . . BECAUSE WHEN <u>YOUR BEST DEAL</u> went into print, the PRIME-RATE was over 13%! When YOU use this example . . . TO COMPUTE YOUR OWN COMPETITIVE PAYMENTS . . . the "going" Add-On Rate" and equivalent simple interest rate will NO DOUBT be DIFFERENT. The formula is <u>perpetually useful</u> ONLY if you "plug-in" the CURRENT, COMPETITIVE ADD-ON RATE!

You can DO THIS in a variety of ways . . . even if you are only doing preliminary planning . . . TO GET A CLOSE IDEA of your payments . . . or, as a <u>CHECK</u>, to make sure the lender is not CONNING-YOU. HOW DO YOU KNOW <u>HOW MUCH</u> SIMPLE INTEREST YOU ARE PAYING, if you don't WORK-OUT a SKIP PAYMENT PLAN FOR YOURSELF?

You can "plug-in" ANY Add-On Rate . . . such as the MAXIMUM you consider FAIR TO PAY <u>at that time</u>. But, for it to make sense . . . you should obtain a CONTEMPORARY "GOING-RATE". Obtain it from the lender(s) with whom you plan to "SHOP". Take it from the existing Prime Rate, add 1 to 3%, or whatever is MARKET or "ideal" for you at that time. Look the desired simple-interest rate up in our RATE CHARTS; to convert to an ADD-ON RATE.

THIS IS HOW TO USE OUR SKIP PAYMENT CALCULATIONS <u>MOST EFFECTIVELY</u> . . . <u>NOW</u> . . . or <u>FIVE YEARS</u> from NOW!

FIGURE 3-6

# HOW TO CALCULATE SKIP PAYMENTS

EXPLANATION AND INSTRUCTIONS TO COMPLETE "SKIP PAYMENT CALCULATOR" - PART 1:

To "set-up" your calculations . . . enter the information about the loan transaction in the spaces provided on the SKIP PAYMENT CALCULATOR - PART 1. (We have inserted sample numbers to illustrate a typical transaction).

Amount of loan to be financed . . . "CASH BALANCE" . . . . . . .$ *154,575.00*
(This is the cash loan advance or cash balance, after down-pymt)

Date Contract will be signed . . . . . . . . . . . . . . . . . . *10-1-79*

Month first payment is scheduled for payment . . . . . . . . . . *11-15-79*
(Enter your own estimated date if actual not known)

Which months are to be SKIPPED? Spell these out, by month's NAME. If different months, in succeeding years, enter month's names for EACH year there will be skips. Otherwise, enter (for instance), JAN., FEB., MAR., or whatever consistent months are skipped each year.

Enter the TOTAL CONTRACT TERM, (including skip months) . . . . . *60*

Enter the TOTAL NUMBER OF PAYMENTS, (excluding skip months) . . *40*

STEPS TO LAYOUT THE SKIP PAYMENTS - (Enter on SKIP PAYMENT CALCULATOR - PART 1)

Step No. 1: Enter the calendar year at the top of each YEAR COLUMN.

Step No. 2: Enter "D.S." next to the proper month, the "Date Signed" . . . or, when you PLAN TO SIGN. If the lender funds the loan or contract at that time, your 1st payment will usually "come-due" in 30 to 45 days. It is possible, of course, that the first month(s), after funding, SKIP MONTHS ARE SCHEDULED.

Step No. 3: Enter a - - (dash), next to the name of each month you PLAN to SKIP.

Step No. 4: Enter, in consecutive order, the numbers 1, 2, 3, 4, etc., for each open month of the contract term, counting each month as ONE . . . BUT BE SURE TO COUNT EACH SKIP MONTH AS "ONE", as you enter the addition numbers. That means, if the first month to be paid turns-out to be a SKIP MONTH, it is counted as ONE, etc. (Refer to our example).

Step No. 5: Add together the SUM of each year's columns, and enter in the "SUM-OF-THE-SERIES" Total. (Also, this answer is to be carried to Step No. 1, Part 2).

Step No. 6: COUNT the actual number of installments where a payment will be made, and ENTER in Step No. 2, Part 2. This is a simple addition count of each month where NO CASH appears).

FIGURE 3-6 (continued)

## SKIP PAYMENT CALCULATOR -- PART 1

PURPOSE OF THESE CALCULATIONS: *Purchase of Cat Dozer $183,075.00*
(Enter here loan details or item(s) to be financed)

DATE CONTRACT TO BE SIGNED: *10-1-79* DOWN PAYMENT PLANNED $ *28,500.00*

UNPAID CASH BALANCE $ *154,575.00* DATE OF 1st PAYMENT *11-15-79*

NUMBER OF INSTALMENTS TO BE PAID *40* NAMES OF SKIP MONTHS

*DEC. JAN. FEB. MAR (same mos. each year)*

| | YEAR | YEAR | YEAR | YEAR | YEAR | YEAR | YEAR | YEAR |
|---|---|---|---|---|---|---|---|---|
| | 1979 | 1980 | 1981 | 1982 | 1983 | 1984 | | |
| JAN | | — | — | — | — | — | | |
| FEB | | — | — | — | — | — | | |
| MAR | | — | — | — | — | — | | |
| APR | | 6 | 18 | 30 | 42 | 54 | | |
| MAY | | 7 | 19 | 31 | 43 | 55 | | |
| JUN | | 8 | 20 | 32 | 44 | 56 | | |
| JUL | | 9 | 21 | 33 | 45 | 57 | | |
| AUG | | 10 | 22 | 34 | 46 | 58 | | |
| SEP | | 11 | 23 | 35 | 47 | 59 | | |
| OCT | D.S. | 12 | 24 | 36 | 48 | 60 | | |
| NOV | 1 | 13 | 25 | 37 | 49 | | | |
| DEC | — | — | — | — | — | | | |
| TOTALS | 1 | 76 | 172 | 268 | 364 | 399 | | |

Add together the amounts appearing in each of the TOTAL COLUMNS . . . the answer is the "SUM-OF-THE-SERIES" . . . ENTER TOTAL here and in Part 2, Step No. 1 . . . . . . . . . . . . . . . . . . . . . . *1,280*

Make an ACTUAL COUNT of INSTALMENTS to be PAID. Count each month as "ONE" to arrive at your answer - - DO NOT COUNT SKIP MONTHS. Enter TOTAL COUNT HERE and in Part 2, Step No. 2 . . . . . . . . . *40*

FIGURE 3-6 (continued)

## SKIP PAYMENT CALCULATOR -- PART 2

EXPLANATION AND TYPICAL TRANSACTION: (You MUST complete Part 1, to start these final calculations).

Step No. 1: Enter here the TOTAL of "SUM-OF-THE-SERIES" from Part 1 1,280

Step No. 2: Enter here the ACTUAL NUMBER OF INSTALMENTS TO BE PAID, 40

Step No. 3: DIVIDE "Sum-of-the-series" BY "Number of Instalments to be Paid" . . . ENTER answer here . . . this provides the "AVERAGE MATURITY" . . . . . . . . . . . . . . . . 32

Step No. 4: Multiply "Average Maturity" by two (2), and SUBTRACT ONE (1), to get "RUNNING MONTHS", ENTER answer here . . 63

Step No. 5: Round-off "Running Months" to the NEAREST WHOLE NUMBER 63

Step No. 6: Multiply "Running Months" by "MONTHLY CHARGE", which is the ANNUAL "ADD-ON RATE", divided by Twelve (12), to obtain the "CHARGE PERCENTAGE". . . . . . . . . . . . . 48.195

(Using 15% A.P.R. on 60 mos. = 9.18 Add-on ÷ 12 = 0.765 X 63 = ↗)

(NOTE: To HANDLE this calculation, we have included an explanation of Step No. 6, on the NEXT PAGE).

Step No. 7: Multiply "Cash Balance", (from top of Part 1 format), $154,575.00, by "Charge Percentage", from Step No. 6, to obtain "CHARGE AMOUNT" . . ENTER answer here . . . . $74,497.42

Step No. 8: ADD "Cash Balance" and "Charge Amount", to arrive at the "UNPAID TIME BALANCE" . . . . . . . . . . . . . . . . . . $229,072.42

Step No. 9: DIVIDE "Unpaid Time Balance", by "Number of Instalments to be Paid", (from Step No. 2, above), to obtain "AMOUNT OF EACH INSTALMENT" . . . . . . . . . . . . . . . . $5,726.81

# 4

# HOW TO NEGOTIATE YOUR BEST DEAL

You are about to buy equipment for your business or need to borrow for working capital purposes. You need money for expansion or remodeling or have specialized money needs, such as accounts receivable financing. What will you do? Do you go to your bank, perhaps with hat in hand, to see what they will offer? Will your bank automatically offer you your best deal, just because it is a bank? Not necessarily!

Choosing between your bank and an outside source is not as simple as it may appear. In negotiating your best deal, the first decision you must make is what is your best source of funds. Your decision should take into consideration several factors which may not be immediately apparent. First, think about each of these open questions:

- What are the funds to be used for?
- Will my bank understand the intended use of those funds?
- Do I need a source with specialized expertise in a particular type of financing?
- Is it likely that a bank will offer terms and conditions that fit into my business plan, budget, or cash flow projections?

## CONSIDERING YOUR BANK YOUR BEST SOURCE

Many companies have learned, to their ultimate sorrow, that it can be a mistake to use their bank for equipment financing. This includes strong, creditworthy companies who readily qualify for bank financing. It can be a costly, troublesome mistake to rely upon your bank, or banks in general, for your every money need. Let's go through the basic considerations, the questions you should ask, and the answers you should get to make your decision.

Let's assume you are well qualified and in excellent standing with your bank. It has always provided you with whatever funds you have needed. Why go elsewhere? This time you need more equipment. You approach your banker for money. Will he fund your purchase? You are in good standing—of course he will! Depending on the credit limit they have already set up for you, based almost entirely on your financial statements, banks generally offer two means of repayment:

1. They will simply loan you the money on a promissory note, requiring payment in full, plus interest, in 30 to 90 days. The note might be renewable, requiring predetermined principal reductions or simply interest-only payments. Little or no consideration is given to the value of the capital goods purchased or their potential to increase profits. The entire unpaid balance financed is generally charged against your credit or borrowing limit. In their minds, they have loaned you "unsecured" money.
2. The second means of repayment might be on an installment-loan basis, giving you months or years to repay. Even though they take the equipment as security, the entire financed balance is usually charged against your financial statement's borrowing strength. The determination as to borrowing strength—your credit limit—is made by a bank credit analyst who may know nothing about your type of business. Very often, the determination is made solely by set formulas and bank policy criteria that permit little deviation despite business type differences.

## Ask These Questions Before You Act

*Can you "roll" that note?*

- If you borrow on a promissory note and cannot pay the bank's required principal and interest when due, will they permit you to renew or "roll" all or part of it? Are you sure?
- Are there even more restrictions they can impose, if you do request renewal?
- If you do not pay the bank within the year, will they require you to do a year-end "clean-up" and be debt-free with them for a prescribed period? This requirement might force you to search out alternate financing, perhaps under adverse circumstances.

*Rates: Watch out for variations!*

- What is the true interest rate—the annual percentage rate (A.P.R.)—they offer you?
- Do you understand that a discount rate is different from simple interest? For instance, on a 36-month contract, a 9.73% discount rate equals a 24% annual actuarial rate!
- Do you know the true effective yield if you are required to maintain a compensating balance? (See our Compensating Balance Chart, Fig. 4-3, at the end of this chapter. From it, you

can readily determine how much additional interest you are paying under varying circumstances.)

*Squeezed by inadequate terms?*

- If they offer an installment loan, is the term of sufficient length to enable you to handle payments comfortably out of normal cash flow? Can you handle still another payment if you finance additional equipment on short terms?
- Are you aware that banks customarily do not offer the length of term that commercial finance or leasing companies routinely offer?

*What's left of your credit line?*

- Having funded your equipment purchase with your bank, how much borrowing capacity do you have left? Many times, business people are unaware that the bank has already determined their limit; it is never discussed. It can be a real shock, even a setback, to learn that a previous purchase of "hard" collateral has used up your credit. Increasing your limit can range from being a nuisance to being downright impossible, especially if the need is sudden and there is little time for bank deliberation. Banks are also restricted by banking regulations in the amount they can lend to any one customer. Their credit decisions are continually subject to review by outside examiners for improprieties, inordinate risk taking, and credit extensions inconsistent with your financial statement ratios and net worth.
- Will you have other short-term borrowing needs in the foreseeable future that might exceed your credit limit?
- If you later require funds for operating expenses, to purchase land or buildings, or to modernize present facilities, will the equipment loans jeopardize new borrowings?

## Watch for Restrictive Covenants

Most bank loan documents will contain restrictions that come into play if your financial condition deteriorates. Others place restraints on dividends, bonuses, salary increases, and others disbursements your company might provide during the time of the loan term. These kinds of restrictions are generally referred to as "restrictive covenants." Some are simply restrictive loan conditions on your company's activities.

The bank may require interim financial statements or at least summary-type financial data. This may be required as often as every month. They always require detailed year-end financial statements, and it is not unusual for them to request quarterly and semiannual statements.

Some banks decide upon the frequency of statement review on the basis of how secure they feel. They consider the extent of risk taken in relation to your financial stability. Others may be influenced by the volatility or rapidity of change likely to occur in your type of business. Quite often, bank policy dictates that every borrower provide statements on a given frequency and spell this out in their standard documents.

Whatever influences the bank's feelings, whatever the frequency of reporting required, the banks use your financial statements to "control the account." They may require you to maintain a certain debt-to-worth ratio or a prescribed "current ratio" of current assets versus current liabilities.

Whatever measurements or standards they may devise or impose, they are all designed to help them decide whether or not they are satisfied with your financial condition. If they are not satisfied and feel insecure, they may make certain additional requirements of you or impose more restraints. By examining your statements, they also look for violations of the restrictive covenants.

If your future statements do not measure up to the agreed criteria—if you have made forbidden expenditures, for example—the bank may "call the loan." Sometimes, because of your violations or their dissatisfaction, they will require you to "make other arrangements"—find a new bank or other lender.

Ask these questions about restrictions the banks may impose:

- Must you subordinate accrued bonuses or refrain from repaying yourself or other officers or owners for loans made to the company?
- Can you be required to refrain from paying dividends? Are dividend payments tightly controlled, subject to the bank's approval?
- Can you merge, consolidate, or change company structure without the bank's permission?
- Must you obtain the bank's consent to lease or borrow from any other source?
- Does the bank insist on being able to enter your business premises to conduct an audit or examine your records? Under what circumstances may examiners enter? What are the conditions of entry as to time and written notice?

It is important for you to look for clauses on these subjects. They are generally discussed in advance by bankers or other lenders. However, they may be swiftly brushed over and dismissed as "just standard loan conditions." On occasion, no mention is made by the lender. If you sign without reading and objecting, the restrictions are there to live with throughout the term of the loan.

Recognize these restrictive clauses and limiting conditions for what they are: in exchange for the loan or special financing, the lender is reserving the right to intrude upon your business. Such intrusion and restraints may be entirely justified. In some cases, the lender's controls and subsequent financial reviews may even prove beneficial. Bankers are capable of good financial counseling; as they review your statements, they may see problems that you are too close to detect.

Lenders are generally entitled to their restrictions. Without them, you may not obtain the loan. But bear in mind, restrictions may be negotiated. If you, or the company you represent, are financially strong enough to be approved for credit, do you really have to stand still for every restriction they choose to invoke?

If the lender is out of line, fight back against restrictions you may feel are unwarranted. Make the lender explain why he needs the protection of extensive controls. Too many business people "take the money and run." Lenders come to expect everything their way. "We did you a favor to lend you our money!" Not necessarily; it should be a fair, two-way street.

You owe it to yourself and your business to eliminate every restrictive covenant you can. Consider negotiating time limits, subject to removal under certain improved financial conditions. Don't let the lenders dismiss restrictions on your business as "just standard." Remember, you have to live with those restrictions for the life of the loan.

Restrictive covenants or other restraints are a valid reason to consider source in negotiating your best deal. Maybe another bank or an outside finance company with fewer restrictions will be a better source.

### The "Routine" Personal Guaranty

Does your bank require your personal guaranty, tying up your personal property and real estate? Every time you go in to sign loan documents, does this personal guaranty form just routinely appear for your signature?

- Read the fine print carefully. What are the lender's remedies—what can he do to you personally—if your company defaults on the loan? Is he able to take measures that may be prohibited by consumer protection laws?
- Does the fine print give the bank a too liberal, easy lien on your real property?
- Be aware that banks may routinely request your personal guaranty and ask your spouse to sign as well. Does the loan extended really justify this request? Does the guaranty also extend to your spouse's separate property?
- They may hold your "continuing guaranty" after the intended need for it has expired, perhaps interfering with plans you enter into months or years later.
- Be aware that finance companies, relying more on collateral values, may dispense with personal guaranties.

Your personal guaranty may be essential to the bank's making the money available to your small corporation. Offering your guaranty may not be a big concern to you and may be fully understandable, especially if it is your personal assets that make loans possible. Don't sign a personal guaranty without reading it, especially if the lender has filled in blanks concerning the continuing nature of the guaranty. Also, if you are not familiar with the lender, read every word. Some of their terms may be negotiable.

Think about these things:

1. Just how long must your corporation be established, how strong must it be, to stand on its own with your bank?
2. Will standing as guarantor, ad infinitum, restrict your flexibility in entering other business ventures?
3. If you are not 100% owner of the stock or are a limited partner, can you negotiate a limited guaranty?
4. Is the bank reaching too far, with all-inclusive claims on all your assets? Don't always treat a personal guarantee as "strictly routine."

**THE UCC FORM CAN GET IN YOUR POCKET!**

We have provided sample Uniform Commercial Code forms required by lenders to familiarize you with their appearance and why they are necessary. (See Figs. 4-1 and 4-2.) You should be aware that many banks utilize these forms with broad language to maximize their security interests. Think about these things before you sign.

- If you borrow from your bank, do any of their documents affect your flexibility? Look particularly at the innocent-appearing UCC-1 Financing Statement.
- Are you aware that many banks will take a security interest in your accounts receivable or inventories, despite the fact you were not borrowing against them?
- Or that they will take, or attempt to take, a security interest in your existing capital equipment—or even in equipment you may acquire later? Look for this clause: ". . . all equipment, now owned or hereafter acquired."
- If you sign this UCC-1, with "all-inclusive" or "after-acquired" property clauses, you have given the bank a lien, a security interest, in whatever assets they have listed on the form!
- Do you know that the bank files this UCC-1 with your secretary of state, putting everyone on notice they have established lien rights in your assets? (In some states, the place of filing differs, but the results are the same.)
- Some banks (and other lenders) have gone to the extent of pre-printing or typing this "all-inclusive" or "after-acquired" language on all their UCC forms. Pay particular attention to the "Description" section of this form. They may have inserted these clauses in type or print, so they are less noticeable.

**The UCC Form Can Send Messages**

The UCC form is another document that banks and other lenders often dismiss as "strictly routine." Usually, it is pretty much of a simple requirement, to which they are entitled in order to establish their security interest or interests. You should be aware of the possible consequences of this document. It is a very strong, important link in establishing lender claims on your assets. Think about these "messages" the UCC form carries:

- The UCC-1 can severely restrict your future financing flexibility; it can "tie you in knots."
- If you decide to finance equipment by borrowing from any other bank or finance company, the new lender will search the UCC filings for prior UCC financing statements. Finding your bank's filing with "all-inclusive" or "after-acquired" clauses, they will contact your bank and request them to release or subordinate their filings.
- This filing, then, is a trigger which alerts your bank to any outside moves you may attempt to make.
- Your bank may refuse to release or subordinate, forcing you to borrow from them, perhaps on less favorable terms, or they may stop you entirely!
- They may agree to the release, but then change your credit limits or impose other disagreeable restrictions.

Figures 4-1 and 4-2 show examples of UCC-1 forms used in different states. We have provided examples of the "all-inclusive" or "after-acquired" language typically inserted by the lenders. Believe it, they will insert this language without your prior knowledge and consent. Don't let them minimize how serious this filing can be to your future financing decisions. It may provide the lender with more security than the amount loaned or risk warrants.

## Words of Caution

Do not assume it is never logical or correct for lenders to expect to insert special terminology on their UCC forms. In order for them to lend in a situation of some risk, they may need the added security of your inventories, accounts receivable, or other equipment.

The point is, if they feel the need for added security, they should tell you about it before putting documents in front of you for signature. We want you to know what to look for. Notice how the assets being taken as security are neatly woven into the other words in our example description sections.

You should have the chance to discuss any security lenders may feel obliged to list on this UCC form. If they are lending money on the assets listed, that's their right. If they arbitrarily list additional assets, never discussed with you, they have taken away your right to negotiate terms and conditions. They should not be able to slip it into the fine print.

If lenders tell you in advance that they plan to take additional assets to secure the loan, insist they explain why they need more security. Have them explain exactly which of your assets they plan to list on the UCC. Do not surrender too easily to their requests. Think of the possible future consequences of having your receivables, inventory, or equipment tied up by one loan. After considering their requests, decide if they are reasonable and if the loan is worth the security taken. If you don't object, how can you get lenders to back off or respect you as a negotiator? If you feel their requests for additional security are unwarranted, shop around. After all, the lender did approve your loan request; perhaps another lender will not be so demanding.

If you learn the lender has inserted objectionable security interest items when you are ready to sign, it may be too late to shop around. If you are financially strong and creditworthy, it is never too late to raise objections. Quite possibly you can force the lender to cross out all or part of the unwarranted security items listed. If you feel your bank is too harsh or tried to slip it into the fine print, you should really consider changing banks.

We repeat these words of caution about the UCC form: (1) Ask for completed documents, with all the blanks typed in, for your preliminary review a day or two before loan closing. (2) If this is impractical or you don't feel the matter is that critical, at least read the description section of every UCC-1 presented before you sign it. A UCC form similar to our examples will accompany virtually every set of loan, lease, or contract documents. It is part of the Uniform Commercial Code adopted by each of the states.

## COMMERCIAL FINANCE COMPANIES: AN ALTERNATE SOURCE?

There is more than one reason why there are so many equipment finance and lease companies competing for your equipment borrowings. Foremost, of course, is that the profits to be earned are generally excellent. Also, commercial financing offers a marvelous opportunity for them to leverage on their borrowing strength. Investment in plant and equipment is minimal. The bigger they are, the less they pay for "other people's money."

Many of the financing organizations are subsidiaries of very large parent companies. General Electric Credit Company and ITT Industrial Credit Company are two familiar examples. Although the financing subsidiaries are able to loan the parent's surplus cash profitably, they are much more likely to utilize their great financial strength. The subsidiaries can borrow at the lowest possible money cost in the commercial paper market. Some of these subsidiaries have become so large and successful they do not need parent backup.

The finance and lease companies proliferate because they are filling a large gap left by the banks. At far less risk than they would have you know, these secured collateral lenders meet definite commercial and industrial money needs. What's important for business people to realize is that finance companies are often capable of doing more for them than banks. It can be worthwhile to pay their somewhat higher rates to maintain bank credit lines or to achieve flexibility in terms and conditions. You should be aware, also, that more and more frequently, finance company rates are the same as or less than the banks' rates.

### Banks Don't Understand Equipment

Banks often lack expertise in collaterally oriented lending. They frequently are uninformed about the intrinsic values of machine tools, heavy construction equipment, specially outfitted truck-tractors, and other profit-making types of equipment. They do not know resale values, how to remarket equipment if returned through default, or how to appraise equipment in order to make adequate loan advances. This is not a blanket indictment of all banks, because there are some who are informed, some who are trying, but many are still woefully weak in this area of lending. Traditionally, banks are not interested in becoming heavily involved in equipment lending based on collateral values. They are generally not known as "secured lenders," they are "balance sheet and income statement" lenders.

Banks are heavily regulated. They are audited by state and federal bank examiners. They are restricted by their capitalization or asset base as to lending limits to any one customer. Some of the limitations placed on banks are imposed by state or federal agencies. The criteria for these limitations are derived from predetermined minimum balance sheet ratios each customer must maintain. Banks must operate within guidelines or regulations of the Federal Reserve Board, their state banking commission, and the Federal Deposit Insurance Corporation. They are lending their depositors' money, which must be controlled.

### Finance Companies Have Fewer Restrictions

The finance companies operate with very few governmental restrictions, federal or state. They are usually working with stockholders' capital, stock or bond issues, or money borrowed in the commercial paper market. Bear in mind that we are not talking about consumer finance companies. They are more heavily regulated by truth-in-lending and consumer protection laws. We are talking only about commercial and industrial finance and leasing companies that make loans to or finance equipment for businesses.

### Finance Companies Understand Equipment

Over the years, some finance companies have built up expertise in certain specialized fields. Almost all finance companies understand equipment better than banks. They are obliged to; they are the secured lenders of the finance world. Many finance companies provide their services in several fields but have personnel with specialized knowledge in construction equipment, machine tools, medical or dental equipment, trucks and trailers, aircraft, marine equipment, store fixtures, or restaurants.

Sometimes this expertise and the finance companies' flexibility can be worked to your benefit. You can take best advantage of this alternative money source by knowing who they are, how they operate, and how to deal with them.

## NEGOTIATING YOUR BEST DEAL WITH A FINANCE COMPANY

If you have been unable to negotiate satisfactorily with your bank or cannot qualify for bank lending, you should consider the finance company as an alternative source. This decision need not be onerous or considered the last resort. There are circumstances in which the finance company makes better money acquisition sense than your bank—even when you are fully qualified to borrow money from the latter.

Have you ever dealt with a finance company? You have a very wide selection to consider in deciding upon your best choice. Even in the remotest parts of the United States, the major national finance companies have local representatives within driving distance or a short airline trip. If they are not in your local Yellow Pages, try the nearest larger city under the headings "Financing," "Loans," or "Leasing." The commercial-industrial finance companies usually list themselves under "Financing," leaving "Loans" to the consumer loan companies. Major finance companies that offer leasing services will also appear under that heading, along with bank-related leasing companies and those that specialize in that type of financing. Negotiating with a leasing company is very much like negotiating with a commercial finance company. Many so-called lease agreements are nothing more than conditional sale contracts—and the leasing companies are secured collateral lenders, just like their sister finance companies. We will differentiate between financing and leasing in chapter seven, "The Inside Scoop on Leasing." The differences in negotiating with these two types of financers is mainly a matter of semantics. Leasing also has more complicated tax implications and tricky structuring of repayment terms.

### Your Present Finance Company: Always Friend, Never Foe?

If you are presently dealing with a finance company and are reasonably satisfied with it, by all means start your negotiations with that company. Or bring the company back in when you are ready for a final decision. If your pay record has been good, chances are you can negotiate an acceptable deal with your present company. It may not be your best deal, however, because things change, sometimes from month to month.

- Finance companies' money costs may be higher than their competition.

- Their changing policies or personnel may have forestalled the flexibility your additional financing requires.
- They may have reached their loan quota for that month.
- They may have loaned all they can to your company, under their credit-extension guidelines.
- They may have enough of your type of equipment in their portfolio (computers, store fixtures, etc.).

### It Pays to Shop

There is no way to be sure you have negotiated your best deal if you always deal with the same bank or finance company. There comes a time when it is prudent to check your lender out against the competition.

Bear in mind that negotiating with two or three additional sources can also put you in contact with a lender who is more flexible, more receptive to your future growth plans. Their rates may be virtually identical, but the availability of money, structured the best way for you, is important.

Make no mistake about how worthwhile negotiating and comparing can be. Do not lull yourself into the belief that "there can't be that much difference between finance companies." There can be significant differences—from company to company, from original quotation to final quotation! These differences can be negotiated right into your bank account, if you know how and try.

Don't tell yourself, "What the hell, it's all tax-deductible anyway." True, finance or interest costs are an expense. So is your telephone bill—don't you try holding that down? You turn out the lights when not needed, don't you? Telephone and electric bill savings can be important pennies; interest costs reduced can be big dollars!

Every day, thousands of business people unknowingly give the banks or finance companies part of their profits by paying excessive interest rates. Or, failing to protect themselves, they have ended up shortchanged by improper refunds when they paid their contract or loan off early.

There is no way to determine how many business owners have found themselves locked into poorly negotiated leases, loans, or contracts. There is no way to calculate how many poorly negotiated loan agreements have seriously damaged mergers, buy-outs, buy-ins, new capital acquisition, or, in extreme cases, the very survival of what was once a viable business. Remember, the deal that looks OK as you sign it today may look terrible to others considering buying your business a year hence.

### Watchwords: Prepare—Don't Hurry!

Let's assume you have considered your bank financing offer and have decided it might be worthwhile to check outside finance sources. Putting first things first, start out by being properly prepared to enter negotiations.

- Do everything you can to avoid being hurried into a decision.
- Start shopping for your best deal as far in advance as possible.
- Don't wait until you desperately need funds before you borrow. Last-minute urgency can make borrowing more expensive and your best deal less likely.
- Don't wait until the last minute to acquire needed equipment and then insist upon "delivery yesterday" and "instant financing."
- Failure to preplan is an open invitation to be "had"—sometimes by both the equipment seller and the financing source.
- Hurry up deals nearly always weaken your control of the buying or financing situation. You lose leverage.

## Your Seller Can Help You

If you are lightly capitalized, have a short business experience track record, or have suffered reverses in prior years, you especially need to avail yourself of all possible assistance. You must exert all possible pressures to get the deal you need and are entitled to have. Along the way, you must do your part by being properly prepared. The seller of the equipment can be your best ally. After working out a satisfactory purchase, what routes are available to you for suitable financing?

Ask your seller if he has had good experiences with one or more finance companies. Get the names of those companies and, if possible, the names of the finance company representatives who service your seller.

If your credit is weak because you are new in business or you are recovering from business reverses, you will be well advised to sell yourself to your seller. Utilize advice given in chapters two and five of this book.

The seller, usually anxious to make a sale, can sometimes be persuaded to become your partner in the financial risk. He can obtain financing and back you in the transaction with the finance company, using his endorsement. This is called "recoursing," and usually takes one of two forms:

- "Full recourse," running for the term of the contract
- "Limited recourse," under which the seller endorses the contract for a predetermined number of contract months or years until your payments have established a safe equity position

In some cases, the lender will be satisfied with the seller's agreement to remarket the equipment, working out a contract settlement from the sale proceeds. In the case of recourse, the seller is assuring the finance company that if you fail to meet the payment obligations, he will pay the finance company off.

If you fail to prepare and are unable to convince the seller you are a reasonable risk, he may decide his potential profit does not warrant lending his endorsement to the financing. On the other hand, unless you are exceptionally weak and plain grateful to have any financing, do not relax and assume you have your best deal, because the seller helped you out!

### Rate Participation: Polite Words for Kickbacks?

Some sellers have "rate participation" plans worked out with the finance companies. These plans may come into play only when the seller has endorsed your contract. For instance, you may have a higher finance rate forced on you, part of which is kicked back to the seller. Perhaps it can be argued that a seller who acts as your guarantor is entitled to participate in the finance charges. However, the profit your seller earns on the equipment sale should be sufficient reward under most circumstances.

By adhering to a plan of unhurried negotiations, you can minimize the risk of "being had" by an unscrupulous seller or finance company, just because you are in a somewhat weak credit position. If the seller strongly recommends only one finance company, it is possible he has a kickback plan with them.

Sometimes the seller wants his recourse endorsement kept secret. He does not want you to know that if you fail to pay, he must buy your defaulted contract back from the finance company. If you are aware that the seller will endorse your contract and you don't like the implication of being directed to one finance company, ask him if he would mind if you called another finance company. If the seller quickly objects, it's probable he has a kickback worked out with his recommended financer.

If he doesn't object, or even volunteers additional finance sources, use the advice outlined under "Be Prepared Before You Negotiate" in this chapter. Of course, some sellers do so much volume, and their recourse endorsement is so dependable, that they may have several finance companies kicking back on the rates. This is all the more reason for you to negotiate carefully.

### Some Pointers on Negotiating

ETHICAL SELLERS ATTRACT GOOD FINANCING Most sellers are interested only in selling their products. Without too much involvement, which uses their sales time, they will try to assist you in obtaining financing at reasonable rates. The finance company, happy to have the seller's flow of referral business, will also cooperate.

DON'T GIVE AWAY THE STORE! Without question, being more knowledgeable in both buying and financing aspects, you will be much more likely to get the seller's respect and cooperation. Still, do not let your guard down and sign contracts blindly. No matter how grateful you may feel for the seller's assistance, do not unnecessarily give anything away with contract terms that can work against you.

DON'T GIVE AWAY YOUR RIGHTS Once the seller has endorsed your contract—or indicated he is willing to do so—the finance company will not want to lose you. It also will not want to anger the seller. Now you can hang tough instead of wilting in gratitude. Negotiate for the best possible rate, length of term, and contractual conditions you can obtain. We are not talking about being ridiculous. If a seller's endorsement has "put you in business," there are ethical limits involved. That doesn't mean you should be careless or needlessly acquiescent.

DON'T GET OUT OF THE DRIVER'S SEAT! In almost every case, your best deal is made when you are in the driver's seat and not dependent on any seller's endorsement. When you are in the control position, you will present yourself and your company in the best possible light. Put this advice into action:

- Arbitrate each of the key elements of the finance or loan contract: the finance or interest rate, the length of term, and the contract conditions.
- Examine and intelligently select the best of two or more finance company proposals.
- Negotiate your best deal on documents worded fairly to you. It must not be a one-way street for the lender.
- Ask in advance for copies of lender documents, preferably completely filled out, so that you can examine them without someone pressuring you to sign them. If you are satisfied just to check the blank documents, make sure the completed documents are the same, not altered. Make sure the blanks that were filled in match the promises you were made by the financer.

## Be Prepared Before You Negotiate

In the real estate business, they say only three things really count in buying or selling buildings or land: location, location, and location! In the finance world, for the buyer, borrower, or lessee, it should be: preparedness, preparedness, and preparedness!

BE PREPARED TO BUY RIGHT Making your best equipment purchase can involve more than collecting quotations. Thousands of major purchases are made each year that are poorly thought out and inadequately researched. Purchases must be realistic to the intended use of the equipment and your company's financial capabilities.

- Get a detailed, written sales quotation. It will prove useful in obtaining satisfactory financing. It will eliminate misunderstandings by the finance company.
- Make sure the equipment description and every seller promise is reduced to writing.
- Make sure the equipment and every component, attachment, or accessory is fully listed and described.

- Nail down delivery dates, freight costs, sales taxes, and any labor or installation costs.
- When you get down to requesting financing, present the finance or lease company with a clear-cut purchase agreement.
- Avoid misunderstandings about whether the lender or lessor has agreed to finance the sales taxes and installation or freight charges.
- If the equipment is specialized or custom-built, prepare a brief explanation of it for the lender, in layman's language. Most lenders do not understand technical terminology.
- If the equipment has a high cost (especially in relation to your net worth), provide the lender with forecasted earnings from the use of this equipment. Justify your decision for selection of such expensive equipment.

BE PREPARED TO PRESENT YOUR FINANCIAL DATA Have your credit references ready and your financial statements well prepared, with good, legible copies on hand. They are essential negotiating tools, and a weak or nonexistent presentation will put you in a lower priority position with any lender.

In times of tight money, when there is a credit crunch, being poorly prepared can eliminate you from consideration. But even when money is plentiful, busy account representatives and their credit managers, will give priority to the most clearly presented financing requests or proposals. They will do so even though the applicant is not extremely strong in net worth or profits earned.

BE PREPARED TO TALK TERMS Decide in advance how you want the finance contract structured as to repayment terms.

- Establish as clearly as you are able the most ideal terms of repayment that are commensurate with your business plans and cash flow.
- If your business has known slow months, work out the relief you may require to maintain prompt payments over this slow period. This relief could consist of interest-only or token payments.
- If you know the equipment being purchased will at first be slow in paying for itself and you do not have adequate funds to support prompt payments, ask for lower payments during the start-up period.
- Do not hesitate to ask for any payment plan that makes good business sense to your circumstances. Finance companies are concerned with being repaid. They do not want collection problems. They will try to work out payments geared to your ability to pay promptly.

Realize that special terms can be more costly due to finance charge adjustments necessary to compensate the lender for those months skipped or repaid at reduced amounts. Don't pay too much for special terms.

When the calculations get complicated, some finance companies will slip in additional finance charges which are more than necessary to cover interest costs for uneven or skipped payments. They do this secure in the knowledge that few business people are capable of checking their arithmetic. You can quickly determine the lender's true simple interest charges by using our skip-payment charts and formulas (Figs. 3-5 and 3-6).

BE PREPARED TO TAKE ALL THE RIGHT STEPS Setting up properly for negotiations as we recommend can make you a month's pay in a few minutes. It is extremely important to prepare for your meetings with the lenders' representatives to the greatest degree possible. You want to be able to concentrate your attention on the actual negotiations, not be diverted by frantic searches for financial statements, credit references, telephone numbers, account numbers, and other mundane details. Avoid chaos and save your time for the meat of the meeting. Don't be running around making photocopies when you should be calmly sitting there looking the lender representative square in the eye!

Review chapter three if you are a bit hazy on rate calculations or terminology. The objective is to gain the lender's respect by exhibiting some financial savvy. Dazzle the representative with your financial footwork. Be ahead of him on the basics of finance mathematics and buzzwords.

Get your presentation ready before the meeting starts. Review chapter two and get the recommended data together commensurate with the size, importance, and complexity of your requirements.

If your financial requirements involve leasing or accounts receivable financing, review our chapters covering these specialized areas. Spend a few minutes on those sections most applicable to your financing proposal or needs. Do whatever is necessary to prepare for negotiating meetings so that you can control what happens. *You* conduct the meetings, not the lender's contact person.

Once you've laid this groundwork—and not before—you're ready to take these steps:

- Call finance company A, the one you have preselected to negotiate with first. (It could just as well be leasing company R or bank Z, if you are having them come to you.)
- Set up an appointment in your office at a time convenient to you. Select a time when you are least likely to be disturbed. Shut off all interruptions and devote total attention to your presentation and to absorbing what the lender representative has to say and offer.
- Have all of your financial data and credit references ready. Be

sure your presentation of data is adequate to the financing being requested.

- Make sure the lender representative gets a complete understanding of what you want to do, how you plan to do it, and why you are borrowing.
- Get him or her to understand what your company does. In some cases a tour of your plant, yard, or other facilities will help. Provide anything you have in the way of brochures or other printed matter that helps to increase prestige, give historical background, or serve as a reminder of what your company is all about.
- Familiarize the representative with the equipment being purchased or the equipment you already own and plan to borrow against. Show and tell as much as possible. Get the rep on your side through each step of your meeting.
- Voluntarily give the representative all available, pertinent information. Do this for your own good. Don't force the rep to drag information out of you. It is more businesslike and more expeditious simply to hand over prepared written information.
- Request that the lender representative reciprocate by providing you with a written financing proposal.

Although the representative's verbal or written proposal is not binding until his or her management approves your credit, you need this quotation to work out your best deal. All outside finance contact people are informed concerning their company's street rate. They will usually quote this going rate to everyone they meet with and feel are reasonably qualified.

This street or going rate is the finance rate or interest rate most readily quoted out on the street, when lender people meet with borrowers in field situations. This rate may also be synonymous with the finance company's standard rate.

Some finance companies establish standard rates applicable to every "usual" finance proposal they normally consider for financing. Sometimes there are standard rates for certain types of equipment, size of the transaction, or type of transaction (such as time-sale contract or loan), and all will be affected by length of term.

They provide these rates to their customer-contact people, and according to the parameters noted above, this is the *only* rate they quote to businesses called upon. This will be particularly true of fixed-rate financing, utilizing an add-on rate factor as discussed in chapter three.

It may be less true if you are quoted a floating rate tied to the prevailing prime rate. Recently, more finance companies have been quoting a floating rate in addition to, or in place of, fixed-rate financing. There has been a tendency for some of the finance companies to ask for, say, 3 to 5 points over prime. If the borrower balks, they are inclined to decrease the spread. A great deal depends upon the desirability of the customer, his creditworthiness, the collateral, and the size of the financing. Of course, in many instances, the number of points over prime rate is just as rigidly standardized as the add-on rate.

The first rate you are quoted, fixed or floating, may be the only rate you ever hear from the lender's representative. It may be exactly, or extremely close to, the rate other lenders quote in subsequent meetings you may schedule. In all candor, each of the rates quoted may also be the final rate, no matter how much negotiating you attempt.

For summary purposes, we are concentrating on negotiating your best interest rate. The basic purpose of your negotiating meetings is to seek credit approval for some form of borrowing. The negotiating procedure fundamentally seeks to obtain approval as expeditiously as possible. Suitable terms and conditions, in their endless variations, are sought as an integral part of your negotiating sessions.

Let's return to your meeting situation with the first lender representative. At this point in time, you do not know if the rate quoted is the final rate from that person's company. Finding out should not take an inordinate amount of your time if you are prepared with a presentation as we suggest. Potential savings on interest costs may be significant or of minor importance. That's your judgment call to make, as you proceed. Just bear in mind that interest savings is not the only factor involved in making your best deal. As you negotiate, you may find that repayment terms and loan conditions may differ, in your favor, and these may outweigh fractional rate differences.

The purpose of your meetings with the lender representatives is to establish favorable communications, first with the contact person and, even more important, with the representative's decision makers.

There is considerable variance in the amount of authority held by the contact person. Some are almost on the level of a messenger. They quote as instructed, and they carry your data and proposal back to their lender. Generally, all contact people are really in the sales marketing end of the lender's operation. Occasionally, your contact will carry credit limits and have rate determination authority.

In most cases, the lender representative has some latitude in quoting rate and terms. Unfortunately, the latitude may be restricted to up-side rate quotes—they have authority or even incentive to offer a higher rate which they may or may not choose later to reduce. It is not uncommon for outside contact people to be uncertain how low their management will go under given favorable circumstances.

Let's summarize by going down the middle of the road. The lender's representative is your link to his or her credit management. Much depends upon how competently this representative carries your message to the credit decision makers. They look to their contact person's recommended interest charge or finance rate for guidance, and it may be the final, conclusive rate they consider along with making their credit determination.

They generally expect a comprehensive summary presentation from their outside contact people. Your safest, wisest course, therefore, is to work carefully and thoroughly with the contact person. In case that person is not experienced or highly motivated, it's up to you to control the situation, always providing a strong presentation and complete financial information. This is your best assurance of reaching your financing objective.

### Negotiating Tips to Remember

- You need the rate quotes, standard or not, for comparison, for future negotiations, and to confirm your planning.
- You can draw closer conclusions as to interest expense, maximum length of terms, and monthly payments and determine if it is worthwhile to proceed with or delay the financing.
- Be aware that the lender contact may be on some type of bonus or commission plan. The commission may be tied directly to the rate charged.
- This tends to be more true of leasing representatives. Many, but not all, finance company representatives are on incentive plans. However, higher rate quotes may not directly affect their bonus earnings.
- Bank loan officers are not directly motivated by special compensation to charge higher rates. Bank subsidiary people, either in their leasing or equipment financing organizations, may be on an incentive program influenced by rates charged.
- Considering the possibilities of being quoted an "up-side" rate—or a "loaded" rate to increase the contact person's earnings—it is essential that you test how firm they stand on their quotes.
- If you can combine pressing hard with an adequate presentation that increases your desirability and apparent ease of credit approval, chances are improved for your best deal.

### Call In the Lucky Company!

After going through two or more negotiating sessions, after allowing sufficient time for "best rate" quotations to have been completed and firmed up to you, you're about ready to make your best deal.

The best situation for you is to obtain written proposals of the rate and terms, firm monthly payments, and credit approval. Request confirmation of how long the rate, terms, and credit approval will stand. If you are not to receive your money for some time, obtain an expression of how the rate might be adjusted if the lender cannot fix it for such an extended period.

If a written approval is not feasible or obtainable, or if the transaction will be concluded swiftly, you can usually trust a verbal commitment. Almost all recognized finance companies will stand true to their managers' commitments.

It's time to call in the lucky company! Naturally, you will select the lowest rate quoted, offering the best terms. If the overall quotations come in virtually identical, think about which company or representative gave you feelings of confidence and rapport.

It's time for another judgment call. Are you satisfied that the quotation selected is your very best deal? All things considered, you may decide to simply ask for completion of documentation.

However, business people, remember that a penny shaved is a penny earned! If you are able to negotiate only fractional decreases in add-on rates or a lease-rate factor, the pennies can rapidly translate into significant dollars. We have endeavored to make this evident in our "Savings at a Glance" charts appearing at the end of chapter one.

The potential savings should also have been evident from our preceding chapter covering finance rates. We are not advocating that everyone become chiselers or nit-pickers. We just feel you should fully appreciate how quickly those pennies add up from the innocent appearing rate factors being quoted.

What steps do you take if you decide to shave the rate? The ideal position to be in is to have, in your hands, three written quotations, including credit approval. Having these in hand, with plenty of time before your actual money need must be filled, you can play some games with those willing lenders.

Call the finance company offering the lowest quotation or the one you prefer to work with. Tell them you would like to meet to discuss the transaction further. We suggest you refrain from rate-shaving efforts on the telephone. When the representative comes out, say that "in checking around," you have found *x* rate and terms readily available to you; however, because you have developed a rapport with them and want them to have your business, if they can match *x* rate, you are ready to sign.

Be sure your bluff is not unrealistic or the representative will know you are fishing. Select a slightly lower rate that will produce a worthwhile savings. Another method is to tell the representative you have been quoted a certain monthly payment—again, not ridiculously lower than that company's quoted payment. Suggest that because you favor them, you want them to have the opportunity of doing the financing. It is usually to your advantage to be complimentary rather than belligerent or threatening. Explain your reasons for wanting to go with them: "You seemed the most knowledgeable about your business"; "Your interest seemed so sincere"; "You reacted so quickly"; and other similar ploys.

The complimentary system motivates them to be more receptive and makes it easier for them to try to go at a lower rate. If you irk them, they may stubbornly stand firm. If they simply cannot go lower, you can comfortably stay with them and they will not necessarily be very upset. I don't think it ever hurts to test and try, especially if worthwhile savings can be achieved.

Sometimes it helps to request that the representative bring along his or her manager, "to get acquainted." On a sizable transaction, in which they may be eager for the loan, lease, or contract volume, the manager could have some latitude to close the deal. Don't be bashful—work on his or her authoritarian ego. If you know your financial standing is very good and credit approval is not even a question, there are occasions when a forceful telephone call to the sales manager will produce favorable results. Again, use compliments and perhaps suggest you just want to be sure their contact person fairly presented your proposal to management. Calling the credit manager about the rate, terms, or conditions is generally not a good approach.

Very often, because of credit bureau feedback or the interchange between finance companies, the company you decide to arbitrate with will be well aware you have negotiated with their competition. They usually will not know if those companies approved your credit or on what rate and terms. If your credit and financial strength are obviously quite strong, your negotiating pressures, coupled with their belief you were indeed approved, will often produce the best rates they can offer.

Don't be too easy-going or too quick to accept a proposed rate as the final rate. The savings in interest expense can add profits to your bottom line. If you are consistently adding equipment on time contracts, the accumulated savings can be very significant. Even slightly reduced monthly payments will also relieve your aggreate debt-service load.

**LOYALTY IS ADMIRABLE, BUT NOTHING IS FOREVER!**

An admonition: Once you have found the best company and have obliged them to provide you with your best deal, do not relax your vigilance! When you go back to that company for more financing, perhaps with every second or third transaction, check it out against its competition. Don't get complacent or let the lender take you for granted.

Watch the prime rate in the financial section of your newspaper or the *Wall Street Journal*. Remember, the finance company you dealt with in bygone years may have the same name, but the people who manage it change, and so do their company policies. Just when you relax, they will change the ball game—and you may once again leave unnecessary dollars on the bargaining table.

FIGURE 4-1

# LONG FORM "UCC-1" FINANCING STATEMENT

STATE OF NEVADA
UNIFORM COMMERCIAL CODE—FINANCING STATEMENT—FORM UCC-1
IMPORTANT—Read instructions on back before filling out form

This FINANCING STATEMENT is presented for filing pursuant to the Nevada Uniform Commercial Code

1. DEBTOR (LAST NAME FIRST): Rongo Manufacturing Company, Inc.
1A. SOCIAL SECURITY OR FEDERAL TAX NO.: 99-97119711
1B. MAILING ADDRESS: 1212 Encumbered Loop, Unit Q
1C. CITY, STATE: Podunk, Any State
1D. ZIP CODE: 00069
1E. RESIDENCE ADDRESS (IF AN INDIVIDUAL AND DIFFERENT THAN 1B)
1F. CITY, STATE
1G. ZIP CODE

2. ADDITIONAL DEBTOR (IF ANY) (LAST NAME FIRST): Fragmeyer, Ferguson F.
2A. SOCIAL SECURITY OR FEDERAL TAX NO.: 999-711-9711
2B. MAILING ADDRESS: 1212 Encumbered Loop, Unit Q (Rear Apt.)
2C. CITY, STATE: Podunk, Any State
2D. ZIP CODE: 00069
2E. RESIDENCE ADDRESS (IF AN INDIVIDUAL AND DIFFERENT THAN 2B)
2F. CITY, STATE
2G. ZIP CODE

3. DEBTOR(S) TRADE NAME OR STYLE (IF ANY)
3A. FEDERAL TAX NO.

4. ADDRESS OF DEBTOR(S) CHIEF PLACE OF BUSINESS (IF ANY)
4A. CITY, STATE
4B. ZIP CODE

5. SECURED PARTY
NAME: Weebytem Finance Company
MAILING ADDRESS: 711 Kitchen Sink Road, Suites 12-18 and Penthouse 69
CITY: Podunk STATE: Any State ZIP CODE: 00079
5A. SOCIAL SECURITY NO., FEDERAL TAX NO. OR BANK TRANSIT AND A.B.A. NO.: 79-69696969

6. ASSIGNEE OF SECURED PARTY (IF ANY)
NAME
MAILING ADDRESS
CITY STATE ZIP CODE
6A. SOCIAL SECURITY NO., FEDERAL TAX NO. OR BANK TRANSIT AND A.B.A. NO.

7. This FINANCING STATEMENT covers the following types or items of property (if crops or timber, include description of real property on which growing or to be grown and name of record owner of such real estate, if fixtures, include description of real property to which affixed or to be affixed and name of record owner of such real estate; if oil, gas or minerals, include description of real property from which to be extracted. (1) All Accounts, Contract Rights, Chattel Paper, and other rights, to payment of money of Debtor, now existing or hereafter acquired, and all Proceeds thereof, and all Goods repossessed or returned in connection therewith. (2) All Inventory Goods, consisting of but not limited to sheet metal, rods, bars, plates, castings, coated parts, assemblies or component parts thereof, or miscellaneous materials, which as raw materials, work in process, finished products, and materials, are used or consumed in Debtor's business, or are to be or have been furnished under contracts of service, and all goods whenever acquired as Inventory goods by way of replacement, substitution, addition or otherwise, and all additions or accessions thereto.

7A. Maximum amount of indebtedness to be secured at any one time (OPTIONAL) $ 696,969.00

8. Check [X] if Applicable
A [X] Proceeds of collateral are also covered
B [X] Products of collateral are also covered
C [ ] Proceeds of above described original collateral in which a security interest was perfected
D [ ] Collateral was brought into this State subject to security interest in another jurisdiction

THIS SPACE FOR USE OF FILING OFFICER

9.
(Date) December 31, 1985

RONGO MANUFACTURING COMPANY, INC.

By: ____________ President
SIGNATURE(S) OF DEBTOR(S) (TITLE)

WEEBYTEM FINANCE COMPANY

By: ____________ Vice-President A/R Department
SIGNATURE(S) OF SECURED PARTY(IES) (TITLE)

10. This Space for Use of Filing Officer (Date, Time, File Number and Filing Officer)

11. Return Copy to
NAME / ADDRESS / CITY, STATE AND ZIP:
Weebytem Finance Company
Attention: Mr. Vise Grips
711 Kitchen Sink Road, Penthouse 69
Podunk, Any State 00079

(3) FILING OFFICER COPY—ALPHABETICAL

UNIFORM COMMERCIAL CODE—FORM UCC-1 (REV. 2-68) Approved by the Secretary of State STANDARD FORM—FILING FEE $2.00

FIGURE 4-2

# SHORT FORM "UCC-1" FINANCING STATEMENTS

**STATE OF IDAHO**
**UNIFORM COMMERCIAL CODE—FINANCING STATEMENT—FORM UCC-1**

INSTRUCTIONS:

1. PLEASE TYPE THIS FORM IN BLACK, FOLD ONLY ON PERFORATION FOR MAILING.
2. Remove secured party and debtor copies and send the other three pages with interleaved carbon paper intact to the filing officer.
3. Enclose filing fee of $1.00. When this form shows an assignment, enclose fee of $2.00.
4. If the space provided for any item(s) on the form is inadequate, the item(s) should be continued on additional sheets preferably 8"x 5". Only one copy of such additional sheets need be presented to the filing officer with a set of three copies of the financing statement. Indicate the number of sheets attached in the space provided.
5. Reasonable identity and description of personal property used as collateral in the space provided below.
6. When a copy of the security agreement is used as a financing statement, it is requested that it be accompanied by a completed, but unsigned, set of these forms. There is no extra fee when security agreement is used, but the security agreement must be signed by both the debtor and the secured party.
7. At the time of the original filing, if the filing is on standard form UCC-1, the filing officer will automatically return the third copy as an acknowledgment. At a later time, the secured party may use the third copy as a termination statement by signing the termination legend, or he may use Form UCC-3 as a termination statement.
8. DO NOT WRITE IN BOX 4.

This FINANCING STATEMENT is presented to filing officer for filing pursuant to the Uniform Commercial Code. | No. of additional sheets presented: | 3. Maturity date (if any):

1. Debtor(s): (last name first, and mailing address(es))

Hasselfree, Harry H.
dba Hasselfree Engineering Co.
69 Last Chance Lane
Podunk, Any State 000069

2. Secured Party(ies) and address(es):

Easy Money Finance Company
1234 Gottcha Court
Suites 1011 - 1017
Podunk, Any State 000069

4. FOR FILING OFFICER ONLY (Date, time, number and filing office)

5. This Financing Statement covers the following types (or items) of property: (Use this space for Real Property legal description and name of record owner, if required.)

One (1) Widget Turning Lathe, Model W, One (1) Framis Milling Machine, Model M and One (1) Robust Forklift, Model RFL, together with all additions, attachments, accessories, modifications or improvements to any or each of them and including, but not limited to all of Debtor's equipment, furniture and fixtures, now owned or hereafter acquired.

6. Assignee(s) of Secured Party(ies) and address(es)

CHECK ☒ IF COVERED ☒ Proceeds of collateral are also covered ☒ Products of collateral are also covered

Filed with: ☒ Secretary of State ☐ County Recorder of ________ County.

☐ The collateral described herein is brought into this state already subject to a security interest in another jurisdiction.

☐ The collateral described herein is proceeds of the original collateral described above in which a security interest was perfected.

Harry H. Hasselfree dba
Hasselfree Engineering Co.

BY: ______________________, Owner
Signature(s) of Debtor(s)

Easy Money Finance Company

BY: ______________________, District Mgr.
SIGNATURE(S) OF SECURED PARTY(IES) OR ASSIGNEE OF RECORD

Idaho Form UCC-1 FORM APPROVED BY PETE T. CENARRUSA, SECRETARY OF STATE

**STATE OF OREGON**
**UNIFORM COMMERCIAL CODE—FINANCING STATEMENT—FORM UCC-1**

INSTRUCTIONS:

1. PLEASE TYPE THIS FORM.
2. Enclose fee of $2.00 for each debtor/or trade name shown.
3. This form is to be filed only with the Secretary of State.
4. Send the Alphabetical, Numerical and Acknowledgment copies with interleaved carbon paper intact to the filing officer. The Debtor(s) and Secured Party(ies) copies are retained by party making the filing.
5. If the space provided for any item(s) on the form is inadequate, the item(s) should be continued on additional sheets, size 5" x 8". Only one copy of such additional sheets need be presented to the filing officer. Long schedules of collateral, indentures, etc. may be on any size paper that is convenient for the secured party. DO NOT STAPLE OR TAPE ANYTHING TO LOWER PORTION OF THIS FORM.
6. At the time of original filing, filing officer will return acknowledgment copy to the assignee if noted on form or secured party. If secured party requires acknowledgment of long schedules of collateral, two copies should be presented and one will be returned.
7. When a copy of the security agreement is used as a financing statement, it is requested that it be accompanied by a completed UCC-21 form. Enclose $3.00 plus $2.00 per debtor more than one.
8. When filing is to be terminated the acknowledgment copy may be sent to the filing officer signed by the secured party or assignee or he may use Form UCC-3 as a Termination Statement.

This FINANCING STATEMENT is presented to filing officer pursuant to the Uniform Commercial Code.

1A. Debtor(s):

WeRgrate Trucking Corporation

1B. Mailing Address(es):

10-4 Fifth Wheel Circle
AlUpHill, Any State, 00069

2A. Secured Party(ies):

FayreForAll Truck Sales Corp.

2B. Address of Secured Party from which security information obtainable:

711 Good Buddy Drive
Aldownhill, Any State, 00033

Filing Officer Use Only

3. This financing statement covers the following types (or items) of collateral (ORS 79.4020):

Twelve (12) STURDIBILT Truck Tractors, NTC 350, w/Jake, 3 axles, 182" W.B., 11x24.5 Tires, (Ten on each unit), 220 Gal. Fuel Cap., P/S, Air Slide, 5th Wheel and Deluxe Interiors, and Twelve (12) FREROLIN 45' Dry Vans, with 11x24.5 Tires (Eight on each unit), Ludd Wheels, 22,500# GUDE Axles, STRONG suspension, Alum. X-Members, 12" O.C., Swing or Roll Doors, CRW 10,600#, each unit.

THE ABOVE LISTED EQUIPMENT IS LEASED EQUIPMENT AND THIS FILING IS FOR INFORMATIONAL PURPOSES ONLY.

4A. Assignee of Secured Party(ies) if any:

First National Bank of
Aldownhill

4B. Address of Assignee from which security information obtainable:

66 Security Blvd.
Aldownhill, Any State
00033

Check box if products of collateral are also covered ☐ No. of additional sheets attached ☐

WeRgrate Trucking Corporation

By: ______________________ Treasurer & Dispatcher
Signature(s) of Debtor(s)*
Signature(s) of Secured Party(ies) or Assignee(s)

*Signature(s) of Debtor(s) required in most cases.
Signature(s) of Secured Party(ies) in cases covered by ORS 79.4020.

FILING OFFICER—ALPHABETICAL This form of Financing Statement approved by the Secretary of State.

STANDARD FORM—UNIFORM COMMERCIAL CODE—FORM UCC-1
7/1/78

REORDER FROM
Registré, Inc.
5284 TAYLOR ST. N.E.
MPLS., MINN. 55421
(612) 571-2903

FIGURE 4-3

## COMPENSATING BALANCES and EQUIVALENT YIELDS

- **"Free" Compensating Balances -- How bankers INCREASE THEIR PROFITS . . . earning on YOUR "FREE" BALANCES!**
- **Compensating Balance Yield Chart . . . An Explanation of the Chart . . . and HOW TO USE IT.**

"FREE" COMPENSATING BALANCES:

This is HOW THE BANKS MAKE THEIR LOANS "YIELD" MORE . . . probably MORE than you THOUGHT POSSIBLE! When you *borrow* from your bank . . . they frequently require YOU to maintain a pre-determined checking account balance. This required balance, may range from 5% to as much as 50% *of the loan extension*. 10% to 20% COMPENSATING BALANCES are COMMON.

"FREE" COMPENSATING BALANCES are defined as NET commercial deposits not used to support other loans . . . AFTER DEDUCTION of "FLOAT" and balances necessary to cover account SERVICING costs.

If the bank requires a 20% COMPENSATING BALANCE, THEY HAVE IT "FREE" TO INVEST . . . BUT YOU CAN'T USE IT, SO IT COSTS YOU. This compensating balance isn't a serious (or costly) problem in small dollar loans because most businesses maintain "reasonable" checking balances anyway. But if you BORROW $100,000. and are required to MAINTAIN A 20% COMPENSATING BALANCE . . . the bank has $20,000. of YOUR MONEY TIED-UP . . . which you could have invested in SHORT-TERM LOANS . . . NOTES . . . Certificates of Deposit . . . Treasury Bills . . . or . . . simply PUT IT TO WORK IN YOUR BUSINESS TO PRODUCE INCOME. So when the bank charges you 14% simple interest . . . AND a 20% COMPENSATING BALANCE . . . the CHART BELOW SHOWS WHAT YOUR TRUE INTEREST COST BECOMES . . . BY BANK STANDARDS . . . 17½%! If you had invested these "tied-up" funds in a high-yield loan . . . these yield "EQUIVALENTS" are CONSERVATIVE . . . your 14% bank loan could be costing 20%. This is ONE REASON a commercial finance company loan . . . where COMPENSATING BALANCES are NOT POSSIBLE . . . can prove less expensive and/or confining.

| INTEREST RATE QUOTED | BANK'S TRUE YIELD WITH "FREE" COMPENSATING BALANCES OF: | | | | | | | |
|---|---|---|---|---|---|---|---|---|
| | 5% | 10% | 15% | 20% | 25% | 30% | 40% | 50% |
| 4 1/2 | 4.7 | 5.0 | 5.3 | 5.6 | 6.0 | 6.4 | 7.5 | 9.0 |
| 4 3/4 | 5.0 | 5.3 | 5.6 | 5.9 | 6.3 | 6.8 | 7.9 | 9.5 |
| 5 | 5.3 | 5.6 | 5.9 | 6.3 | 6.7 | 7.1 | 8.3 | 10.0 |
| 5 1/4 | 5.5 | 5.8 | 6.2 | 6.6 | 7.0 | 7.5 | 8.8 | 10.5 |
| 5 1/2 | 5.8 | 6.1 | 6.5 | 6.9 | 7.3 | 7.9 | 9.1 | 11.0 |
| 5 3/4 | 6.0 | 6.4 | 6.8 | 7.2 | 7.7 | 8.2 | 9.6 | 11.5 |
| 6 | 6.3 | 6.7 | 7.1 | 7.5 | 8.0 | 8.6 | 10.0 | 12.0 |
| 6 1/4 | 6.6 | 6.9 | 7.4 | 7.8 | 8.3 | 8.9 | 10.4 | 12.5 |
| 6 1/2 | 6.8 | 7.2 | 7.7 | 8.1 | 8.7 | 9.3 | 10.8 | 13.0 |
| 6 3/4 | 7.1 | 7.5 | 7.9 | 8.4 | 9.0 | 9.6 | 11.3 | 13.5 |
| 7 | 7.3 | 7.8 | 8.2 | 8.7 | 9.3 | 10.0 | 11.7 | 14.0 |
| 7 1/4 | 7.6 | 8.1 | 8.5 | 9.1 | 9.7 | 10.4 | 12.1 | 14.5 |
| 7 1/2 | 7.9 | 8.3 | 8.8 | 9.3 | 10.0 | 10.7 | 12.5 | 15.0 |
| 7 3/4 | 8.2 | 8.6 | 9.1 | 9.7 | 10.3 | 11.1 | 12.9 | 15.5 |
| 8 | 8.4 | 8.9 | 9.4 | 10.0 | 10.7 | 11.4 | 13.3 | 16.0 |
| 8 1/4 | 8.7 | 9.2 | 9.7 | 10.3 | 11.0 | 11.8 | 13.7 | 16.5 |
| 8 1/2 | 8.9 | 9.4 | 10.0 | 10.6 | 11.3 | 12.1 | 14.5 | 17.0 |
| 8 3/4 | 9.2 | 9.7 | 10.3 | 10.9 | 11.7 | 12.5 | 14.8 | 17.5 |
| 9 | 9.5 | 10.0 | 10.6 | 11.2 | 12.0 | 12.9 | 15.0 | 18.0 |
| 9 1/4 | 9.7 | 10.3 | 10.9 | 11.6 | 12.3 | 13.2 | 15.4 | 18.5 |
| 9 1/2 | 10.0 | 10.6 | 11.2 | 11.9 | 12.7 | 13.6 | 15.8 | 19.0 |
| 9 3/4 | 10.2 | 10.8 | 11.5 | 12.2 | 13.0 | 13.9 | 16.3 | 19.5 |
| 10 | 10.5 | 11.1 | 11.8 | 12.5 | 13.3 | 14.3 | 16.7 | 20.0 |
| 10 1/4 | 10.8 | 11.4 | 12.1 | 12.8 | 13.7 | 14.6 | 17.1 | 20.5 |
| 10 1/2 | 11.1 | 11.7 | 12.4 | 13.1 | 14.0 | 15.0 | 17.5 | 21.0 |
| 10 3/4 | 11.3 | 11.9 | 12.6 | 13.4 | 14.3 | 15.4 | 17.9 | 21.5 |
| 11 | 11.6 | 12.2 | 12.9 | 13.8 | 14.7 | 15.7 | 18.3 | 22.0 |
| 11 1/4 | 11.8 | 12.5 | 13.2 | 14.1 | 15.0 | 16.1 | 18.8 | 22.5 |
| 11 1/2 | 12.1 | 12.8 | 13.5 | 14.4 | 15.3 | 16.4 | 19.2 | 23.0 |
| 11 3/4 | 12.4 | 13.1 | 13.8 | 14.7 | 15.7 | 16.8 | 19.6 | 23.5 |
| 12 | 12.6 | 13.3 | 14.1 | 15.0 | 16.0 | 17.1 | 20.0 | 24.0 |
| 12 1/4 | 12.9 | 13.6 | 14.4 | 15.3 | 16.3 | 17.5 | 20.4 | 24.5 |
| 12 1/2 | 13.2 | 13.9 | 14.7 | 15.6 | 16.7 | 17.9 | 20.8 | 25.0 |
| 12 3/4 | 13.4 | 14.2 | 15.0 | 15.9 | 17.0 | 18.2 | 21.3 | 25.5 |
| 13 | 13.7 | 14.4 | 15.3 | 16.3 | 17.3 | 18.6 | 21.7 | 26.0 |
| 13 1/4 | 13.9 | 14.7 | 15.6 | 16.6 | 17.7 | 18.9 | 22.1 | 26.5 |
| 13 1/2 | 14.2 | 15.0 | 15.9 | 16.9 | 18.0 | 19.3 | 22.5 | 27.0 |
| 13 3/4 | 14.5 | 15.3 | 16.2 | 17.2 | 18.3 | 19.6 | 22.9 | 27.5 |
| 14 | 14.7 | 15.6 | 16.5 | 17.5 | 18.7 | 20.0 | 23.3 | 28.0 |
| 14 1/4 | 15.0 | 15.8 | 16.8 | 17.8 | 19.0 | 20.4 | 23.8 | 28.5 |
| 14 1/2 | 15.3 | 16.1 | 17.1 | 18.1 | 19.3 | 20.7 | 24.2 | 29.0 |
| 14 3/4 | 15.5 | 16.4 | 17.4 | 18.4 | 19.7 | 21.1 | 24.6 | 29.5 |
| 15 | 15.8 | 16.7 | 17.6 | 18.8 | 20.0 | 21.4 | 25.0 | 30.0 |

# 5

# YOUR CREDIT AND FINANCIAL STATEMENTS

Without credit your business cannot grow. Without good financial controls and well-prepared financial statements, obtaining credit can be difficult and expensive. On the surface, these may appear to be obvious observations. Why, then, do so many business people do such a terrible job of maintaining their credit performance? Why are so little effort and attention directed toward preparation and presentation of their financial statements?

Your credit performance and financial statements have become more interwoven than ever before. They represent the only available written and checkable proof of who you are, what you are doing, how you are doing, and where you are going—as an individual or a business. These performance records are the only way lenders can make a credit determination on you or your business.

To the credit managers or loan administrators—decision makers you rarely meet and who seldom see your business operation—you are just pieces of paper, with columns of numbers, ratios, and credit bureau reports! They must have something to read and analyze. Why don't you give them something well prepared, accurately stated, and neatly packaged?

Credit performance and financial statements are critical. Loan pricing, with interest rate quoted, depends on the quality of these records. "Yes" or "No" depends on their analysis. Your business future is wrapped into your credit reports and financial statements.

To get what you want, when you want it, at a reasonable cost, you must compete for the time and attention of that credit authority.

You must do it with demonstrated credit performance and pieces of paper. They see nothing else. To them, nothing else really counts!

## HOW MUCH IS THE PAYMENT?

Too many business people are in the habit of saying, "If I can afford the payment, I'm going to get me that new widget machine." That isn't financial planning, that's consumer thinking. If you can't afford the payment, of course you shouldn't buy.

Making your decision on the basis of being able to handle the payment is likely to prove costly. Deciding on that basis is often an ego response. It is more emotional than analytical. Think about the car salesman who closes the deal by challenging your financial capacity: "The payment on your Super Dooper 8 is *only* $385.00 a month. That's not too much for you, is it?" Certainly not! Following that line of reasoning, $395.00 is also not too much, nor is $399.85.

The point is that the finance and leasing companies make a great deal of extra income from business people who essentially decide on financing on the basis of "affording" the monthly payment. Somewhere down the financing trail, these unfortunates wake up to the fact they have ten or twelve monthly payments that individually are easy but in the aggregate are difficult or impossible to afford. To make matters worse, if the payments are analyzed, each of them contains a bonus few dollars for the lender.

Business people who claim they want to grow and prosper but persist in playing it by ear and making decisions day by day are living in the past. Those who continue to handle their financial affairs like they did in the good old days are apparently blissfully ignorant of pure fact: the times are not a-changing, they have changed!

## FIVE FAMILIAR MISTAKES

These business people are the old-time thinkers who persist in making one or more of the following mistakes.

- *Mistake No. 1:* They try to pull the wool over the lender's eyes, verbally or in writing, and do not realize the full impact of today's computerized credit reporting. They have not made the transition from the early days of less sophisticated, friendly lenders to the numbers-regimented present.
- *Mistake No. 2:* They present poorly prepared financial statements that are inaccurate, unsigned, and often illegibly copied. They expect them to suffice as before, not realizing how many more businesses are competing for lender money.
- *Mistake No. 3:* They fail to handle their receivables properly, use poor collection procedures, and either do not maintain an aging of their receivables or do not take full advantage of a systematic aging.

- *Mistake No. 4:* They pay their bills haphazardly, "when time permits." Or, if cash is tight, they fail to develop a comprehensive payables priority plan.
- *Mistake No. 5:* They fail to consider, or even begin to understand, the importance of knowing the lender's vantage point.

It is important to understand the far-reaching effects of making one or more of these five mistakes. On the surface, they may appear simplistic and not the kind of errors expected from owners of established businesses. Unfortunately, to some degree, these mistakes are repeated over and over by many business people, each time causing unnecessary borrowing difficulties. To appreciate the ramifications of these mistakes, we will expand upon each of them.

## Mistake No. 1: Compromising Your Credit Performance

The times have changed. Computerized, instant credit reporting is now honed razor-sharp and more detailed than ever.

There are few secrets anymore. Putting on a front is generally a waste of time. The credit bureau computer is sending lightninglike messages: Measure-up! Perform! Or pay through the nose for interest charges because you're reported as a "marginal credit risk."

As an individual, on the consumer level, you cannot make one single move, one single slip, one slow payment, without its being duly recorded on a credit bureau report.

In addition to computerized individual credit reporting, the tremendously efficient TRW Information Services has also established NACIS (National Credit Information Service), featuring computerized business credit reporting in competition with venerable Dun & Bradstreet.

"D. & B.," always stalwart business-rating reporters, have streamlined their operations. They are now more computerized, with even more current payment reporting. They report what you are doing, how you are paying your accounts. They list your UCC-1 financing statements which disclose your prior borrowings. Whether you like it or not, your business and personal financial life is undergoing daily open-heart surgery!

Most commercial lending organizations subscribe to Dun & Bradstreet's services. It is a valuable source of credit and historical data they can quickly obtain on virtually any potential borrower. Business people, especially those who haven't changed with the times, still show resistance to providing D. & B. reporters with complete and accurate information. This can be a mistake for businesses, large or small. To misinform or underinform D. & B. can work against a business. The modern way is to make sure D. & B. and all other credit agencies have adequate, accurate information about your business. There are many borrowers competing in a swiftly moving, more complex financial community than just a short decade ago. The lenders must increasingly rely on rapid credit bureau reporting to assist in their decision-making process.

LENDERS TALK TO EACH OTHER The lenders are becoming increasingly cooperative with each other and the credit bureaus. Almost unanimously, they report every delinquency, every problem, every credit inquiry. This is particularly true of the banks and major finance companies.

If one lender calls another for a direct check, the interchange information will include the average balance in your checking account, overdraft experience, loan performance, actual number of first notices (of payment due), and the number of times late charges were incurred.

Banks and finance companies, though in competition, protect each other through interchange, with detailed performance history on almost every individual or business. Loans are revealed: when, how much, terms, date last paid, performance ratings. Lenders never want to inherit another lender's collection problems. They interchange to prevent poor performers from moving from lender to lender.

EVERYONE GETS CHECKED OUT If you are a proprietorship, a partnership, a sub-Chapter S corporation, a major stockholder in a closely held corporation, a principal managing stockholder—even if holding only a small percentage of stock—expect lenders to check you out personally, just like any consumer buying a car or refrigerator on payments.

The individuals who own unlisted corporations, even those with strong net worth and $20 million annual sales, are coming under increasingly close personal investigation. Their personal financial statements are often required by lenders. As for the smaller businesses—proprietorships, partnerships, two- to ten-man corporations—it is almost a foregone conclusion that lenders will require personal financial statements, copies of income tax returns, and personal guaranties.

So much for "wool-pulling" with your credit performance. Don't bother—they've already got your number!

## Mistake No. 2: Short-Circuiting Your Financial Statement

Lenders are increasingly requiring personal guaranties. Many times they are required more for moral, "good faith" reasons than out of any desire to chase your personal assets or to depend upon your personal net worth to pay off a defaulted loan. This is not to say that many lenders do not collect from the guarantors when they grant their approval on the basis of personal net worth.

The lenders want to assure themselves that you will put forth your best efforts where their money is invested. Your personal guaranty says you believe in your business and your abilities. If you don't, why should the lender?

Here are the common mistakes and "wool-pulling" attempted by many individuals in preparing a personal financial statement:

They overstate their cash position.

*Comment*: Depending on the size of loan or financing required, lenders usually verify every checking or savings account balance.

They put big, fat round-number valuations on their home-furnishings, jewelry, stamp and coin collections, and automobiles.

*Comment*: A statement loaded with round numbers, quite apparently on the high side, suggests statement puffery and detracts from the analyst's opinion of you and your moral rectitude. The lender begins to wonder how much can he rely on your promise to pay.

They overstate the cash value of their life insurance, sometimes to the point of unbelievability.

*Comment*: On the liability side, many individuals simply omit any life insurance loans, even though life insurance is factually an excellent, inexpensive borrowing source. If you owe on your policies, insert at least a close estimate.

They invent notes receivables from individuals who, if they do owe, may never pay.

*Comment*: Don't bother inventing personal notes due you. It's OK to list legitimate notes, but the analyst ignores virtually all personal notes.

They overvalue every piece of real estate listed.

*Comment*: Real estate holdings are often an important part of your net worth. The lender is more interested in your credibility and personal acumen than in cash-out values—unless he is taking a secured interest in your real estate, in which case he obtains an appraisal. This is a place in your statement to be realistic, even conservative, to gain the analyst's respect for the statement as a whole.

They list stocks, at inflated values, that aren't even over-the-counter. They list traded stocks at incorrect prices, in round numbers.

*Comment*: Again, credibility counts. The lender couldn't care less about unlisted stocks. Listed ones, including over-the-counter stocks, if they make up a significant part of your net worth, are checked for true present market value.

They conveniently forget or minimize MasterCard, Visa, and department store balances.

*Comment*: It's foolhardy to omit these little items. They all show up on the credit reports. If of some substance, the omissions or misrepresentations hurt your credibility more than their subtraction helps your net worth.

They guess—usually on the low side—what their loan balances are.

*Comment*: It pays to be accurate with car loans, notes payable, and other extended-term debts. The analyst figures if you don't have a good grip on your personal affairs, it reflects on your business judgment. The lender gets a full report on all loans anyway—why become suspect by reason of errors and omissions?

THEY'RE LOOKING AT YOU WITH A JAUNDICED EYE What is the net result of a statement filled with inaccuracies or round numbers? The credit manager, or whoever is deciding on your credit application, immediately casts a jaundiced eye on you, your credibility, your business, and your creditworthiness.

What happens next? If your financial statement is obviously inflated, you may get turned down. If the credit analyst is busy, your loan request is sidetracked "for more investigation" and you go to the bottom of his priority list!

"Wool-pulling" on your personal financial statement is self-defeating and can backfire, having exactly the opposite effect to the one you hoped to achieve.

## Mistake No. 3: Neglecting Your Receivables

For peace of mind and perhaps sheer survival, every business person must stop thinking in the 1950s and '60s.

When in Rome, do as the Romans do. When computerized business methods surround you, if you want to borrow, buy, or lease equipment on payments, do what smart business people are doing: shape up the credit and financial end of your business!

Quit kidding yourself; quit trying to snow any bank, any lessor or finance company. Don't be satisfied with an incompetent, old-fashioned bookkeeper or antiquated financial statements. Pay more attention to your financial systems and bill-paying habits. Learn how to check your business for leaks. Try to put yourself in the lender's chair once in a while, so you can get what you want—when you need it!

CLEAN UP YOUR CREDIT ACT Most business people know it pays to pay your bills. Unfortunately, the best laid plans of mice and men forestall good intentions. Those are what the road to hell are paved with. In the world of business, you cannot pay bills with clichés or good intentions.

If your business is operating profitably and you still cannot pay according to terms, you must do something about it.

- Maybe it is something simple, like an incompetent accounts payable clerk or bookkeeper. Your paying habits have become a much larger factor in determining your borrowing costs and in getting the funds you need. You cannot afford an inefficient accounting system or incompetent help.
- If you are adequately capitalized, if you have the money and you are still not a prompt payer, it is up to you to tighten up your system. If you are missing your trade discounts—shame on you! Losing 2% on a "2%—10 days" invoice costs you 36.73% in interest. That's unnecessary cash lost, and it really adds up!
- Maybe it is not so simple. Maybe you are operating profitably but are undercapitalized. Undercapitalization, the curse of the new business, the prime cause of business failure, also plagues more established businesses.
- When your business is growing, it becomes increasingly difficult to handle growing accounts receivable, to "buy smart," to pay for work in process and carry adequate inventories.
- The best solution for a growing, profitable business that is undercapitalized is to borrow working capital. Working capital is synonymous with liquidity. It is the difference between your current assets and current liabilities. Very often, an excellent source of working capital is your accounts receivable. Don't cringe! Borrowing against your receivables can be a smart move, not one step away from bankruptcy! If the funds are negotiated and used properly, to take your discounts, buy smart, modernize, or operate efficiently, accounts receivable financing can solve your undercapitilization problems. (See chapter eight for accounts receivable financing techniques.)

BORROW WORKING CAPITAL—IT SOUNDS SO EASY! It isn't. The hardest money to come by is often adequate, reasonably priced working capital, especially on comfortable extended payback terms.

Especially for the business with nothing paid for, no "rich uncle" to turn to, just good prospects.

Without a rich uncle and realizing that Uncle Sam's Small Business Administration loans are often difficult and slow to obtain, you are left with just a few choices:

- Go see your friendly banker. (Good luck! You're credit-weak.)
- Try for outside private capital. (Watch out! They may want a piece of your business.)
- Seek out high-risk lenders (sophisticated pawn shop operators whose interest costs and fees could break you!).
- Find an accounts receivable finance company, assuming you have assignable receivables, and see what they can offer.

You don't have much of a prayer with any of the lenders if your financial statements are poorly prepared, lacking in detail, or far behind in their completion. Lenders understand that if you need money, especially for working capital, you are in some degree of difficulty. But they expect you to have at least a coherent plan to extricate yourself. They want to see that you have at least tried to cope with your payables. Your financial statements must be at least presentable for their analysis.

You can go to the lender of your choice with the greatest verbal story of coming successes, big growth plans, "if only I had more money to work with"—and you will strike out or struggle hard to find a lender. You must present a believable plan and be prepared on paper.

GETTING READY TO BORROW If your cash flow is tight—if you are doing the juggling act so many undercapitalized businesses must do, robbing Peter to pay Paul—at least develop a master plan to juggle intelligently.

Whether you are aiming for that time when you can borrow working capital to smooth things out or if you prefer to pull yourself up by the bootstraps, consider the suggestions that follow. Adapt those that fit.

- Analyze your accounts receivable. How long do your customers take to pay? Are they consistently going beyond your normal selling terms? What do the excess days cost you? Our Average Collection Period Calculator (Fig. 8-2) at the end of chapter eight gives you the answers.
- Make an aging worksheet of your receivables. Work it properly. A suggested format appears in Fig. 8-1. Adapt it to your business—perhaps providing other informational columns or headings more applicable to your needs. An aging should become a working tool.
- Put one person in charge of maintaining the aging in constant updated order. Preferably have the same person do all the collection follow-up. If this person is an employee, consider adapting a system that requires you, as owner, to take over tough collections. It is very important, for whomever is collecting, to elicit promises from your slow-paying customers and to write down the promised date of payment and dollars promised in the comments column.
- Follow-up, done the right way, is as important as eliciting promises. You must be systematic in collections. If customers break promises, they must be called promptly and reminded. You cannot be systematic if you trust your memory. Use that "Comments" column and always call them on broken promises. When you take your vacation, hand the aging worksheet to an assistant for uninterrupted follow-up. Your assistant will know right where you were if you've kept the comments updated.
- Some people hate to collect and are just not suited for collections. Others thrive on being the hard-nosed collector, but even those who enjoy it need some training and diplomacy

lessons. If at all possible, select an employee who can adapt to the horrors of collections and do it diplomatically, forcefully, and—most importantly—systematically. You know receivables are your lifeblood. Don't let lackadaisical, inefficient collection procedures put you in trouble or out of business!

- Get the most modern, most recently printed reference books on credits and collection procedures you can find.

  Good credit and collection procedures are almost a science nowadays. If your system is nonexistent or antiquated, it's time to modernize!

- Use your well-kept aging as a management tool. Naturally, some of you cannot afford the luxury of a separate collection employee. If you, as owner or manager-executive, are stuck with the task or are the most logical person to do collections, develop the skills necessary to get the job done.
- Don't attempt to carry several account stories in your head! Use the aging worksheet and write things down as they occur.
- Make command decisions on every problem account. Set deadlines and plan your ultimatums, if required. Shut off unprofitable accounts before they hurt you!
- If you have one or more employees doing the collections, designate at least two days per month for meetings. Take enough time to plan strategies. You will be surprised how much your interest inspires and helps your employees.
- If you have a number of accounts, it sometimes helps to make account cards or collection cards, rather than working from an aging list. Some companies find it helps to place all problem accounts on cards. Others use a receivables calendar which records the date each payment should arrive from each customer. The main thing is to be systematic.

ACCOUNTS RECEIVABLE AGING: A MANAGEMENT TOOL Aside from the obvious fact that it is difficult to pay your bills if your customers are slow-paying, systematic, religious attention to accounts receivable will accomplish other desirable things for you as owner or manager:

- Logging your collections on a daily-receipts basis, by account, assists in cash-flow projections. You can see patterns and paying habits more clearly.
- Pinpoint undesirable customers who should be cut off or straightened out.
- Your continuing follow-up comments provide phone numbers and names of the right person to get that check made out. They provide insight into the payment procedures of larger corporations. Sometimes you just have to learn how to cooperate with each company's internal procedures.
- A good accounts receivable aging, actively worked, is inval-

uable and is almost a mandatory requirement of lenders you ask to loan money on your receivables.

- It is very damaging to your loan request to approach a lender without an aging or to offer a poorly prepared listing that evidences poor procedures. You still must collect your accounts receivable to repay the loan, and the lender considers your abilities carefully.
- A well-maintained aging, which evidences your concerted, intelligent effort, is a very positive factor in your favor when reviewed by a credit analyst.
- Whenever your accounts receivable are an important part of your assets, a legible, current copy of your aging worksheets, belongs in every loan package presented to the lenders.
- If you plan to finance your receivables, a major reason to have and work on the aging worksheet is to get your accounts in a salable condition. You cannot sell ineligible accounts receivable. (Ineligible accounts are explained in chapter eight.)

## Mistake No. 4: Playing Games with Your Payables

Controlling your accounts receivable is only half the battle. It's the most important half, but controlling your payables is also important, especially when prepping up for a loan.

If you are cash-tight but trying to get ready for that loan, it is imperative that you develop a written, planned system for handling your payables. Receivables and payables control should become an integrated program, done with as much professionalism as possible.

Most businessmen who are in a cash-tight position know the old game of riding their suppliers, using them for working capital. Unquestionably, it is sometimes the only way. Many suppliers know it, expect it, and go along. Some suppliers are not so cooperative and will cut you off if you go too long or break your promises. You usually know who they are.

These elementary considerations, second nature to many business people, must still become part of your written priority plan.

Your priority plan must be flexible and will probably have to be changed occasionally. But if written down, it prevents oversights and provides management control and discipline. The plan enables you to leave on vacation, take business trips, and feel reasonably assured an employee or partner is less likely to damage your credit standing.

YOUR BEST CREDIT PICTURE Here are suggestions for a priority plan that will produce your best credit picture and make it more probable that your loan or lease requests will receive favorable consideration. The suggestions assume a very tight cash-flow situation, but they can prove suitable for any business, even without cash-flow problems.

Make a list of every fixed payment that repeats on a regular schedule—monthly, bimonthly, or quarterly payments, skip payments, whatever. This list, which is a preliminary to your priority plan, should include:

- Rent or mortgage payments
- Utilities
- Taxes of all kinds
- Loan payments
- Lease payments
- Supply or maintenance payments.

Your list should include the following information:

- Account number
- Dollar amounts, if payment is fixed, or estimates from prior years' experience if you wish to prepare a budget or cash disbursement forecast
- Scheduled due date
- Last mailing date or number of days after due date to avoid late charges or last date to mail and still be on time
- Amount of preset late charges (as with loan payments) or any known penalties for late payment (as with taxes)
- Complete address for paying bills. Many companies maintain a separate post office box or a department number for incoming payments. Avoid being late due to improperly addressed payments.
- Phone numbers and name of right person to contact, including service department, accounting department, managers' names and phone extensions—all appropriate information for efficient, easy communication with each account.

This list, properly prepared, becomes your easy reference guide to all payables. It eliminates constant, time-wasting file searches, relieves references to an overburdened Rolodex or card file, improves your efficiency, and expedites giving references. Using the reference guide enables any employee to maintain communications in your absence.

YOUR PAYABLES CALENDAR The next step in using your reference guide to payables is to turn your priority plan into a payables calendar. This can just be a continuation of your reference guide—perhaps a list which chronologically consolidates the above payable data on a clipboard hung in your office or in any other place that is readily accessible to you or whomever is in charge.

Use a format that makes for easy reference, that serves as a constant reminder, whatever works best for your business.

Here are some other suggested formats for your payables calendar:

- The "come-up" file sits flat on the desk top. Tabs are numbered 1 to 31 (days), for current month or for payables due on a particular day in future months. This simple system works well provided it is reviewed each business day. Payment coupon books are not forgotten in a desk or file drawer. Reminder notes can be placed several days in advance of due date or mailing date. Checks can be made out in advance and placed under scheduled mailing date.
- A large, desk-pad-sized calendar which provides large squares to write in planned daily reminder information for each known payable for the entire year. Fixed obligations can be totaled and entered on the calendar on the first of each month, providing at-a-glance cash requirements, which simplifies planning. Combining fixed obligations with the less predictable material and supply payables and fluctuating labor costs, you have a basic money-management planner. Entries can be pushed back to a later date and rescheduled. Payments made can be crossed off as they are mailed. By reviewing this calendar, or any calendar system you might devise, you can more readily and accurately forecast money requirements. You can prevent panic short-term borrowings and give the bank or other lender more time to meet your needs.

BANK OVERDRAFTS ARE RED FLAGS Avoid bank overdrafts if you possibly can. Even when the bank is friendly and covers your checks, overdrafts are still a stigma on your record. Many banks, if asked by another lender, will report all overdrafts. If these overdrafts occur on the last day of the accounting year or last day of any month for which you have financial statements prepared, most accountants enter "CURRENT LIABILITIES–BANK OVERDRAFT" and the dollar amount.

Your bank might understand and not be very concerned, but what if you decide to change banks or must go to an outside lender?

You are generally better off to borrow on a short-term basis and pay the interest than to show up with overdrafts or comments such as "30 days slow," "doesn't take discounts," or "is always paying late fees." And remember, late fees can add up to 24% to 36% simple interest.

Overdrafts, late payments, and missed discounts are red flags to outside lenders. They may indicate more than a cash-tight situation: they may imply poor planning, lack of management controls, a poor businessman, and a risky loan. "Turn him down, or charge plenty for the increased risk"!

MAKE YOUR PRIORITY PLAN WORK FOR YOU It doesn't matter what system you devise—31-day pocket files, "come-up" desk-top files, desk-top calendar, computer display of day, week, month, year at a glance—you need a system that is written down and open to periodic review. It should assist in preplanning and not fail you like your memory. It avoids payables lost in desk or file drawers.

Most important of all, even if you're extremely cash-tight, priority planning can help you look your "credit-best"—even better than you really are—if you follow this advice:

> Do not necessarily pay the accounts who squawk the loudest just because they irritated you or forced you into a promise.
>
> Do everything you possibly can to make equipment-contract or lease payments on time so as to avoid late fees. Not only are late fees expensive, but these payments receive the most consistent credit bureau reporting and lender interchange. All lenders look very closely at your "secured obligation performance" or unsecured bank loan paying habits.
>
> If you are doing a tough juggling act with available cash, pay utilities just prior to disconnect, pay the oil company just prior to credit card cancellation—then turn right around and pay a key supplier who offers a 2% discount.
>
> Know this: Very few lenders check into how you pay utilities or oil companies. Very few utilities report payment records to credit bureaus. Oil company credit cards usually report only serious problem accounts.
>
> With suppliers, some lenders do check directly or analyze credit bureau reports, but unless you are shown as running extremely slow or on C.O.D. with several, much less weight is placed on trade slowness than on bank, finance company, or lease company payment delinquency.

Your priority plan must be tough-minded, geared to saving you money whenever possible on late charges or by taking discounts; always with the express knowledge of what does the most for your checkable credit picture.

A well-executed priority plan can help set you up for the least expensive working capital loan or accounts receivable financing obtainable for a business of your size and profit potential.

Anticipation of problem periods, be they weeks or months in duration, if written down and forecast, can go a long way toward painting a good picture. It can prevent you or an automated payables clerk from cranking out checks to payables who could have waited.

Your priority plan can provide you with forewarning and enough time to prepare for any loan or financing your business requires.

## Mistake No. 5: Misunderstanding Your Lender

Understanding lenders involves much more than being empathetic, although simple empathy can sometimes get you what you want *if* your business credentials are in good order.

In case it hasn't already occurred to you, bankers, credit managers, and all those people who have the power of the pen, the authority to lend you money or say no—they're "different." They are a breed apart from you, the business person. Usually, they're lending someone else's money. This is an obvious but real factor in their attitude and interplay with you. These people have been hired, trained, and promoted to guard the vault! They dole out their employers' money, and with nary a loss, nary a mistake, they must put the money back in the vault—with a profit.

There are virtually no rewards for employee lenders, except they get to keep their job, provided they seldom, if ever, tout a bad loan. Sometimes they get an "atta-boy" for making loan quota, landing a new account, getting a higher-than-average yield, or for running a tight ship, but that's about it. If they hang in there and avoid mistakes, they get to be assistant vice-presidents or even full vice-presidents!

Many bankers are harried, especially branch bank managers. While trying to make good loans to less-than-helpful or understanding business people, they have their hands full. They must cope with tellers who are lower paid and turnover-prone. Endless meetings and reports are a way of life. Besides their own auditors, government agencies watch their every move. They must run a tight ship, even with the computer down half the time! With all their problems, they must retain your goodwill after saying no and keep those checking accounts filled with free lendable money.

Then there are the credit managers—also called credit analysts or loan administrators and sometimes less complimentary names. These are the suffering souls who receive the loan proposals recommended by the bankers, finance company account executives, or other similar go-fers. Credit managers don't have breakfast, they get ice-water injections. They are not paid to get emotional and they never cry for you. Credit people are beat over the head by impatient bank officers, finance company managers, field representatives, and account executives. They nearly always are paid less than any of the loan getters. These final arbiters have a tough, virtually thankless job. The buck stops with these credit decision makers. You must put your best foot forward to get their favorable consideration.

I'm on your side. You may think I'm making excuses for the banks and finance companies and the people who manage them because I was one of them for over twenty years—*not so*!

Those twenty years gave me ample opportunity to learn the lender's strengths and weaknesses. They do have many weaknesses, and sometimes it seemed they never wanted to say yes. Their only strength was they had what the borrower needed—money!

Whenever I thought I had seen it all, along would come another business person with a new self-defeating twist! Hoping to lend at least some insight to the lender's point of view, I list a few of those defeatist moves, with comments:

I have seen some business owners who were the best truck fleet owners, parts manufacturers, auto dealers, shirt makers, and gourmet chef restaurant operators commit every financial blunder known to "lenderkind."

*Comment*: These business people, very talented in their particular skill or industry, are the same ones who neglect their accounting and financial controls. They invariably made the lender beg for financial statements and reference data. Even when finally obtained, this information was still lacking in many ways.

These are the same business people who complain about slow lender service and often get turned down. They are the ones who are forced into shopping around—and end up paying a higher rate than they would have if their accounting had been in order.

I have seen some very wild-eyed business people come in with some pretty far-out financing requests—people whose strongest suit was a gift of gab and "wool-pulling" on personal financial statements.

*Comment*: These are the people who say, "The only time the banks are willing to loan money is when you don't really need it." They seem blissfully ignorant; they are their own worst enemies. It is sad, because some of these supreme optimists often had basically good ideas or businesses, but they irritated the lenders and killed their chances with a poorly prepared presentation. They turned the lenders off with their verbal assaults and without the facts to back their stories up.

I have had businessmen give me a knowing wink and an elbow nudge; "I can't show you my real profits, I'd pay too much in taxes if I do that. But you guys know how to read between the lines. Couldn't afford the 'Caddy' if I was losing money, could I?"

*Comment*: This sort of comment is usually a real no-no. Truth or not, if you were a bank officer, would you try telling that story to a credit analyst? He's the poor soul who is driving a 1967 V.W., makes 15K a year, and pays his full taxes by payroll deduction!

Every intelligent business person is expected to use every legal means to minimize taxes. Every credit analyst knows the places where a business person can hide profits, that depreciation is additional cash flow, and that the company buys that Caddy and pays for trips and club memberships.

Unless you are in a cash-type business, the story about "no profits because you hate to pay taxes" is usually a smoke-screen. It is offensive to all lenders, bankers in particular. Credit analysts are unimpressed because they make their decisions based on visible cash flow and ability to service a debt, not stories.

I have seen some otherwise excellent business owners sign bad loan agreements. They let their giant egos get in the way of commonsense questions they should have asked. That is the whole point of knowing where the lender is coming from. Don't *you* be self-defeating. Help that lender be as good as he wants to be—he can't make a dime unless he loans you money! Help him say yes. Don't waste your valuable time and energy being exasperated, angry, or frustrated by what may appear to be lender inadequacies.

WHAT ABOUT LENDER INADEQUACIES? Every lender has some shortcomings or lacks of expertise that you must either live with, go around, or change as best you can. Knowing the nature of the lender is very important to your digestion. It can also help promote business tranquility, saving you valuable time and effort. Most business people are already buried under tax reporting, labor problems, government rules and regulations, reports of all kinds. Who has time to struggle with an incompetent lender?

The reasons for knowing where your lender is coming from are to get the financing or loans you need with the fewest problems and delays, after expending as little time and effort as possible. That would be Utopia, but as many of us learn, the lenders don't always cooperate. Let's examine common complaints about lender inadequacies, to see if *Creative Business Financing* can help you achieve Utopia—or at least improve your digestion!

Bankers are sometimes accused of being lazy, aloof, or disinterested. Their major interest seems to lie in protecting their careers and keeping their noses clean with upper management. Some have been compared to frightened sparrows, lacking in vision and courage, possessing little enthusiasm for new or difficult financing situations of any kind. They are not known for having much knowledge of machine tools, trucks, construction equipment, or other special kinds of commercial or industrial equipment. Right or wrong, business people often complain their banker is unsympathetic, with little understanding of what they're up against.

There are many bankers who have entered banking careers because it seemed so suitable to their conservative natures. Sometimes the bankers richly deserve the criticism of business people. However, we would like to suggest that it might help business owners and managers to look at the other side and consider the banker's plight. Many bankers who would truly enjoy being aggressive and enthusiastic learn rather early that maintaining such spirit is far from easy. They get caught up in the banking bureaucracy. There are few rewards for fearless performance, and it is simple to get knocked down for being slightly wrong or out of step.

In addition to banking's numerous checks and balances, causing feelings of futility on an internal basis, there are external discouragements they also must cope with. These negative influences result from trying to deal with the general business public, day after day. Not only are many business people unreasonable in their expectations, but they are also too often unbusinesslike in their approach. Business people are essentially risk takers. They can be extremely abrasive, especially when viewed by conservative, security-minded bankers. The bankers are constantly confronted with demanding, woefully unprepared business owners. Many of them seem to have little appreciation for the banker's side of the story.

We have experienced tremendous growth over the last twenty years in the number of businesses competing for lendable dollars. The degree of borrower sophistication has also shown remarkable improvement. As much as most competitive bankers would like to loan their available funds, they are showing a growing impatience with business people who persist in approaching them on an adversary basis. Indeed there are lender inadequacies—but we suggest that all business people reexamine their attitudes and approach to their banker to be sure they are not contributing to the problems.

ARE YOU PART OF THE PROBLEM OR THE SOLUTION? If a banker seems lazy, too slow, or inept, and this is hurting you, consider changing bankers. But realize that if you have done your homework, even the lazy banker can be inspired and speeded up. A good presentation, financial statements that are legible and complete, prepared as we recommend, will give courage to that sparrowlike loan officer.

Think about these employees' situations. Those branch managers, with $10,000 or $20,000 lending limits, personally can't do much for you if you need more than they can approve. They may only appear lazy or disinterested because they feel so powerless and are tired of shoveling sand against the tide. They look at your financial statements, consider your verbal request for a loan or financing, think about the hours it will take to shape it up for their credit people, and mentally give up!

Inadequately prepared smaller business people are driving the lenders to the larger businesses. Those individual bankers are either taking the path of least resistance or doing what they are told to do. Their top management says, "Go after those big accounts, with big checking account balances. They have financial reports our credit committee can read, analyze, and believe."

Sure, it's true, happening more and more: big business is swallowing up the little fish. The lenders often shunt the smaller businesses aside or to their junior people. Still, as an ex-banker, I feel there is hope for smaller businesses. I've witnessed numerous examples of the "little guy" receiving excellent treatment, very favorable rates, and quick service.

THUMBNAIL SKETCH OF THE FAVORED LITTLE GUY Keeps his promises. If unexpected troubles arise, he has a plan. He has receivables and payables controls. Never asks for money "yesterday." His financial statements are carefully prepared, and he knows every number on them. When needing money, he always presents the lender with coherent facts and reasons for his request. Voluntarily keeps the bank informed; sends or drops off financial statements at least every six months, whether borrowing or not. Doesn't maintain a very large checking account balance; never overdrafts. Net worth less than $100,000, but his thoroughness and dependability make him stand tall with his banker. Mr. Little Guy meets his banker at least halfway; doesn't overrate or sell himself short. Branch manager wishes he had a thousand small businesses just like Mr. Little Guy!

DESPITE INADEQUACIES, EVERY BUSINESS NEEDS A BANK Yes, there is a love-hate relationship between bankers and business people. It runs both ways. Their shortcomings—real, imagined, or provoked by you or their regulations—are what you must cope with. You need them and they need you. If you can find a reasonably cooperative bank, so much the better. The extent of cooperation and assistance you get requires your contribution as well as the bank's willingness and understanding.

Despite bank-to-bank competition, in some areas very intense, the least efficient businesses uniformly receive minimal service and attention. When money is loose and credit readily available, the poorly managed, less knowledgeable business owners usually pay too much or agree to inordinately tough restrictions.

When money is tight, the situation worsens for all of the lightly capitalized, slow-paying businesses with typically poor financial controls. Even if they manage to obtain needed monies, they pay maximum rates, which only worsen their condition. They are pushed into very unpalatable alternative financing. Those with basically attractive operations, though unprofitable due to insufficient capital or inefficient use of capital, are swallowed up by big business.

We cannot offer a ready cure for businesses that are undercapitalized; they always suffer in a tight-money market. We do know that when money gets tight, the undercapitalized must tighten up their operations. It is a time when knowing where your lender is coming from is imperative. Not only are money costs extremely high—made purposely high to slow loan demand—but credit requirements become increasingly stringent. The lenders, particularly the banks, stiffen up, insisting on better-quality credits and more sizable down payments.

This book offers a whole series of treatments because there is no ready cure. It may sound simplistic, but a lot depends upon how much ammunition you provide the lender. The tighter money and credit become, the more necessary it is to plan well in advance, providing lenders with ample notice of your money needs.

## PREPARING YOUR PERSONAL FINANCIAL STATEMENTS

Small to medium-sized businesses are seldom publicly traded stock companies. Even when incorporated, with some stock sold outside, the strength of the company is often the managerial and financial strength of one or two individuals. Each of these key principals should prepare a good, complete, current personal financial statement.

We have developed forms for your instruction and use. You will find that banks and other lenders want the details these forms provide. Frequently, your personally or accountant-prepared individual statements come up lacking facts or other explanatory details. Grand-appearing statements, with very impressive assets and large net worths, are so uncheckable that they are virtually a collection of numbers. Why be bothered with lender questions? Why pay for or labor over a personal statement that fails to accomplish its mission? Give the lender what he needs in the first place!

The simplest solution is to use our form or your bank's form. Do a careful, thorough job in completing it. If there is inadequate space on the form, take the time to attach schedules or explanations. If you make copies—and you should always make at least one extra copy—do not use cheap or coated paper for copies. Use nothing less than good-quality bond paper.

Illegible, coated-paper copies say to the lender, "The borrower is chintzy, dumb, or really doesn't care." If you are working with a broker or financial consultant, insist on a good presentation. This starts with quality paper and copies the lender can read. Tell that broker you want to see the quality of his presentation of your company. Would you show up for a business appointment with an unshaven face and tennis shoes? When you're going for the money, presenting a good image requires only a small but extremely important investment.

Many business people are intimidated by a personal financial statement form. They are not quite sure what many of the terms mean or exactly what should be inserted in all of those blanks. It is not uncommon for people to puzzle over how to arrive at their net worth. Others find it too formidable or think it is too much trouble to bother completing. Taken line by line, a statement form is mostly common sense. To some it may seem terribly troublesome to complete because their personal financial affairs are not very well organized. Preparation or updating of a personal statement should be relatively simple if your filing system is in order. The lenders all place considerable reliance on an accurately completed personal financial statement. For that reason alone, it is worth doing it up properly.

To assist those who are unsure about the line-by-line entry requirements and the meaning of terminology used, we have included an explanatory model personal financial statement (Fig. 5-1). This statement appears at the end of this chapter in two parts: "Income and Expense Statement" and "Balance Sheet." You will find these forms instructional in completing any lender's statement forms. They will also prove useful in assembling your data for future reference.

Immediately after our model personal financial statement is a personal financial statement form you may use, confident that most lenders will find it all they could possibly require (Fig. 5-2). Occasionally a bank will insist on use of their own form. If so, this layout is readily transferrable. We suggest that you make copies, supplying original signatures and current date of signing.

Personal statements should be made up at least annually. Those who are borrowing frequently should not wait until the lender insists on a statement. Update twice a year, and keep copies handy for your negotiations or inclusion in a presentation. Develop a system of tracking the changes that take place in your more important assets. When prepping for a loan, put in the same file as your personal statement current information such as stock prices, real estate values, loan amortization schedules, new note balances due you, and all significant asset or liability changes affecting your net worth.

## HOW'S YOUR (COMPANY) HEALTH?

It is important to review your business financial statements to detect problem areas. Like preventive medicine, if at all possible, begin corrective measures immediately upon identifying the financial illness.

One of the most effective ways of watching financial statements is to focus on trends over time periods in several ratios and other tests of your balance sheet and income statement. These ratios and tests can warn of problem areas requiring corrective action. Sometimes you are only vaguely aware that things just aren't right. Studying your statements with a system can help you see more clearly what you only suspected originally.

You can analyze your own financial statements. It is really quite easy and can prove beneficial in familiarizing you with your business. It helps you spot trends, and you will be able to talk like a professional manager. Sounding like you know what you're talking about is still important to the lenders, though that which is written is still the predominant influence.

Whenever you borrow or request equipment financing of any sizable amount (usually $25,000 or more), the credit analyst will "spread" your statements. They will come up with ratios, test answers, percentages, cash flow, and ability to service the debt.

We have provided a "Balance Sheet Analysis" form in a single-page format containing the most important ratios and measurements

(Fig. 5-3). You should be familiar enough with your statements to know what the lenders are looking for, how they make their calculations, and, equally important, what they should mean to you. You should become familiar with the words, phrases, and meanings of the most commonly employed measurements.

You could put your lender into shock if you were to present your statements and your own analysis along with them! Your ability to verbalize the answers from your own analysis is also impressive in discussions with lenders, particularly your banker.

Some of these measurements and ratios are commonly known, but they are all included because they are part of a step-by-step procedure that renders a composite picture of your business. From the analyst's spread sheet comes one main answer to any borrowing request: *Yes* or *No*.

## ANALYZING YOUR BUSINESS FINANCIAL REPORTS

Financial statements are more than ancient history or a necessary evil to keep the lenders and IRS happy. Your statements are like a road map. They show where you have been, aid in telling how you got there, and, if you will just read them, will tell you where you are heading.

The smallest business should not keep books only so that they can do their tax returns and make various payroll reports; these records should also be referred to at regular intervals for management decisions. It is a mistake to make up statements or receive them from your accountant and toss them in a drawer!

Take those statements out of the drawer and get some use out of them! They cost you money, perhaps a considerable amount, if you used an outside accountant. In any case, getting all those numbers on paper represents some expense and effort, and you should benefit from them. What follows is not intended as a quick course in accounting. But we think you'll find it helpful in understanding how lenders look at your business through your financial statements.

Just to read the terminology can help you see that ratio calculations and other statement measurements are not very complicated. It may be useful for you to run through the basic calculations personally on a quarterly, semiannual, or annual basis, so that the answers stay in mind. Or run through a quick analysis before approaching the lenders for an important loan. Just being able to verbalize about your numbers will help to impress the lenders that you have a handle on your finances. If you can make corrections in your business's operation, so much the better!

### Balance Sheet Analysis

To assist you in making your own analysis, or to simplify reviewing the terminology and calculations, use our blank form, "Balance Sheet Analysis" (Fig. 5-3). This form covers the key ratios and measurements every lender commonly uses in an analysis. In preparing your analysis, as the lenders do it, you will need to know what ingredients they put into their calculations and what they throw out.

For instance, there are certain of your assets which you may consider current assets but the lenders typically consider as "other assets." They may even disagree with your accountant as to his categories or asset treatment. To be effective, you should revise your current assets to conform to the usual conservative treatment of the lenders.

Listed below are the assets usually removed from current assets before calculating the current ratio:

1. Cash and claims for cash which are (a) restricted as to withdrawal or use for other than current operations, (b) earmarked for expenditure in the acquisition or construction of noncurrent assets, (c) segregated for the liquidation of long-term debts, and (d) funds set aside to be used in the near future for the liquidation of long-term debt, sinking fund payments, or other similar purposes.
2. Investments in securities (marketable or not) or advances which have been made for the purposes of control, affiliation, or other continuing business advantage.
3. Receivables arising from unusual transactions not expected to be collected within a one-year period, such as sales of assets and loans or advances to affiliate companies, officers, or employees.
4. Cash surrender value of life insurance policies.
5. Land and other natural resources.
6. Depreciable assets.
7. Long-term prepayments which are chargeable to the operations of several years, or deferred charges such as unamortized discount expenses, bonus payments under a long-term lease, costs of rearranging a factory or removal to a new location, and certain types of research and development costs.

Prepaid expenses are not current assets, but if *not* paid in advance they would require use of current assets otherwise available during that year. Therefore, most prepaid expenses can properly be included as current assets, and the lender should not exclude prepaids from the current operating cycle.

THE ACID TEST: ADEQUACY OF WORKING CAPITAL The acid test ratio is done to remove inventory from consideration. Your quick-asset total should consist only of cash, marketable securities, and good accounts receivable. The tighter the ratio, the tighter will be your real working capital position.

ACCENTUATE THE POSITIVE; ELIMINATE THE INTANGIBLES Another category the lenders will adjust prior to calculation is assets considered as intangibles. They do this to arrive at your correct tangible net worth. This is preliminary to calculation of an important ratio called the debt-to-worth ratio.

To arrive at tangible net worth as the lenders do it, listed below are the assets considered as intangible. These are subtracted from your net worth, as in our sample analysis at the end of this chapter.

- Patents, copyrights, and trademarks
- Franchise valuations
- Goodwill
- Leasehold improvements
- Organization expenses
- Secret formulas and processes.

After arriving at your correct tangible net worth, you only need to total your debts and divide by tangible net worth to arrive at your debt-to-worth ratio. Be sure you correctly list and total all debts of the following categories:

- All liabilities classified as "current"
- All long-term debt (less current portion already included under current liabilities)
- All noncancelable, fully amortizing equipment lease obligations (those leases not being treated as lease or rental expenses).

## FUNDS DERIVED FROM OPERATIONS EQUALS CASH FLOW

Cash flow is a relatively simple calculation, but extremely important to you and to the lenders. It is arrived at from two main historical items, your prior net earnings (also called net income or net profit) and your prior depreciation. We use the word "prior" because the cash flow can be from any previous period. That is, if your accounting is completed quarterly, you will have three months' net earnings and three months' allocated depreciation. The answer, of course, will be a quarterly cash flow. Normally, the lenders work with the prior year-end figures to determine annualized cash flow. They may update your more recent cash-flow results from a late interim financial statement, especially if six or more months have passed since your year-end statements.

Simply add your earnings to the major noncash expense of depreciation. There are other noncash items which can logically be added to depreciation and earnings to arrive at cash flow.

- Amortization
- Depletion allowances
- Drilling or other exploratory write-offs
- Deferred tooling improvements

RATIOS, PERCENTAGES, RELATIONSHIPS, MEASUREMENTS—JUST MORE NUMBERS? It doesn't take a managerial genius to figure out that your business is experiencing declining profitability. Smaller businesses notice declining profits just by looking at a shrinking checking account balance. Detection of declining profits is one thing; prescribing a cure is where management skill comes in.

The primary interest of management is to determine how efficiently company assets are being used. To make valid determinations that are useful, so that corrective action may be intelligently planned and started, the balance sheet analyses are necessary. All of the key ratios and income statement measurements are most critical and revealing.

What is important are the factors contributing to lower profits. And, even more important, what steps you must take to turn things around.

If you are unaccustomed to playing with numbers, we urge you to become familiar with income statement analysis. The real meaning of the numbers can only be ascertained by comparisons. These comparisons should be made with your prior year's statements and, if possible, with the corresponding figures and percentages of companies in businesses similar to your own.

## Income Statement Analysis

Balance sheet analysis is very revealing, but we think close inspection of your income statement is more useful if you are checking for leaks. Small to medium-sized businesses can more practically eyeball their sales performance, cost of goods sold, labor costs, and operating expenses. If you operate on them, as you resolve the income statement leakage problems, your balance sheet ratios should start to improve. It is also fairly easy to prepare and work with sales, manufacturing, and operating expense budgets with information straight off your income statements from prior years.

For your convenience in spreading your own financial statements, we have included spread sheets at the end of this chapter (Figs. 5-4, 5-5, and 5-6). These forms are used by most lenders for balance sheet and income statement analysis. You can do the same thing, using these forms, and obtain management answers to work with.

30-DAY TERMS, 60-DAY COLLECTIONS? Even without mathematics, most business managers become quickly and painfully aware that their slow-paying accounts receivables are causing a real drag on working capital. It shows up as a serious case of cash-shortness, because the business cannot carry the slow-receivable load.

The turnover, or number of days outstanding, of accounts receivable is readily calculated:

$$\frac{\text{annual sales}}{\text{365 (days)}} = \text{sales per day}$$

$$\frac{\text{sales per day}}{\text{accounts receivable (year end)}} = \text{average number of days A/R are outstanding}$$

You may also make the calculation at the end of the month or the quarter or for any other period, as long as you take the total A/R at the period end and compare them with sales for the same time period.

For Example: Assume accounts receivable of $350,000 at year-end.
Assume annual sales of $3,000,000 for that year.

$$\frac{\$3{,}000{,}000}{365 \text{ (days)}} = \$8{,}219.18 \text{ (sales per day)}$$

$$\frac{\$8{,}219.18}{\$350{,}000} = 42.58 \text{ average number of days outstanding}$$

In this example, your A/R are paying on an average of 42 to 43 days. If your terms are net 30 days, there is a 12- to 13-day lag. You are therefore carrying some $100,000, which naturally restricts your working capital by that amount!

A twelve day lag isn't too bad an average, but if you can't afford it, it hurts! Whenever you apply for credit, this is an important measurement used by the credit analysts. (Use the form in Fig. 8–2, at the end of chapter eight, for your own A/R calculations.)

You should know and memorize this average. You should understand that the longer it exceeds your normal billing terms, the less competent your or your A/R collection department will appear. If the average gets too far out of whack, here are the negatives reflected:

- Your products are not up to par.
- Your controls are nonexistent or ineffective.
- Your customers are not of good credit quality.
- Some of the A/R will prove uncollectable, reducing your liquidity even more in future months.

## Key Ratios and Measurements

What are the factors contributing to lower profits? Declining sales? Rising merchandising or manufacturing costs? What are labor costs? Too much paperwork? Too much duplication of effort? Front-office costs getting disproportionate to production and sales?

Here are the key ratios and measurements you should take from your income statement:

Cost of Goods Sold ÷ Average inventory = inventory turnover rate
Net Profits ÷ Net sales = Net profits on net sales
Net Profits ÷ Tangible net worth = Net profits on tangible net worth
Operating expenses ÷ Net sales = Operating expenses to sales

*Note*: You can perform the operating expenses measurement, using the dollar amount of each expense item, to determine individual expenses as a percentage of sales.

Rather than raising prices, which may be impossible or unwise at best, you should take corrective action to fix the problem areas. Before you can act effectively, you have to zero in on the expenses that are eating into your bottom line. Prior-year comparisons, working with expense as a percentage of sales, is an easy, accurate way to approach the problem areas.

INCOME STATEMENT LEVERAGE RATIOS These ratios are often called coverage ratios. Ratios in this analysis category compare a company's ability to pay a particular expense to the level of that expense.

To see how well a particular expense is covered, take your total earnings and subtract the particular expense you want to check out for coverage from those earnings, then divide remaining earnings by the expense item:

$$\frac{\text{Net earnings} - \text{Expense item}}{\text{Expense item}} = \text{times covered}$$

One particular expense item the analysts check out for times covered is interest expense, which, of course, includes finance or lease charges. This ratio is called times-interest-earned. To find this ratio, subtract both income taxes and interest from your net earnings, then divide by total interest charges.

This ratio will tell you how far earnings can decline before you will have trouble meeting annual interest costs. Since payments are made from earnings over a period of time, this ratio measures your company's ability to service its debt. This is of particular interest to your long-term lenders.

To be a more professional manager, you need to have at least a working knowledge of the ratios and measurements set forth above. These are the yardsticks used by the credit analysts to measure your business. If your business fails to measure up, consistently falling short when compared to similar businesses, you will encounter increasing difficulty in obtaining the loans or financing you require

If you are currently working with lenders in any major financing or borrowing programs, they may be expecting or insisting on improvement in some or all of these key ratios. It behooves you to know what they are talking about and what you are talking about and trying to accomplish.

FINANCIAL STATEMENT CONSIDERATIONS Your business financial statements are critical to internal management controls and decision making. When displayed to the lenders, they become *you*—your on-paper representatives. They can make a good first impression or a lasting bad impression.

So you're not G.M. or Ford! Not everyone can afford impressive CPA-prepared financial statements. Most small to medium-sized businesses have no need for audited statements which a CPA certifies as true and correct. Certified statements are quite expensive because the CPA firm must expend great amounts of time and effort, verifying inventories and receivables, and, in general, satisfying themselves as to the authenticity of your internally prepared accounting entries. They can be held liable for certifying figures improperly investigated. Their reputations are on the line.

This is not to say that you shouldn't consider using a CPA firm or an individual CPA to prepare your financial statements. If you do not need certified statements, the CPA will prepare them unaudited, without expressing an opinion. These statements will cost less than certified, but will accomplish as much as you probably need for continuing operations. If you are about to sell out or merge, audited statements may be required or at least a worthwhile investment.

All business persons should periodically reexamine their financial statement preparation and reconsider who is doing them. Recheck the costs and reflect upon what you're getting for your money.

The net effect of inadequate or poorly prepared statements is an area frequently underrated by small to medium-sized businesses. Even larger businesses, with sales volumes running to the high six figures, fail to recognize what it really costs them when they cut corners or persist in coming out with half-baked internally prepared statements.

If you are paying an outside public accountant or bookkeeping service for shoddy statements, lacking in details, improperly footnoted, containing no percentages or comparisons to prior years, you could be costing yourself money in higher borrowing costs and your precious time spent in answering questions, not to mention shortchanging yourself by not having useful management measuring tools.

This is not to say there aren't some very good, completely adequate public accountants and bookkeeping services out there; nor is it to say all CPAs are automatically better or worth their charges. Overall, the CPAs, through training and experience, will do a better job, often for only a little more money. If you are actively buying or leasing equipment or borrowing substantial amounts, the professionalism of a good CPA can wipe out cost differences. As a smaller business, you don't have to go to the "big eight" CPA firms to get the professional assistance of a CPA.

## Creative Business Financing Recommendations

- Do not underestimate the positive or negative impact your financial statements can have on the lenders, no matter what your net worth.
- Use your financial statements as an important management tool.
- Don't cut costs on financial statements and the preliminary accounting that goes into their preparation. It isn't worth it unless you have insignificant credit and borrowing requirements and anticipate none.
- Have them prepared as best you can afford. Duplicate them only on high-grade bond paper; use a cover and staple or rivet them into a booklet presentation format.
- Try to come out with a reasonably detailed quarterly—or at least semiannual—statement, plus a very complete year-end statement.
- If prepared by an outside accountant or service, insist upon an ample supply of quality duplicates. File them where you can find them!

MINIMIZING ACCOUNTING SERVICE COSTS CAN BE A FALSE ECONOMY If your business is struggling and is marginally profitable, every expense item becomes critical. Struggling or not, we recommend holding down interest and finance charges as one way to decrease operating costs.

Now we are going to recommend the possibility of spending a little more to save more. We are talking about your accounting procedures and services. Business people, especially those anxious to hold down expenses, perhaps to increase their own take-home pay, have a tendency to trim back on accounting costs. Others, not so much influenced by the cost factor, tend to underrate the value and importance of well-prepared financial statements and internal accounting systems.

This can be counterproductive to your growth, your management systems and controls, and your efforts to reduce the cost of borrowed money. In fact, because of poorly prepared statements and lack of adequate internal accounting systems, you may be unnecessarily increasing other costs.

If you are purchasing materials on special extended terms, many suppliers require financial statements in addition to bank and trade references before granting credit. It is entirely possible that your overall material costs will go up when the supplier's opinion of your statements goes down.

Consider the following suggestions; fit them to your business and ability to pay.

- Take a critical look at the statements you are now producing from your own efforts or those prepared by your company bookkeeper. With a little effort, can you make them look more like our model CPA-style statements (Figs. 5-5 and 5-6)?

  If you are getting outside assistance from a bookkeeper or accountant, is he or she capable of upgrading or changing to a better, more useful format, like our model?

- Are you partially or fully responsible for the inadequacies or slowness of your outside statement preparation? Sit down with your outside accountant and try to improve upon what you provide to make up your statements and what you get back in completed form. In your discussions, determine how you can improve on your daily record keeping and preliminary preparations. Most outside accounting services will tell you if you will turn over all data in an organized fashion, it will definitely save time and money.
- Reconsider the limitations of your existing internal accounting and those of your present outside accounting person or firm.

  Aside from typing up a bunch of statements or handing you inadequate computerized printouts devoid of helpful percentages, explanations, and facts, what assistance do they offer as advisers? Do they assist with depreciation guidelines, provide IRS insight, keep you abreast of regulation changes, or provide any tax guidance?

  Do they know anything about finance rates, yield equivalents, leasing rates, the technicalities of investment tax credits (used in a lease transaction), or true lease versus lease-purchase?

TIME FOR A CHANGE? If you are not happy with the answers you are getting from this little survey, it is time to consider changing your internal systems or your outside accounting service.

Shop around! You need the best financial and accounting assistance you can find and afford!

- Try to upgrade to a small CPA firm or a local independent CPA. Compare costs and what you get for your precious dollars.
- If you can't afford the CPA, look for a public accountant.

  Try to locate an accountant who has clientele and experience in your industry or type of business. If at all possible, check his references. See if others are pleased with his services and results. As a minimum, have him provide samples of his actual completed products.

- If you can't locate or afford an accountant, search for a qualified bookkeeping service. It is imperative that you check out a bookkeeping service carefully. Don't do business with a bookkeeping service without having one or more local business owners tell you they are well satisfied. See several actual copies of the statements they have prepared or complete formats of the exact products they will provide you. Although there are some good ones, certainly worth the modest fees they charge, many business services are nationally franchised, with a good sales pitch and little else.

They gather up your data, punch it into a computer or bookkeeping machine, and call it accounting. Many of these companies are constantly late in completing your statements. Many know next to nothing about your business, tax problems, the latest accounting changes, or how to provide you with reports you can use in decision making.

- Many accounting service firms and accountants are now providing businesses with the necessary forms and instructions to assist with daily or monthly accounting entries and tax returns.

  If your office staff consists of only a receptionist-secretary, consider utilizing her "free" time with a posting system set up by the outside accounting service. Make sure the service is available to provide assistance to resolve problem entries or special situations as they occur.

- Most business people are aware of bank services, such as complete payroll handling. If you are not, check with your bank to learn what duties they can take over or assist you with.

## IS THERE A COMPUTER IN YOUR FUTURE?

There is another solution to handling your accounting, reporting, and management control problems: a computer! More and more businesses are turning to their own in-house computer systems either to replace outside accounting services entirely or to prepare monthly financial reports and invoices, control receivables, and handle payables. Advantages include closer management control and the ability to take out or input information whenever needed.

If an outside public accountant or CPA is used, the computer data are utilized to simplify and perhaps shorten their time spent and reduce outside accounting expenses.

We would like to acquaint you with some of the problems and pitfalls inherent in the selection of a computer and getting it programmed to do what you want it to do and not present more problems. We also provide some financing tips and areas to guard against in obtaining computer financing.

A BIT OF COMPUTER HISTORY Back about 1954 or 1955, computers were locked up in separate rooms about the size of the corner drugstore. Only people with specialized knowledge were able to operate the complex beasts.

Those computers were called mainframes and were very expensive. Only large companies could afford their own in-house computer.

Many equally large and successful companies utilized the computer on a time-share basis. Numerous computer companies sprouted up, purchasing or leasing one or more large computers and selling available time to companies. They usually provided computerized accounting or billing services for companies with hundreds of thousands of charge account customers. But few of them provided package accounting services, statement preparation, and the daily controls needed by smaller businesses.

Today, those mainframes are in-house for many more companies and they are called maxis, to differentiate them from the smaller computers. These are referred to as super-minis, minicomputers, or microcomputers, depending on size.

Businesses with hundreds of thousands of inventory items and numerous accounts receivable are now buying a medium-sized computer called a super-minicomputer. These systems can have memory locations of 64,000 bytes, with a 10-million-byte disc-drive capacity, called disc storage. The computers we will be discussing are in the mini and micro size range. These computer systems, including all hardware and specialized software, are in the $15,000 to $100,000 price category. There are even computers being offered in the hobby and home sector for under $10,000 that are being adapted to business use.

Back in 1964 or 1965, the minicomputer was in its infancy. These much smaller computers were followed by the microcomputer around 1974 or 1975. User acceptance and sales have rapidly accelerated every year since. Miniaturized circuitry, advances in disc storage, printers that produce error-free copy at 180 characters per second, and improved video display units have all served to reduce the size, cost, and operating complexity of a computer. In the very near future the remarkable assistance of a total computer system will be within affordable reach of most small businesses.

We recommend that all businesses with numerous accounts receivable, varied or troublesome inventories, manufacturing or scheduling flow problems, departmental coordination problems, and the need for in-house accounting capabilities immediately begin consideration of a mini or microcomputer. But we also urge you to proceed with extreme caution. Don't jump in too fast, without adequate investigation!

### Watch Out for Hardware and Software "Nurds"!

Businesses are buying or leasing computers the way the public went after hula hoops. Sales have reached "fad" proportions, but, as you are aware or may soon find out, the investment can be substantial. Perhaps equally important, selection of an inadequate system or an incompetent software specialist can cause serious business disruption. It can be very costly to quickly outgrow your system and find you cannot increase the capacity. Finding out you cannot readily obtain service and parts can also prove disastrous. Learning that the software programs will not perform all that was promised can prove an expensive disappointment.

The recent technological breakthroughs we have mentioned have caused numerous fly-by-night software specialists to emerge. Many of them, tied loosely to hardware manufacturing or distributor sources, have sprung up to share in the quick-money aspects of packaged computer sales. Unfortunately, many small software specialist companies are either undercapitalized or not technically competent—or both. They cannot service what they sell and often cannot give you all the wonderful results promised. These are the "nurds" you must look out for, and it seems they are the types who inevitably come on the scene of every new, fast-selling product.

If you were selecting a maxicomputer (mainframe type), there would not be problems or major concerns as outlined above. There are ten leading manufacturers, all providing quality equipment. They all back up their products with service contracts which guarantee the performance of the equipment. They have nationwide service and parts networks. They generally provide the software programming through their own people or at least control the preparation, always using trained professionals. This is not to say maxi or super-minicomputers are trouble-free; it's that this area is not relevant to the problems confronting small to medium-sized businesses now shopping for a computer.

## Problem Solver or Another Problem?

Mini and microcomputer problems begin with the selection of a hardware manufacturer. There are now about five hundred manufacturers cranking out these electronic wizards. Although a reliable count is not available, there are probably five thousand software "specialists" peddling their services along with a variety of hardware.

By 1983, through merger or business failure, the experts are predicting that only about thirty manufacturers will survive. It is imperative that you thoroughly investigate the hardware manufacturer.

Don't get locked into a five- to seven-year lease or contract only to learn that service and parts are difficult or impossible to obtain. Computers do break down, as we all know—who hasn't heard, "Sorry, our computer is down"?

To make your selection even more difficult, many of these manufacturers are selling their products through software specialist companies and franchised vendors. Some of these companies are very much like the old blue-suede-shoe salesmen of the '50s. Underfinanced, lacking training, guilty of overselling the equipment and their own capabilities, and overcharging for their services, these get-rich-quick artists can cost you a bundle!

There is an additional risk in working with these "specialists" and their vendor sales-oriented companies: many manufacturers make only the CPU, the central processing unit. The vendors or programming companies must select and assemble the peripheral equipment. This equipment includes disc storage, printer, video screen or viewer, plotter, and various remote station units. This may not necessarily be bad, except you *can* end up with peripheral equipment from either a foreign manufacturer or one that later goes bankrupt—making obtaining parts and service difficult. You also want to have a well-assembled system, fully integrated with your computer. The larger manufacturers, including those who produce only the CPU, usually marry their equipment with selected, quality peripherals.

As a business owner who can really use and benefit from a good, in-house computer system, the need for careful selection and well-considered buyer-beware negotiating should be obvious.

### Tips on Selecting a Reliable Hardware Manufacturer

- Check manufacturers out by determining their financial strength.
- Find out how long they have been in the computer manufacturing business.
- Get customer references. Where do they now have installations? Call or visit these references and see if the users are satisfied. What problems were encountered? What promises broken? How have parts and service been?
- If you are spending $50,000 or more and still have reason for concern, get a copy of each manufacturer's annual report. Ask for a copy at any stockbroker's office, have your banker obtain one, or request a copy from the manufacturer's representative or the software-vendor company.
- You can also check manufacturers out the same way if they're over-the-counter companies, but it may be more difficult to obtain their financial and background information. If the hardware manufacturer is not either an OTC American or well-known foreign manufacturer with established parts and service—*take care*! Go slow with unlisted companies with which you encounter difficulty in checking customer or financial references. Do not buy a sales pitch; buy only proof. If you aren't completely satisfied—pass! Continue to shop and look at the major, well-advertised equipment. The prices might be somewhat higher, but bargain-priced computers may not be a bargain if they interrupt your business's continuity.

Consider ordering the *Benchmark Report*, published by the Association of Computer Users. This not-for-profit corporation is a membership-type monthly-report publication. Nonmembers can also order complete analysis-type reports, which evaluate and report on tests of small to medium-sized computers. The association will provide nonmembers with a fee schedule for separate reports.

In addition to specific information sections on small, medium, and large computers, which you may order separately according to your interests, *Benchmark Reports* has sections on distributed processing, word processing, time sharing, and home and hobbyist computers. Also available to members are *Interactive Computing* (a bimonthly newsletter), *Remote Computing Directory*, and *Computer Terminals Directory*. Contributor-authors of these reports include Peat, Marwick, Mitchell & Co. (CPAs); the Business Research Division of the University of Colorado; and Real Decisions Corporation.

If you are considering a computer, want to upgrade your present system, or simply want to keep informed as to the latest technology, these reasonably priced memberships and reports can help you. Quite possibly, you may save valuable time and money and prevent expensive mistakes. Remember, you must not only consider the initial cost of a computer but also the ongoing costs of training people, converting your existing systems and methods, business interruption, and perhaps struggling with an unsuitable system that does not perform as anticipated. To obtain membership and report information, write to the Association of Computer Users, P.O. Box 9003, Boulder, CO 80301. We are not affiliated with this publication in any way. We have researched their informational services and feel they are unbiased and factual. They provide a reliable reference source in a volatile, rapidly changing industry that is unusually short on comparisons business people can rely upon.

## Computer Services Buying Tips

- Obtain a copy of the manufacturer's warranty or guarantee. Read it and compare it with others as you shop.
- Have the manufacturer's sales organization or the software vendor prepare a detailed quotation. Do not settle for an abbreviated quick list—especially one that reads like computerese. If they do this to you, insist on an interpretation, translated into plain English. The quotation should include the manufacturer's name or a recognizable trade name, all major components—described in common terms, not abbreviations or buzzword computer letters and phrases. Have them provide model numbers, all separately priced (if not part of a package) and packaged items broken down as to components or parts included in the package. You will need this quotation to make valid shopping comparisons. The bank, finance company, or lease company will need it for their credit consideration and proper documentation.
- Get the software programming in as much written detail as possible. What business functions will the programs perform, and in what detail? Make sure to get a price quotation. Know how much each add-on function will cost. Lenders do not like to

receive vague hardware or software quotations. They want to know what they are financing and what you are getting. As a minimum, have the programming functions spelled out: accounts receivable, inventory control, financial statements, production scheduling, and all other capabilities. Many quotations have been presented to lenders that briefly list the hardware in computerese, plus, to make matters worse, the statement "complete with software." What does the software consist of? Isn't it bad enough that lenders are wary of financing "soft" collateral?

- Get a delivery date for both hardware and software. Pin this down as exactly as possible. Don't be pressured by the salesman who says, "Give me the order and I'll get you a delivery date." Tell this salesman, "Put it in the order. Delivery will be within *X* days after acceptance of this quotation."
- Avoid surprises: have the quotation indicate any other costs such as freight, taxes, and installation charges.
- If you are going to have a separate maintenance and service policy, get it in writing, including the exact cost per month, per year, or per call.

  Find out where the service center is located. How long will it take for the serviceman to get to you and put your computer back into operation? Do they have parts in stock or must they order them from a distant city or foreign country?

- Try to locate software specialists who are experienced in your business or industry. Some software programmers specialize in serving doctors, dentists, or other professionals. Others do automobile dealers, parts manufacturers, real estate brokers, etc. Some prepare highly specialized programs for engineering studies and related models. Others have expertise in environmental, energy, or water-conservation programming. Programming for these industries and for parts manufacturers requires someone expert in applicable software systems. In addition, a good "plotter" peripheral hardware unit must be selected suitable to their needs. If your major concerns are financial statements or accounting functions, the programming is often most satisfactory when prepared by an accountant or people with accountancy backgrounds.
- When considering the hardware, watch out for manufacturers offering a system that locks you into their computer language. Some systems, including those offered by prominent manufacturers, were devised so that your software will work properly only on their equipment. When it comes time to upgrade or make add-ons, you must stay with your first manufacturer's products.

## Computer Financing or Leasing Can Be Tricky

Historically, leasing has played a dominant role in computer financing. Because of the risks inherent in financing high-technology equipment, lease brokers have gravitated toward the sellers to get a first shot at the fledgling new users.

Computers, much like other office equipment, are frequently sold on the basis of monthly or annual savings: reductions in or elimination of labor, outside services, paper and file cabinets, or management time. Logically, then, the financing is presented on a monthly-cost basis. Simplified, the financing presentation asserts that the savings make the payments of little or no importance. "The savings make the payments."

The computer salesman's pitch is: "You can have this entire system, software included, installed, for only $598 per month! All you have to do is lease it. You only need the first and last months in advance!"

The user's decision process goes something like this: "Can I afford the payments? Let's see, I get rid of that expensive accountant, for starters. I cut my office staff down by one or two people. Gee, I can't afford not to afford it!"

Enter lease brokers! Seller puts broker onto the potential user, who says, "Get me financed! My bank doesn't understand computers, seven-year terms, or no-money-down leases."

The broker says, "No problem! I've got finance sources who do understand computers and love seven-year leases! Just give me a security deposit, sign this commitment, and I'll get you financed." And they sure do!

Many of these users, innocent and unsuspecting, end up paying 25% to 30% interest (or more), neatly buried in those monthly "rental" payments! Some neophyte computer buyers also give away their investment tax credit, without even thinking about the value of it or about how much the rate should have been dropped for allowing the lessor to have it!

Virtually the same thing holds true for some of the "factory-lease" plans being offered by manufacturers. The interest-rate "pack" may not be quite as high, but those users who are reasonably creditworthy should definitely look behind those "easy monthly rental payments."

We repeat: it pays to shop. If a broker can get you financed, why can't you locate your own financing?

FIGURE 5-1

# INCOME AND EXPENSE STATEMENT

From ______________ ____, 19 ___ to ______________ ____, 19 ___

## INCOME Money you receive for your use.

| | | |
|---|---|---|
| GROSS SALARY/WAGES | $______ | |
| LESS DEDUCTIONS Federal and state income tax, FICA, unemployment compensation. | –$______ | |
| TAKE-HOME PAY | | $______ |
| SPOUSE OR OTHER GROSS SALARY/WAGES | $______ | |
| LESS DEDUCTIONS | –$______ | |
| TAKE-HOME PAY | | $______ |
| COMMISSIONS, TIPS, BONUSES | | $______ |
| NET PROFIT FROM BUSINESS, FARM, TRADE, PROFESSION | | $______ |
| INTEREST OR DIVIDENDS FROM SAVINGS, STOCKS, BONDS, OTHER SECURITIES, NOTES | | $______ |
| NET PROFIT FROM SALE OF ASSETS | | $______ |
| NET PROFIT FROM RENTAL PROPERTY | | $______ |
| INCOME FROM ALIMONY/CHILD SUPPORT/MAINTENANCE (Court ordered.) | | $______ |
| REFUNDS/REBATES | | $______ |
| CASH GIFTS | | $______ |
| OTHER INCOME | | |
| Social Security benefits | | $______ |
| Pensions, annuities | | $______ |
| Veterans benefits | | $______ |
| Unemployment benefits | | $______ |
| Disability benefits | | $______ |
| Life insurance benefits | | $______ |
| Income from trusts | | $______ |
| Royalties/residuals | | $______ |
| **TOTAL INCOME** | | $______ |

| | |
|---|---|
| TOTAL INCOME | $______ |
| LESS TOTAL EXPENSES (FIXED AND VARIABLE) | –$______ |
| **Amount available for savings, investments or debt payment** | $______ |

## FIXED EXPENSES Payments you must make, usually set by written agreement, at regular times for set amounts.

| | |
|---|---|
| RENT OR MORTGAGE PAYMENTS Include property tax and insurance if automatically included in payment. | $______ |
| OTHER REAL ESTATE PAYMENT Second mortgage, home improvement loan (if secured by home), vacation home, storage rental, homeowner association fees. | $______ |
| INCOME TAXES Federal and state taxes due in addition to withholding taxes; past taxes. | $______ |
| PROPERTY TAXES If not part of house payment. | $______ |
| OTHER TAXES Gift or estate taxes. | $______ |
| INSTALLMENT CONTRACT PAYMENTS Fixed payments made at regular intervals over specific time periods for purchase of vehicles, mobile home, furniture, appliances, etc. | $______ |
| PERSONAL PROPERTY LEASE PAYMENTS Auto, furniture, equipment. | $______ |
| INSURANCE Real property (fire, liability, theft, etc., if not included in house payment), personal property (homeowner's, renter's, auto), life, health, other. | $______ |
| REGULAR PAYMENTS TO OTHERS Alimony, child support, maintenance. | $______ |
| REGULAR CONTRIBUTIONS Church, charities, etc. | $______ |
| DUES Union, club and other memberships. | $______ |
| TOTAL FIXED EXPENSES | $______ |

## VARIABLE EXPENSES Regular expenses that may fluctuate from month to month or year to year.

| | |
|---|---|
| UTILITIES Gas, electricity, heating, fuel, phone, water, cable TV, garbage. | $______ |
| CHARGE ACCOUNTS Store account and credit card payments. | $______ |
| MEDICAL/DENTAL Drugs and treatment not covered by insurance. | $______ |
| TRANSPORTATION Car operating expenses (gas, oil, repairs, servicing), parking, public transportation. | $______ |
| HOUSEHOLD MAINTENANCE/REPAIR Gardening, cleaning, house/appliance repairs (material, labor). | $______ |
| CHILD CARE Day care, nursery school, housekeeper, babysitter. | $______ |
| FOOD Groceries, nonfood items in supermarket bill. | $______ |
| PERSONAL MAINTENANCE Clothing, laundry, barber, beauty salon, health and beauty products. | $______ |
| SELF-IMPROVEMENT/EDUCATION Books, magazines, newspapers, seminars, lessons, tuition, room and board away from home. | $______ |
| RECREATION/ENTERTAINMENT Restaurants, movies, sports, vacations, weekends, parties, etc. | $______ |
| TOTAL VARIABLE EXPENSES | $______ |
| **TOTAL EXPENSES (FIXED AND VARIABLE)** | $______ |

FIGURE 5-1 (continued)

# BALANCE SHEET

__________ ____, 19 ___

## ASSETS Everything you own with cash value.

**CASH** Money you have on hand. Include cash at home, today's checking and savings account balances. $________

**STOCKS, BONDS, OTHER SECURITIES** U.S. Savings Bonds, Treasury issues, other money market and stock market investments. Check your records for documentation of current holdings. Current market value for some types of securities may be found in newspaper financial pages; for others, contact your broker. $________

**CASH SURRENDER VALUE LIFE INSURANCE** Investment or equity built up in your whole or straight life insurance policy; not face value. (Term life insurance has no cash surrender value.) Find the cash surrender value from the chart on your policy. $________

**ACCOUNTS RECEIVABLE** Money owed to you for goods and/or services. Check your files for bills outstanding. $________

**NOTES RECEIVABLE** Money owed to you and documented by promissory notes. Check your records for the balance of any note due you. $________

**REBATES/REFUNDS** Money owed to you for refundable deposits, sales or tax refunds or rebates. Check your files for receipts and current 1040 income tax form. $________

**AUTOS/OTHER VEHICLES** Trucks, trailers, mobile homes, motorcycles, campers, boats and airplanes. Vehicle dealers and some libraries carry special price books such as the Kelley Blue Book for new and used automobiles. If no published information is available, dealers may be able to tell you the current market value. $________

**REAL ESTATE** Any land and/or structures affixed to land. Also, legal rights you may have to resources in the land: growing crops, water, minerals, etc. For an estimate of the current market value, you may contact a local real estate agent or hire a professional appraiser. $________

**VESTED PENSION** Nonforfeitable rights to benefits you accumulate after a certain time under your employer's pension plan. To find the current amount of your benefits, you must submit a written request to your employer or plan administrator. $________

**KEOGH OR INDIVIDUAL RETIREMENT ACCOUNT** Available to those without employer pension plans or the self-employed. Record your account balance. $________

**OTHER ASSETS** Any property other than real estate that has cash value, estimated in terms of what it is worth today. To find an item's value, check classified ads for comparable items or get estimates from dealers or special appraisers.

**Home furnishings/household goods/appliances** $________

**Hobby/sports equipment** $________

**Art/antiques/collections/jewelry/furs** $________

**Trade/professional tools and equipment** $________

**Livestock/pets for show or breeding** $________

**Trusts/patents/memberships/interest in estate** $________

**Interest in business/farm/commercial operation/investment club.** (Any whole or part ownership.) $________

**TOTAL ASSETS** $________

## LIABILITIES What you owe: your debts.

**ACCOUNTS PAYABLE** Total balance of what you owe today on bills for goods and services (such as doctor bills) and credit card and store accounts. A credit card company or store usually lists the account's total balance due on the monthly statement mailed to you. If you do not have these records, contact the credit departments of firms where you have accounts. $________

**CONTRACTS PAYABLE** Total remaining balance on installment credit contracts for goods such as a car, furniture, appliances, or services of someone working for you under contract. To figure the total amount due, multiply your monthly payment by the number of months remaining on the contract. $________

**NOTES PAYABLE** Total balance due on cash loans, both secured and unsecured. Contact the office where you received the loan if you don't have these figures. $________

**TAXES** Federal and state income or property taxes due as of today (including any past due taxes). Do not list property taxes if they are automatically included with your mortgage payments. Self-employed people should include any Social Security taxes due. Check your income tax or property tax statements. $________

**REAL ESTATE LOANS** Balance you owe on deeds of trust (mortgages) on your property. Contact the office where you received the loan if you don't have these figures. Also list any liens on property that you are liable for and must pay. $________

**OTHER LIABILITIES** Court-ordered judgments of payments you must make, lawsuit settlements, past due accounts, etc. $________

**TOTAL LIABILITIES** $________

**CONTINGENT LIABILITIES** **Debts you may or may not come to owe sometime in the future. If you cosigned a note and the other signer doesn't pay, you may be responsible for paying the debt. If a suit is pending against you, you may be liable to pay a settlement.** $________

## NET WORTH Your assets less your liabilities.

ASSETS $________

LESS LIABILITIES −$________

**NET WORTH** $________

**To check your figures, make sure:**
**Assets = Liabilities + Net Worth**

FIGURE 5-2

# *Personal Financial Statement*

Name ______________________________

Address ______________________________

Social Security No. ______________________ Date of Birth ______________________

Present Employer ______________________ Position ______________________

Address Of Employer ______________________________

Marital Status (answer only if this financial statement is provided in connection with a request for secured credit or if you live in a community property state ):

☐ Married ☐ Separated

☐ Unmarried (unmarried includes single, divorced, widowed)

**YOU MAY APPLY FOR CREDIT EXTENSION OR FINANCIAL ACCOMMODATION SEPARATELY OR JOINTLY.**

Are you requesting this financial accommodation: ☐ Separately? ☐ Jointly with your spouse?

☐ Jointly with another person. (Please submit separate financial statements attached together)

Reflect in this statement the financial condition of your spouse as well as your own financial condition if:

**1.** You are seeking this financial accommodation jointly with your spouse, or

**2.** You are relying on your spouse's assets or income in requesting this financial accommodation, or

**3.** You live in a community property state.

FIGURE 5-2 (continued)

**DATE OF VALUATIONS** ______________________

- List all amounts in dollars. Omit cents.
- Please attach a separate sheet if you need more space to complete a detail schedule.

| ASSETS | AMOUNT | LIABILITIES | AMOUNT |
|---|---|---|---|
| Cash in Bank | | Accounts Payable | |
| Cash in Other Banks (Detail) | | | |
| | | Notes Payable to Bank | |
| | | | |
| | | Notes Payable to Others (Schedule 7) | |
| Accounts Receivable | | Income Taxes Payable | |
| | | | |
| Notes Receivable (Schedule 1) | | Other Taxes Payable | |
| Mortgages & Deeds of Trust Owned (Sched. 2) | | | |
| Securities Owned (Schedule 3) | | | |
| Cash Surrender Value of Life Insur. (Sched. 4) | | Loans on Life Insurance (Schedule 4) | |
| Real Estate (Schedule 5) | | Mortgages or Liens on Real Estate (Schedule 6) | |
| Automobiles | | Instalment Contracts Payable | |
| | | | |
| Personal Property | | | |
| | | Other Liabilities (Detail) | |
| Other Assets (Detail) | | | |
| | | | |
| | | | |
| | | TOTAL LIABILITIES | |
| | | NET WORTH | |
| **TOTAL** | | **TOTAL** | |

| ANNUAL INCOME | | ANNUAL EXPENDITURES | | CONTINGENT LIABILITIES | |
|---|---|---|---|---|---|
| Employment Income | | Property Taxes/Assessments | | As Endorser | |
| | | Income and Other Taxes | | As Guarantor | |
| Dividends | | Mortgage Payments & Interest | | On Damage Claims | |
| Interest | | Other Contract Payments | | For Taxes | |
| Rentals | | Insurance | | Other (Detail) | |
| Alimony, child support or separate maintenance (you need not show this income unless you wish us to consider it). | | Living Expense | | | |
| | | Alimony, child support/maint | | | |
| | | Other | | | |
| Other | | | | ☐ Check here if "None" | |
| **TOTAL INCOME** | | **TOTAL EXPENDITURES** | | **TOTAL CONTINGENT LIABILITIES** | |

**SCHEDULE 1** Notes Receivable

| Name of Debtor | Collateral | Payable | Maturity Date | Total Amount Due |
|---|---|---|---|---|
| | | $ per | | |
| | | $ per | | |
| | | $ per | | |
| | | | **TOTAL** | |

**SCHEDULE 2** Mortgages and Deeds of Trust Owned

| Name of Debtor | Type of Property | 1st or 2nd Lien | Value of Property | How Payable | Unpaid Balance |
|---|---|---|---|---|---|
| | | | | $ per | |
| | | | | $ per | |
| | | | | $ per | |
| | | | | $ per | |

FIGURE 5-2 (continued)

**SCHEDULE 3** Securities Owned

| No. Shares or Bond Amount | Description | Title in Name of | How Held Code* | Amount at Which Carried on this Statement | Present Market Value | L–Listed U–Unlisted |
|---|---|---|---|---|---|---|
| | | | | | | |
| | | | | | | |
| | | | | | | |
| | | | | | | |
| | | | | | | |
| | | | | | | |
| | | | | | | |
| | | | | | | |
| | | | **TOTAL** | | | |

**SCHEDULE 4** Life Insurance

| Insured | Face Amount Of Policy | Insurance Company | Beneficiary | Cash Value | Loans |
|---|---|---|---|---|---|
| | | | | | |
| | | | | | |
| | | | | |
| | | | **TOTAL** | | |

**SCHEDULE 5** Real Estate

| Address and Type of Property | Title in Name of | How Held Code* | Monthly Income | Cost / Year Acquired | Present Market Value | Total Balance Owed (Detail in Schedule 6) |
|---|---|---|---|---|---|---|
| | | | | $ | | |
| | | | | Year | | |
| | | | | $ | | |
| | | | | Year | | |
| | | | | $ | | |
| | | | | Year | | |
| | | | | $ | | |
| | | | | Year | | |
| | | | **TOTAL** | | | |

**SCHEDULE 6** Mortgages or Liens on Real Estate

| To Whom Payable | Indicate 1st or 2nd Mortgage | How Payable | Interest Rate | Maturity Date | Balance Owing |
|---|---|---|---|---|---|
| | | $ per | | | |
| | | $ per | | | |
| | | $ per | | | |
| | | $ per | | | |
| | | $ per | | | |

**SCHEDULE 7** Notes Payable

| To Whom | Address | Collateral | Interest Rate | Unpaid Balance |
|---|---|---|---|---|
| | | | | |
| | | | | |
| | | | | |

| *HOW HELD CODES | COMMUNITY PROPERTY | SEPARATE PROPERTY (indicate applicable abbreviation) | | |
|---|---|---|---|---|
| | ALWAYS INDICATE "CP" | "SO"–SINGLE OWNERSHIP | "JT"–JOINT TENANTS | "TIC"–TENANTS IN COMMON |

FIGURE 5-2 (continued)

Have you ever gone through bankruptcy or had a judgment against you? ☐ Yes ☐ No

Are any assets pledged or debts secured except as shown? ☐ Yes ☐ No

Have you made a will? ☐ Yes ☐ No

**YOUR REPRESENTATIONS AND WARRANTIES**

I understand that ________________ is relying on the information in this financial statement (including the designation of my property as separate or community property) in deciding to give or continue the financial accommodation or extension of credit I have requested or received. I promise that this is a true statement of my financial condition as of the date of valuations. You may rely on it as being true and correct until I otherwise notify you in writing. If this statement is not true in any material respect, or if I should die, file for bankruptcy, if any other creditor tries to seize my property, or if any adverse change occurs in my financial condition, at your election any or all of my indebtedness and obligations to you, direct or contingent, shall become immediately due and payable without demand or notice. You may retain and verify this statement. I understand that from time to time you may receive information about me from others and may answer questions and requests from others seeking credit and experience information about me and my relationships with you, but that you will try to protect our confidential relationship in handling other requests, like those from government agencies. If this is a joint financial statement, these representations and warranties are from each of us.

**I HAVE READ, UNDERSTAND AND AGREE TO MAKE THESE REPRESENTATIONS AND WARRANTIES.**

________________ Date

________________ Your Signature

________________ Date

________________ Your Spouse's Signature (if you are requesting the financial accommodation jointly with your spouse)

FIGURE 5-3

# BALANCE SHEET ANALYSIS

**CURRENT RATIO:**

____________ ÷ ____________ = Current Ratio
(Current Assets) (Current Liabilities)

**WORKING CAPITAL:**

____________ – ____________ = Working Capital
(Current Assets) (Current Liabilities)

**"ACID TEST" RATIO:**

____________ ÷ ____________ = Acid Test Ratio
("Quick" Assets) (Current Liabilities)

**NET WORTH:**

____________ – ____________ = $ YOUR NET WORTH
(Total Assets) (Total Liabilities)

**TANGIBLE NET WORTH:**

____________ – ____________ = Tangible Net Worth
(Net Worth) (Intangible Assets)

**DEBT TO WORTH RATIO:**

____________ ÷ ____________ = Debt/Worth Ratio
(Total Debt) (Tangible Net Worth)

**CASH FLOW:**

____________ + ____________ = Cash Flow
(Net Earnings) (Depreciation)

**DEBT SERVICE:**

____________ – ____________ = Dollars Available for Debt Service
(Cash Flow) (Current Portion of) (Long Term Debt)

FIGURE 5-4

# "SPREAD SHEET" FORMS

To properly analyze your financial statements, credit analysts use "spread sheet" forms. These forms facilitate the credit-decision process by summarizing your financial statement parts into the same organized sequence of assets, liabilities, net worth, expenses, sales, cost of goods sold, etc. The numbers are rounded . . . pennies and zeroes eliminated . . . thus $1,900 appears as 1.9, or rounded-up to 2.0, and $100,000. appears as 100.0, etc.

On these spread-sheets, lenders *"properly categorize"* your assets and liabilities and make varying adjustments to show your "corrected" financial position. At the bottom of each spread-sheet are the most commonly employed ratios and measurements lenders use to see how your business MEASURES-UP.

YOUR BEST DEAL has included the "typical" Balance Sheet and Income Statement "spread sheets" many lenders require completed prior to most CREDIT DECISIONS . . . or to CONTINUALLY REVIEW your business' performance, if you are presently borrowing or leasing.

Many businesses internally complete similar spread sheets to facilitate management decision-making processes or simply to make their more complicated financial statements easy to understand. We have included these BLANK FORMS for YOUR USE. You will find it helpful in analyzing your current year financial results . . . and the ease with which you can compare several prior years in the adjoining columns.

FIGURE 5-4 (continued)

# OPERATING STATEMENT

| | | | | | | |
|---|---|---|---|---|---|---|
| 1 | Net Sales | | | | | 1 |
| 2 | Cost of Goods Sold | | | | | 2 |
| 3 | Gross Profit | | | | | 3 |
| 4 | General and Administrative Expenses | | | | | 4 |
| 5 | Executive Salaries | | | | | 5 |
| 6 | Interest | | | | | 6 |
| 7 | Bad Debts | | | | | 7 |
| 8 | | | | | | 8 |
| 9 | | | | | | 9 |
| 10 | | | | | | 10 |
| 11 | Total Expenses | | | | | 11 |
| 12 | Operating Profit | | | | | 12 |
| 13 | Other Income | | | | | 13 |
| 14 | | | | | | 14 |
| 15 | Other Charges | | | | | 15 |
| 16 | | | | | | 16 |
| 17 | Net Profit before Income Taxes | | | | | 17 |
| 18 | Income Taxes | | | | | 18 |
| 19 | Net Profit | | | | | 19 |
| 20 | Beginning Surplus or Net Worth | | | | | 20 |
| 21 | Dividends or Withdrawals | | | | | 21 |
| 22 | | | | | | 22 |
| 23 | | | | | | 23 |
| 24 | | | | | | 24 |
| 25 | | | | | | 25 |
| 26 | | | | | | 26 |
| 27 | | | | | | 27 |
| 28 | Ending Surplus or Net Worth | | | | | 28 |
| 29 | WORKING CAPITAL RECONCILEMENT | | | | | 29 |
| 30 | Working Capital Beginning | | | | | 30 |
| 31 | Funds Provided: | | | | | 31 |
| 32 | Net Profit | | | | | 32 |
| 33 | Depreciation | | | | | 33 |
| 34 | | | | | | 34 |
| 35 | | | | | | 35 |
| 36 | | | | | | 36 |
| 37 | | | | | | 37 |
| 38 | | | | | | 38 |
| 39 | Funds Applied: | | | | | 39 |
| 40 | Dividends or Withdrawals | | | | | 40 |
| 41 | Fixed Assets | | | | | 41 |
| 42 | | | | | | 42 |
| 43 | | | | | | 43 |
| 44 | | | | | | 44 |
| 45 | | | | | | 45 |
| 46 | | | | | | 46 |
| 47 | Working Capital -- Ending | | | | | 47 |
| 48 | RATIOS | | | | | 48 |
| 49 | Current Ratio | | | | | 49 |
| 50 | Cash and Rec. ÷ Current Debt | | | | | 50 |
| 51 | Receivables ÷ Av. Days Sales | | | | | 51 |
| 52 | Inventory Supply (Days) | | | | | 52 |
| 53 | Tangible Net Worth to Total Debt | | | | | 53 |
| 54 | Fixed Assets to Tangible Net Worth | | | | | 54 |
| 55 | Net Profit to Sales | | | | | 55 |
| 56 | Net Profit to Net Worth | | | | | 56 |
| 57 | Net Sales to Net Worth | | | | | 57 |
| 58 | | | | | | 58 |

FIGURE 5-4 (continued)

# BALANCE SHEET

| | ASSETS | | | | | |
|---|---|---|---|---|---|---|
| 1 | Cash | | | | | 1 |
| 2 | | | | | | 2 |
| 3 | Notes Receivable | | | | | 3 |
| 4 | Account Receivable | | | | | 4 |
| 5 | Less Reserve for Bad Debts | | | | | 5 |
| 6 | Inventory | | | | | 6 |
| 7 | | | | | | 7 |
| 8 | | | | | | 8 |
| 9 | | | | | | 9 |
| 10 | | | | | | 10 |
| 11 | Prepaid Items | | | | | 11 |
| 12 | Current Assets | | | | | 12 |
| 13 | Land and Buildings | | | | | 13 |
| 14 | Machinery and Equipment | | | | | 14 |
| 15 | | | | | | 15 |
| 16 | Less Reserve for Depreciation | | | | | 16 |
| 17 | | | | | | 17 |
| 18 | Miscellaneous Receivables | | | | | 18 |
| 19 | | | | | | 19 |
| 20 | Investments | | | | | 20 |
| 21 | | | | | | 21 |
| 22 | | | | | | 22 |
| 23 | | | | | | 23 |
| 24 | Deferred and Miscellaneous Assets | | | | | 24 |
| 25 | Intangibles | | | | | 25 |
| 26 | Total Assets | | | | | 26 |
| 27 | LIABILITIES | | | | | 27 |
| 28 | Notes Payable to Banks | | | | | 28 |
| 29 | | | | | | 29 |
| 30 | Accounts Payable | | | | | 30 |
| 31 | Accruals | | | | | 31 |
| 32 | Income Taxes | | | | | 32 |
| 33 | | | | | | 33 |
| 34 | | | | | | 34 |
| 35 | | | | | | 35 |
| 36 | | | | | | 36 |
| 37 | Current Portion Term Debt | | | | | 37 |
| 38 | Current Liabilities | | | | | 38 |
| 39 | | | | | | 39 |
| 40 | | | | | | 40 |
| 41 | | | | | | 41 |
| 42 | Total Liabilities | | | | | 42 |
| 43 | | | | | | 43 |
| 44 | | | | | | 44 |
| 45 | | | | | | 45 |
| 46 | | | | | | 46 |
| 47 | | | | | | 47 |
| 48 | | | | | | 48 |
| 49 | Net Worth | | | | | 49 |
| 50 | Total Liabilities and Net Worth | | | | | 50 |
| 51 | Working Capital | | | | | 51 |
| 52 | Tangible Net Worth | | | | | 52 |
| 53 | Net Sales | | | | | 53 |
| 54 | Depreciation | | | | | 54 |
| 55 | Profit, Before or After Taxes | | | | | 55 |
| 56 | Dividends or Withdrawals | | | | | 56 |
| 57 | Contingent Liabilities | | | | | 57 |
| 58 | | | | | | 58 |

FIGURE 5-5

# MODEL FINANCIAL STATEMENTS

We have prepared "model" BALANCE SHEET and INCOME STATEMENTS for your guidance. These formats are a composite of several CPA prepared reports which we feel represent the best appearance and are most USEFUL for REFERENCE . . . *for you* . . . *for the lenders*.

Businesses have account classifications or categories of assets, liabilities and expense items which are peculiar to only their business. These differences will have to be worked into our suggested layouts, as suitable and necessary. The purpose of financial statements are to be concise . . . not overly condensed . . . and informative. You may be perfectly happy with your present statements. However, if they always CREATE questions . . . you should re-assess them to find out WHY.

If you are preparing your own statement . . . either for interim and/or internal purposes . . . or in full, including fiscal year-endings and for tax returns . . . we think you will find these suggested formats helpful. You may wish to have your present bookkeeper or accountant incorporate some of the suggestions. You may choose to require a newly selected bookkeeping service or accounting firm provide you with all or part of the suggested formats.

We particularly draw your attention to the two yearly column headings . . . the YEAR-ENDING being reported. . . AND . . . the comparative figures from the PRIOR year-ending. If your present statements do not have prior year comparative figures . . . you will find this column a useful addition. They assist in your own review and management decision . . . and they expedite lender analysis.

You should also give consideration to placing "NOTES" to your account entries . . . when more explanation is appropriate. These notes will definitely reduce or STOP "20 QUESTIONS". (Refer to our section on NOTES TO FINANCIAL STATEMENTS following our EXAMPLE -- WORKING CAPITAL FLOW STATEMENT).

FIGURE 5-5 (continued)

VERI-RITE MANUFACTURING COMPANY, INC.

Balance Sheet
December 31, 1979 and 1978

*(Some accountants specify "For the Years-Ending" . . . "For the Periods Ending" . . . "For the Twelve Months Ending December 31, 1979 and 1978").*

| ASSETS | 1979 | 1978 |
|---|---|---|
| CURRENT ASSETS: | | |
| Cash . . . . . . . . . . . . . . . . . . . . . . . . . . | $ | $ |
| Receivables (Notes 1 and ___): | | |
| Accounts, Pledged as Collateral for Note Payable *(If an item appears in more than one note explanation, enter "Note" numbers. If Accounts Receivable are financed, this entry is proper way to so indicate)* | | |
| Refundable income taxes . . . . . . . . . . . . . . . | ______ | ______ |
| Less allowance for doubtful accounts . . . . . . . | ______ | ______ |
| Inventories: | | |
| Finished Goods . . . . . . . . . . . . . . . . . . . | | |
| Work in Process . . . . . . . . . . . . . . . . . . . | | |
| Raw Materials . . . . . . . . . . . . . . . . . . . . | | |
| *(If inventories are pledged, add Notes, to explain how, to whom).* | | |
| Prepaid Expenses . . . . . . . . . . . . . . . . . . | ______ | ______ |
| Total current assets . . . . . . . . . . . . . | ______ | ______ |
| Long term notes and interest receivable (Notes __ and __) . . . . . . . . . . . . . . . . . | | |
| Investments (Note __) . . . . . . . . . . . . . . . . | | |
| Land, equipment and leasehold improvements, at cost less accumulated depreciation and amortization (Notes ___ and __) . . . . . . . . . . . . . . . . . | | |
| Other assets (Note __) . . . . . . . . . . . . . . . | | |
| Intangible Assets . . . . . . . . . . . . . . . . . . . | | |
| Membership in ______________ . . . . . . . . . . . | | |
| Organization expense, net of amortization (Note __) . . . . . . . . . . . . . . . . . . . . . . | ______ | ______ |
| TOTAL . . . . . . . . . . . . | $______ | $______ |

FIGURE 5-5 (continued)

VERI-RITE MANUFACTURING COMPANY, INC.

Balance Sheet
December 31, 1979 and 1978

LIABILITIES AND STOCKHOLDER'S EQUITY

| | | |
|---|---|---|
| CURRENT LIABILITIES: | | |
| Note Payable (Notes __and__) . . . . . . . . . . . | $ | $ |
| _____Bank, Collateralized by accounts receivable and inventories . . . . . . . . . . . . | | |
| _____Bank, unsecured . . . . . . . . . . . . . . | | |
| Current instalments of long-term debt (Note__). . | | |
| Accounts payable and Accrued Expenses . . . . . . | | |
| Trade . . . . . . . . . . . . . . . . . . . . . . | | |
| Sales Tax . . . . . . . . . . . . . . . . . . . . | | |
| Payroll Taxes . . . . . . . . . . . . . . . . . . | | |
| Bonuses (Note __) . . . . . . . . . . . . . . . . | | |
| Income Taxes . . . . . . . . . . . . . . . . . . . | ________ | ________ |
| Total current liabilities . . . . . . . . . . | ________ | ________ |
| LONG-TERM DEBT (Notes __and__) . . . . . . . . . . | | |
| Notes Payable *(collateralized by__)* . . . . . . . | | |
| Capitalized long-term lease obligations . . . . . | ________ | ________ |
| Less current maturities . . . . . . . . . . . . . . | ________ | ________ |
| Long-term debt, net . . . . . . . . . . . . . . | ________ | ________ |
| STOCKHOLDER'S EQUITY: (Notes __and__) . . . . . . | | |
| Common stock, $___ par value; authorized . . . . | | |
| _____shares; issued and outstanding . . . . . . | | |
| _____shares . . . . . . . . . . . . . . . . . . | | |
| Additional paid - in capital . . . . . . . . . . . | | |
| Retained earnings . . . . . . . . . . . . . . . . . | | |
| Less cost of ___shares in treasury . . . . . . . | ________ | ________ |
| Total stockholder's equity . . . . . . . . . | ________ | ________ |
| Commitments and Contingent Liabilities (Note __) | ________ | ________ |
| Subsequent event(s) (Note __) *(If these entries are used they do not include dollar amounts, except in "Notes").* | | |
| TOTAL . . . . . . . . . | $________ | $________ |

See notes to financial statements.

FIGURE 5-5 (continued)

VERI-RITE MANUFACTURING COMPANY, INC.

Statement of Income and Retained Earnings
Years ended December 31, 1979 and 1978

| | 1979 | 1978 |
|---|---|---|
| NET SALES | $ | $ |
| Cost of sales (Note __) . . . . . . . . . . . . . . . | | |
| Gross Profit . . . . . . . . . . . . . . . . . . | | |
| OPERATING EXPENSES: | | |
| Warehouse and shipping expenses . . . . . . . . . . | | |
| Direct selling expenses . . . . . . . . . . . . . . | | |
| Other selling expenses . . . . . . . . . . . . . . | | |
| Office expenses . . . . . . . . . . . . . . . . . | | |
| Executive management expenses . . . . . . . . . . . | | |
| General and financial expenses . . . . . . . . . . | | |
| *(These general categories are broken-out in the back of the financial statement, after the Notes. If there is room . . . or no expense allocations between departments or functions . . . expenses are itemized below OPERATING EXPENSES).* | | |
| OPERATING PROFIT . . . . . . . . . . . . . . . . . | | |
| OTHER INCOME (DEDUCTIONS): | | |
| Interest income . . . . . . . . . . . . . . . . . . | | |
| Bonuses and profit-share deductions . . . . . . . . | | |
| Miscellaneous income, net . . . . . . . . . . . . . | | |
| Interest Expense (if not included under G and A) | | |
| Earnings before income taxes . . . . . . . . . . | | |
| INCOME TAXES (Notes __ and __) . . . . . . . . . . | | |
| Current: | | |
| Federal . . . . . . . . . . . . . . . . . . . . . | | |
| State . . . . . . . . . . . . . . . . . . . . . . | | |
| Deferred: | | |
| Federal, net . . . . . . . . . . . . . . . . . . | | |
| State, net . . . . . . . . . . . . . . . . . . . | | |
| Net earnings (or, Net Income) (Note __). . | | |
| RETAINED EARNINGS, BEGINNING OF YEAR . . . . . . . | | |
| *(Plus or minus exchanges of capital stock for fixed assets, over or under par value)* | | |
| RETAINED EARNINGS, END OF YEAR . . . . . . . . . . | $ | $ |
| Earnings per common shares . . . . . . . . . . . | $ | $ |

See notes to financial statements

*These statements are for corporations. Proprietorships and partnerships can utilize all except the stock, equity and retained earnings portions . . . replaced by partnership accounts, drawing and NET WORTH.*

FIGURE 5-6

# "FLOW-OF-FUNDS" STATEMENTS

There are two statement forms accountants generally use to show the net flow of funds INTO a business from ALL SOURCES . . . and the flow of funds OUT OF THE BUSINESS.

- ➤ Working Capital Flow Statement
- ➤ Cash-Flow Statement

- WORKING CAPITAL FLOW STATEMENT

Many CPA firms prefer the working capital flow statement. This statement lists the CHANGES in NON-CURRENT ITEMS . . . which require either the GENERATION or USE of WORKING CAPITAL. This form of summarizing the use of funds is also called the STATEMENT OF CHANGES IN FINANCIAL STATEMENT.

The Working Capital "Flow" statement shows CHANGES of SOURCES and USES of funds affecting *NET WORKING CAPITAL* available to the business during the accounting period of the statement.

Bankers prefer the Working Capital basis because they often *require* term loan borrowers maintain a *prescribed* MINIMUM NET WORKING CAPITAL.

On the next page, YOUR BEST DEAL presents a "typical" WORKING CAPITAL FLOW STATEMENT for your guidance. Our statement has many of the entries common to businesses . . . but there are many other possibilities which are peculiar to certain industries or commercial businesses . . . which may be inserted when appropriate.

- CASH-FLOW STATEMENT

YOUR BEST DEAL prefers this format . . . *especially* for small to medium-sized businesses who are "upgrading" the appearance and completeness of their financial statements. We also like this CASH-FLOW STATEMENT because it WORKS BETTER as a MANAGEMENT INFORMATION TOOL.

- ➤ Illustrates the business' *ability* to generate cash.
- ➤ Summarizes clearly where the money CAME FROM and HOW it was UTILIZED.
- ➤ Assists in forecasting future cash requirements . . . ability to handle financing . . . facilitates CASH BUDGET preparation.

The key to CASH-FLOW STATEMENT preparation involves conversion of NET INCOME . . . (computed on an accrual basis) . . . to net income on a CASH BASIS. You can *look* at our "typical" CASH-FLOW STATEMENT appearing on the NEXT PAGE . . . *and see how the "adjustments" section readily accomplishes this requirement.*

FIGURE 5-6 (continued)

## EXAMPLE

# WORKING CAPITAL FLOW STATEMENT

VERI-RITE MANUFACTURING COMPANY, INC.

Statement of Changes in Financial Position
Years Ended December 31, 19___ and 19___ .

| | 19___ | 19___ |
|---|---|---|
| SOURCES OF WORKING CAPITAL *(or, Source of Funds)*: | | |
| Operations: | | |
| Net Earnings *(or, Net Income)* . . . . . . . . . . | $ | $ |
| Items which do not use *(provide)* working capital: | | |
| Depreciation . . . . . . . . . . . . . . . . . . . . | | |
| Amortization*(of leasehold improvements, trademarks, etc.)* . . . . . . . . . . . . . . . . . . | | |
| Gain *(or Loss)* on sale of equipment . . . . . . . | | |
| Provision for deferred income taxes . . . . . . . | | |
| Working capital provided by operation . . . . . . | | |
| Additions to long-term debt . . . . . . . . . . | | |
| APPLICATION OF FUNDS: | | |
| Purchase of equipment . . . . . . . . . . . . . . . . | | |
| Current instalments and repayment of long-term debt | | |
| Deposits . . . . . . . . . . . . . . . . . . . . . | | |
| Additional investment in . . . *(indicate investment)* | | |
| Purchase of leasehold improvements . . . . . . . . | | |
| Retirement of _____ shares . . . . . . . . . . . | | |
| INCREASE IN WORKING CAPITAL . . . . . . . . . . . . | | |
| WORKING CAPITAL, BEGINNING OF YEAR . . . . . . . . | | |
| WORKING CAPITAL, END OF YEAR . . . . . . . . . . . | $ | $ |
| CHANGES IN COMPONENTS OF WORKING CAPITAL: | | |
| Increase (decrease) in current assets: | | |
| Cash . . . . . . . . . . . . . . . . . . . . . . . | $ | |
| Customer receivables . . . . . . . . . . . . . . . . | | |
| Refundable income taxes . . . . . . . . . . . . . . | | |
| Inventory . . . . . . . . . . . . . . . . . . . . . | | |
| Prepaid expenses . . . . . . . . . . . . . . . . . . | | |
| *(List ALL other increases or decreases in C/A)* . | | |
| Increase (decrease) in current liabilities: | | |
| Notes payable . . . . . . . . . . . . . . . . . . . | $ | |
| Accounts payable . . . . . . . . . . . . . . . . . . | | |
| Accrued expenses . . . . . . . . . . . . . . . . . . | | |
| Current maturities of long-term debt . . . . . . . | | |
| Income taxes . . . . . . . . . . . . . . . . . . . . | | |
| *(List ALL other increases or decreases in C/L)* . | | |
| Increase (decrease) in working capital . . . . . . . | $ | $ |

See accompanying notes to financial statements.

FIGURE 5-6 (continued)

## EXAMPLE

# CASH-FLOW STATEMENT

VERI-RITE MANUFACTURING COMPANY, INC.

Cash - Flow Statement
For the Year Ending December 31, 19___

| | | | |
|---|---|---|---|
| Beginning cash balance (January 1, 19__) . . . . | | | $ 60,000 |
| Cash provided by operations: | | | |
| Net income . . . . . . . . . . . . . . . . . . . . | | $144,000 | |
| Adjustments to convert income from accrual to a cash basis: | | | |
| Depreciation . . . . . . . . . . . . . . . . | $ 36,500 | | |
| Increase in prepaid insurance . . . . . | (1,000) | | |
| Increase in prepaid rent . . . . . . . . . | ( 750) | | |
| Provision for bad debts . . . . . . . . . | 1,200 | | |
| Increase in inventories . . . . . . . . . | (9,000) | | |
| Decrease in receivables . . . . . . . . . | 38,000 | | |
| Decrease in payables . . . . . . . . . . . | (5,200) | | |
| Loss on sale of fixed assets . . . . . . | 1,500 | | |
| Net adjustment to income . . . . . . . | | 61,250 | |
| Cash generated by current operations . . . . . . | | $205,250 | |
| Nonrecurring sources of cash: | | | |
| Sale of fixed assets . . . . . . . . . . . | $ 6,000 | | |
| Sale of short-term notes . . . . . . . . . | 6,500 | | |
| Total other sources . . . . . . . . | | $ 12,500 | |
| Total cash provided, 19__ . . . . | | | 217,750 |
| Total cash . . . . . . . . . . . . . . . . . . . . . . | | | $277,750 |
| Cash used for: | | | |
| Increase in sinking fund . . . . . . . . | $ 19,000 | | |
| Payment on short-term bank notes . . . | 40,000 | | |
| Payment on long-term notes . . . . . . . | 30,000 | | |
| Purchase of land . . . . . . . . . . . . | 105,000 | | |
| Payment of dividends (19__) . . . . . . . | 34,000 | | |
| Total cash used during year . . . . | | | $228,000 |
| Ending cash balance (December 31, 19__) . . . . | | | $ 49.750 |

FIGURE 5-7

# NOTES TO FINANCIAL STATEMENTS

Summarized below are the typical "notes" which CPA firms traditionally include in the financial report, immediately following the Statements of Changes in Financial Position. These notes are often very extensive and we suggest the businesses who are not using a CPA or Public Accountant simply CONSIDER the usefulness or desirability of including these "notes" in their internally or bookkeeping service prepared statements. Some of the comments and explanations are extremely useful to credit analysts. In many cases, they will eliminate "20 questions" and expedite credit approval.

The reader should bear in mind there are a number of acceptable formats used to present "notes". We are presenting . . . in the usual order they appear . . . and comment only briefly as to content of "note" entries.

## EXAMPLE -- NOTES

SUMMARY OF SIGNIFICANT ACCOUNTING POLICIES

- ➤ Inventories -- How inventories are stated . . . LIFO, last-in, first-out . . . FIFO, first-in, first-out, etc.
- ➤ Depreciation -- Method(s) of depreciation.
- ➤ Amortization -- Covers "write-off" of trade-marks, organization expense, leaseholds . . . over what period of years.
- ➤ Income Taxes and/or Investment Tax Credits -- Generally covers how ITC is used to reduce income taxes . . . using "flow-through" method, etc.

CHANGE(S) IN ACCOUNTING PRINCIPLE(S)

- ➤ Inventory Cost Determinations -- Changes from FIFO to LIFO . . in valuing inventories . . . reasons for change . . . when changed . . . effects of change.

"OTHER NOTES" -- *(Appearing by captioned category, in their usual order)*

- ➤ Receivables Summarized -- When receivables consist of several types . . . a *dollar amount* summary appears under this note.
- ➤ Inventories Summarized -- Raw materials, finished goods and supplies . . . and the related *dollar amounts* are indicated.

FIGURE 5-7 (continued)

- Investments -- Marketable securities, land or building purchases, uses of cash surrender value of life insurance pledged, included in sale of assets . . . are summarized, including dollar amounts.

- Land, Equipment and Leasehold Improvements -- An explanation of lives in years . . . and *dollar amounts* for each are listed. This is followed by total amount of accumulated depreciation . . . deducted from the total asset values.

- Notes Payable -- Notes are summarized as to *dollar amounts* . . terms . . . interest rates . . . due dates.

  Bankers Acceptances, or similar payable instruments, often are included in summary, with Notes Payable.

- Income Taxes -- Differences or changes in computation . . . State and Federal broken-out . . . Investment Tax Credit . . . New jobs credit . . . and other income tax adjustments are summarized by plus-or-minus *dollar amounts. The last year-ending and prior year are presented in dollar amount columns.*

- Employees' Pension and Profit-Sharing Plans -- An explanation of the plan(s) . . . . company and employee contributions . . . employees qualified . . . actuarial value . . . *dollar amounts* involved. This summary is often presented in narrative form.

- Commitments and Contingent Liabilities -- Joint ventures are summarized . . . with dates . . . dollar amounts of any commitments . . . lease or rent expenses are broken-out for future years. Possible contingent liabilities of guaranties are outlined as to scope . . . length of liability, etc.

- Lease Financing -- Long-term . . . (and generally non-cancellable) . . . lease commitments are outlined . . . in *dollar amounts* . . . *length of terms* . . . *rates* . . . broken-down into categories, such as Real Property and Equipment. These categories are usually listed *by year* . . . indicating the amounts due . . . extending out as far as the lease term agreements.

- Letters of Credit -- Amounts . . . uses . . . expiration dates and name of source.

FIGURE 5-7 (continued)

- Stockholder's Equity -- Sometimes a narrative explanation is inserted to explain equity positions . . . names and percentages . . . sales of equity positions or other stockholder changes are outlined.

- Bonuses Payable -- Details of bonuses being accrued are provided . . particularly those involving officers and share issuances. The number of shares . . . agreed price . . dates accrued . . . conditions of, when and how paid . . . also including cash bonuses.

- Related Party Transactions -- This category usually outlines officer or related parties providing guaranties of Notes Payable . . . or other company obligations.

- Subsequent Events -- There are events that sometimes occur shortly after the accounting/fiscal period of the financial statement . . . which should be revealed to anyone relying upon the statement for information. These events generally relate to sale of company assets . . . in full or part . . . transfer of licenses . . . changes in operations or other factors about which outsiders should be informed . . . in considering the statements in hand.

RELATED SCHEDULES; *(Relating to "Notes" inserted in the financial statement Balance Sheet or Income Statement):*

Sometimes the categories shown in the Income Statement . . . (or, Statement of Income and Retained Earnings) . . . are consolidations of more extensive accounts or expense categories . . . which require more explicit "breakdown".

Examples include the general categories of "Warehouse and Shipping Expenses" . . . "Direct Selling Expenses" . . . "Other Selling Expenses" . . . "Office Expenses" . . . "Executive Management Expenses" . . . "General and Financial Expenses".

These "general" categories will vary from company to company . . . but a good Schedule of Operating Expenses . . . will break-down the generalized expense groupings to explain the summary totals appearing in the Income Statement. For instance, each summarized entry may consist of salaries, payroll taxes, rent, depreciation, auto expense, truck or delivery expense, advertising, travel and entertainment . . . literally dozens of expense items . . . which are allocated to various departments or company functions.

# 6

# GAMES LENDERS PLAY

Have you ever paid off a car, home improvement, or equipment loan months or even years ahead of time? Were you shocked to learn how much in finance charges your lender claimed to have earned prior to your early pay-off? Was it possible—or even legal—you might have asked, for the lender to give such a meager "interest refund"? You used their money for a shorter time than originally agreed; how could they justify their apparently disproportionate earnings?

Did you protest, questioning the lender's integrity? Did you demand an explanation? Were you given an understandable, satisfactory answer? Chances are, if you took issue with their refund, you were told about the rule of 78ths. Just as likely, after they explained this rule, your doubts continued. There are reasons business people remain skeptical after encountering the rule of 78ths and the lender's ensuing explanations.

Many in banking and finance are incapable of providing an explanation understandable to business people. This is particularly true of lender people on the clerical level, commonly first contacted on telephone inquiry. However, it is not unusual to find officer-level finance people equally tongue-tied. Their difficulty in providing an explanation is not necessarily from knowing too little but too much.

Business people can relate to principal, interest, and amortization tables, as seen in home mortgages. The lender's interest earnings are the greatest in the first month of the loan term. As the principal payments reduce the amount originally loaned, the amount of interest being earned declines. But when the loan officer starts explaining the rule of 78ths, using the sum of the digits in relation to a refund, business people may think about acceleration, as in depreciation. There is an understandable presumption that the rule may be founded on a prepayment-penalty theory. The fact is, the rule of 78th refund tables, properly applied, will produce a remarkably accurate answer as to interest earned or the amount of original finance charge to be refunded.

The percentage refunded leaves the lender with finance charges very close to what their interest earnings would have been at the same number of elapsed months to point of early prepayment. There are no built-in penalties when the refund is computed properly, based on the correct number of elapsed months. (See Fig. 6-1.)

## RULE OF 78THS: LICENSE TO STEAL?

Simply put, the rule of 78ths works very much like amortization of an interest-bearing loan. The interest charge is the largest when the loan is first extended—and, incidentally, when the lender's risk is the greatest. This rule is also known as the 78ths method or sum-of-the-digits refund method. It is the standard formula used by most banks and finance companies to determine the amount of finance charges which remain unearned if a loan or contract is paid off earlier than the original agreed term.

Bear in mind that the 78ths method is used to determine a refund whenever the finance charge is added on to the original loan or unpaid contract balance after a down payment. The rule is employed when a borrower prepays any contract containing such noninterest finance charges. Coincidentally, the lenders usually program their earnings in the rule of 78ths throughout the contract's term. There are variations to this, differing from lender to lender, which is one game lenders play and which we will explain further.

The more knowledgeable bankers and finance company officers may mumble and stumble when queried about their refund policy because of their familiarity with how the rule is bent. These upper-level people are intimately privy to their company or bank refund policy. Wouldn't you be hesitant or embarrassed, trying to explain a refund that was intentionally—"by policy"—hundreds of dollars short of the correct amount? Think it doesn't happen? It does, with regularity! And short refunds are not confined to the smaller finance companies. There are major, big-name companies who make a practice of increasing their "sundry income" by shortchanging those who prepay loans or conditional-sale contracts!

Some bank and finance company officers are uncomfortable with their refund policy because they know how tightly their organization interprets and controls the calculations. That is, top management may dictate very stringent rules about counting the elapsed months. In some cases, this may involve counting off a full month if the customer's payoff check comes in one single day into the next month.

(The lender should begin counting months with the day and month they put out their money on a finance charge-type loan or contract.) That isn't bad at all compared to other lenders' refund-policy calculations. For example, even in this mild case, the lender makes 2½% to 3% on the earned charges.

Tangible example: Assuming an original finance charge of $25,000.00 on a 60-month contract prepaid in the ninth month, the refund should be 72.46%, or $18,115.00. If the lender refunds by counting another elapsed month, 69.67%, or $17,417.50, is rebated: a difference of $697.50—not bad for a single day, if the lender plays it that way!

Now, ask yourself this: What if the lender decides to "accidentally or on purpose" use the *eleventh* elapsed-month column on the refund chart? The percentage of the original charge to be refunded becomes 66.94%. That's a refund of $16,735.00—$1,380.00 *less* than should have been returned to the borrower.

Rare case? Not at all! How would you even know if the close-out calculation was correctly computed? As a borrower, do you have a rule of 78ths refund chart? You do now—right at the end of this chapter!

Unfortunately for those of you who are able to prepay your loan or contract, the lender's taking one or more extra elapsed months is only the tip of the iceberg. We are going to show you the rest of that iceberg in explicit detail. What's more, we'll explain what to do if you should bump into it! First, to assist you in grasping the procedures, we will recount some fundamentals.

This refund or rebate calculation method, often not understood by business people, is frequently bent, distorted, and improperly applied by the lenders. It is used to extract untold dollars from American businesses every year! How many dollars, it is impossible to determine. This is a secret, buried within the lender organizations, who not only permit the abuses but actually encourage their employees to learn how to shortchange borrowers on loan closeouts! Short rebates are purposely perpetrated on unsuspecting borrowers all the time—by some of the most prominent equipment finance companies in the lending business!

## Add-On or Discount—It's Not Interest

Because your finance charge was stated in dollars, not in terms of interest or percent interest, it's an "add-on" finance charge. This charge is added to your unpaid cash balance, after down payment on a contract. In the case of a loan, it's added to the amount loaned. If a discount rate was employed, the finance charge was deducted from the loan proceeds before you received the money. The charges were still stated in dollars—and if you prepay, a portion is unearned and should be rebated by the 78ths method. There are variances from state to state, but in consumer-type loans and some kinds of commercial financing, the simple interest equivalent of the add-on or discount rate *must be separately stated.* This has become known as the annual percentage rate, or A.P.R.

### A.P.R.—That's True Interest

A.P.R. has become familiar to most people because of the Federal truth-in-lending laws enacted in 1969. It is mentioned in bold print in automobile, motor home, and small truck financing, which commonly use add-on rates. There are numerous consumer protection laws, both state and federal, requiring A.P.R. to be clearly stated. We will not cover these matters in this commercial financing guidebook. The point is, in most situations involving commercial-type financing—conditional sale contracts, loans on equipment, and leases to acquire equipment—the A.P.R. is *not* separately stated, nor is it required to be separately stated. That means it is up to each business person to find out what the A.P.R. is from the add-on or discount rate quoted.

Getting back to the refund calculation, understand the A.P.R. has nothing to do with calculating your rebate. A.P.R. relates only to the equivalent yield of the dollar charges added on at the time the loan is funded. To obtain the desired yield, the lender selects an add-on or discount rate that will provide the desired interest earnings. If the equivalent of, say, 18% simple interest is added on to the unpaid balance, the rule of 78ths percentages insure that interest rate will be earned on the investment, no matter when the loan is closed out.

### THE LENDER GIVETH—AND TAKETH AWAY!

Show the lenders a loosely written regulation, such as how and when to employ the rule of 78ths, and I'll show you abuses. When it comes to rebating unearned finance charges, explicit regulations and formulas range from nonexistent to vague, depending on various state laws. At best, those states that require a rebate of any kind have regulations with large loopholes. That's the way it is in commercial financing and leasing.

Therefore, what appears to be your best deal going in may not stay that way. If you are able to prepay and literally get ripped off on the refund, your low best-deal rate can evaporate! And remember, whenever you consolidate loans or refinance, a closeout calculation is made on the old loans to determine rebates. The lenders may get you on these closeouts even more readily. Your attention is not on that aspect, it's on getting new money, refinancing, or alleviating a heavy payment situation. The calculations are not brought to your attention. Often you may not even suspect being shortchanged!

We are going to tell you, in advance, what to do going into and out of these deals: how to calculate the correct amount of unearned finance charges, what tricks and subterfuges the lenders may resort to, and how to straighten them out if you are shortchanged.

**What to Do Going In**

Let's assume you have already negotiated your best deal as far as rate and terms are concerned. Let's assume your credit has been approved, perhaps by more than one lender. They want your business!

The chosen lender provides all the documents for your signature. As usual, there is considerable fine print. Look for a provision, clause, or section dealing with prepayment or rebates. Good luck! Chances are, no such provision exists. Why?

As far as I know at the time of this writing, in most states, if not all, there are *no* legal requirements compelling a commercial lender to state in writing a method of rebating—or, for that matter, if any rebate will be made under any circumstances!

Some bank and finance contracts now read something like this: "*NOTICE TO BUYER*: Under the state law regulating installment sales, you have certain rights, among them, the right to pay off the full amount due in advance and to obtain a partial rebate of the financing charge." Does that sound a little vague? Try to find even that much promise in a commercial loan contract, using finance charges rather than a stated interest rate!

If you have the slightest intention or possibility of prepaying an installment contract or a loan containing finance charges, we recommend you consider going over these "hurdles":

*First hurdle:* Get the lender to do one of two things:

1. Have the lender insert our recommended provisions (outlined below) in the body of the contract; or
2. Have an authorized lending manager or officer provide you with a separate letter—on the lender's letterhead or in the form of an addendum, cross-referenced to the original documents—containing our recommended provisions.

Do not accept verbal assurances. Do not accept even written assurances from lender representatives who are not managers or officers.

*Second hurdle:* Get the lender to see it *your* way and do it *our* way! No matter how it is done—in the contract, a letter, or an addendum—here is the essence of the desired written assurance:

". . . in the event of prepayment of the loan (or contract) balance, lender will compute a rebate of the unearned finance charges, using the rule of 78ths method, and deduct the unearned finance charges from the gross balance due lender at the time loan is prepaid."

In addition, have the lender define any charges that he will consider nonrefundable or that will be added back to the closeout balance. Why? Because even under consumer protection laws, which usually do not apply to commercial loans, lenders are permitted to charge back certain acquisition costs and fees.

Of course, they cannot be expected to refund fees for such things as appraisals, document preparation, searching public records

(UCC filing search and county recorder files, for instance), or certain legal fees for setting up a complex transaction, etc.

All lenders have acquisition costs, and justifiably so, to cover the normal, explainable costs of setting up the loan or contract. If a lender does not have the opportunity to earn the intended finance charges—if you contract for, say, sixty months and prepay after twelve months—the lender did incur costs of acquiring the transaction. These include credit search, documentation, clerical and accounting costs, and a certain amount of overhead just to be there with money to lend. An early closeout causes repetition of these costs at closer intervals than anticipated. In all fairness, lenders are generally entitled to reasonable acquisition costs. Now, however, we are talking about the rest of that iceberg.

## Acquisition Costs: How Much?

Some lenders, without hesitation, will add hundreds or even thousands of dollars in acquisition costs! If you do not detect that you are being shortchanged, or if you fail to complain, that lender has just increased his interest earnings or sundry income dramatically.

What is reasonable? This is a tough question. Generalizations can be unfair to you or the lender. Each situation is different; so tailor your written requirements to our suggestions. The important thing for each of you is to get this matter out on the table. You are entitled to be informed. It is, or should be, a matter of open negotiation, not a surprise the lender can spring on you when you are fortunate enough to prepay or unfortunate enough to have to refinance!

ACQUISITION COST GUIDELINES Consider the circumstances of your particular loan or sales contract. Was it a routine transaction, not large dollars in relation to your usual borrowings? How many and how complex were the documents? Did the transaction arise from a simple referral from your vendor to the lender? Was the credit decision easy—perhaps because you are a repeat customer or one of excellent credit standing? Considering these relative circumstances, all of which indicate an inexpensive loan or contract to acquire, the acquisition cost can be eliminated or kept to a reasonable minimum. In this context, a reasonable minimum acquisition fee should not exceed $500.

At this stage of your negotiations, the lender is presumably eager to complete the transaction. He is more likely to make contractual concessions to finalize the deal than if you attempt to arbitrate a year or so later when you announce your early prepayment of the extended terms originally granted.

"TIME LIMIT" THE ACQUISITION COST Another way to negotiate a minimal or zero acquisition cost is to work out a time limit that spells out the decreasing charges the lender will impose. For instance, if the original term is, say, sixty months, negotiate a loan acquisition cost if prepaid in twelve months, twenty-four months, and thirty-six months, decreasing each year. Perhaps you can stipulate that after the second or third year, the lender will waive all acquisition costs except certain fees.

The point is, you must nail down the intended acquisition charge in advance—in writing—because if you fail to do this, the lender can conjure up some heavy costs, greatly reducing the amount of your rebate. In many states, you are vulnerable because of loose regulations—or no regulations pertaining to commercial borrowing. Besides, even though the amount may be substantial, how many of us have the time and patience to do court battle?

If you get in a bind and must refinance with your present lender, be aware that some lenders, knowing you are trapped, will close out the original loan and lay on a heavy acquisition charge. They stick it into the refinanced loan, and you pay through the nose!

Supposing interest rates come down? What if you are able to find better financing elsewhere, after making a portion of the payments? Unless lenders are compelled by law in your particular state or you have negotiated an explicit understanding in writing, they can make it impossibly expensive to prepay—by refusing to give any rebate (if not unlawful) or by wiping out the rebate with heavy acquisition charges. You will think twice about prepaying or going elsewhere for a lower rate.

With interest rates at extremely high levels, with many businesses paying 18% to 26% or more, it is imperative that you examine any contract, loan, or lease that contains finance charges. Unless your transaction, in whatever form or style, involves principal and interest, the finance costs are built in by an add-on, discount, or lease rate.

### Protect Yourself Going In

Get the rebate method in writing. Negotiate and define all charges, fees, and acquisition costs in advance. Get these things in writing. If that conditional sale contract, loan document, or lease does not contain explicit terminology as to the rebate method, the lender can require you to pay the full gross balance due!

Consider financing on a prime-rate-plus basis, with any prepayment costs defined in the contract or promissory note. If the lender refuses to define, negotiate, or loan on a principal-and-interest basis, you should look for another lender. Or, be awfully certain you will not want to prepay. Naturally, on what is to you a small finance charge, getting it in writing may not seem worth the effort. That is an individual decision. We recommend getting written assurances as a matter of principle and good business. With equipment costs bloated by inflation (and higher because of improved technology), the accompanying finance charges are also very high. Why let the lenders get you because you failed to negotiate or read your documents?

## Protect Yourself Coming Out

The best way to protect yourself coming out of a transaction is to have protected yourself going in. Assuming you did get everything in writing and assuming you prepay, you can further protect yourself by being capable of computing your own closeout and unearned finance charge rebate. How do you know if you are being short-rebated if you are unable to compute a proper rule of 78ths closeout? You can't, unless you have the charts and proper instructions to make the calculations. We'll make it easy for you to do so with the following instructions. Use them in conjunction with the rule of 78ths charts at the end of this chapter (see Fig. 6-2).

*Step-by-Step Closeout Procedure*

1. Determine the original amount of finance charges which were added on to the original unpaid cash balance or original loan advance.
2. Determine the exact date the lender advanced your loan proceeds or paid your vendor—the date when the lender put out his money. That is the date the lender should begin earning his finance charges; it is the control date for starting "elapsed months."
3. Know the exact date the lender actually received your closeout monies. It is best to pay closeouts with a certified check so that the lender cannot readily take another month while waiting for your check to clear. If you pay by mail, consider using certified or registered mail, return receipt requested, to get the exact date the lender received your money.
4. Count the number of months that elapsed from the date the lender put his money out to the date lender received your funds.
   a. Lenders generally count as the first month any monies advanced on or before the fifteenth day of the month. Some lenders count a full month even if the investment was made on the last day of a month.
      Technically, the count should start in thirty-day increments, from whatever date the investment is made to the date the lender receives good funds in loan repayment.
   b. Lenders will generally end their count of elapsed months if your money is received on or before the fifteenth and take another month if it is received after the fifteenth day of the month or after fifteen days of the thirty-day incremental count.
5. Refer to Fig. 6-2 at the end of this chapter. Follow the instructions for actual calculation of your own closeout.
6. Subtract the amount of unearned finance charges from the gross balance you owed to the lender at the time you repaid the balance. Remember, the gross balance included the total original finance charge and may have included certain nonrefundable fees or charges such as appraisals, document fees, or filing

fees. In some instances, fees or other charges are stated separately. If so, the finance charges are isolated and readily ascertained. But, unless you paid for those additional fees and costs, they are in your gross balance, along with the finance charges. All payments made are deducted from original gross balance to arrive at the ending gross balance. A word of caution: Do not deduct as payments any late charges sent in along with your regular monthly payments. They do not reduce your gross balance.

7. Working with our closeout chart, you will have arrived at a closeout balance due the lender. To obtain a corrected, true closeout, two adjustments may be necessary:
   a. Add back any legitimate unpaid late charges you may have neglected to pay the lender during the course of regular payments.
   b. Add back any legitimate preagreed nonrefundable fees or acquisition costs.
8. The answer is the correct closeout actually due the lender. By your calculations, were you short-refunded?

In practice, when you intend to prepay and request that the lender provide a closeout quotation, he will usually provide it and give you a "good until" date. If there is sufficient time—and there usually is—insist upon a *written* closeout quotation. Immediately double-check his arithmetic. Do not pay if dissatisfied with the closeout. If you pay and then disagree, you may have much more difficulty obtaining a corrected rebate. If there is insufficient time prior to closeout expiration, pay the requested amount under written protest. Depending on the size of the alleged discrepancy, you may elect to pay through an attorney. Have him file a written protest, outlining the disputed amount.

WHAT TO DO IF SHORT-REFUNDED Any time you prepay a loan, contract, or finance-type lease or request an advance closeout quotation in preparation to prepay, always recalculate the lender's quotation. If you think the closeout is incorrect, take the following actions:

Call the lender. Find out who is responsible for closeout calculations. Get that person on the telephone. Be careful now; you can win or lose in these early stages. At this point, you don't want the calculator person on the defensive. You don't want to force him or her to invent acquisition charges or place any roadblocks in the way of a legitimate closeout and rebate.

You want to sneak up on the calculator person. Don't say, "I think your calculations are wrong" or "I think you shorted or cheated me." Say, "I received your closeout quotation today. It appears OK, but I'd like to get some information for my own satisfaction." Continue with questions like these:

1. Did you use the 78ths method?

2. What date did you put out your money? Or, What was the date of your loan investment?
3. What date did you receive my payoff check? (If you have already paid them off.)
4. Or, if just quoted a closeout, How many elapsed months did you figure to the closeout date or the "good until" date?

Don't argue; don't accuse. By your intelligent questioning, the calculator person will almost certainly review the computations. Because your questioning sounded authoritative, not threatening, an honest error may be discovered—or an honest policy error may be discovered and reversed without further argument.

You see, if they purposely shorted you, they know by exactly how much! If the calculator person volunteers the correction on your first friendly phone call, have him or her send you a revised closeout. Or have him or her telephone the other lender who is awaiting the closeout to make your new loan. If you have already paid off—and paid too much—request that you immediately be sent a check for the corrected difference. Unfortunately, once you are short-refunded, the lenders have a strong inclination to stick to their guns. It isn't easy to back them down from an incorrect closeout quotation. And it is more difficult still to get them to send you a check if you've already paid them off.

Take the calculator person's answers and carefully review your calculations and related facts. If you still come up short-refunded, call the lender again. Ask for the top manager—preferably by name. Tell this manager you disagree with the closeout calculation. Explain why you disagree. Explain how you arrived at your answer. Dazzle that manager with your know-how. Use all the buzzwords: "78ths method," "your investment date," "elapsed months."

## Be Ready for Stalls

"I'll have to get your account card and call you back." "We just tell you what the computer comes up with. Our calculator person is really in Pittsburgh!" "I'll call headquarters and see what they say or what we can work out." Or, the really tough reply, "That's our policy, pal. You closeout early with us and it costs you! Show me in our contract where we say anything about rebates, refunds, or the rule of 78ths!"

Do not be easily stalled. No matter what the manager says to you, other than agreeing to the corrected closeout, keep boring right in! If he or she must get the account card, you will wait. If he or she must call someone of higher authority, ask the name of that authority. Be tough, because if the lender shorted you on purpose, he won't give it back easily!

Let's assume the manager stands fast—and he or she probably will. Suppose the manager hits you with reasons: "We have acquisition costs, you know." "You probably forgot to figure our closeout fees."

Or, "You just don't know how to figure a closeout—they're very complicated!" Whatever that manager may dream up or have as a perfectly "legal" excuse, you may still feel cheated. It may only be a few hundred dollars, but the principle of being shorted is important to many of us. It could also be up to several thousand dollars—which is important to most of us. What's next?

**Threaten—But Make It Meaningful!**

Threaten the manager's company's lending license. Every finance company operates under the regulations of some form of state lending license. Usually this license is issued by the corporations department. Do not indulge in idle threats. If you don't know where this license comes from, find out. This license, naming the issuing agency or department, is usually posted on the lender's office wall. Read it. Phone the various state agencies until you locate the issuing source.

Reiterate to the highest-level manager you can locate how much you were short-refunded. Specifically ask for rebate of that amount—*no* compromise. Put your demand in a letter, addressed and sent to this manager by certified mail, return receipt requested. Tell the lender manager verbally or in writing, or both, that you will be writing to the licensing agency with the facts and exact calculations of the short refund. Name the agency and its address. Add this threat: "I am also sending a carbon copy of this letter to the president of your company." Name him and spell out the headquarters address as an additional convincer.

Most upper-management people are sensitive to good public relations. They value their license privileges and do not want black marks registered, even if they have operated within the law. As stated earlier, in many states, there are no laws which require commercial lenders to provide any written refund assurances!

Don't waste your time with idle threats. The commercial lenders are not intimidated by the Better Business Bureau. Personal loan companies might be; but business people seldom check out a commercial finance company for bad marks or complaints. However, we would encourage all businesses to report every instance of impropriety, such as a short refund, to the B.B.B.—just don't expect your threat to change the commercial lender's ways.

Don't tell them you are "turning this over to your attorney" unless you mean it. Be sure the refund correction is worth it. Don't permit unreasonable stalls, and don't get sidetracked. Write that demand letter. If the shortage warrants an attorney, or you already have one, have him send the demand letter. A strongly worded notice, with facts, will get the lender's attention.

The most flagrant offenders with short refunds are finance companies. They are the ones who are most likely to allege outrageous acquisition costs. But banks have been known to short-refund, too. In their case, the minimized refund is generally caused by a tight policy of counting elapsed months in their favor. Also, banks and finance companies employ lower-paid, less competent people. Most closeouts are manually computed by these clerical people. They sometimes make mistakes. Recalculate every closeout, be it bank or finance company.

Remember, it is your money the lender may be keeping. If only for the principle involved—be it $20 or $2,000—if shorted, go after them! After all, if you paid them early, perhaps struggling hard to do so, why stand still when being penalized? Why pay more interest than you originally agreed to?

## FINE PRINT

There is fine print and then there is "fine" fine print. Every loan agreement, conditional sale contract, and lease contains covenants and provisions covering a variety of standard requirements. This legal language spells out the rights and obligations of the several possible parties to every contractual agreement. In the finance industry, this "legalese" is often referred to as the "boilerplate." Typically, the participants are the lender and debtor or lessor who leases to a lessee. In the case of a conditional sale contract, there are three parties involved: The seller, who is also the original secured party, the lender, who acquires the contract from the seller by assignment, and the buyer/debtor. Upon assignment of the conditional sale contract, the lender becomes the assignee of the secured party seller.

All documents contain considerable fine print, most of it designed to protect the lender or lessor. Hence, "boilerplate." Nothing unfair about that—or is there? After all, you are borrowing *their* money!

It's true, most of the provisions are necessary to protect the lender or lessor. It is also true that documents are worded so that if problems develop, the lenders' moves can be legally undertaken. That is, lenders must have legally enforceable documents. By terms of agreement, they can do only what they are legally entitled to do to enforce or collect on your obligation. They must abide by your state laws, as provided for in the documents or by license regulations.

### Twenty Years and $125,000,000 Later ...

Over my twenty years in finance and banking, I have probably put together some $125 million dollars in loans, leases, and sale contracts. These documents were completed for a variety of banks, leasing companies, and commercial finance companies. Some of these money-lenders were extremely hard-nosed, one-way street types of financiers. The legalese was put together by a variety of lawyers who specialized in turning the English language into foreignlike gibberish.

Although I was sometimes involved in big-ticket transactions of a million dollars or more, typically the average financing or lease was about $40,000. That means I personally supervised the signing of over three thousand transactions. With all of those sign-up experiences involving bank, finance company, or leasing company documents, you can imagine the variety of fine print I encountered!

It is impossible to summarize the diversity of complaints, challenges, criticism, and plain trouble caused by contract boilerplate! *Creative Business Financing* will zero in on what you should look out for, where you can get hurt, and the negotiable or deletable clauses. We will endeavor to make it easy to scan any document, so you can skip over the unalterable and usual boilerplate—enabling you to concentrate on the parts that vitally concern you.

Many of the business people I signed up did not attempt to read the fine print. Some of them did not even check the payments or the aggregate loan, lease, or contract balance. They made no attempt to verify the interest or finance rate charged. They didn't give even a passing glance at any entry on the documents. They just signed! I suppose this was sometimes a case of trust in me or my lender. Perhaps such faith was complimentary, but *Creative Business Financing* does *not* recommend unquestioning blind trust.

Signing without reading, more often than not, was due to resignation. Why fight the lender's system? Clients often said to me, "Look, I don't have time to read all those 'whereases,' 'wherefores' and other legal gobbleygook. Let's face it, if I don't pay you people, it is very simple: you repossess the collateral. If you don't recover on the collateral, you sue me. If you can't recover from me, you write it off! So why in hell read all that stuff? I always pay. Then the fine print doesn't mean a thing. And I know I will pay!"

I never argued with this reasoning. Why should I? There is merit to it—and such thinking made my job a lot easier. If you pay as agreed, the lender is happy. He doesn't have to resort to collection efforts or legally enforcing the contract. He doesn't have to worry about the fine print either.

The trouble starts when the unexpected happens. The lenders must protect themselves against well-intentioned debtors who encounter unexpected business or personal problems. Only a tiny percentage of debtors start out with the intention of defaulting or frauding the lender.

### Fine Print Can Get in Your Pocket

The reality is, there *is* fine print. It is inescapable and necessary to minimize pages of documents. But the lenders do sometimes take extreme protective measures! There is a necessity to read at least parts of the boilerplate. And not just because the lenders put in iron-clad collection and enforcement provisions to assure themselves of repayment. Lenders are entitled to expect trouble-free repayment. They are entitled to provide for maximum legal flexibility in making collections, recovering by repossession or accelerating the balance due.

Nevertheless, the fine print can get in your pocket. It can cause you unnecessary grief and infringe on your business operation in many other ways. Just because the documents were printed by Bank of the World or Rock of Gibraltar Finance Corporation does not make them sainted, untainted, or unchangeable, nor does that mean that they could not possibly work against you in several ways.

Consider and be aware of the following:

- Lenders will make themselves extra secure with fine-print legal language in the contract or UCC filings by taking a security interest in present or after-acquired assets. They often do this without prior discussion or without revealing these inserted provisions to you. They will go unreasonably beyond the value of the financing involved. They will control your business by forcing other lenders you may deal with to get their permission to extend additional financing.
- They will insert restrictive covenants which can become extremely burdensome to your daily operations. If feeling insecure, they can use some pretext contracted in legalese to enter your business premises, inspect and audit your books, or question or stop pay raises, bonuses, or dividends. If the clauses are worded too liberally or are out of line compared to the size and value of the financing, you may have unnecessarily agreed to disruption and interference.
- Many bankers and other lenders love to control the account. They like to make it easy on themselves—using fine print—to dictate and help you run your business.
- They will impose unreasonably high insurance requirements. In addition to the usual fire, theft, vandalism, or other comprehensive loss or damage coverages, lenders or lessors will often require public liability coverage in amounts many businesses do not normally maintain. The reason behind these sometimes excessive requirements may be the lender's concern that an injured party will seek larger damages when they learn that Bank of the World holds the loss payable endorsement or actually owns the equipment as lessor—even though you, as debtor or lessee, must provide full insurance and pay the premiums! Sometimes unreasonably high insurance requirements are the result of a lender's legal department's or the lower-level departmental employees' wanting to play it extra safe. Whatever the reason, take a close look at the insurance coverage requirements whenever you lease, borrow, or purchase on extended payments. High-limit insurance can be very costly. The lender's "standard" initial requirement may be negotiable.
- Married women who sign as guarantor or as an additional debtor or lessee will often find, hidden in the fine print, that she has given the lender unqualified access to her separate property! As a married woman, if it is your intention to commit only your community property assets, the separate property clause

should be deleted. This is especially true if the married woman has little or no control over the business operation or if she has significant, readily accessible assets. Remember, lenders can and will take the easiest route to full recovery of a loss. This may include selling the collateral "quick and cheap," then suing for the deficiency. It is difficult to prove that the lender did not sell the collateral "in a commercially reasonable manner to obtain the best possible price," so guard against the extensive separate property guarantee when you first sign!

There are many other fine-print clauses lenders may insert. Most of them are of the nuisance type, buried in the legalese by lenders who just aren't happy unless the boilerplate is eighteen inches thick. All borrowers or lessees should be on the lookout for these legal gems. However, the stronger, more creditworthy borrowers are in the best position to resist being pushed around.

These fine-print nuisances deserve your scrutiny:

- *Financial statements*: Some lenders' documents require audited CPA statements. Others require additional monthly or semiannual statements, which they may also specify must be in their hands within a specified number of days after the period end. This kind of requirement may be difficult for them to enforce—but it is expensive for you if they insist. The lender can use this clause on you for harassment or the beginnings of feeling "insecure." The tardiness of required financial statements or interim reports can trigger the lender's first stages of feeling insecure about his loan or other credit extension. The lender can utilize infraction of this clause to harass you to an extent not anticipated. If you are late delivering statements, he may threaten to call the loan immediately due and payable. Some lenders enforce their threat by actually calling the loan. Others may serve notice that you immediately find a new bank or other lender source. Or, feeling insecure in the absence of financial statements, they may demand an immediate review of your books by their auditors. These surprise audits can prove embarrassing and extremely disruptive to your normal business operations.
- *Right of audit*: Some lenders specifically reserve the right to enter your business premises and conduct an audit of your books "any time during normal business hours."

  Lenders have rights, but they shouldn't too readily be given the key to your front door, especially in cases of relatively small-scale financing. Watch out for liberally worded clauses permitting lenders unrealistic, easy access.

- *Right of acceleration*: Every loan and contract and many leases contain acceleration and default clauses. These provisions establish the lender's right to declare the entire unpaid balance (or remaining lease rentals) immediately due and payable in full.

You will recognize this particular chunk of fine print because it generally starts out, "Time is of the essence" or "In the event of default." Lenders must have the right of acceleration. They must be able to charge additional interest and recoup attorneys' costs. They must abide by state law and document provisions as to giving notice, sale of collateral, handling of sale proceeds, and establishing a deficiency balance. You should at least scan the default clause to see if the lender has inserted unreasonable fine print as to what it takes for him to feel or deem himself "insecure." Although most of the acceleration clause rights are prescribed by law—covering such items as what constitutes default, time and means of proper notice, extent of interest penalties, and costs that may be added—there can be variations in how short a fuse the lender places on "feeling insecure." You cannot negotiate and change these clauses if you fail even to read the fine print.

FIGURE 6-1

# RULE of 78ths

## EXPLANATION OF

## 100% PRO-RATA REFUND

THIS IS THE "SUGGESTED" EXPLANATION ONE FINANCE COMPANY HAS PROVIDED FOR CUSTOMERS WHO DO NOT UNDERSTAND THE BASICS OF THE RULE OF 78ths:

Under the "Point 78" pro-rata refund plan, the customer is allowed the full unearned finance charge when the account is prepaid. Often, the customer asks for an explanation of the method used in computing the refund and this Exhibit will help explain to the customer that he is getting back everything to which he is entitled.

Many customers confuse an INSTALMENT CONTRACT with a one-payment contract. On a one-payment contract, because the total amount outstanding is constant each month, the charge is pro-rated evenly over each instalment. On a contract calling for one payment at the end of 12 months, the earned charge each month is 1/12 of the total charge and, if prepaid at the end of three months, it is easy to see that the earned charge is 3/12 of the total charge, and the unearned charge, or refund is 9/12 of the total charge.

However, on an INSTALMENT CONTRACT, the amount outstanding varies each month, with the greater amount outstanding at the beginning. Therefore, the earned charge per month is greater at the beginning than at the end of the contract. For example, assume the unpaid balance on a 12 monthly payment transaction is $1,200 and the finance charge is $72. We are obviously entitled to more charges per month during the first portion of the contract when $1,200 is outstanding, than we are for the last month, when only $100 is due.

In other words, we earn charges during the first month on 12 instalments for one month. Similarly, we earn charges on 11 instalments for one month during the second month of the contract, etc. It follows therefore, that during the first month, when 12 instalments are outstanding, we are entitled to twelve times as much for charges as for the twelfth month when only one instalment is outstanding. The second month, we are entitled to eleven times as much, etc.

FIGURE 6-1 (continued)

SEE THE FOLLOWING TABLE, WHICH EXPRESSES THIS CLEARLY:

| MONTH | INSTALMENTS REMAINING | AMOUNTS OWING |
|---|---|---|
| First | 12 | $ 1,200 |
| Second | 11 | 1,100 |
| Third | 10 | 1,000 |
| Fourth | 9 | 900 |
| Fifth | 8 | 800 |
| Sixth | 7 | 700 |
| Seventh | 6 | 600 |
| Eighth | 5 | 500 |
| Ninth | 4 | 400 |
| Tenth | 3 | 300 |
| Eleventh | 2 | 200 |
| Twelfth | 1 | 100 |
| Total | 78 | |

By adding the instalments outstanding over a 12 months' contract, we arrive at 78. Accordingly, it can be seen that our charges on a 12 months' contract are earned in 78 parts -- 12 during the first month, 11 during the second month, etc. If a customer prepays at the end of one month, we have earned 12/78 of the total charge and the customer is entitled to a refund of 66/78 of the total charge. Similarly, at the end of six months, we have earned 12/78, plus 11/78, plus 10/78, plus 9/78, plus 8/78, plus 7/78, or 57/78 of the total charge and the customer is entitled to a refund of 21/78. (These fractions are translated into percentages on the Refund Chart.) Because the earned and unearned charges in connection with a 12 months' contract are stated in 78ths, this method is known as "Point 78" or "Rule of 78" refund.

The same principle applies to equal monthly payment contracts of all maturities. For example, in a 24 months' contract payable at $100 a month, the customer has the use of $2,400. During the first month when there are 24 instalments outstanding. Over a 24 months' contract there are a total of 300 instalments outstanding (totaled in the same way as illustrated by the table preceding) and, therefore, the charge is spread over 300 parts. During the first month, the earned charge is 24/300 of the total and the unearned charge is 276/300 of the total. At the end of three months, the earned charge is 69/300 and the unearned charge or refund is 231/300.

FIGURE 6-2

# RULE OF 78ths

## PERCENTAGE REFUND CHARTS

HOW TO USE THESE REFUND CHARTS:

- Find the table based on the ORIGINAL TERM of your CONTRACT . . as indicated at the TOP OF EACH PAGE.
- Next . . . using the ORIGINAL TERM COLUMN . . . (STATED IN MONTHS ON THE RIGHT-HAND SIDE) . . . LOCATE YOUR ORIGINAL TERM.
- Moving across the chart . . . locate the NUMBER OF INSTALMENTS MATURED on the HORIZONTAL LINE at the TOP of the page.
- Read the PERCENTAGE of the CHARGE to be REFUNDED at the intersecting LINE and COLUMN.
- Take the PERCENTAGE REFUND NUMBER you have located at the desired intersection . . . and . . . MULTIPLY THIS NUMBER TIMES YOUR ORIGINAL FINANCE CHARGE . . . the PRODUCT is the DOLLAR AMOUNT you should receive as a REFUND OF UNEARNED FINANCE CHARGES.

BE SURE TO REFER TO CHAPTER 6, ON REFUNDS . . . WHICH PROVIDES FULL-DETAILS ON DETERMINATION OF MATURED MONTHS AND CERTAIN NON-REFUNDABLE CHARGE CONSIDERATIONS.

FIGURE 6-2 (continued)

# RULE of 78ths REFUND CHARTS

## ORIGINAL TERM 1 to 60 MONTHS

| ORIGINAL TERM | NUMBER OF INSTALLMENTS MATURED | | | | | | | | | | | | | | | | | | | | | | | | | | | | | |
|---|---|---|---|---|---|---|---|---|---|---|---|---|---|---|---|---|---|---|---|---|---|---|---|---|---|---|---|---|---|---|
| | 1 | 2 | 3 | 4 | 5 | 6 | 7 | 8 | 9 | 10 | 11 | 12 | 13 | 14 | 15 | 16 | 17 | 18 | 19 | 20 | 21 | 22 | 23 | 24 | 25 | 26 | 27 | 28 | 29 | 30 |
| 1 | | | | | | | | | | | | | | | | | | | | | | | | | | | | | | |
| 2 | 33.33 | | | | | | | | | | | | | | | | | | | | | | | | | | | | | |
| 3 | 50.00 | 16.67 | | | | | | | | | | | | | | | | | | | | | | | | | | | | |
| 4 | 60.00 | 30.00 | 10.00 | | | | | | | | | | | | | | | | | | | | | | | | | | | |
| 5 | 66.67 | 40.00 | 20.00 | 6.67 | | | | | | | | | | | | | | | | | | | | | | | | | | |
| 6 | 71.43 | 47.62 | 28.57 | 14.29 | 4.76 | | | | | | | | | | | | | | | | | | | | | | | | | |
| 7 | 75.00 | 53.57 | 35.71 | 21.43 | 10.71 | 3.57 | | | | | | | | | | | | | | | | | | | | | | | | |
| 8 | 77.78 | 58.33 | 41.67 | 27.78 | 16.67 | 8.33 | 2.78 | | | | | | | | | | | | | | | | | | | | | | | |
| 9 | 80.00 | 62.22 | 46.67 | 33.33 | 22.22 | 13.33 | 6.67 | 2.22 | | | | | | | | | | | | | | | | | | | | | | |
| 10 | 81.82 | 65.45 | 50.91 | 38.18 | 27.27 | 18.18 | 10.91 | 5.45 | 1.82 | | | | | | | | | | | | | | | | | | | | | |
| 11 | 83.33 | 68.18 | 54.55 | 42.42 | 31.82 | 22.73 | 15.15 | 9.09 | 4.55 | 1.52 | | | | | | | | | | | | | | | | | | | | |
| 12 | 84.62 | 70.51 | 57.69 | 46.15 | 35.90 | 26.92 | 19.23 | 12.82 | 7.69 | 3.85 | 1.28 | | | | | | | | | | | | | | | | | | | |
| 13 | 85.71 | 72.53 | 60.44 | 49.45 | 39.56 | 30.77 | 23.08 | 16.48 | 10.99 | 6.59 | 3.30 | 1.10 | | | | | | | | | | | | | | | | | | |
| 14 | 86.67 | 74.29 | 62.86 | 52.38 | 42.86 | 34.29 | 26.67 | 20.00 | 14.29 | 9.52 | 5.71 | 2.86 | .95 | | | | | | | | | | | | | | | | | |
| 15 | 87.50 | 75.83 | 65.00 | 55.00 | 45.83 | 37.50 | 30.00 | 23.33 | 17.50 | 12.50 | 8.33 | 5.00 | 2.50 | .83 | | | | | | | | | | | | | | | | |
| 16 | 88.24 | 77.21 | 66.91 | 57.35 | 48.53 | 40.44 | 33.09 | 26.47 | 20.59 | 15.44 | 11.03 | 7.35 | 4.41 | 2.21 | .74 | | | | | | | | | | | | | | | |
| 17 | 88.89 | 78.43 | 68.63 | 59.48 | 50.98 | 43.14 | 35.95 | 29.41 | 23.53 | 18.30 | 13.73 | 9.80 | 6.54 | 3.92 | 1.96 | .65 | | | | | | | | | | | | | | |
| 18 | 89.47 | 79.53 | 70.18 | 61.40 | 53.22 | 45.61 | 38.60 | 32.16 | 26.32 | 21.05 | 16.37 | 12.28 | 8.77 | 5.85 | 3.51 | 1.75 | .58 | | | | | | | | | | | | | |
| 19 | 90.00 | 80.53 | 71.58 | 63.16 | 55.26 | 47.89 | 41.05 | 34.74 | 28.95 | 23.68 | 18.95 | 14.74 | 11.05 | 7.89 | 5.26 | 3.16 | 1.58 | .53 | | | | | | | | | | | | |
| 20 | 90.48 | 81.43 | 72.86 | 64.76 | 57.14 | 50.00 | 43.33 | 37.14 | 31.43 | 26.19 | 21.43 | 17.14 | 13.33 | 10.00 | 7.14 | 4.76 | 2.86 | 1.43 | .48 | | | | | | | | | | | |
| 21 | 90.91 | 82.25 | 74.03 | 66.23 | 58.87 | 51.95 | 45.45 | 39.39 | 33.77 | 28.57 | 23.81 | 19.48 | 15.58 | 12.12 | 9.09 | 6.49 | 4.33 | 2.60 | 1.30 | .43 | | | | | | | | | | |
| 22 | 91.30 | 83.00 | 75.10 | 67.59 | 60.47 | 53.75 | 47.43 | 41.50 | 35.97 | 30.83 | 26.09 | 21.74 | 17.79 | 14.23 | 11.07 | 8.30 | 5.93 | 3.95 | 2.37 | 1.19 | .40 | | | | | | | | | |
| 23 | 91.67 | 83.70 | 76.09 | 68.84 | 61.96 | 55.43 | 49.28 | 43.48 | 38.04 | 32.97 | 28.26 | 23.91 | 19.93 | 16.30 | 13.04 | 10.14 | 7.61 | 5.43 | 3.62 | 2.17 | 1.09 | .36 | | | | | | | | |
| 24 | 92.00 | 84.33 | 77.00 | 70.00 | 63.33 | 57.00 | 51.00 | 45.33 | 40.00 | 35.00 | 30.33 | 26.00 | 22.00 | 18.33 | 15.00 | 12.00 | 9.33 | 7.00 | 5.00 | 3.33 | 2.00 | 1.00 | .33 | | | | | | | |
| 25 | 92.31 | 84.92 | 77.85 | 71.08 | 64.62 | 58.46 | 52.62 | 47.08 | 41.85 | 36.92 | 32.31 | 28.00 | 24.00 | 20.31 | 16.92 | 13.85 | 11.08 | 8.62 | 6.46 | 4.62 | 3.08 | 1.85 | .92 | .31 | | | | | | |
| 26 | 92.59 | 85.47 | 78.63 | 72.08 | 65.81 | 59.83 | 54.13 | 48.72 | 43.59 | 38.75 | 34.19 | 29.91 | 25.93 | 22.22 | 18.80 | 15.67 | 12.82 | 10.26 | 7.98 | 5.98 | 4.27 | 2.85 | 1.71 | .85 | .28 | | | | | |
| 27 | 92.86 | 85.98 | 79.37 | 73.02 | 66.93 | 61.11 | 55.56 | 50.26 | 45.24 | 40.48 | 35.98 | 31.75 | 27.78 | 24.07 | 20.63 | 17.46 | 14.55 | 11.90 | 9.52 | 7.41 | 5.56 | 3.97 | 2.65 | 1.59 | .79 | .26 | | | | |
| 28 | 93.10 | 86.45 | 80.05 | 73.89 | 67.98 | 62.32 | 56.90 | 51.72 | 46.80 | 42.12 | 37.68 | 33.50 | 29.56 | 25.86 | 22.41 | 19.21 | 16.26 | 13.55 | 11.08 | 8.87 | 6.90 | 5.17 | 3.69 | 2.46 | 1.48 | .74 | .25 | | | |
| 29 | 93.33 | 86.90 | 80.69 | 74.71 | 68.97 | 63.45 | 58.16 | 53.10 | 48.28 | 43.68 | 39.31 | 35.17 | 31.26 | 27.59 | 24.14 | 20.92 | 17.93 | 15.17 | 12.64 | 10.34 | 8.28 | 6.44 | 4.83 | 3.45 | 2.30 | 1.38 | .69 | .23 | | |
| 30 | 93.55 | 87.31 | 81.29 | 75.48 | 69.89 | 64.52 | 59.35 | 54.41 | 49.68 | 45.16 | 40.86 | 36.77 | 32.90 | 29.25 | 25.81 | 22.58 | 19.57 | 16.77 | 14.19 | 11.83 | 9.68 | 7.74 | 6.02 | 4.52 | 3.23 | 2.15 | 1.29 | .65 | .22 | |
| 31 | 93.75 | 87.70 | 81.85 | 76.21 | 70.77 | 65.52 | 60.48 | 55.65 | 51.01 | 46.57 | 42.34 | 38.31 | 34.48 | 30.85 | 27.42 | 24.19 | 21.17 | 18.35 | 15.73 | 13.31 | 11.09 | 9.07 | 7.26 | 5.65 | 4.23 | 3.02 | 2.02 | 1.21 | .60 | .20 |
| 32 | 93.94 | 88.07 | 82.39 | 76.89 | 71.59 | 66.48 | 61.55 | 56.82 | 52.27 | 47.92 | 43.75 | 39.77 | 35.98 | 32.39 | 28.98 | 25.76 | 22.73 | 19.89 | 17.23 | 14.77 | 12.50 | 10.42 | 8.52 | 6.82 | 5.30 | 3.98 | 2.84 | 1.89 | 1.14 | .57 |
| 33 | 94.12 | 88.41 | 82.89 | 77.54 | 72.37 | 67.38 | 62.57 | 57.93 | 53.48 | 49.20 | 45.10 | 41.18 | 37.43 | 33.87 | 30.48 | 27.27 | 24.24 | 21.39 | 18.72 | 16.22 | 13.90 | 11.76 | 9.80 | 8.02 | 6.42 | 4.99 | 3.74 | 2.67 | 1.78 | 1.07 |
| 34 | 94.29 | 88.74 | 83.36 | 78.15 | 73.11 | 68.24 | 63.53 | 58.99 | 54.62 | 50.42 | 46.39 | 42.52 | 38.82 | 35.29 | 31.93 | 28.74 | 25.71 | 22.86 | 20.17 | 17.65 | 15.29 | 13.11 | 11.09 | 9.24 | 7.56 | 6.05 | 4.71 | 3.53 | 2.52 | 1.68 |
| 35 | 94.44 | 89.05 | 83.81 | 78.73 | 73.81 | 69.05 | 64.44 | 60.00 | 55.71 | 51.59 | 47.62 | 43.81 | 40.16 | 36.67 | 33.33 | 30.16 | 27.14 | 24.29 | 21.59 | 19.05 | 16.67 | 14.44 | 12.38 | 10.48 | 8.73 | 7.14 | 5.71 | 4.44 | 3.33 | 2.38 |
| 36 | 94.59 | 89.34 | 84.23 | 79.28 | 74.47 | 69.82 | 65.32 | 60.96 | 56.76 | 52.70 | 48.80 | 45.05 | 41.44 | 37.99 | 34.68 | 31.53 | 28.53 | 25.68 | 22.97 | 20.42 | 18.02 | 15.77 | 13.66 | 11.71 | 9.91 | 8.26 | 6.76 | 5.41 | 4.20 | 3.15 |
| 37 | 94.74 | 89.62 | 84.64 | 79.80 | 75.11 | 70.55 | 66.15 | 61.88 | 57.75 | 53.77 | 49.93 | 46.23 | 42.67 | 39.26 | 35.99 | 32.86 | 29.87 | 27.03 | 24.32 | 21.76 | 19.35 | 17.07 | 14.94 | 12.94 | 11.10 | 9.39 | 7.82 | 6.40 | 5.12 | 3.98 |
| 38 | 94.87 | 89.88 | 85.02 | 80.30 | 75.71 | 71.26 | 66.94 | 62.75 | 58.70 | 54.79 | 51.01 | 47.37 | 43.86 | 40.49 | 37.25 | 34.14 | 31.17 | 28.34 | 25.64 | 23.08 | 20.65 | 18.35 | 16.19 | 14.17 | 12.28 | 10.53 | 8.91 | 7.42 | 6.07 | 4.86 |
| 39 | 95.00 | 90.13 | 85.38 | 80.77 | 76.28 | 71.92 | 67.69 | 63.59 | 59.62 | 55.77 | 52.05 | 48.46 | 45.00 | 41.67 | 38.46 | 35.38 | 32.44 | 29.62 | 26.92 | 24.36 | 21.92 | 19.62 | 17.44 | 15.38 | 13.46 | 11.67 | 10.00 | 8.46 | 7.05 | 5.77 |
| 40 | 95.12 | 90.37 | 85.73 | 81.22 | 76.83 | 72.56 | 68.41 | 64.39 | 60.49 | 56.71 | 53.05 | 49.51 | 46.10 | 42.80 | 39.63 | 36.59 | 33.66 | 30.85 | 28.17 | 25.61 | 23.17 | 20.85 | 18.66 | 16.59 | 14.63 | 12.80 | 11.10 | 9.51 | 8.05 | 6.71 |
| 41 | 95.24 | 90.59 | 86.06 | 81.65 | 77.35 | 73.17 | 69.11 | 65.16 | 61.32 | 57.61 | 54.01 | 50.52 | 47.15 | 43.90 | 40.77 | 37.75 | 34.84 | 32.06 | 29.38 | 26.83 | 24.39 | 22.07 | 19.86 | 17.77 | 15.80 | 13.94 | 12.20 | 10.57 | 9.06 | 7.67 |
| 42 | 95.35 | 90.81 | 86.38 | 82.06 | 77.85 | 73.75 | 69.77 | 65.89 | 62.13 | 58.47 | 54.93 | 51.50 | 48.17 | 44.96 | 41.86 | 38.87 | 35.99 | 33.22 | 30.56 | 28.02 | 25.58 | 23.26 | 21.04 | 18.94 | 16.94 | 15.06 | 13.29 | 11.63 | 10.08 | 8.64 |
| 43 | 95.45 | 91.01 | 86.68 | 82.45 | 78.33 | 74.31 | 70.40 | 66.60 | 62.90 | 59.30 | 55.81 | 52.43 | 49.15 | 45.98 | 42.92 | 39.96 | 37.10 | 34.36 | 31.71 | 29.18 | 26.74 | 24.42 | 22.20 | 20.08 | 18.08 | 16.17 | 14.38 | 12.68 | 11.10 | 9.62 |
| 44 | 95.56 | 91.21 | 86.97 | 82.83 | 78.79 | 74.85 | 71.01 | 67.27 | 63.64 | 60.10 | 56.67 | 53.33 | 50.10 | 46.97 | 43.94 | 41.01 | 38.18 | 35.45 | 32.83 | 30.30 | 27.88 | 25.56 | 23.33 | 21.21 | 19.19 | 17.27 | 15.45 | 13.74 | 12.12 | 10.61 |
| 45 | 95.65 | 91.40 | 87.25 | 83.19 | 79.23 | 75.36 | 71.59 | 67.92 | 64.35 | 60.87 | 57.49 | 54.20 | 51.01 | 47.92 | 44.93 | 42.03 | 39.23 | 36.52 | 33.91 | 31.40 | 28.99 | 26.67 | 24.44 | 22.32 | 20.29 | 18.36 | 16.52 | 14.78 | 13.14 | 11.59 |
| 46 | 95.74 | 91.58 | 87.51 | 83.53 | 79.65 | 75.86 | 72.16 | 68.55 | 65.03 | 61.61 | 58.28 | 55.04 | 51.90 | 48.84 | 45.88 | 43.02 | 40.24 | 37.56 | 34.97 | 32.47 | 30.06 | 27.75 | 25.53 | 23.40 | 21.37 | 19.43 | 17.58 | 15.82 | 14.15 | 12.58 |
| 47 | 95.83 | 91.76 | 87.77 | 83.87 | 80.05 | 76.33 | 72.70 | 69.15 | 65.69 | 62.32 | 59.04 | 55.85 | 52.75 | 49.73 | 46.81 | 43.97 | 41.22 | 38.56 | 35.99 | 33.51 | 31.12 | 28.81 | 26.60 | 24.47 | 22.43 | 20.48 | 18.62 | 16.84 | 15.16 | 13.56 |
| 48 | 95.92 | 91.92 | 88.01 | 84.18 | 80.44 | 76.79 | 73.21 | 69.73 | 66.33 | 63.01 | 59.78 | 56.63 | 53.57 | 50.60 | 47.70 | 44.90 | 42.18 | 39.54 | 36.99 | 34.52 | 32.14 | 29.85 | 27.64 | 25.51 | 23.47 | 21.51 | 19.64 | 17.86 | 16.16 | 14.54 |
| 49 | 96.00 | 92.08 | 88.24 | 84.49 | 80.82 | 77.22 | 73.71 | 70.29 | 66.94 | 63.67 | 60.49 | 57.39 | 54.37 | 51.43 | 48.57 | 45.80 | 43.10 | 40.49 | 37.96 | 35.51 | 33.14 | 30.86 | 28.65 | 26.53 | 24.49 | 22.53 | 20.65 | 18.86 | 17.14 | 15.51 |
| 50 | 96.08 | 92.24 | 88.47 | 84.78 | 81.18 | 77.65 | 74.20 | 70.82 | 67.53 | 64.31 | 61.18 | 58.12 | 55.14 | 52.24 | 49.41 | 46.67 | 44.00 | 41.41 | 38.90 | 36.47 | 34.12 | 31.84 | 29.65 | 27.53 | 25.49 | 23.53 | 21.65 | 19.84 | 18.12 | 16.47 |
| 51 | 96.15 | 92.38 | 88.69 | 85.07 | 81.52 | 78.05 | 74.66 | 71.34 | 68.10 | 64.93 | 61.84 | 58.82 | 55.88 | 53.02 | 50.23 | 47.51 | 44.87 | 42.31 | 39.82 | 37.41 | 35.07 | 32.81 | 30.62 | 28.51 | 26.47 | 24.51 | 22.62 | 20.81 | 19.08 | 17.42 |
| 52 | 96.23 | 92.53 | 88.90 | 85.34 | 81.86 | 78.45 | 75.11 | 71.84 | 68.65 | 65.53 | 62.48 | 59.51 | 56.60 | 53.77 | 51.02 | 48.33 | 45.72 | 43.18 | 40.71 | 38.32 | 35.99 | 33.74 | 31.57 | 29.46 | 27.43 | 25.47 | 23.58 | 21.77 | 20.03 | 18.36 |
| 53 | 96.30 | 92.66 | 89.10 | 85.60 | 82.18 | 78.83 | 75.54 | 72.33 | 69.18 | 66.11 | 63.10 | 60.17 | 57.30 | 54.51 | 51.78 | 49.13 | 46.54 | 44.03 | 41.58 | 39.20 | 36.90 | 34.66 | 32.49 | 30.40 | 28.37 | 26.42 | 24.53 | 22.71 | 20.96 | 19.29 |
| 54 | 96.36 | 92.79 | 89.29 | 85.86 | 82.49 | 79.19 | 75.96 | 72.79 | 69.70 | 66.67 | 63.70 | 60.81 | 57.98 | 55.22 | 52.53 | 49.90 | 47.34 | 44.85 | 42.42 | 40.07 | 37.78 | 35.56 | 33.40 | 31.31 | 29.29 | 27.34 | 25.45 | 23.64 | 21.89 | 20.20 |
| 55 | 96.43 | 92.92 | 89.48 | 86.10 | 82.79 | 79.55 | 76.36 | 73.25 | 70.19 | 67.21 | 64.29 | 61.43 | 58.64 | 55.91 | 53.25 | 50.65 | 48.12 | 45.65 | 43.25 | 40.91 | 38.64 | 36.43 | 34.29 | 32.21 | 30.19 | 28.25 | 26.36 | 24.55 | 22.79 | 21.10 |
| 56 | 96.49 | 93.05 | 89.66 | 86.34 | 83.08 | 79.89 | 76.75 | 73.68 | 70.68 | 67.73 | 64.85 | 62.03 | 59.27 | 56.58 | 53.95 | 51.38 | 48.87 | 46.43 | 44.05 | 41.73 | 39.47 | 37.28 | 35.15 | 33.08 | 31.08 | 29.14 | 27.26 | 25.44 | 23.68 | 21.99 |
| 57 | 96.55 | 93.16 | 89.84 | 86.57 | 83.36 | 80.22 | 77.13 | 74.11 | 71.14 | 68.24 | 65.40 | 62.61 | 59.89 | 57.23 | 54.63 | 52.09 | 49.61 | 47.19 | 44.83 | 42.53 | 40.29 | 38.11 | 36.00 | 33.94 | 31.94 | 30.01 | 28.13 | 26.32 | 24.56 | 22.87 |
| 58 | 96.61 | 93.28 | 90.01 | 86.79 | 83.64 | 80.54 | 77.50 | 74.52 | 71.60 | 68.73 | 65.93 | 63.18 | 60.49 | 57.86 | 55.29 | 52.78 | 50.32 | 47.93 | 45.59 | 43.31 | 41.09 | 38.92 | 36.82 | 34.77 | 32.79 | 30.86 | 28.99 | 27.18 | 25.42 | 23.73 |
| 59 | 96.67 | 93.39 | 90.17 | 87.01 | 83.90 | 80.85 | 77.85 | 74.92 | 72.03 | 69.21 | 66.44 | 63.73 | 61.07 | 58.47 | 55.93 | 53.45 | 51.02 | 48.64 | 46.33 | 44.07 | 41.86 | 39.72 | 37.63 | 35.59 | 33.62 | 31.69 | 29.83 | 28.02 | 26.27 | 24.58 |
| 60 | 96.72 | 93.50 | 90.33 | 87.21 | 84.15 | 81.15 | 78.20 | 75.30 | 72.46 | 69.67 | 66.94 | 64.26 | 61.64 | 59.07 | 56.56 | 54.10 | 51.69 | 49.34 | 47.05 | 44.81 | 42.62 | 40.49 | 38.42 | 36.39 | 34.43 | 32.51 | 30.66 | 28.85 | 27.10 | 25.41 |

FIGURE 6-2 (continued)

# RULE of 78ths REFUND CHARTS

## ORIGINAL TERM 1 to 60 MONTHS

| ORIG-INAL TERM | NUMBER OF INSTALLMENTS MATURED | | | | | | | | | | | | | | | | | | NUMBER OF INSTALLMENTS MATURED | | | | | | | | | | | |
|---|---|---|---|---|---|---|---|---|---|---|---|---|---|---|---|---|---|---|---|---|---|---|---|---|---|---|---|---|---|
| | 31 | 32 | 33 | 34 | 35 | 36 | 37 | 38 | 39 | 40 | 41 | 42 | 43 | 44 | 45 | 46 | 47 | 48 | 49 | 50 | 51 | 52 | 53 | 54 | 55 | 56 | 57 | 58 | 59 | 60 |
| 1 | | | | | | | | | | | | | | | | | | | | | | | | | | | | | | |
| 2 | | | | | | | | | | | | | | | | | | | | | | | | | | | | | | |
| 3 | | | | | | | | | | | | | | | | | | | | | | | | | | | | | | |
| 4 | | | | | | | | | | | | | | | | | | | | | | | | | | | | | | |
| 5 | | | | | | | | | | | | | | | | | | | | | | | | | | | | | | |
| 6 | | | | | | | | | | | | | | | | | | | | | | | | | | | | | | |
| 7 | | | | | | | | | | | | | | | | | | | | | | | | | | | | | | |
| 8 | | | | | | | | | | | | | | | | | | | | | | | | | | | | | | |
| 9 | | | | | | | | | | | | | | | | | | | | | | | | | | | | | | |
| 10 | | | | | | | | | | | | | | | | | | | | | | | | | | | | | | |
| 11 | | | | | | | | | | | | | | | | | | | | | | | | | | | | | | |
| 12 | | | | | | | | | | | | | | | | | | | | | | | | | | | | | | |
| 13 | | | | | | | | | | | | | | | | | | | | | | | | | | | | | | |
| 14 | | | | | | | | | | | | | | | | | | | | | | | | | | | | | | |
| 15 | | | | | | | | | | | | | | | | | | | | | | | | | | | | | | |
| 16 | | | | | | | | | | | | | | | | | | | | | | | | | | | | | | |
| 17 | | | | | | | | | | | | | | | | | | | | | | | | | | | | | | |
| 18 | | | | | | | | | | | | | | | | | | | | | | | | | | | | | | |
| 19 | | | | | | | | | | | | | | | | | | | | | | | | | | | | | | |
| 20 | | | | | | | | | | | | | | | | | | | | | | | | | | | | | | |
| 21 | | | | | | | | | | | | | | | | | | | | | | | | | | | | | | |
| 22 | | | | | | | | | | | | | | | | | | | | | | | | | | | | | | |
| 23 | | | | | | | | | | | | | | | | | | | | | | | | | | | | | | |
| 24 | | | | | | | | | | | | | | | | | | | | | | | | | | | | | | |
| 25 | | | | | | | | | | | | | | | | | | | | | | | | | | | | | | |
| 26 | | | | | | | | | | | | | | | | | | | | | | | | | | | | | | |
| 27 | | | | | | | | | | | | | | | | | | | | | | | | | | | | | | |
| 28 | | | | | | | | | | | | | | | | | | | | | | | | | | | | | | |
| 29 | | | | | | | | | | | | | | | | | | | | | | | | | | | | | | |
| 30 | | | | | | | | | | | | | | | | | | | | | | | | | | | | | | |
| 31 | | | | | | | | | | | | | | | | | | | | | | | | | | | | | | |
| 32 | .19 | | | | | | | | | | | | | | | | | | | | | | | | | | | | | |
| 33 | .53 | .18 | | | | | | | | | | | | | | | | | | | | | | | | | | | | |
| 34 | 1.01 | .50 | .17 | | | | | | | | | | | | | | | | | | | | | | | | | | | |
| 35 | 1.59 | .95 | .48 | .16 | | | | | | | | | | | | | | | | | | | | | | | | | | |
| 36 | 2.25 | 1.50 | .90 | .45 | .15 | | | | | | | | | | | | | | | | | | | | | | | | | |
| 37 | 2.99 | 2.13 | 1.42 | .85 | .43 | .14 | | | | | | | | | | | | | | | | | | | | | | | | |
| 38 | 3.78 | 2.83 | 2.02 | 1.35 | .81 | .40 | .13 | | | | | | | | | | | | | | | | | | | | | | | |
| 39 | 4.62 | 3.59 | 2.69 | 1.92 | 1.28 | .77 | .38 | .13 | | | | | | | | | | | | | | | | | | | | | | |
| 40 | 5.49 | 4.39 | 3.41 | 2.56 | 1.83 | 1.22 | .73 | .37 | .12 | | | | | | | | | | | | | | | | | | | | | |
| 41 | 6.39 | 5.23 | 4.18 | 3.25 | 2.44 | 1.74 | 1.16 | .70 | .35 | .12 | | | | | | | | | | | | | | | | | | | | |
| 42 | 7.31 | 6.09 | 4.98 | 3.99 | 3.10 | 2.33 | 1.66 | 1.11 | .66 | .33 | .11 | | | | | | | | | | | | | | | | | | | |
| 43 | 8.25 | 6.98 | 5.81 | 4.76 | 3.81 | 2.96 | 2.22 | 1.59 | 1.06 | .63 | .32 | .11 | | | | | | | | | | | | | | | | | | |
| 44 | 9.19 | 7.88 | 6.67 | 5.56 | 4.55 | 3.64 | 2.83 | 2.12 | 1.52 | 1.01 | .61 | .30 | .10 | | | | | | | | | | | | | | | | | |
| 45 | 10.14 | 8.79 | 7.54 | 6.38 | 5.31 | 4.35 | 3.48 | 2.71 | 2.03 | 1.45 | .97 | .58 | .29 | .10 | | | | | | | | | | | | | | | | |
| 46 | 11.10 | 9.71 | 8.42 | 7.22 | 6.11 | 5.09 | 4.16 | 3.33 | 2.59 | 1.94 | 1.39 | .93 | .56 | .28 | .09 | | | | | | | | | | | | | | | |
| 47 | 12.06 | 10.64 | 9.31 | 8.07 | 6.91 | 5.85 | 4.88 | 3.99 | 3.19 | 2.48 | 1.86 | 1.33 | .89 | .53 | .27 | .09 | | | | | | | | | | | | | | |
| 48 | 13.01 | 11.56 | 10.20 | 8.93 | 7.74 | 6.63 | 5.61 | 4.68 | 3.83 | 3.06 | 2.38 | 1.79 | 1.28 | .85 | .51 | .26 | .09 | | | | | | | | | | | | | |
| 49 | 13.96 | 12.49 | 11.10 | 9.80 | 8.57 | 7.43 | 6.37 | 5.39 | 4.49 | 3.67 | 2.94 | 2.29 | 1.71 | 1.22 | .82 | .49 | .24 | .08 | | | | | | | | | | | | |
| 50 | 14.90 | 13.41 | 12.00 | 10.67 | 9.41 | 8.24 | 7.14 | 6.12 | 5.18 | 4.31 | 3.53 | 2.82 | 2.20 | 1.65 | 1.18 | .78 | .47 | .24 | .08 | | | | | | | | | | | |
| 51 | 15.84 | 14.33 | 12.90 | 11.54 | 10.26 | 9.05 | 7.92 | 6.86 | 5.88 | 4.98 | 4.15 | 3.39 | 2.71 | 2.11 | 1.58 | 1.13 | .75 | .45 | .23 | .08 | | | | | | | | | | |
| 52 | 16.76 | 15.24 | 13.79 | 12.41 | 11.10 | 9.87 | 8.71 | 7.62 | 6.60 | 5.66 | 4.79 | 3.99 | 3.27 | 2.61 | 2.03 | 1.52 | 1.09 | .73 | .44 | .22 | .07 | | | | | | | | | |
| 53 | 17.68 | 16.14 | 14.68 | 13.28 | 11.95 | 10.69 | 9.50 | 8.39 | 7.34 | 6.36 | 5.45 | 4.61 | 3.84 | 3.14 | 2.52 | 1.96 | 1.47 | 1.05 | .70 | .42 | .21 | .07 | | | | | | | | |
| 54 | 18.59 | 17.04 | 15.56 | 14.14 | 12.79 | 11.52 | 10.30 | 9.16 | 8.08 | 7.07 | 6.13 | 5.25 | 4.44 | 3.70 | 3.03 | 2.42 | 1.89 | 1.41 | 1.01 | .67 | .40 | .20 | .07 | | | | | | | |
| 55 | 19.48 | 17.92 | 16.43 | 15.00 | 13.64 | 12.34 | 11.10 | 9.94 | 8.83 | 7.79 | 6.82 | 5.91 | 5.06 | 4.29 | 3.57 | 2.92 | 2.34 | 1.82 | 1.36 | .97 | .65 | .39 | .19 | .06 | | | | | | |
| 56 | 20.36 | 18.80 | 17.29 | 15.85 | 14.47 | 13.16 | 11.90 | 10.71 | 9.59 | 8.52 | 7.52 | 6.58 | 5.70 | 4.89 | 4.14 | 3.45 | 2.82 | 2.26 | 1.75 | 1.32 | .94 | .63 | .38 | .19 | .06 | | | | | |
| 57 | 21.23 | 19.66 | 18.15 | 16.70 | 15.31 | 13.97 | 12.70 | 11.49 | 10.34 | 9.26 | 8.23 | 7.26 | 6.35 | 5.51 | 4.72 | 3.99 | 3.33 | 2.72 | 2.18 | 1.69 | 1.27 | .91 | .60 | .36 | .18 | .06 | | | | |
| 58 | 22.09 | 20.51 | 18.99 | 17.53 | 16.13 | 14.79 | 13.50 | 12.27 | 11.10 | 9.99 | 8.94 | 7.95 | 7.01 | 6.14 | 5.32 | 4.56 | 3.86 | 3.21 | 2.63 | 2.10 | 1.64 | 1.23 | .88 | .58 | .35 | .18 | .06 | | | |
| 59 | 22.94 | 21.36 | 19.83 | 18.36 | 16.95 | 15.59 | 14.29 | 13.05 | 11.86 | 10.73 | 9.66 | 8.64 | 7.68 | 6.78 | 5.93 | 5.14 | 4.41 | 3.73 | 3.11 | 2.54 | 2.03 | 1.58 | 1.19 | .85 | .56 | .34 | .17 | .06 | | |
| 60 | 23.77 | 22.19 | 20.66 | 19.18 | 17.76 | 16.39 | 15.08 | 13.83 | 12.62 | 11.48 | 10.38 | 9.34 | 8.36 | 7.43 | 6.56 | 5.74 | 4.97 | 4.26 | 3.61 | 3.01 | 2.46 | 1.97 | 1.53 | 1.15 | .82 | .55 | .33 | .16 | .05 | |

FIGURE 6–2 (continued)

# RULE of 78ths REFUND CHARTS

## ORIGINAL TERM 61 to 120 MONTHS

| ORIG-INAL TERM | NUMBER OF INSTALLMENTS MATURED | | | | | | | | | | | | | | | | | | | | NUMBER OF INSTALLMENTS MATURED | | | | | | | | | |
|---|---|---|---|---|---|---|---|---|---|---|---|---|---|---|---|---|---|---|---|---|---|---|---|---|---|---|---|---|---|---|
| | 1 | 2 | 3 | 4 | 5 | 6 | 7 | 8 | 9 | 10 | 11 | 12 | 13 | 14 | 15 | 16 | 17 | 18 | 19 | 20 | 21 | 22 | 23 | 24 | 25 | 26 | 27 | 28 | 29 | 30 |
| 61 | 96.77 | 93.60 | 90.48 | 87.41 | 84.40 | 81.44 | 78.53 | 75.67 | 72.87 | 70.12 | 67.42 | 64.78 | 62.19 | 59.65 | 57.17 | 54.73 | 52.35 | 50.03 | 47.75 | 45.53 | 43.36 | 41.25 | 39.19 | 37.18 | 35.22 | 33.32 | 31.46 | 29.67 | 27.92 | 26.23 |
| 62 | 96.83 | 93.70 | 90.63 | 87.61 | 84.64 | 81.72 | 78.85 | 76.04 | 73.27 | 70.56 | 67.90 | 65.28 | 62.72 | 60.22 | 57.76 | 55.35 | 53.00 | 50.69 | 48.44 | 46.24 | 44.09 | 41.99 | 39.94 | 37.94 | 36.00 | 34.10 | 32.26 | 30.47 | 28.73 | 27.04 |
| 63 | 96.88 | 93.80 | 90.77 | 87.80 | 84.87 | 81.99 | 79.17 | 76.39 | 73.66 | 70.98 | 68.35 | 65.77 | 63.24 | 60.76 | 58.33 | 55.95 | 53.62 | 51.34 | 49.11 | 46.92 | 44.79 | 42.71 | 40.67 | 38.69 | 36.76 | 34.87 | 33.04 | 31.25 | 29.51 | 27.83 |
| 64 | 96.92 | 93.89 | 90.91 | 87.98 | 85.10 | 82.26 | 79.47 | 76.73 | 74.04 | 71.39 | 68.80 | 66.25 | 63.75 | 61.30 | 58.89 | 56.54 | 54.23 | 51.97 | 49.76 | 47.60 | 45.48 | 43.41 | 41.39 | 39.42 | 37.50 | 35.63 | 33.80 | 32.02 | 30.29 | 28.61 |
| 65 | 96.97 | 93.99 | 91.05 | 88.16 | 85.31 | 82.52 | 79.77 | 77.06 | 74.41 | 71.79 | 69.23 | 66.71 | 64.24 | 61.82 | 59.44 | 57.11 | 54.83 | 52.59 | 50.40 | 48.25 | 46.15 | 44.10 | 42.10 | 40.14 | 38.23 | 36.36 | 34.55 | 32.77 | 31.05 | 29.37 |
| 66 | 97.01 | 94.08 | 91.18 | 88.33 | 85.53 | 82.77 | 80.05 | 77.39 | 74.76 | 72.18 | 69.65 | 67.16 | 64.72 | 62.32 | 59.97 | 57.67 | 55.40 | 53.19 | 51.02 | 48.89 | 46.81 | 44.78 | 42.79 | 40.84 | 38.94 | 37.09 | 35.28 | 33.51 | 31.80 | 30.12 |
| 67 | 97.06 | 94.16 | 91.31 | 88.50 | 85.73 | 83.01 | 80.33 | 77.70 | 75.11 | 72.56 | 70.06 | 67.60 | 65.19 | 62.82 | 60.49 | 58.21 | 55.97 | 53.78 | 51.62 | 49.52 | 47.45 | 45.43 | 43.46 | 41.53 | 39.64 | 37.80 | 36.00 | 34.24 | 32.53 | 30.86 |
| 68 | 97.10 | 94.25 | 91.43 | 88.66 | 85.93 | 83.25 | 80.61 | 78.01 | 75.45 | 72.93 | 70.46 | 68.03 | 65.64 | 63.30 | 61.00 | 58.74 | 56.52 | 54.35 | 52.22 | 50.13 | 48.08 | 46.08 | 44.12 | 42.20 | 40.32 | 38.49 | 36.70 | 34.95 | 33.25 | 31.59 |
| 69 | 97.14 | 94.33 | 91.55 | 88.82 | 86.13 | 83.48 | 80.87 | 78.30 | 75.78 | 73.29 | 70.85 | 68.45 | 66.09 | 63.77 | 61.49 | 59.25 | 57.06 | 54.91 | 52.80 | 50.72 | 48.70 | 46.71 | 44.76 | 42.86 | 40.99 | 39.17 | 37.39 | 35.65 | 33.95 | 32.30 |
| 70 | 97.18 | 94.41 | 91.67 | 88.97 | 86.32 | 83.70 | 81.13 | 78.59 | 76.10 | 73.64 | 71.23 | 68.85 | 66.52 | 64.23 | 61.97 | 59.76 | 57.59 | 55.45 | 53.36 | 51.31 | 49.30 | 47.32 | 45.39 | 43.50 | 41.65 | 39.84 | 38.07 | 36.34 | 34.65 | 33.00 |
| 71 | 97.22 | 94.48 | 91.78 | 89.12 | 86.50 | 83.92 | 81.38 | 78.87 | 76.41 | 73.98 | 71.60 | 69.25 | 66.94 | 64.67 | 62.44 | 60.25 | 58.10 | 55.99 | 53.91 | 51.88 | 49.88 | 47.93 | 46.01 | 44.13 | 42.29 | 40.49 | 38.73 | 37.01 | 35.33 | 33.69 |
| 72 | 97.26 | 94.56 | 91.89 | 89.27 | 86.68 | 84.13 | 81.62 | 79.15 | 76.71 | 74.32 | 71.96 | 69.63 | 67.35 | 65.11 | 62.90 | 60.73 | 58.60 | 56.51 | 54.45 | 52.44 | 50.46 | 48.52 | 46.61 | 44.75 | 42.92 | 41.13 | 39.38 | 37.67 | 36.00 | 34.36 |
| 73 | 97.30 | 94.63 | 92.00 | 89.41 | 86.86 | 84.34 | 81.86 | 79.42 | 77.01 | 74.64 | 72.31 | 70.01 | 67.75 | 65.53 | 63.35 | 61.20 | 59.09 | 57.02 | 54.98 | 52.98 | 51.02 | 49.09 | 47.20 | 45.35 | 43.54 | 41.76 | 40.02 | 38.32 | 36.65 | 35.02 |
| 74 | 97.33 | 94.70 | 92.11 | 89.55 | 87.03 | 84.54 | 82.09 | 79.68 | 77.30 | 74.95 | 72.65 | 70.38 | 68.14 | 65.95 | 63.78 | 61.66 | 59.57 | 57.51 | 55.50 | 53.51 | 51.57 | 49.66 | 47.78 | 45.95 | 44.14 | 42.38 | 40.65 | 38.95 | 37.30 | 35.68 |
| 75 | 97.37 | 94.77 | 92.21 | 89.68 | 87.19 | 84.74 | 82.32 | 79.93 | 77.58 | 75.26 | 72.98 | 70.74 | 68.53 | 66.35 | 64.21 | 62.11 | 60.04 | 58.00 | 56.00 | 54.04 | 52.11 | 50.21 | 48.35 | 46.53 | 44.74 | 42.98 | 41.26 | 39.58 | 37.93 | 36.32 |
| 76 | 97.40 | 94.84 | 92.31 | 89.82 | 87.35 | 84.93 | 82.54 | 80.18 | 77.85 | 75.56 | 73.31 | 71.09 | 68.90 | 66.75 | 64.63 | 62.54 | 60.49 | 58.48 | 56.49 | 54.55 | 52.63 | 50.75 | 48.91 | 47.10 | 45.32 | 43.57 | 41.87 | 40.19 | 38.55 | 36.94 |
| 77 | 97.44 | 94.91 | 92.41 | 89.94 | 87.51 | 85.11 | 82.75 | 80.42 | 78.12 | 75.86 | 73.63 | 71.43 | 69.26 | 67.13 | 65.03 | 62.97 | 60.94 | 58.94 | 56.98 | 55.04 | 53.15 | 51.28 | 49.45 | 47.65 | 45.89 | 44.16 | 42.46 | 40.79 | 39.16 | 37.56 |
| 78 | 97.47 | 94.97 | 92.50 | 90.07 | 87.67 | 85.30 | 82.96 | 80.66 | 78.38 | 76.14 | 73.94 | 71.76 | 69.62 | 67.51 | 65.43 | 63.39 | 61.38 | 59.40 | 57.45 | 55.53 | 53.65 | 51.80 | 49.98 | 48.20 | 46.45 | 44.73 | 43.04 | 41.38 | 39.76 | 38.17 |
| 79 | 97.50 | 95.03 | 92.59 | 90.19 | 87.82 | 85.47 | 83.16 | 80.89 | 78.64 | 76.42 | 74.24 | 72.09 | 69.97 | 67.88 | 65.82 | 63.80 | 61.80 | 59.84 | 57.91 | 56.01 | 54.15 | 52.31 | 50.51 | 48.73 | 46.99 | 45.28 | 43.61 | 41.96 | 40.35 | 38.77 |
| 80 | 97.53 | 95.09 | 92.69 | 90.31 | 87.96 | 85.65 | 83.36 | 81.11 | 78.89 | 76.70 | 74.54 | 72.41 | 70.31 | 68.24 | 66.20 | 64.20 | 62.22 | 60.28 | 58.36 | 56.48 | 54.63 | 52.81 | 51.02 | 49.26 | 47.53 | 45.83 | 44.17 | 42.53 | 40.93 | 39.35 |
| 81 | 97.56 | 95.15 | 92.77 | 90.42 | 88.11 | 85.82 | 83.56 | 81.33 | 79.13 | 76.96 | 74.83 | 72.72 | 70.64 | 68.59 | 66.58 | 64.59 | 62.63 | 60.70 | 58.81 | 56.94 | 55.10 | 53.30 | 51.52 | 49.77 | 48.06 | 46.37 | 44.72 | 43.09 | 41.49 | 39.93 |
| 82 | 97.59 | 95.21 | 92.86 | 90.54 | 88.25 | 85.98 | 83.75 | 81.55 | 79.37 | 77.23 | 75.11 | 73.02 | 70.97 | 68.94 | 66.94 | 64.97 | 63.03 | 61.12 | 59.24 | 57.39 | 55.57 | 53.78 | 52.01 | 50.28 | 48.57 | 46.90 | 45.25 | 43.64 | 42.05 | 40.49 |
| 83 | 97.62 | 95.27 | 92.94 | 90.65 | 88.38 | 86.14 | 83.94 | 81.76 | 79.60 | 77.48 | 75.39 | 73.32 | 71.29 | 69.28 | 67.30 | 65.35 | 63.43 | 61.53 | 59.67 | 57.83 | 56.02 | 54.25 | 52.50 | 50.77 | 49.08 | 47.42 | 45.78 | 44.18 | 42.60 | 41.05 |
| 84 | 97.65 | 95.32 | 93.03 | 90.76 | 88.52 | 86.30 | 84.12 | 81.96 | 79.83 | 77.73 | 75.66 | 73.61 | 71.60 | 69.61 | 67.65 | 65.71 | 63.81 | 61.93 | 60.08 | 58.26 | 56.47 | 54.71 | 52.97 | 51.26 | 49.58 | 47.93 | 46.30 | 44.71 | 43.14 | 41.60 |
| 85 | 97.67 | 95.38 | 93.11 | 90.86 | 88.65 | 86.46 | 84.30 | 82.16 | 80.05 | 77.98 | 75.92 | 73.90 | 71.90 | 69.93 | 67.99 | 66.07 | 64.19 | 62.33 | 60.49 | 58.69 | 56.91 | 55.16 | 53.43 | 51.74 | 50.07 | 48.43 | 46.81 | 45.23 | 43.67 | 42.13 |
| 86 | 97.70 | 95.43 | 93.18 | 90.96 | 88.77 | 86.61 | 84.47 | 82.36 | 80.27 | 78.21 | 76.18 | 74.18 | 72.20 | 70.25 | 68.32 | 66.43 | 64.55 | 62.71 | 60.89 | 59.10 | 57.34 | 55.60 | 53.89 | 52.21 | 50.55 | 48.92 | 47.31 | 45.74 | 44.19 | 42.66 |
| 87 | 97.73 | 95.48 | 93.26 | 91.07 | 88.90 | 86.76 | 84.64 | 82.55 | 80.49 | 78.45 | 76.44 | 74.45 | 72.49 | 70.56 | 68.65 | 66.77 | 64.92 | 63.09 | 61.29 | 59.51 | 57.76 | 56.03 | 54.34 | 52.66 | 51.02 | 49.40 | 47.81 | 46.24 | 44.70 | 43.18 |
| 88 | 97.75 | 95.53 | 93.34 | 91.16 | 89.02 | 86.90 | 84.81 | 82.74 | 80.69 | 78.68 | 76.69 | 74.72 | 72.78 | 70.86 | 68.97 | 67.11 | 65.27 | 63.46 | 61.67 | 59.91 | 58.17 | 56.46 | 54.78 | 53.12 | 51.48 | 49.87 | 48.29 | 46.73 | 45.20 | 43.69 |
| 89 | 97.78 | 95.58 | 93.41 | 91.26 | 89.14 | 87.04 | 84.97 | 82.92 | 80.90 | 78.90 | 76.93 | 74.98 | 73.06 | 71.16 | 69.29 | 67.44 | 65.62 | 63.82 | 62.05 | 60.30 | 58.58 | 56.88 | 55.21 | 53.56 | 51.94 | 50.34 | 48.76 | 47.22 | 45.69 | 44.19 |
| 90 | 97.80 | 95.63 | 93.48 | 91.36 | 89.26 | 87.18 | 85.13 | 83.10 | 81.10 | 79.12 | 77.17 | 75.24 | 73.33 | 71.45 | 69.60 | 67.77 | 65.96 | 64.18 | 62.42 | 60.68 | 58.97 | 57.29 | 55.63 | 53.99 | 52.38 | 50.79 | 49.23 | 47.69 | 46.18 | 44.69 |
| 91 | 97.83 | 95.68 | 93.55 | 91.45 | 89.37 | 87.31 | 85.28 | 83.28 | 81.29 | 79.34 | 77.40 | 75.49 | 73.60 | 71.74 | 69.90 | 68.08 | 66.29 | 64.52 | 62.78 | 61.06 | 59.36 | 57.69 | 56.04 | 54.42 | 52.82 | 51.24 | 49.69 | 48.16 | 46.66 | 45.17 |
| 92 | 97.85 | 95.72 | 93.62 | 91.54 | 89.48 | 87.45 | 85.44 | 83.45 | 81.49 | 79.55 | 77.63 | 75.74 | 73.87 | 72.02 | 70.20 | 68.40 | 66.62 | 64.87 | 63.14 | 61.43 | 59.75 | 58.09 | 56.45 | 54.84 | 53.25 | 51.68 | 50.14 | 48.62 | 47.12 | 45.65 |
| 93 | 97.87 | 95.77 | 93.69 | 91.63 | 89.59 | 87.58 | 85.59 | 83.62 | 81.67 | 79.75 | 77.85 | 75.98 | 74.12 | 72.29 | 70.49 | 68.70 | 66.94 | 65.20 | 63.49 | 61.79 | 60.12 | 58.48 | 56.85 | 55.25 | 53.67 | 52.12 | 50.58 | 49.07 | 47.59 | 46.12 |
| 94 | 97.89 | 95.81 | 93.75 | 91.71 | 89.70 | 87.70 | 85.73 | 83.78 | 81.86 | 79.96 | 78.07 | 76.22 | 74.38 | 72.56 | 70.77 | 69.00 | 67.26 | 65.53 | 63.83 | 62.15 | 60.49 | 58.86 | 57.25 | 55.66 | 54.09 | 52.54 | 51.02 | 49.52 | 48.04 | 46.58 |
| 95 | 97.92 | 95.86 | 93.82 | 91.80 | 89.80 | 87.83 | 85.88 | 83.95 | 82.04 | 80.15 | 78.29 | 76.45 | 74.63 | 72.83 | 71.05 | 69.30 | 67.57 | 65.86 | 64.17 | 62.50 | 60.86 | 59.23 | 57.63 | 56.05 | 54.50 | 52.96 | 51.45 | 49.96 | 48.49 | 47.04 |
| 96 | 97.94 | 95.90 | 93.88 | 91.88 | 89.91 | 87.95 | 86.02 | 84.11 | 82.22 | 80.35 | 78.50 | 76.68 | 74.87 | 73.09 | 71.33 | 69.59 | 67.87 | 66.17 | 64.50 | 62.84 | 61.21 | 59.60 | 58.01 | 56.44 | 54.90 | 53.37 | 51.87 | 50.39 | 48.93 | 47.49 |
| 97 | 97.96 | 95.94 | 93.94 | 91.96 | 90.01 | 88.07 | 86.16 | 84.26 | 82.39 | 80.54 | 78.71 | 76.90 | 75.11 | 73.34 | 71.60 | 69.87 | 68.17 | 66.48 | 64.82 | 63.18 | 61.56 | 59.96 | 58.38 | 56.83 | 55.29 | 53.78 | 52.28 | 50.81 | 49.36 | 47.93 |
| 98 | 97.98 | 95.98 | 94.00 | 92.04 | 90.11 | 88.19 | 86.29 | 84.42 | 82.56 | 80.73 | 78.91 | 77.12 | 75.35 | 73.59 | 71.86 | 70.15 | 68.46 | 66.79 | 65.14 | 63.51 | 61.90 | 60.32 | 58.75 | 57.20 | 55.68 | 54.17 | 52.69 | 51.23 | 49.78 | 48.36 |
| 99 | 98.00 | 96.02 | 94.06 | 92.12 | 90.20 | 88.30 | 86.42 | 84.57 | 82.73 | 80.91 | 79.11 | 77.33 | 75.58 | 73.84 | 72.12 | 70.42 | 68.75 | 67.09 | 65.45 | 63.84 | 62.24 | 60.67 | 59.11 | 57.58 | 56.06 | 54.57 | 53.09 | 51.64 | 50.20 | 48.79 |
| 100 | 98.02 | 96.06 | 94.12 | 92.20 | 90.30 | 88.42 | 86.55 | 84.71 | 82.89 | 81.09 | 79.31 | 77.54 | 75.80 | 74.08 | 72.38 | 70.69 | 69.03 | 67.39 | 65.76 | 64.16 | 62.57 | 61.01 | 59.47 | 57.94 | 56.44 | 54.95 | 53.49 | 52.04 | 50.61 | 49.21 |
| 101 | 98.04 | 96.10 | 94.18 | 92.27 | 90.39 | 88.53 | 86.68 | 84.86 | 83.05 | 81.27 | 79.50 | 77.75 | 76.02 | 74.32 | 72.63 | 70.96 | 69.31 | 67.68 | 66.06 | 64.47 | 62.90 | 61.35 | 59.81 | 58.30 | 56.80 | 55.33 | 53.87 | 52.44 | 51.02 | 49.62 |
| 102 | 98.06 | 96.14 | 94.23 | 92.35 | 90.48 | 88.64 | 86.81 | 85.00 | 83.21 | 81.44 | 79.69 | 77.96 | 76.24 | 74.55 | 72.87 | 71.22 | 69.58 | 67.96 | 66.36 | 64.78 | 63.22 | 61.68 | 60.16 | 58.65 | 57.17 | 55.70 | 54.25 | 52.83 | 51.42 | 50.03 |
| 103 | 98.08 | 96.17 | 94.29 | 92.42 | 90.57 | 88.74 | 86.93 | 85.14 | 83.36 | 81.61 | 79.87 | 78.16 | 76.46 | 74.78 | 73.11 | 71.47 | 69.85 | 68.24 | 66.65 | 65.09 | 63.54 | 62.01 | 60.49 | 59.00 | 57.52 | 56.07 | 54.63 | 53.21 | 51.81 | 50.43 |
| 104 | 98.10 | 96.21 | 94.34 | 92.49 | 90.66 | 88.85 | 87.05 | 85.27 | 83.52 | 81.78 | 80.05 | 78.35 | 76.67 | 75.00 | 73.35 | 71.72 | 70.11 | 68.52 | 66.94 | 65.38 | 63.85 | 62.33 | 60.82 | 59.34 | 57.88 | 56.43 | 55.00 | 53.59 | 52.20 | 50.82 |
| 105 | 98.11 | 96.24 | 94.39 | 92.56 | 90.75 | 88.95 | 87.17 | 85.41 | 83.67 | 81.94 | 80.23 | 78.54 | 76.87 | 75.22 | 73.58 | 71.97 | 70.37 | 68.79 | 67.22 | 65.68 | 64.15 | 62.64 | 61.15 | 59.68 | 58.22 | 56.78 | 55.36 | 53.96 | 52.58 | 51.21 |
| 106 | 98.13 | 96.28 | 94.45 | 92.63 | 90.83 | 89.05 | 87.29 | 85.54 | 83.81 | 82.10 | 80.41 | 78.73 | 77.08 | 75.44 | 73.81 | 72.21 | 70.62 | 69.05 | 67.50 | 65.97 | 64.45 | 62.95 | 61.47 | 60.01 | 58.56 | 57.13 | 55.72 | 54.33 | 52.95 | 51.60 |
| 107 | 98.15 | 96.31 | 94.50 | 92.70 | 90.91 | 89.15 | 87.40 | 85.67 | 83.96 | 82.26 | 80.58 | 78.92 | 77.28 | 75.65 | 74.04 | 72.45 | 70.87 | 69.31 | 67.77 | 66.25 | 64.75 | 63.26 | 61.79 | 60.33 | 58.90 | 57.48 | 56.07 | 54.69 | 53.32 | 51.97 |
| 108 | 98.17 | 96.35 | 94.55 | 92.76 | 91.00 | 89.25 | 87.51 | 85.80 | 84.10 | 82.42 | 80.75 | 79.10 | 77.47 | 75.86 | 74.26 | 72.68 | 71.12 | 69.57 | 68.04 | 66.53 | 65.04 | 63.56 | 62.10 | 60.65 | 59.23 | 57.82 | 56.42 | 55.05 | 53.69 | 52.34 |
| 109 | 98.18 | 96.38 | 94.60 | 92.83 | 91.08 | 89.34 | 87.62 | 85.92 | 84.24 | 82.57 | 80.92 | 79.28 | 77.66 | 76.06 | 74.48 | 72.91 | 71.36 | 69.82 | 68.31 | 66.81 | 65.32 | 63.85 | 62.40 | 60.97 | 59.55 | 58.15 | 56.76 | 55.40 | 54.05 | 52.71 |
| 110 | 98.20 | 96.41 | 94.64 | 92.89 | 91.15 | 89.43 | 87.73 | 86.04 | 84.37 | 82.72 | 81.08 | 79.46 | 77.85 | 76.27 | 74.69 | 73.14 | 71.60 | 70.07 | 68.57 | 67.08 | 65.60 | 64.14 | 62.70 | 61.28 | 59.87 | 58.48 | 57.10 | 55.74 | 54.40 | 53.07 |
| 111 | 98.21 | 96.44 | 94.69 | 92.95 | 91.23 | 89.53 | 87.84 | 86.16 | 84.51 | 82.87 | 81.24 | 79.63 | 78.04 | 76.46 | 74.90 | 73.36 | 71.83 | 70.32 | 68.82 | 67.34 | 65.88 | 64.43 | 63.00 | 61.58 | 60.18 | 58.80 | 57.43 | 56.08 | 54.75 | 53.43 |
| 112 | 98.23 | 96.48 | 94.74 | 93.02 | 91.31 | 89.62 | 87.94 | 86.28 | 84.64 | 83.01 | 81.40 | 79.80 | 78.22 | 76.66 | 75.11 | 73.58 | 72.06 | 70.56 | 69.07 | 67.60 | 66.15 | 64.71 | 63.29 | 61.88 | 60.49 | 59.12 | 57.76 | 56.42 | 55.09 | 53.78 |
| 113 | 98.25 | 96.51 | 94.78 | 93.08 | 91.38 | 89.71 | 88.05 | 86.40 | 84.77 | 83.15 | 81.56 | 79.97 | 78.40 | 76.85 | 75.31 | 73.79 | 72.29 | 70.80 | 69.32 | 67.86 | 66.42 | 64.99 | 63.58 | 62.18 | 60.80 | 59.43 | 58.08 | 56.75 | 55.43 | 54.12 |
| 114 | 98.26 | 96.54 | 94.83 | 93.14 | 91.46 | 89.79 | 88.15 | 86.51 | 84.90 | 83.30 | 81.71 | 80.14 | 78.58 | 77.04 | 75.51 | 74.00 | 72.51 | 71.03 | 69.57 | 68.12 | 66.68 | 65.26 | 63.86 | 62.47 | 61.10 | 59.74 | 58.40 | 57.07 | 55.76 | 54.46 |
| 115 | 98.28 | 96.57 | 94.87 | 93.19 | 91.53 | 89.88 | 88.25 | 86.63 | 85.02 | 83.43 | 81.86 | 80.30 | 78.76 | 77.23 | 75.71 | 74.21 | 72.73 | 71.26 | 69.81 | 68.37 | 66.94 | 65.53 | 64.14 | 62.76 | 61.39 | 60.04 | 58.71 | 57.39 | 56.09 | 54.80 |
| 116 | 98.29 | 96.60 | 94.92 | 93.25 | 91.60 | 89.96 | 88.34 | 86.74 | 85.15 | 83.57 | 82.01 | 80.46 | 78.93 | 77.41 | 75.91 | 74.42 | 72.94 | 71.49 | 70.04 | 68.61 | 67.20 | 65.80 | 64.41 | 63.04 | 61.69 | 60.34 | 59.02 | 57.71 | 56.41 | 55.13 |
| 117 | 98.31 | 96.62 | 94.96 | 93.31 | 91.67 | 90.05 | 88.44 | 86.85 | 85.27 | 83.70 | 82.15 | 80.62 | 79.10 | 77.59 | 76.10 | 74.62 | 73.16 | 71.71 | 70.27 | 68.85 | 67.45 | 66.06 | 64.68 | 63.32 | 61.97 | 60.64 | 59.32 | 58.02 | 56.73 | 55.45 |
| 118 | 98.32 | 96.65 | 95.00 | 93.36 | 91.74 | 90.13 | 88.53 | 86.95 | 85.39 | 83.83 | 82.30 | 80.77 | 79.26 | 77.77 | 76.29 | 74.82 | 73.37 | 71.93 | 70.50 | 69.09 | 67.70 | 66.32 | 64.95 | 63.59 | 62.26 | 60.93 | 59.62 | 58.33 | 57.04 | 55.78 |
| 119 | 98.33 | 96.68 | 95.04 | 93.42 | 91.81 | 90.21 | 88.63 | 87.06 | 85.50 | 83.96 | 82.44 | 80.92 | 79.43 | 77.94 | 76.47 | 75.01 | 73.57 | 72.14 | 70.73 | 69.33 | 67.94 | 66.57 | 65.21 | 63.87 | 62.54 | 61.22 | 59.92 | 58.63 | 57.35 | 56.09 |
| 120 | 98.35 | 96.71 | 95.08 | 93.47 | 91.87 | 90.29 | 88.72 | 87.16 | 85.62 | 84.09 | 82.58 | 81.07 | 79.59 | 78.11 | 76.65 | 75.21 | 73.77 | 72.36 | 70.95 | 69.56 | 68.18 | 66.82 | 65.47 | 64.13 | 62.81 | 61.50 | 60.21 | 58.93 | 57.66 | 56.40 |

FIGURE 6-2 (continued)

# RULE of 78ths REFUND CHARTS

## ORIGINAL TERM 61 to 120 MONTHS

| ORIGINAL TERM | NUMBER OF INSTALLMENTS MATURED | | | | | | | | | | | | | | |
|---|---|---|---|---|---|---|---|---|---|---|---|---|---|---|---|
| | 31 | 32 | 33 | 34 | 35 | 36 | 37 | 38 | 39 | 40 | 41 | 42 | 43 | 44 | 45 |
| 61 | 24.59 | 23.00 | 21.47 | 19.99 | 18.56 | 17.19 | 15.86 | 14.60 | 13.38 | 12.22 | 11.11 | 10.05 | 9.04 | 8.09 | 7.19 |
| 62 | 25.40 | 23.81 | 22.27 | 20.79 | 19.35 | 17.97 | 16.64 | 15.36 | 14.13 | 12.95 | 11.83 | 10.75 | 9.73 | 8.76 | 7.83 |
| 63 | 26.19 | 24.60 | 23.07 | 21.58 | 20.14 | 18.75 | 17.41 | 16.12 | 14.88 | 13.69 | 12.55 | 11.46 | 10.42 | 9.42 | 8.48 |
| 64 | 26.97 | 25.38 | 23.85 | 22.36 | 20.91 | 19.52 | 18.17 | 16.88 | 15.63 | 14.42 | 13.27 | 12.16 | 11.11 | 10.10 | 9.13 |
| 65 | 27.74 | 26.15 | 24.62 | 23.12 | 21.68 | 20.28 | 18.93 | 17.62 | 16.36 | 15.15 | 13.99 | 12.87 | 11.79 | 10.77 | 9.79 |
| 66 | 28.49 | 26.91 | 25.37 | 23.88 | 22.43 | 21.03 | 19.67 | 18.36 | 17.10 | 15.88 | 14.70 | 13.57 | 12.48 | 11.44 | 10.45 |
| 67 | 29.24 | 27.66 | 26.12 | 24.63 | 23.18 | 21.77 | 20.41 | 19.10 | 17.82 | 16.59 | 15.41 | 14.27 | 13.17 | 12.12 | 11.11 |
| 68 | 29.97 | 28.39 | 26.85 | 25.36 | 23.91 | 22.51 | 21.14 | 19.82 | 18.54 | 17.31 | 16.11 | 14.96 | 13.85 | 12.79 | 11.76 |
| 69 | 30.68 | 29.11 | 27.58 | 26.09 | 24.64 | 23.23 | 21.86 | 20.54 | 19.25 | 18.01 | 16.81 | 15.65 | 14.53 | 13.46 | 12.42 |
| 70 | 31.39 | 29.82 | 28.29 | 26.80 | 25.35 | 23.94 | 22.58 | 21.25 | 19.96 | 18.71 | 17.51 | 16.34 | 15.21 | 14.12 | 13.08 |
| 71 | 32.08 | 30.52 | 28.99 | 27.50 | 26.06 | 24.65 | 23.28 | 21.95 | 20.66 | 19.41 | 18.19 | 17.02 | 15.88 | 14.79 | 13.73 |
| 72 | 32.76 | 31.20 | 29.68 | 28.20 | 26.75 | 25.34 | 23.97 | 22.64 | 21.35 | 20.09 | 18.87 | 17.69 | 16.55 | 15.45 | 14.38 |
| 73 | 33.43 | 31.88 | 30.36 | 28.88 | 27.43 | 26.03 | 24.66 | 23.32 | 22.03 | 20.77 | 19.55 | 18.36 | 17.22 | 16.11 | 15.03 |
| 74 | 34.09 | 32.54 | 31.03 | 29.55 | 28.11 | 26.70 | 25.33 | 24.00 | 22.70 | 21.44 | 20.22 | 19.03 | 17.87 | 16.76 | 15.68 |
| 75 | 34.74 | 33.19 | 31.68 | 30.21 | 28.77 | 27.37 | 26.00 | 24.67 | 23.37 | 22.11 | 20.88 | 19.68 | 18.53 | 17.40 | 16.32 |
| 76 | 35.37 | 33.83 | 32.33 | 30.86 | 29.43 | 28.02 | 26.66 | 25.32 | 24.03 | 22.76 | 21.53 | 20.33 | 19.17 | 18.05 | 16.95 |
| 77 | 36.00 | 34.47 | 32.97 | 31.50 | 30.07 | 28.67 | 27.31 | 25.97 | 24.68 | 23.41 | 22.18 | 20.98 | 19.81 | 18.68 | 17.58 |
| 78 | 36.61 | 35.09 | 33.59 | 32.13 | 30.70 | 29.31 | 27.95 | 26.61 | 25.32 | 24.05 | 22.82 | 21.62 | 20.45 | 19.31 | 18.21 |
| 79 | 37.22 | 35.70 | 34.21 | 32.75 | 31.33 | 29.94 | 28.58 | 27.25 | 25.95 | 24.68 | 23.45 | 22.25 | 21.08 | 19.94 | 18.83 |
| 80 | 37.81 | 36.30 | 34.81 | 33.36 | 31.94 | 30.56 | 29.20 | 27.87 | 26.57 | 25.31 | 24.07 | 22.87 | 21.70 | 20.56 | 19.44 |
| 81 | 38.39 | 36.89 | 35.41 | 33.97 | 32.55 | 31.17 | 29.81 | 28.49 | 27.19 | 25.93 | 24.69 | 23.49 | 22.31 | 21.17 | 20.05 |
| 82 | 38.97 | 37.47 | 36.00 | 34.56 | 33.15 | 31.77 | 30.41 | 29.09 | 27.80 | 26.54 | 25.30 | 24.10 | 22.92 | 21.77 | 20.66 |
| 83 | 39.53 | 38.04 | 36.57 | 35.14 | 33.73 | 32.36 | 31.01 | 29.69 | 28.40 | 27.14 | 25.90 | 24.70 | 23.52 | 22.38 | 21.26 |
| 84 | 40.08 | 38.60 | 37.14 | 35.71 | 34.31 | 32.94 | 31.60 | 30.28 | 28.99 | 27.73 | 26.50 | 25.29 | 24.12 | 22.97 | 21.85 |
| 85 | 40.63 | 39.15 | 37.70 | 36.28 | 34.88 | 33.52 | 32.18 | 30.86 | 29.58 | 28.32 | 27.09 | 25.88 | 24.71 | 23.56 | 22.44 |
| 86 | 41.17 | 39.70 | 38.25 | 36.84 | 35.45 | 34.08 | 32.75 | 31.44 | 30.15 | 28.90 | 27.67 | 26.46 | 25.29 | 24.14 | 23.02 |
| 87 | 41.69 | 40.23 | 38.79 | 37.38 | 36.00 | 34.64 | 33.31 | 32.00 | 30.72 | 29.47 | 28.24 | 27.04 | 25.86 | 24.71 | 23.59 |
| 88 | 42.21 | 40.76 | 39.33 | 37.92 | 36.54 | 35.19 | 33.86 | 32.56 | 31.28 | 30.03 | 28.80 | 27.60 | 26.43 | 25.28 | 24.16 |
| 89 | 42.72 | 41.27 | 39.85 | 38.45 | 37.08 | 35.73 | 34.41 | 33.11 | 31.84 | 30.59 | 29.36 | 28.16 | 26.99 | 25.84 | 24.72 |
| 90 | 43.22 | 41.78 | 40.37 | 38.97 | 37.61 | 36.26 | 34.95 | 33.65 | 32.38 | 31.14 | 29.91 | 28.72 | 27.55 | 26.40 | 25.27 |
| 91 | 43.72 | 42.28 | 40.87 | 39.49 | 38.13 | 36.79 | 35.48 | 34.19 | 32.92 | 31.68 | 30.46 | 29.26 | 28.09 | 26.95 | 25.82 |
| 92 | 44.20 | 42.78 | 41.37 | 40.00 | 38.64 | 37.31 | 36.00 | 34.71 | 33.45 | 32.21 | 31.00 | 29.80 | 28.63 | 27.49 | 26.37 |
| 93 | 44.68 | 43.26 | 41.87 | 40.49 | 39.14 | 37.82 | 36.51 | 35.23 | 33.97 | 32.74 | 31.53 | 30.34 | 29.17 | 28.03 | 26.90 |
| 94 | 45.15 | 43.74 | 42.35 | 40.99 | 39.64 | 38.32 | 37.02 | 35.74 | 34.49 | 33.26 | 32.05 | 30.86 | 29.70 | 28.56 | 27.44 |
| 95 | 45.61 | 44.21 | 42.83 | 41.47 | 40.13 | 38.82 | 37.52 | 36.25 | 35.00 | 33.77 | 32.57 | 31.38 | 30.22 | 29.08 | 27.96 |
| 96 | 46.07 | 44.67 | 43.30 | 41.95 | 40.61 | 39.30 | 38.02 | 36.75 | 35.50 | 34.28 | 33.08 | 31.89 | 30.73 | 29.60 | 28.48 |
| 97 | 46.52 | 45.13 | 43.76 | 42.42 | 41.09 | 39.79 | 38.50 | 37.24 | 36.00 | 34.78 | 33.58 | 32.40 | 31.24 | 30.11 | 28.99 |
| 98 | 46.96 | 45.58 | 44.22 | 42.88 | 41.56 | 40.26 | 38.98 | 37.72 | 36.49 | 35.27 | 34.08 | 32.90 | 31.75 | 30.61 | 29.50 |
| 99 | 47.39 | 46.02 | 44.67 | 43.33 | 42.02 | 40.73 | 39.45 | 38.20 | 36.97 | 35.76 | 34.57 | 33.39 | 32.24 | 31.11 | 30.00 |
| 100 | 47.82 | 46.46 | 45.11 | 43.78 | 42.48 | 41.19 | 39.92 | 38.67 | 37.45 | 36.24 | 35.05 | 33.88 | 32.73 | 31.60 | 30.50 |
| 101 | 48.24 | 46.88 | 45.54 | 44.22 | 42.92 | 41.64 | 40.38 | 39.14 | 37.91 | 36.71 | 35.53 | 34.36 | 33.22 | 32.09 | 30.98 |
| 102 | 48.66 | 47.31 | 45.97 | 44.66 | 43.37 | 42.09 | 40.83 | 39.60 | 38.38 | 37.18 | 36.00 | 34.84 | 33.70 | 32.57 | 31.47 |
| 103 | 49.07 | 47.72 | 46.40 | 45.09 | 43.80 | 42.53 | 41.28 | 40.05 | 38.83 | 37.64 | 36.46 | 35.31 | 34.17 | 33.05 | 31.95 |
| 104 | 49.47 | 48.13 | 46.81 | 45.51 | 44.23 | 42.97 | 41.72 | 40.49 | 39.29 | 38.10 | 36.92 | 35.77 | 34.63 | 33.52 | 32.42 |
| 105 | 49.87 | 48.54 | 47.22 | 45.93 | 44.65 | 43.40 | 42.16 | 40.93 | 39.73 | 38.54 | 37.38 | 36.23 | 35.09 | 33.98 | 32.88 |
| 106 | 50.26 | 48.93 | 47.63 | 46.34 | 45.07 | 43.82 | 42.59 | 41.37 | 40.17 | 38.99 | 37.82 | 36.68 | 35.55 | 34.44 | 33.35 |
| 107 | 50.64 | 49.33 | 48.03 | 46.75 | 45.48 | 44.24 | 43.01 | 41.80 | 40.60 | 39.43 | 38.27 | 37.12 | 36.00 | 34.89 | 33.80 |
| 108 | 51.02 | 49.71 | 48.42 | 47.15 | 45.89 | 44.65 | 43.43 | 42.22 | 41.03 | 39.86 | 38.70 | 37.56 | 36.44 | 35.34 | 34.25 |
| 109 | 51.39 | 50.09 | 48.81 | 47.54 | 46.29 | 45.05 | 43.84 | 42.64 | 41.45 | 40.28 | 39.13 | 38.00 | 36.88 | 35.78 | 34.70 |
| 110 | 51.76 | 50.47 | 49.19 | 47.93 | 46.68 | 45.45 | 44.24 | 43.05 | 41.87 | 40.70 | 39.56 | 38.43 | 37.31 | 36.22 | 35.14 |
| 111 | 52.12 | 50.84 | 49.57 | 48.31 | 47.07 | 45.85 | 44.64 | 43.45 | 42.28 | 41.12 | 39.98 | 38.85 | 37.74 | 36.65 | 35.57 |
| 112 | 52.48 | 51.20 | 49.94 | 48.69 | 47.46 | 46.24 | 45.04 | 43.85 | 42.68 | 41.53 | 40.39 | 39.27 | 38.16 | 37.07 | 36.00 |
| 113 | 52.83 | 51.56 | 50.30 | 49.06 | 47.83 | 46.62 | 45.43 | 44.25 | 43.08 | 41.93 | 40.80 | 39.68 | 38.58 | 37.49 | 36.42 |
| 114 | 53.18 | 51.91 | 50.66 | 49.43 | 48.21 | 47.00 | 45.81 | 44.64 | 43.48 | 42.33 | 41.21 | 40.09 | 38.99 | 37.91 | 36.84 |
| 115 | 53.52 | 52.26 | 51.02 | 49.79 | 48.58 | 47.38 | 46.19 | 45.02 | 43.87 | 42.73 | 41.60 | 40.49 | 39.40 | 38.32 | 37.26 |
| 116 | 53.86 | 52.61 | 51.37 | 50.15 | 48.94 | 47.75 | 46.57 | 45.40 | 44.25 | 43.12 | 42.00 | 40.89 | 39.80 | 38.73 | 37.67 |
| 117 | 54.19 | 52.95 | 51.72 | 50.50 | 49.30 | 48.11 | 46.94 | 45.78 | 44.63 | 43.50 | 42.39 | 41.29 | 40.20 | 39.13 | 38.07 |
| 118 | 54.52 | 53.28 | 52.06 | 50.85 | 49.65 | 48.47 | 47.30 | 46.15 | 45.01 | 43.88 | 42.77 | 41.67 | 40.59 | 39.52 | 38.47 |
| 119 | 54.85 | 53.61 | 52.39 | 51.19 | 50.00 | 48.82 | 47.66 | 46.51 | 45.38 | 44.26 | 43.15 | 42.06 | 40.98 | 39.92 | 38.87 |
| 120 | 55.17 | 53.94 | 52.73 | 51.53 | 50.34 | 49.17 | 48.02 | 46.87 | 45.74 | 44.63 | 43.53 | 42.44 | 41.36 | 40.30 | 39.26 |

| ORIGINAL TERM | NUMBER OF INSTALLMENTS MATURED | | | | | | | | | | | | | | |
|---|---|---|---|---|---|---|---|---|---|---|---|---|---|---|---|
| | 46 | 47 | 48 | 49 | 50 | 51 | 52 | 53 | 54 | 55 | 56 | 57 | 58 | 59 | 60 |
| 61 | 6.35 | 5.55 | 4.81 | 4.12 | 3.49 | 2.91 | 2.38 | 1.90 | 1.48 | 1.11 | .79 | .53 | .32 | .16 | .05 |
| 62 | 6.96 | 6.14 | 5.38 | 4.66 | 3.99 | 3.38 | 2.82 | 2.30 | 1.84 | 1.43 | 1.08 | .77 | .51 | .31 | .15 |
| 63 | 7.59 | 6.75 | 5.95 | 5.21 | 4.51 | 3.87 | 3.27 | 2.73 | 2.23 | 1.79 | 1.39 | 1.04 | .74 | .50 | .30 |
| 64 | 8.22 | 7.36 | 6.54 | 5.77 | 5.05 | 4.38 | 3.75 | 3.17 | 2.64 | 2.16 | 1.73 | 1.35 | 1.01 | .72 | .48 |
| 65 | 8.86 | 7.97 | 7.13 | 6.34 | 5.59 | 4.90 | 4.24 | 3.64 | 3.08 | 2.56 | 2.10 | 1.68 | 1.31 | .98 | .70 |
| 66 | 9.50 | 8.59 | 7.73 | 6.92 | 6.15 | 5.43 | 4.75 | 4.12 | 3.53 | 2.99 | 2.49 | 2.04 | 1.63 | 1.27 | .95 |
| 67 | 10.14 | 9.22 | 8.34 | 7.51 | 6.72 | 5.97 | 5.27 | 4.61 | 3.99 | 3.42 | 2.90 | 2.41 | 1.98 | 1.58 | 1.23 |
| 68 | 10.78 | 9.85 | 8.95 | 8.10 | 7.29 | 6.52 | 5.80 | 5.12 | 4.48 | 3.88 | 3.32 | 2.81 | 2.34 | 1.92 | 1.53 |
| 69 | 11.43 | 10.48 | 9.57 | 8.70 | 7.87 | 7.08 | 6.34 | 5.63 | 4.97 | 4.35 | 3.77 | 3.23 | 2.73 | 2.28 | 1.86 |
| 70 | 12.07 | 11.11 | 10.18 | 9.30 | 8.45 | 7.65 | 6.88 | 6.16 | 5.47 | 4.83 | 4.23 | 3.66 | 3.14 | 2.66 | 2.21 |
| 71 | 12.72 | 11.74 | 10.80 | 9.90 | 9.04 | 8.22 | 7.43 | 6.69 | 5.99 | 5.32 | 4.69 | 4.11 | 3.56 | 3.05 | 2.58 |
| 72 | 13.36 | 12.37 | 11.42 | 10.50 | 9.63 | 8.79 | 7.99 | 7.23 | 6.51 | 5.82 | 5.18 | 4.57 | 4.00 | 3.46 | 2.97 |
| 73 | 13.99 | 13.00 | 12.03 | 11.11 | 10.22 | 9.37 | 8.55 | 7.77 | 7.03 | 6.33 | 5.66 | 5.04 | 4.44 | 3.89 | 3.37 |
| 74 | 14.63 | 13.62 | 12.65 | 11.71 | 10.81 | 9.95 | 9.12 | 8.32 | 7.57 | 6.85 | 6.16 | 5.51 | 4.90 | 4.32 | 3.78 |
| 75 | 15.26 | 14.25 | 13.26 | 12.32 | 11.40 | 10.53 | 9.68 | 8.88 | 8.11 | 7.37 | 6.67 | 6.00 | 5.37 | 4.77 | 4.21 |
| 76 | 15.89 | 14.87 | 13.88 | 12.92 | 12.00 | 11.11 | 10.25 | 9.43 | 8.65 | 7.89 | 7.18 | 6.49 | 5.84 | 5.23 | 4.65 |
| 77 | 16.52 | 15.48 | 14.49 | 13.52 | 12.59 | 11.69 | 10.82 | 9.99 | 9.19 | 8.42 | 7.69 | 6.99 | 6.33 | 5.69 | 5.09 |
| 78 | 17.14 | 16.10 | 15.09 | 14.12 | 13.18 | 12.27 | 11.39 | 10.55 | 9.74 | 8.96 | 8.21 | 7.50 | 6.82 | 6.17 | 5.55 |
| 79 | 17.75 | 16.71 | 15.70 | 14.72 | 13.77 | 12.85 | 11.96 | 11.11 | 10.28 | 9.49 | 8.73 | 8.01 | 7.31 | 6.65 | 6.01 |
| 80 | 18.36 | 17.31 | 16.30 | 15.31 | 14.35 | 13.43 | 12.53 | 11.67 | 10.83 | 10.03 | 9.26 | 8.52 | 7.81 | 7.13 | 6.48 |
| 81 | 18.97 | 17.92 | 16.89 | 15.90 | 14.94 | 14.00 | 13.10 | 12.23 | 11.38 | 10.57 | 9.79 | 9.03 | 8.31 | 7.62 | 6.96 |
| 82 | 19.57 | 18.51 | 17.48 | 16.49 | 15.52 | 14.58 | 13.66 | 12.78 | 11.93 | 11.11 | 10.31 | 9.55 | 8.82 | 8.11 | 7.43 |
| 83 | 20.17 | 19.10 | 18.07 | 17.07 | 16.09 | 15.15 | 14.23 | 13.34 | 12.48 | 11.65 | 10.84 | 10.07 | 9.32 | 8.61 | 7.92 |
| 84 | 20.76 | 19.69 | 18.66 | 17.65 | 16.67 | 15.71 | 14.79 | 13.89 | 13.03 | 12.18 | 11.37 | 10.59 | 9.83 | 9.10 | 8.40 |
| 85 | 21.34 | 20.27 | 19.23 | 18.22 | 17.24 | 16.28 | 15.35 | 14.45 | 13.57 | 12.72 | 11.90 | 11.11 | 10.34 | 9.60 | 8.89 |
| 86 | 21.92 | 20.85 | 19.81 | 18.79 | 17.80 | 16.84 | 15.90 | 15.00 | 14.11 | 13.26 | 12.43 | 11.63 | 10.85 | 10.10 | 9.38 |
| 87 | 22.49 | 21.42 | 20.38 | 19.36 | 18.36 | 17.40 | 16.46 | 15.54 | 14.66 | 13.79 | 12.96 | 12.15 | 11.36 | 10.61 | 9.87 |
| 88 | 23.06 | 21.99 | 20.94 | 19.92 | 18.92 | 17.95 | 17.01 | 16.09 | 15.19 | 14.33 | 13.48 | 12.67 | 11.87 | 11.11 | 10.37 |
| 89 | 23.62 | 22.55 | 21.50 | 20.47 | 19.48 | 18.50 | 17.55 | 16.63 | 15.73 | 14.86 | 14.01 | 13.18 | 12.38 | 11.61 | 10.86 |
| 90 | 24.18 | 23.10 | 22.05 | 21.03 | 20.02 | 19.05 | 18.10 | 17.17 | 16.26 | 15.38 | 14.53 | 13.70 | 12.89 | 12.11 | 11.36 |
| 91 | 24.73 | 23.65 | 22.60 | 21.57 | 20.57 | 19.59 | 18.63 | 17.70 | 16.79 | 15.91 | 15.05 | 14.21 | 13.40 | 12.61 | 11.85 |
| 92 | 25.27 | 24.19 | 23.14 | 22.11 | 21.11 | 20.13 | 19.17 | 18.23 | 17.32 | 16.43 | 15.57 | 14.73 | 13.91 | 13.11 | 12.34 |
| 93 | 25.81 | 24.73 | 23.68 | 22.65 | 21.64 | 20.66 | 19.70 | 18.76 | 17.84 | 16.95 | 16.08 | 15.24 | 14.41 | 13.61 | 12.83 |
| 94 | 26.34 | 25.26 | 24.21 | 23.18 | 22.17 | 21.19 | 20.22 | 19.28 | 18.37 | 17.47 | 16.60 | 15.74 | 14.92 | 14.11 | 13.33 |
| 95 | 26.86 | 25.79 | 24.74 | 23.71 | 22.70 | 21.71 | 20.75 | 19.80 | 18.88 | 17.98 | 17.11 | 16.25 | 15.42 | 14.61 | 13.82 |
| 96 | 27.38 | 26.31 | 25.26 | 24.23 | 23.22 | 22.23 | 21.26 | 20.32 | 19.39 | 18.49 | 17.61 | 16.75 | 15.91 | 15.10 | 14.30 |
| 97 | 27.90 | 26.83 | 25.77 | 24.74 | 23.73 | 22.74 | 21.78 | 20.83 | 19.90 | 19.00 | 18.11 | 17.25 | 16.41 | 15.59 | 14.79 |
| 98 | 28.41 | 27.33 | 26.28 | 25.25 | 24.24 | 23.25 | 22.28 | 21.34 | 20.41 | 19.50 | 18.61 | 17.75 | 16.90 | 16.08 | 15.28 |
| 99 | 28.91 | 27.84 | 26.79 | 25.76 | 24.75 | 23.76 | 22.79 | 21.84 | 20.91 | 20.00 | 19.11 | 18.24 | 17.39 | 16.57 | 15.76 |
| 100 | 29.41 | 28.34 | 27.29 | 26.26 | 25.25 | 24.26 | 23.29 | 22.34 | 21.41 | 20.50 | 19.60 | 18.73 | 17.88 | 17.05 | 16.24 |
| 101 | 29.90 | 28.83 | 27.78 | 26.75 | 25.74 | 24.75 | 23.78 | 22.83 | 21.90 | 20.99 | 20.09 | 19.22 | 18.37 | 17.53 | 16.72 |
| 102 | 30.38 | 29.32 | 28.27 | 27.24 | 26.23 | 25.24 | 24.27 | 23.32 | 22.39 | 21.47 | 20.58 | 19.70 | 18.85 | 18.01 | 17.19 |
| 103 | 30.86 | 29.80 | 28.75 | 27.73 | 26.72 | 25.73 | 24.76 | 23.81 | 22.87 | 21.96 | 21.06 | 20.18 | 19.32 | 18.48 | 17.66 |
| 104 | 31.34 | 30.27 | 29.23 | 28.21 | 27.20 | 26.21 | 25.24 | 24.29 | 23.35 | 22.44 | 21.54 | 20.66 | 19.80 | 18.96 | 18.13 |
| 105 | 31.81 | 30.75 | 29.70 | 28.68 | 27.67 | 26.68 | 25.71 | 24.76 | 23.83 | 22.91 | 22.01 | 21.13 | 20.27 | 19.42 | 18.60 |
| 106 | 32.27 | 31.21 | 30.17 | 29.15 | 28.14 | 27.16 | 26.19 | 25.23 | 24.30 | 23.38 | 22.48 | 21.60 | 20.74 | 19.89 | 19.06 |
| 107 | 32.73 | 31.67 | 30.63 | 29.61 | 28.61 | 27.62 | 26.65 | 25.70 | 24.77 | 23.85 | 22.95 | 22.07 | 21.20 | 20.35 | 19.52 |
| 108 | 33.18 | 32.13 | 31.09 | 30.07 | 29.07 | 28.08 | 27.12 | 26.16 | 25.23 | 24.31 | 23.41 | 22.53 | 21.66 | 20.81 | 19.98 |
| 109 | 33.63 | 32.58 | 31.54 | 30.53 | 29.52 | 28.54 | 27.57 | 26.62 | 25.69 | 24.77 | 23.87 | 22.99 | 22.12 | 21.27 | 20.43 |
| 110 | 34.07 | 33.02 | 31.99 | 30.97 | 29.98 | 28.99 | 28.03 | 27.08 | 26.14 | 25.23 | 24.32 | 23.44 | 22.57 | 21.72 | 20.88 |
| 111 | 34.51 | 33.46 | 32.43 | 31.42 | 30.42 | 29.44 | 28.47 | 27.53 | 26.59 | 25.68 | 24.77 | 23.89 | 23.02 | 22.17 | 21.33 |
| 112 | 34.94 | 33.90 | 32.87 | 31.86 | 30.86 | 29.88 | 28.92 | 27.97 | 27.04 | 26.12 | 25.22 | 24.34 | 23.47 | 22.61 | 21.78 |
| 113 | 35.37 | 34.33 | 33.30 | 32.29 | 31.30 | 30.32 | 29.36 | 28.41 | 27.48 | 26.56 | 25.66 | 24.78 | 23.91 | 23.06 | 22.22 |
| 114 | 35.79 | 34.75 | 33.73 | 32.72 | 31.73 | 30.76 | 29.79 | 28.85 | 27.92 | 27.00 | 26.10 | 25.22 | 24.35 | 23.49 | 22.65 |
| 115 | 36.21 | 35.17 | 34.15 | 33.15 | 32.16 | 31.18 | 30.22 | 29.28 | 28.35 | 27.44 | 26.54 | 25.65 | 24.78 | 23.93 | 23.09 |
| 116 | 36.62 | 35.59 | 34.57 | 33.57 | 32.58 | 31.61 | 30.65 | 29.71 | 28.78 | 27.87 | 26.97 | 26.08 | 25.21 | 24.36 | 23.52 |
| 117 | 37.03 | 36.00 | 34.98 | 33.99 | 33.00 | 32.03 | 31.07 | 30.13 | 29.20 | 28.29 | 27.39 | 26.51 | 25.64 | 24.79 | 23.95 |
| 118 | 37.43 | 36.41 | 35.39 | 34.40 | 33.41 | 32.45 | 31.49 | 30.55 | 29.63 | 28.71 | 27.82 | 26.93 | 26.06 | 25.21 | 24.37 |
| 119 | 37.83 | 36.81 | 35.80 | 34.80 | 33.82 | 32.86 | 31.90 | 30.97 | 30.04 | 29.13 | 28.24 | 27.35 | 26.48 | 25.63 | 24.79 |
| 120 | 38.22 | 37.20 | 36.20 | 35.21 | 34.23 | 33.26 | 32.31 | 31.38 | 30.45 | 29.55 | 28.65 | 27.77 | 26.90 | 26.05 | 25.21 |

FIGURE 6-2 (continued)

# RULE of 78ths REFUND CHARTS

## ORIGINAL TERM 61 to 120 MONTHS

| ORIGINAL TERM | NUMBER OF INSTALLMENTS MATURED 61 | 62 | 63 | 64 | 65 | 66 | 67 | 68 | 69 | 70 | 71 | 72 | 73 | 74 | 75 |
|---|---|---|---|---|---|---|---|---|---|---|---|---|---|---|---|
| 61 | | | | | | | | | | | | | | | |
| 62 | .05 | | | | | | | | | | | | | | |
| 63 | .15 | .05 | | | | | | | | | | | | | |
| 64 | .29 | .14 | .05 | | | | | | | | | | | | |
| 65 | .47 | .28 | .14 | .05 | | | | | | | | | | | |
| 66 | .68 | .45 | .27 | .14 | .05 | | | | | | | | | | |
| 67 | .92 | .66 | .44 | .26 | .13 | .04 | | | | | | | | | |
| 68 | 1.19 | .90 | .64 | .43 | .26 | .13 | .04 | | | | | | | | |
| 69 | 1.49 | 1.16 | .87 | .62 | .41 | .25 | .12 | .04 | | | | | | | |
| 70 | 1.81 | 1.45 | 1.13 | .85 | .60 | .40 | .24 | .12 | .04 | | | | | | |
| 71 | 2.15 | 1.76 | 1.41 | 1.10 | .82 | .59 | .39 | .23 | .12 | .04 | | | | | |
| 72 | 2.51 | 2.09 | 1.71 | 1.37 | 1.07 | .80 | .57 | .38 | .23 | .11 | .04 | | | | |
| 73 | 2.89 | 2.44 | 2.04 | 1.67 | 1.33 | 1.04 | .78 | .56 | .37 | .22 | .11 | .04 | | | |
| 74 | 3.28 | 2.81 | 2.38 | 1.98 | 1.62 | 1.30 | 1.01 | .76 | .54 | .36 | .22 | .11 | .04 | | |
| 75 | 3.68 | 3.19 | 2.74 | 2.32 | 1.93 | 1.58 | 1.26 | .98 | .74 | .53 | .35 | .21 | .11 | .04 | |
| 76 | 4.10 | 3.59 | 3.11 | 2.67 | 2.26 | 1.88 | 1.54 | 1.23 | .96 | .72 | .51 | .34 | .21 | .10 | .03 |
| 77 | 4.53 | 4.00 | 3.50 | 3.03 | 2.60 | 2.20 | 1.83 | 1.50 | 1.20 | .93 | .70 | .50 | .33 | .20 | .10 |
| 78 | 4.97 | 4.41 | 3.89 | 3.41 | 2.95 | 2.53 | 2.14 | 1.79 | 1.46 | 1.17 | .91 | .68 | .49 | .32 | .19 |
| 79 | 5.41 | 4.84 | 4.30 | 3.80 | 3.32 | 2.88 | 2.47 | 2.09 | 1.74 | 1.42 | 1.14 | .89 | .66 | .47 | .32 |
| 80 | 5.86 | 5.28 | 4.72 | 4.20 | 3.70 | 3.24 | 2.81 | 2.41 | 2.04 | 1.70 | 1.39 | 1.11 | .86 | .65 | .46 |
| 81 | 6.32 | 5.72 | 5.15 | 4.61 | 4.10 | 3.61 | 3.16 | 2.74 | 2.35 | 1.99 | 1.66 | 1.36 | 1.08 | .84 | .63 |
| 82 | 6.79 | 6.17 | 5.58 | 5.02 | 4.50 | 4.00 | 3.53 | 3.09 | 2.67 | 2.29 | 1.94 | 1.62 | 1.32 | 1.06 | .82 |
| 83 | 7.26 | 6.63 | 6.02 | 5.45 | 4.91 | 4.39 | 3.90 | 3.44 | 3.01 | 2.61 | 2.24 | 1.89 | 1.58 | 1.29 | 1.03 |
| 84 | 7.73 | 7.09 | 6.47 | 5.88 | 5.32 | 4.79 | 4.29 | 3.81 | 3.36 | 2.94 | 2.55 | 2.18 | 1.85 | 1.54 | 1.26 |
| 85 | 8.21 | 7.55 | 6.92 | 6.32 | 5.75 | 5.20 | 4.68 | 4.19 | 3.72 | 3.28 | 2.87 | 2.49 | 2.13 | 1.81 | 1.50 |
| 86 | 8.69 | 8.02 | 7.38 | 6.76 | 6.17 | 5.61 | 5.08 | 4.57 | 4.09 | 3.64 | 3.21 | 2.81 | 2.43 | 2.09 | 1.76 |
| 87 | 9.17 | 8.49 | 7.84 | 7.21 | 6.61 | 6.03 | 5.49 | 4.96 | 4.47 | 4.00 | 3.55 | 3.13 | 2.74 | 2.38 | 2.04 |
| 88 | 9.65 | 8.96 | 8.30 | 7.66 | 7.05 | 6.46 | 5.90 | 5.36 | 4.85 | 4.37 | 3.91 | 3.47 | 3.06 | 2.68 | 2.32 |
| 89 | 10.14 | 9.44 | 8.76 | 8.11 | 7.49 | 6.89 | 6.32 | 5.77 | 5.24 | 4.74 | 4.27 | 3.82 | 3.40 | 3.00 | 2.62 |
| 90 | 10.62 | 9.91 | 9.23 | 8.57 | 7.94 | 7.33 | 6.74 | 6.18 | 5.64 | 5.13 | 4.64 | 4.18 | 3.74 | 3.32 | 2.93 |
| 91 | 11.11 | 10.39 | 9.70 | 9.03 | 8.39 | 7.76 | 7.17 | 6.59 | 6.04 | 5.52 | 5.02 | 4.54 | 4.09 | 3.66 | 3.25 |
| 92 | 11.59 | 10.87 | 10.17 | 9.49 | 8.84 | 8.20 | 7.60 | 7.01 | 6.45 | 5.91 | 5.40 | 4.91 | 4.44 | 4.00 | 3.58 |
| 93 | 12.08 | 11.35 | 10.64 | 9.95 | 9.29 | 8.65 | 8.03 | 7.44 | 6.86 | 6.31 | 5.79 | 5.28 | 4.80 | 4.35 | 3.91 |
| 94 | 12.56 | 11.83 | 11.11 | 10.41 | 9.74 | 9.09 | 8.47 | 7.86 | 7.28 | 6.72 | 6.18 | 5.67 | 5.17 | 4.70 | 4.26 |
| 95 | 13.05 | 12.30 | 11.58 | 10.88 | 10.20 | 9.54 | 8.90 | 8.29 | 7.70 | 7.13 | 6.58 | 6.05 | 5.55 | 5.07 | 4.61 |
| 96 | 13.53 | 12.78 | 12.05 | 11.34 | 10.65 | 9.99 | 9.34 | 8.72 | 8.12 | 7.54 | 6.98 | 6.44 | 5.93 | 5.43 | 4.96 |
| 97 | 14.01 | 13.25 | 12.52 | 11.80 | 11.11 | 10.44 | 9.78 | 9.15 | 8.54 | 7.95 | 7.38 | 6.84 | 6.31 | 5.81 | 5.32 |
| 98 | 14.49 | 13.73 | 12.99 | 12.27 | 11.56 | 10.88 | 10.22 | 9.59 | 8.97 | 8.37 | 7.79 | 7.24 | 6.70 | 6.18 | 5.69 |
| 99 | 14.97 | 14.20 | 13.45 | 12.73 | 12.02 | 11.33 | 10.67 | 10.02 | 9.39 | 8.79 | 8.20 | 7.64 | 7.09 | 6.57 | 6.06 |
| 100 | 15.45 | 14.67 | 13.92 | 13.19 | 12.48 | 11.78 | 11.11 | 10.46 | 9.82 | 9.21 | 8.61 | 8.04 | 7.49 | 6.95 | 6.44 |
| 101 | 15.92 | 15.14 | 14.39 | 13.65 | 12.93 | 12.23 | 11.55 | 10.89 | 10.25 | 9.63 | 9.03 | 8.44 | 7.88 | 7.34 | 6.81 |
| 102 | 16.39 | 15.61 | 14.85 | 14.11 | 13.38 | 12.68 | 11.99 | 11.33 | 10.68 | 10.05 | 9.44 | 8.85 | 8.28 | 7.73 | 7.20 |
| 103 | 16.86 | 16.08 | 15.31 | 14.56 | 13.83 | 13.13 | 12.43 | 11.76 | 11.11 | 10.47 | 9.86 | 9.26 | 8.68 | 8.12 | 7.58 |
| 104 | 17.33 | 16.54 | 15.77 | 15.02 | 14.29 | 13.57 | 12.88 | 12.20 | 11.54 | 10.90 | 10.27 | 9.67 | 9.08 | 8.52 | 7.97 |
| 105 | 17.79 | 17.00 | 16.23 | 15.47 | 14.73 | 14.02 | 13.32 | 12.63 | 11.97 | 11.32 | 10.69 | 10.08 | 9.49 | 8.91 | 8.36 |
| 106 | 18.25 | 17.46 | 16.68 | 15.92 | 15.18 | 14.46 | 13.75 | 13.07 | 12.40 | 11.74 | 11.11 | 10.49 | 9.89 | 9.31 | 8.75 |
| 107 | 18.71 | 17.91 | 17.13 | 16.37 | 15.63 | 14.90 | 14.19 | 13.50 | 12.82 | 12.17 | 11.53 | 10.90 | 10.30 | 9.71 | 9.14 |
| 108 | 19.16 | 18.37 | 17.58 | 16.82 | 16.07 | 15.34 | 14.63 | 13.93 | 13.25 | 12.59 | 11.94 | 11.31 | 10.70 | 10.11 | 9.53 |
| 109 | 19.62 | 18.82 | 18.03 | 17.26 | 16.51 | 15.78 | 15.06 | 14.36 | 13.68 | 13.01 | 12.36 | 11.73 | 11.11 | 10.51 | 9.92 |
| 110 | 20.07 | 19.26 | 18.48 | 17.71 | 16.95 | 16.22 | 15.50 | 14.79 | 14.10 | 13.43 | 12.78 | 12.14 | 11.52 | 10.91 | 10.32 |
| 111 | 20.51 | 19.71 | 18.92 | 18.15 | 17.39 | 16.65 | 15.93 | 15.22 | 14.53 | 13.85 | 13.19 | 12.55 | 11.92 | 11.31 | 10.71 |
| 112 | 20.95 | 20.15 | 19.36 | 18.58 | 17.83 | 17.08 | 16.36 | 15.64 | 14.95 | 14.27 | 13.61 | 12.96 | 12.33 | 11.71 | 11.11 |
| 113 | 21.39 | 20.59 | 19.80 | 19.02 | 18.26 | 17.51 | 16.78 | 16.07 | 15.37 | 14.69 | 14.02 | 13.37 | 12.73 | 12.11 | 11.50 |
| 114 | 21.83 | 21.02 | 20.23 | 19.45 | 18.69 | 17.94 | 17.21 | 16.49 | 15.79 | 15.10 | 14.43 | 13.78 | 13.14 | 12.51 | 11.90 |
| 115 | 22.26 | 21.45 | 20.66 | 19.88 | 19.12 | 18.37 | 17.63 | 16.91 | 16.21 | 15.52 | 14.84 | 14.18 | 13.54 | 12.91 | 12.29 |
| 116 | 22.69 | 21.88 | 21.09 | 20.31 | 19.54 | 18.79 | 18.05 | 17.33 | 16.62 | 15.93 | 15.25 | 14.59 | 13.94 | 13.31 | 12.69 |
| 117 | 23.12 | 22.31 | 21.51 | 20.73 | 19.96 | 19.21 | 18.47 | 17.75 | 17.04 | 16.34 | 15.66 | 14.99 | 14.34 | 13.70 | 13.08 |
| 118 | 23.54 | 22.73 | 21.93 | 21.15 | 20.38 | 19.63 | 18.89 | 18.16 | 17.45 | 16.75 | 16.07 | 15.40 | 14.74 | 14.10 | 13.47 |
| 119 | 23.96 | 23.15 | 22.35 | 21.57 | 20.80 | 20.04 | 19.30 | 18.57 | 17.86 | 17.16 | 16.47 | 15.80 | 15.14 | 14.50 | 13.87 |
| 120 | 24.38 | 23.57 | 22.77 | 21.98 | 21.21 | 20.45 | 19.71 | 18.98 | 18.26 | 17.56 | 16.87 | 16.20 | 15.54 | 14.89 | 14.26 |

| ORIGINAL TERM | NUMBER OF INSTALLMENTS MATURED 76 | 77 | 78 | 79 | 80 | 81 | 82 | 83 | 84 | 85 | 86 | 87 | 88 | 89 | 90 |
|---|---|---|---|---|---|---|---|---|---|---|---|---|---|---|---|
| 61 | | | | | | | | | | | | | | | |
| 62 | | | | | | | | | | | | | | | |
| 63 | | | | | | | | | | | | | | | |
| 64 | | | | | | | | | | | | | | | |
| 65 | | | | | | | | | | | | | | | |
| 66 | | | | | | | | | | | | | | | |
| 67 | | | | | | | | | | | | | | | |
| 68 | | | | | | | | | | | | | | | |
| 69 | | | | | | | | | | | | | | | |
| 70 | | | | | | | | | | | | | | | |
| 71 | | | | | | | | | | | | | | | |
| 72 | | | | | | | | | | | | | | | |
| 73 | | | | | | | | | | | | | | | |
| 74 | | | | | | | | | | | | | | | |
| 75 | | | | | | | | | | | | | | | |
| 76 | | | | | | | | | | | | | | | |
| 77 | .03 | | | | | | | | | | | | | | |
| 78 | .10 | .03 | | | | | | | | | | | | | |
| 79 | .19 | .09 | .03 | | | | | | | | | | | | |
| 80 | .31 | .19 | .09 | .03 | | | | | | | | | | | |
| 81 | .45 | .30 | .18 | .09 | .03 | | | | | | | | | | |
| 82 | .62 | .44 | .29 | .18 | .09 | .03 | | | | | | | | | |
| 83 | .80 | .60 | .43 | .29 | .17 | .09 | .03 | | | | | | | | |
| 84 | 1.01 | .78 | .59 | .42 | .28 | .17 | .08 | .03 | | | | | | | |
| 85 | 1.23 | .98 | .77 | .57 | .41 | .27 | .16 | .08 | .03 | | | | | | |
| 86 | 1.47 | 1.20 | .96 | .75 | .56 | .40 | .27 | .16 | .08 | .03 | | | | | |
| 87 | 1.72 | 1.44 | 1.18 | .94 | .73 | .55 | .39 | .26 | .16 | .08 | .03 | | | | |
| 88 | 1.99 | 1.69 | 1.40 | 1.15 | .92 | .72 | .54 | .38 | .26 | .15 | .08 | .03 | | | |
| 89 | 2.27 | 1.95 | 1.65 | 1.37 | 1.12 | .90 | .70 | .52 | .37 | .25 | .15 | .07 | .02 | | |
| 90 | 2.56 | 2.22 | 1.90 | 1.61 | 1.34 | 1.10 | .88 | .68 | .51 | .37 | .24 | .15 | .07 | .02 | |
| 91 | 2.87 | 2.51 | 2.17 | 1.86 | 1.58 | 1.31 | 1.08 | .86 | .67 | .50 | .36 | .24 | .14 | .07 | .02 |
| 92 | 3.18 | 2.81 | 2.45 | 2.13 | 1.82 | 1.54 | 1.29 | 1.05 | .84 | .65 | .49 | .35 | .23 | .14 | .07 |
| 93 | 3.50 | 3.11 | 2.75 | 2.40 | 2.08 | 1.78 | 1.51 | 1.26 | 1.03 | .82 | .64 | .48 | .34 | .23 | .14 |
| 94 | 3.83 | 3.43 | 3.05 | 2.69 | 2.35 | 2.04 | 1.75 | 1.48 | 1.23 | 1.01 | .81 | .63 | .47 | .34 | .22 |
| 95 | 4.17 | 3.75 | 3.36 | 2.98 | 2.63 | 2.30 | 2.00 | 1.71 | 1.45 | 1.21 | .99 | .79 | .61 | .46 | .33 |
| 96 | 4.51 | 4.08 | 3.67 | 3.29 | 2.92 | 2.58 | 2.26 | 1.95 | 1.68 | 1.42 | 1.18 | .97 | .77 | .60 | .45 |
| 97 | 4.86 | 4.42 | 4.00 | 3.60 | 3.22 | 2.86 | 2.52 | 2.21 | 1.91 | 1.64 | 1.39 | 1.16 | .95 | .76 | .59 |
| 98 | 5.22 | 4.76 | 4.33 | 3.92 | 3.53 | 3.15 | 2.80 | 2.47 | 2.16 | 1.88 | 1.61 | 1.36 | 1.13 | .93 | .74 |
| 99 | 5.58 | 5.11 | 4.67 | 4.24 | 3.84 | 3.45 | 3.09 | 2.75 | 2.42 | 2.12 | 1.84 | 1.58 | 1.33 | 1.11 | .91 |
| 100 | 5.94 | 5.47 | 5.01 | 4.57 | 4.16 | 3.76 | 3.39 | 3.03 | 2.69 | 2.38 | 2.08 | 1.80 | 1.54 | 1.31 | 1.09 |
| 101 | 6.31 | 5.82 | 5.36 | 4.91 | 4.48 | 4.08 | 3.69 | 3.32 | 2.97 | 2.64 | 2.33 | 2.04 | 1.77 | 1.51 | 1.28 |
| 102 | 6.68 | 6.19 | 5.71 | 5.25 | 4.82 | 4.40 | 4.00 | 3.62 | 3.26 | 2.91 | 2.59 | 2.28 | 2.00 | 1.73 | 1.48 |
| 103 | 7.06 | 6.55 | 6.07 | 5.60 | 5.15 | 4.72 | 4.31 | 3.92 | 3.55 | 3.19 | 2.86 | 2.54 | 2.24 | 1.96 | 1.70 |
| 104 | 7.44 | 6.92 | 6.43 | 5.95 | 5.49 | 5.05 | 4.63 | 4.23 | 3.85 | 3.48 | 3.13 | 2.80 | 2.49 | 2.20 | 1.92 |
| 105 | 7.82 | 7.30 | 6.79 | 6.31 | 5.84 | 5.39 | 4.96 | 4.55 | 4.15 | 3.77 | 3.41 | 3.07 | 2.75 | 2.44 | 2.16 |
| 106 | 8.20 | 7.67 | 7.16 | 6.67 | 6.19 | 5.73 | 5.29 | 4.87 | 4.46 | 4.07 | 3.70 | 3.35 | 3.02 | 2.70 | 2.40 |
| 107 | 8.58 | 8.05 | 7.53 | 7.03 | 6.54 | 6.07 | 5.62 | 5.19 | 4.78 | 4.38 | 4.00 | 3.63 | 3.29 | 2.96 | 2.65 |
| 108 | 8.97 | 8.43 | 7.90 | 7.39 | 6.90 | 6.42 | 5.96 | 5.52 | 5.10 | 4.69 | 4.30 | 3.92 | 3.57 | 3.23 | 2.91 |
| 109 | 9.36 | 8.81 | 8.27 | 7.76 | 7.26 | 6.77 | 6.31 | 5.85 | 5.42 | 5.00 | 4.60 | 4.22 | 3.85 | 3.50 | 3.17 |
| 110 | 9.75 | 9.19 | 8.65 | 8.12 | 7.62 | 7.13 | 6.65 | 6.19 | 5.75 | 5.32 | 4.91 | 4.52 | 4.14 | 3.78 | 3.44 |
| 111 | 10.14 | 9.57 | 9.03 | 8.49 | 7.98 | 7.48 | 7.00 | 6.53 | 6.08 | 5.65 | 5.23 | 4.83 | 4.44 | 4.07 | 3.72 |
| 112 | 10.52 | 9.96 | 9.40 | 8.87 | 8.34 | 7.84 | 7.35 | 6.87 | 6.42 | 5.97 | 5.55 | 5.14 | 4.74 | 4.36 | 4.00 |
| 113 | 10.91 | 10.34 | 9.78 | 9.24 | 8.71 | 8.20 | 7.70 | 7.22 | 6.75 | 6.30 | 5.87 | 5.45 | 5.05 | 4.66 | 4.29 |
| 114 | 11.30 | 10.72 | 10.16 | 9.61 | 9.08 | 8.56 | 8.05 | 7.57 | 7.09 | 6.64 | 6.19 | 5.77 | 5.35 | 4.96 | 4.58 |
| 115 | 11.69 | 11.11 | 10.54 | 9.99 | 9.45 | 8.92 | 8.41 | 7.92 | 7.44 | 6.97 | 6.52 | 6.09 | 5.67 | 5.26 | 4.87 |
| 116 | 12.08 | 11.49 | 10.92 | 10.36 | 9.81 | 9.28 | 8.77 | 8.27 | 7.78 | 7.31 | 6.85 | 6.41 | 5.98 | 5.57 | 5.17 |
| 117 | 12.47 | 11.88 | 11.30 | 10.73 | 10.18 | 9.65 | 9.13 | 8.62 | 8.13 | 7.65 | 7.19 | 6.74 | 6.30 | 5.88 | 5.48 |
| 118 | 12.86 | 12.26 | 11.68 | 11.11 | 10.55 | 10.01 | 9.49 | 8.97 | 8.47 | 7.99 | 7.52 | 7.06 | 6.62 | 6.20 | 5.78 |
| 119 | 13.25 | 12.65 | 12.06 | 11.48 | 10.92 | 10.38 | 9.85 | 9.33 | 8.82 | 8.33 | 7.86 | 7.39 | 6.95 | 6.51 | 6.09 |
| 120 | 13.64 | 13.03 | 12.44 | 11.86 | 11.29 | 10.74 | 10.21 | 9.68 | 9.17 | 8.68 | 8.20 | 7.73 | 7.27 | 6.83 | 6.40 |

FIGURE 6–2 (continued)

# RULE OF 78ths REFUND CHARTS

## ORIGINAL TERM 61 to 120 MONTHS

| ORIG-INAL TERM | NUMBER OF INSTALLMENTS MATURED | | | | | | | | | | | | | | | | | | NUMBER OF INSTALLMENTS MATURED | | | | | | | | | | | |
|---|---|---|---|---|---|---|---|---|---|---|---|---|---|---|---|---|---|---|---|---|---|---|---|---|---|---|---|---|---|---|
| | 91 | 92 | 93 | 94 | 95 | 96 | 97 | 98 | 99 | 100 | 101 | 102 | 103 | 104 | 105 | 106 | 107 | 108 | 109 | 110 | 111 | 112 | 113 | 114 | 115 | 116 | 117 | 118 | 119 | 120 |
| 61 | | | | | | | | | | | | | | | | | | | | | | | | | | | | | | |
| 62 | | | | | | | | | | | | | | | | | | | | | | | | | | | | | | |
| 63 | | | | | | | | | | | | | | | | | | | | | | | | | | | | | | |
| 64 | | | | | | | | | | | | | | | | | | | | | | | | | | | | | | |
| 65 | | | | | | | | | | | | | | | | | | | | | | | | | | | | | | |
| 66 | | | | | | | | | | | | | | | | | | | | | | | | | | | | | | |
| 67 | | | | | | | | | | | | | | | | | | | | | | | | | | | | | | |
| 68 | | | | | | | | | | | | | | | | | | | | | | | | | | | | | | |
| 69 | | | | | | | | | | | | | | | | | | | | | | | | | | | | | | |
| 70 | | | | | | | | | | | | | | | | | | | | | | | | | | | | | | |
| 71 | | | | | | | | | | | | | | | | | | | | | | | | | | | | | | |
| 72 | | | | | | | | | | | | | | | | | | | | | | | | | | | | | | |
| 73 | | | | | | | | | | | | | | | | | | | | | | | | | | | | | | |
| 74 | | | | | | | | | | | | | | | | | | | | | | | | | | | | | | |
| 75 | | | | | | | | | | | | | | | | | | | | | | | | | | | | | | |
| 76 | | | | | | | | | | | | | | | | | | | | | | | | | | | | | | |
| 77 | | | | | | | | | | | | | | | | | | | | | | | | | | | | | | |
| 78 | | | | | | | | | | | | | | | | | | | | | | | | | | | | | | |
| 79 | | | | | | | | | | | | | | | | | | | | | | | | | | | | | | |
| 80 | | | | | | | | | | | | | | | | | | | | | | | | | | | | | | |
| 81 | | | | | | | | | | | | | | | | | | | | | | | | | | | | | | |
| 82 | | | | | | | | | | | | | | | | | | | | | | | | | | | | | | |
| 83 | | | | | | | | | | | | | | | | | | | | | | | | | | | | | | |
| 84 | | | | | | | | | | | | | | | | | | | | | | | | | | | | | | |
| 85 | | | | | | | | | | | | | | | | | | | | | | | | | | | | | | |
| 86 | | | | | | | | | | | | | | | | | | | | | | | | | | | | | | |
| 87 | | | | | | | | | | | | | | | | | | | | | | | | | | | | | | |
| 88 | | | | | | | | | | | | | | | | | | | | | | | | | | | | | | |
| 89 | | | | | | | | | | | | | | | | | | | | | | | | | | | | | | |
| 90 | | | | | | | | | | | | | | | | | | | | | | | | | | | | | | |
| 91 | | | | | | | | | | | | | | | | | | | | | | | | | | | | | | |
| 92 | .02 | | | | | | | | | | | | | | | | | | | | | | | | | | | | | |
| 93 | .07 | .02 | | | | | | | | | | | | | | | | | | | | | | | | | | | | |
| 94 | .13 | .07 | .02 | | | | | | | | | | | | | | | | | | | | | | | | | | | |
| 95 | .22 | .13 | .07 | .02 | | | | | | | | | | | | | | | | | | | | | | | | | | |
| 96 | .32 | .21 | .13 | .06 | .02 | | | | | | | | | | | | | | | | | | | | | | | | | |
| 97 | .44 | .32 | .21 | .13 | .06 | .02 | | | | | | | | | | | | | | | | | | | | | | | | |
| 98 | .58 | .43 | .31 | .21 | .12 | .06 | .02 | | | | | | | | | | | | | | | | | | | | | | | |
| 99 | .73 | .57 | .42 | .30 | .20 | .12 | .06 | .02 | | | | | | | | | | | | | | | | | | | | | | |
| 100 | .89 | .71 | .55 | .42 | .30 | .20 | .12 | .06 | .02 | | | | | | | | | | | | | | | | | | | | | |
| 101 | 1.07 | .87 | .70 | .54 | .41 | .29 | .19 | .12 | .06 | .02 | | | | | | | | | | | | | | | | | | | | |
| 102 | 1.26 | 1.05 | .86 | .69 | .53 | .40 | .29 | .19 | .11 | .06 | .02 | | | | | | | | | | | | | | | | | | | |
| 103 | 1.46 | 1.23 | 1.03 | .84 | .67 | .52 | .39 | .28 | .19 | .11 | .06 | .02 | | | | | | | | | | | | | | | | | | |
| 104 | 1.67 | 1.43 | 1.21 | 1.01 | .82 | .66 | .51 | .38 | .27 | .18 | .11 | .05 | .02 | | | | | | | | | | | | | | | | | |
| 105 | 1.89 | 1.64 | 1.40 | 1.19 | .99 | .81 | .65 | .50 | .38 | .27 | .18 | .11 | .05 | .02 | | | | | | | | | | | | | | | | |
| 106 | 2.12 | 1.85 | 1.60 | 1.38 | 1.16 | .97 | .79 | .63 | .49 | .37 | .26 | .18 | .11 | .05 | .02 | | | | | | | | | | | | | | | |
| 107 | 2.35 | 2.08 | 1.82 | 1.57 | 1.35 | 1.14 | .95 | .78 | .62 | .48 | .36 | .26 | .17 | .10 | .05 | .02 | | | | | | | | | | | | | | |
| 108 | 2.60 | 2.31 | 2.04 | 1.78 | 1.55 | 1.33 | 1.12 | .93 | .76 | .61 | .48 | .36 | .25 | .17 | .10 | .05 | .02 | | | | | | | | | | | | | |
| 109 | 2.85 | 2.55 | 2.27 | 2.00 | 1.75 | 1.52 | 1.30 | 1.10 | .92 | .75 | .60 | .47 | .35 | .25 | .17 | .10 | .05 | .02 | | | | | | | | | | | | |
| 110 | 3.11 | 2.80 | 2.51 | 2.23 | 1.97 | 1.72 | 1.49 | 1.28 | 1.08 | .90 | .74 | .59 | .46 | .34 | .25 | .16 | .10 | .05 | .02 | | | | | | | | | | | |
| 111 | 3.38 | 3.06 | 2.75 | 2.46 | 2.19 | 1.93 | 1.69 | 1.46 | 1.25 | 1.06 | .88 | .72 | .58 | .45 | .34 | .24 | .16 | .10 | .05 | .02 | | | | | | | | | | |
| 112 | 3.65 | 3.32 | 3.00 | 2.70 | 2.42 | 2.15 | 1.90 | 1.66 | 1.44 | 1.23 | 1.04 | .87 | .71 | .57 | .44 | .33 | .24 | .16 | .09 | .05 | .02 | | | | | | | | | |
| 113 | 3.93 | 3.59 | 3.26 | 2.95 | 2.65 | 2.38 | 2.11 | 1.86 | 1.63 | 1.41 | 1.21 | 1.02 | .85 | .70 | .56 | .43 | .33 | .23 | .16 | .09 | .05 | .02 | | | | | | | | |
| 114 | 4.21 | 3.86 | 3.52 | 3.20 | 2.90 | 2.61 | 2.33 | 2.07 | 1.83 | 1.60 | 1.39 | 1.19 | 1.01 | .84 | .69 | .55 | .43 | .32 | .23 | .15 | .09 | .05 | .02 | | | | | | | |
| 115 | 4.50 | 4.14 | 3.79 | 3.46 | 3.15 | 2.85 | 2.56 | 2.29 | 2.04 | 1.80 | 1.57 | 1.36 | 1.17 | .99 | .82 | .67 | .54 | .42 | .31 | .22 | .15 | .09 | .04 | .01 | | | | | | |
| 116 | 4.79 | 4.42 | 4.07 | 3.73 | 3.40 | 3.09 | 2.80 | 2.52 | 2.25 | 2.00 | 1.77 | 1.55 | 1.34 | 1.15 | .97 | .81 | .66 | .53 | .41 | .31 | .22 | .15 | .09 | .04 | .01 | | | | | |
| 117 | 5.08 | 4.71 | 4.35 | 4.00 | 3.67 | 3.35 | 3.04 | 2.75 | 2.48 | 2.22 | 1.97 | 1.74 | 1.52 | 1.32 | 1.13 | .96 | .80 | .65 | .52 | .41 | .30 | .22 | .14 | .09 | .04 | .01 | | | | |
| 118 | 5.38 | 5.00 | 4.63 | 4.27 | 3.93 | 3.60 | 3.29 | 2.99 | 2.71 | 2.44 | 2.18 | 1.94 | 1.71 | 1.50 | 1.30 | 1.11 | .94 | .78 | .64 | .51 | .40 | .30 | .21 | .14 | .09 | .04 | .01 | | | |
| 119 | 5.69 | 5.29 | 4.92 | 4.55 | 4.20 | 3.87 | 3.54 | 3.24 | 2.94 | 2.66 | 2.39 | 2.14 | 1.90 | 1.68 | 1.47 | 1.27 | 1.09 | .92 | .77 | .63 | .50 | .39 | .29 | .21 | .14 | .08 | .04 | .01 | | |
| 120 | 5.99 | 5.59 | 5.21 | 4.83 | 4.48 | 4.13 | 3.80 | 3.48 | 3.18 | 2.89 | 2.62 | 2.36 | 2.11 | 1.87 | 1.65 | 1.45 | 1.25 | 1.07 | .91 | .76 | .62 | .50 | .39 | .29 | .21 | .14 | .08 | .04 | .01 | |

# 7

# THE INSIDE SCOOP ON LEASING

Where does fiction end and fact begin? Leasing is full of misconceptions, misapplications, misuse, abuse, tax trickery, accounting disagreements, funny terminology, and, believe it or not, it's been one of the fastest growing, most profitable businesses in the United States for the past several years!

## THE WONDERFUL WORLD OF EQUIPMENT LEASING

Yes, leasing is a huge, powerful segment of the finance industry, involving over 20 billion dollars annually in equipment acquisitions. Exotic deals are made for jetliners, ships, and computer systems connecting industries, government bureaus, even nations.

You name it, and someone will lease it: photocopy machines, telephone systems, postage meters, forklift trucks, X-ray machines, hospital beds (complete with bedpans), even the partitions in offices. It is almost impossible to name a commercial item of equipment that someone has not leased.

Banks, normally confined to doing business within their state, have established leasing subsidiaries operating worldwide. Starting in the 1950s, finance companies established nationwide leasing arms. Insurance companies, seeking places to invest their vast flow of money and wanting to tax-shelter their profits, are now participating with major leasing companies.

Thousands of independent leasing companies have sprung up, funded by banks, private capital, foreign money, investment capital from a hundred sources. Manufacturers and sellers of every imaginable kind of equipment have set up "captive" leasing companies, increasing their sales and profits. All told, a very big game.

### Modern Money Magic?

Why is all of this happening? Is leasing really a financing panacea? Is it "modern money magic"—or just a financing device? Are the much-touted advantages real or imaginary? Like anything so popular, it's a little of each. Some black, some white—and a lot that's gray.

Great marketing phrases have been manufactured out of truthful sounding premises:

- "Profits are made from the use of equipment, not ownership." True enough, but if a lease is fully amortizing and noncancelable, with a nominal purchase option at the end, what do you have, a rental plan or another way to buy on time payments?
- "Rent what you need today, trade up when technology develops a better widget." Sounds good—but what will it cost to get out of the original lease?
- "Get the equipment you need without one cent down." Not one cent? Well, what do you call the first and last month in advance or a 10% security deposit, Monopoly money?
- "Leasing is an expense item; you don't have to show the debt on your balance sheet." Really? Try telling *that* to the IRS, if it isn't really a true lease—or your bank, when you borrow. "Well, maybe just put in a little footnote . . . ."
- "If you have a cost-plus contract (usually with Uncle Sam), need equipment to perform? Lease it! Expense the equipment against the job. After the contract ends, buy the equipment back 'for a song.'" This one isn't fiction—it's been done many times—at taxpayer expense, of course.
- "Budgetary problems? Can't borrow money?" Don't worry—lease it!

### Let's Dissolve the Mystery

The truth is, leasing can be an extremely useful financing alternative. It can be the answer to budgetary problems. An example of a budgetary problem that leasing can solve is the situation where your company division or other unit needs equipment, cannot borrow, and has already used up the amount budgeted for cash purchases.

It is sometimes the best way to take advantage of our tax laws and at the same time acquire needed equipment. For instance, in a given year you may have bought enough new equipment to have wiped out your tax obligation with investment tax credits. You still want to add more equipment, and having that equipment immediately is more important than having ITCs to carry forward. There are lessors with ample funds who are eager for those tax credits. These lessors will often offer you an excellent rate and ready credit approval to get your ITC.

The accounting profession, working against diverse and immense pressures, is struggling to remedy some of the abuses and irregularities of reporting lease obligations. The Internal Revenue Service is constantly striving to inform its staff, close loopholes, interpret the law, and still work with business and industry as prudently as possible.

The Economic Recovery Act (ERTA), which became law on August 31, 1981, will undoubtedly simplify the mutual problems of the accounting profession and the Internal Revenue Service, at least to the extent of interpreting and regulating equipment lease transactions. Basically, this legislation greatly reduced the complexities of defining a lease versus a conditional sale contract. There remains, however, the multitude of leases executed prior to August 31, 1981 (provided the leased equipment was also placed in service prior to that date). Generally, these leases may be interpreted by IRS and the accounting profession as being under tax regulations then in place. In addition, the ERTA itself will be the subject of considerable technical interpretation and implementation as post-Act leases are transacted. There will be treasury regulations that will clarify the language of the Act. These will be followed by Internal Revenue Service rulings, resulting from their own interpretations and the actual examination of business taxpayers' treatment of leases executed after the Act became effective.

The objective of *Creative Business Financing* is to clarify the use of leasing by taking away the mystery. We are going to tell you everything you need to know about this financing alternative for everyday equipment acquisition purposes. We will explain how the extensive changes of ERTA affect leasing, especially those changes which may influence your decision to utilize this alternative or choose some other means of acquiring equipment. But through all of the explanations, we want you to recognize leasing for what it really is—just another means of acquiring equipment. Or, in the case of a sale-and-lease-back arrangement, another means of borrowing money. Recognize that a sale of your equipment to a lessor from whom you lease it back is generally an expensive way to borrow. Why? Because in most states, you must pay a new sales tax on the sale, and you may have a capital gain, also taxable.

As a business owner or corporate officer with the responsibility of deciding whether to buy outright (using your cash resources), lease, or borrow, you need a logical process to work through. Although lease finance calculations can be complicated, or made to appear complicated, we will provide easy-to-comprehend facts, charts, and formulas to aid you in your decision process.

## TO LEASE OR NOT TO LEASE, THAT IS THE QUESTION

Leasing has definite advantages . . . and some costly disadvantages. Leasing is not for everyone. Under some circumstances, it's not for anyone!

We are going to review the most commonly touted advantages, weighing the pros and cons—including the literal cons. We cover these real or imagined advantages to debunk often-advertised benefits that sound better than they really are. We point out those which can be truly beneficial. Many of the points covered depend on where you or your business stands taxwise. Other variances occur because of anticipated growth resulting from use of equipment, future cash flow versus present cash flow, a host of factors which must be answered before a valid lease, buy, or borrow decision can be made.

Consider each of these leasing advantages and our comments on them. They will help you decide if leasing is right for you.

### Conserve Your Cash

Cash conservation is one of the most valid reasons to select leasing as a financing alternative:

- . . . If your credit strength qualifies you for a lease with only one or two advance rentals and no security deposit.
- . . . If you know how to negotiate a rate equal to regular loan financing—which usually requires a down payment.
- . . . If you can use the conserved cash in your business in profitable ways. Leasing rates tend to be higher than time-sale financing or loan rates, especially in amounts below $15,000. Why pay more rate charges and higher payments if all you accomplish is a decrease in profits?

If you are temporarily cash-short, have good credit and financial strength, and can acquire cost-saving or profit-making equipment, by all means lease it. But don't end up paying so many advance rentals or such a big security deposit that you might as well make a down payment and save money on the time-contract rate and lower monthly payments.

BE AWARE OF THE COST DIFFERENTIALS Most leases are computed by multiplying the lease rate factor times the total equipment cost.

- Advance rentals do not a down payment make. If you pay the lessor five advance rentals, you still pay lease finance charges on the entire equipment cost.
- Security deposits do not a down payment make. If you pay the lessor a 10% security deposit, you still pay the lease finance charges on the entire equipment cost. Indeed, the lessor usually holds your deposit until lease termination, interest free! Some

lessors reduce the lease rate factor to compensate you, in full or part, for your money which they hold throughout the lease term.

Arrange to pay the vendor separately for components, accessories, freight, installation, and any separable part. Let the lessor figure his lease rate against only the remaining "hard equipment" costs.

This may sound contrary to cash conservation, but it can be compatible because the cash paid saves you lease charges. You get the lease terms you were after, including another valid cash conserver—the fixed purchase option. Reason: You have deferred the payment of 10% of the equipment cost until the end of the lease.

When you exercise your option to buy, you pay with future dollars—quite possibly cheaper dollars. Not only are the dollars less valuable, but they come due when you are probably in a better position to pay.

## Hedge Against Inflation

It is a sad commentary on our eroding dollar's value, but inflation is another reason leasing is growing in popularity.

Recognize the fixed-percentage purchase option for what it is: a balloon payment, pushed off three to ten years into the future.

A balloon payment on a loan is a deferment of some portion of the principal balance to be repaid in one lump sum. During the term of payments, your regular payments are smaller because of the amount to come due in the balloon. Sometimes the lender will refinance the balloon into a new series of payments.

There is little or no difference between a purchase option and a balloon payment if the option is a fixed percentage or dollar amount.

Furthermore, the so-called renewal option payments, if applied to the purchase option due, serve the same purpose as refinancing the balloon. (More on that aspect later.)

Cash conservation? Hedge against inflation? You bet! So why not try to obtain a 15% or a 20% purchase option? You will pay something for deferring a greater percentage of the equipment's cost, but a higher option aids cash flow and improves on your inflation hedge. You won't pay too much for the larger purchase option if you refer to our lease rate charts or formulas at the end of this chapter.

- A larger purchase option drops your monthly or other regular payments during the lease term.
- If the equipment has a long, useful life and is readily resalable, the lessor can usually be persuaded to offer a larger purchase option percentage.
- A large purchase option (from a lessor) is often more attainable than a balloon payment on a bank equipment loan.

### Longer Terms

Leasing generally allows longer terms—kind of crazy, but usually true, and another reason for the popularity of leasing.

Leasing is more realistically tied to equipment use. Use is tied to depreciable life, which translates into longer terms, generally five to ten years, with terms of up to fifteen years not unusual.

It appears strange that few banks make equipment loans for more than five years. (Many prefer three years.) Yet their leasing subsidiaries will do the same financing as a lease for seven years!

Inconsistent or stupid? Not really. Longer terms offer profit opportunities to all lessors, not just in more lease rate charges, but also from what they really like: investment tax credits, depreciation, and deferred earnings from residuals paid at the end of the lease.

Longer terms provide for full investment tax credit and long depreciation schedules. Complexities mean a better chance to outnegotiate business people unfamiliar with intricate tax laws and complex lease calculations.

DON'T FORGET, YOU'RE PLAYING *THEIR* GAME Unwittingly, some business people give away their investment tax credit. Others may trade it off too cheap, for a lower rate that is not lowered enough to compensate for giving it away. Loans do not offer these tax-shelter and added profit possibilities to banks. Uncomplicated bank loans do not confuse business people, but leasing can be difficult to understand.

We will suggest how you can locate the lowest possible rate in those rare cases where giving up your ITC makes any sense. We will also discuss how to retain the ITC when leasing and still make a good deal.

### Leasing Preserves Your Credit Lines

"Acquire the equipment you need, without disturbing your regular credit lines." Leasing companies often advertise this as a sales point. We offer our viewpoint on this touted advantage:

- Hogwash! Most leases are a firm obligation to pay. The payments come out of cash flow, just like any payment. If your bank or leasing company investigates and feels you cannot service the debt, it will not approve the lease.
- If you have a noncancelable lease—and most leases are—your bank definitely considers the lease as a credit extension. It counts the lease obligation against your credit limit.
- What if you don't show it on your balance sheet? It is an expense, isn't it? It is only if it is written as an operating lease (a rental arrangement) or structured as a true lease under the guidelines prior to the ERTA or if it complies as an expensable lease under the safe harbor rules of the 1981 Act. Otherwise, the asset should have been capitalized and depreciated, not expensed. Don't think lenders ignore equipment rental expenses when analyzing your financial statements. If consistently

sizable, this is a sure indication that long-term lease obligations are being "expensed off." (See ERTA summary at the end of this chapter.)

- With today's credit interchange information, almost totally computerized, don't kid yourself—virtually all lessors report to credit bureaus on leases they complete. They also file UCC-1 Financing Statements, at least for "information purposes."

Occasionally banks will maintain your short-term credit lines even though you enter into leases with them or an outside lessor. If you are working well within debt limits, a lease will of course not disturb your credit limits. The problems start when the lease pushes against or past the debt limits established by the bank for your company.

### You Pay with Pretax Dollars

- Sounds good: you expense off the rentals using pretax dollars, then, at the end of the lease, you buy the equipment for fair market value. Or, under the new Tax Act, even with a nominal option, if the lease is properly structured as expensable under safe harbor rules. No question, this usually works out all right.
- You must be sure you have a lease that is acceptable to the Internal Revenue Service as expensable. Otherwise, be prepared for the IRS to reverse all those rapidly expensed-off pretax dollars.
- If you expense off rental payments on an unqualified lease and the IRS audit picks up on this, they make you start over! After calculating the normal depreciation tax deduction value, you pay taxes and perhaps penalties on the incorrectly reported adjusted income.

### You're Never Bogged Down with Obsolete Equipment

This is another claim advanced by lessors. Unless you have a straight rental agreement or a carefully structured regular lease,. it simply does not hold water.

- Ever try giving back obsolete equipment to the lessor? Are you kidding? What is the lessor going to do with it?
- Ever try canceling a lease and getting a refund of "unearned lease finance charges"?
- You could be bogged down with an obsolete lease, if you went into it thinking it was a miracle way to avoid obsolescence. There is always a price to be paid for the privilege of escaping a lease involving equipment that has become obsolete.

Here are three ways to protect yourself when leasing equipment with rapid obsolescence probability:

1. Lease from the manufacturer or an authorized vendor. Obtain a written "trade in and trade up" agreement. Reach a reasona-

ble understanding as to application of rentals paid in and what must be paid to achieve trade-up to the new equipment.

2. Negotiate a lease with a lessor who will provide, in writing, a predetermined method to close out the original lease, giving you credit for a portion of the rentals paid in. Or, have the lessor agree to compute by the rule of 78ths the amount of unearned lease finance charges to be credited you. (You, as lessee, must dispose of the obsolete equipment.)
3. Enter into a "fair market value" purchase option type of lease. This option should be written so that you are assured you can surrender the equipment if you choose not to pay the option price. If you must get rid of obsolete equipment, at least you are not stuck with a fixed percentage amount due at the end of the lease. That is why you must watch out for "put"-type options that may look like a fair market value agreement but in reality require you to buy the equipment at the predetermined price.

If you are contemplating acquiring equipment with rapid changing technology, don't enter into a lease without predetermined escape clauses. We recommend acquiring this type of equipment on a loan or contract. When it starts reaching obsolescence, you won't have the complications of closing out a lease. At least with a loan or contract, you can be sure of stopping or minimizing interest costs, and you have more freedom with the resale of the equipment.

## IS A LEASE YOUR BEST DEAL?

We would like to present you with a nicely organized response to that question. Unfortunately, in many equipment lease financing situations, a good answer is not so easy to come by as you might think. There are a number of unusual factors peculiar only to leasing that may influence your decision. However, it is important to bear in mind that leasing is just another financing alternative. That is all it is: another way to acquire equipment on finance-type terms.

There are tax implications to be considered even in the simplest leasing arrangement. In the more complex "tax-oriented" or "leveraged" leases, consideration must be given to your tax position, the lessor's tax status, and even the tax shelter needs of third-party investors in the leveraged lease. We are going to confine ourselves to the usual types of leasing arrangements business people encounter in acquiring equipment to operate their business or in production, to produce income. Tax considerations will be covered to define and create an awareness of what to look for and what questions to ask. Beyond that, individual situations vary so greatly that business people should look to their accountant or tax attorney to resolve questions of tax consequences.

Every financing arrangement has a cost-of-money factor. Leasing is no different, but it is sometimes more difficult to determine the inherent costs involved. Also, because leases often require less of your cash, the "time value" of money retained in your business can be a factor worth considering. (See Fig. 7-1 at the end of this chapter.) So does the purchase option you will probably exercise two to ten years later. Renewal option clauses and their costs can also be a variable to consider. Any time you push final acquisition costs out into the future, you will have variance in your true interest costs.

As we demonstrated in chapter three, lease payments are determined by using a rate factor. (Even when your lease payments are tied to prime, the lessor will generally relate changes in the prime to an equivalent rate factor.) The rate factor is usually expressed as a multiplier: so much per hundred or per thousand dollars per month, times the total equipment cost. (The rate factor could also be based on a quarterly or semiannual cost per hundred or thousand, if that is how your payment schedule will be structured.) Inherent in every rate factor is the money cost—the annual simple interest rate you will pay. Call it lease finance charges or whatever, the lessor is going to earn interest on the money they pay to whomever they purchase equipment to be leased to you. The interest earned by the lessor is generally referred to as his yield, or return on investment; of course, this is the gross on the investment, prior to his own money costs and expenses.

A lease can be your best deal, even though you pay more lease finance charges than you would in loan interest or finance charges on a time-sale contract. It could also be an unnecessarily expensive means of acquiring equipment, if a loan or contract would have served the same purpose at lower inherent interest costs—if the lease vehicle fails to show other benefits from tax or cash-conserved standpoints. To protect yourself from overpaying, you should become familiar with the several factors that enter into lease payment calculations.

## Any Variation Changes the Yield

To understand this, refer to our Lease Rate Charts (Fig. 3-4). You will note that the rate changes with every variation in security deposits paid, the purchase option, and, of course, length of term. Our lease charts contain constantly varying rate factors so that the lessor will earn the designated yield despite variations.

Consider each of these factors in relation to leases you may be negotiating:

- How many months in the lease term and how many security deposits or advance rentals will you be required to pay?

  Remember, when you pay the lessor one or more advance rentals, he can then earn interest on your money because until he puts out his money to pay for your equipment, he has no investment.

- Lessor pays you no interest for advance rentals or security deposits held until the end of the lease. Therefore, the more you pay him up front, the lower should be the rate factor. The proper, adequate adjustment of the rate factor is what you must watch carefully in order to pay the desired interest rate.

- Strictly speaking, if the rentals are called advance rentals, all rentals beyond the first month should actually pay the last month or months. For instance, if you pay the first and last three months at lease inception, you would assume the final three months are prepaid, right? Should be, but that isn't necessarily what lessors do. Many times, you will be expected to pay those three months as they come due. At lease termination, having run the full term, the lessor either refunds those advance rentals or applies them against the purchase option you will probably then be exercising.
- If you are required to pay five security deposits, which usually are equivalent to five monthly rental payments, you lay out *six* rental payments. The first goes to pay the first month in advance, and the other five security deposits go into the lessor's coffers. They are held there—interest free—right to the end of the lease.

Our Lease Rate Charts are based on security deposits held to the end because this is the method used by many major leasing companies. Leasing often loses its cash-conservation usefulness when you get into four to six advance rentals or security deposits. Often, the lower cash requirement is the only reason to choose leasing over a contract requiring a larger down payment.

Some lessors do apply additional advance rentals to the final month or months. Be sure the lease says so specifically: for example, on a 60-month lease, if upon signing you pay "the first and last two months," make sure the fifty-ninth and sixtieth months are paid for in advance. To help you check out the lessor's quotations, we have included a Lease Yield Calculator at the end of this chapter (Fig. 7–2). In the event you cannot backtrack into our Lease Rate Charts for reasonably close rate factors, use our Lease Yield Calculator to learn the true lessor yield, even with differing advance rentals, purchase options, or unusual terms such as 66 months, rather than the more standard 36, 48, 60, or 84 months.

### Get Compensation for Up Front Monies

You should be compensated for all advance rentals or security deposits in the form of lower rental rate factors. Your rate reflects the value to the lessor of your first month in advance. Thus, at 20% yield, for example, if you paid one security deposit your rate factor would drop from 25.09 to 24.69 per thousand per month. The lessor's yield remains at 20%, and you have been exactly compensated for lessor's holding your security deposit.

Thousands of lessees have been shortchanged—or not compensated at all—by lessors who do not voluntarily correct the rate to reflect the lessee's cash they receive and hold. This happens most often when, in negotiating, the lessor changes the advance or security deposit requirements. Some change the rate only slightly, others not at all!

### Purchase Option or Buy-Back Price

How much does it cost to buy the equipment from the lessor at lease termination?

- In our example, the cost is 10% of the total *original* equipment cost.
- In our example in Fig. 7-2 (and in our Lease Rate Chart), it is called a purchase option. Sometimes lessors use phrases like "residual of purchase price" or "buy-back price." If the option is a prestated percentage or dollar amount, these terms are synonymous.
- In our example, we are using a full-payout lease. Many leases are written so that you, as lessee, will pay the stated 10% purchase option price. This isn't a residual value, it is a fixed buy-out price. A residual value comes from the fair market value type of option.

Most full-payout leases are written with no possibility of surrendering the equipment to the lessor. Of course, with good, well-maintained equipment, a lessee would be crazy to surrender it and not pay the 10% option price, anyway! The leases that do not allow return of equipment often use a "put" option clause. This document or lease clause states how much you *must* pay upon lease termination or at end of lease term.

### Sales or Use Taxes Add to Lease Costs

Finally—and many lessees forget to consider this—when it comes time for the lessor to go through the procedure of selling the equipment back to the lessee, in most states you must pay sales tax on the purchase option price paid.

Think about this forgotten cost and what has taken place: The lessor buys your equipment for you and pays the sales tax. The tax becomes part of the total equipment cost. At lease end, to buy the equipment back from the lessor, you must pay 10% of the lessor's original equipment cost, plus sales tax on that amount.

There are exceptions. Some states do not require the lessor to pay sales tax initially but allow him to charge a use tax on each payment, generally the same as the prevailing sales tax rate. The lessor collects this tax and remits it to the taxing authority on a monthly or quarterly basis.

Some states have tax option laws. That is, you are given the choice of paying the usual sales tax at time of purchase by lessor or, by your election or at the lessor's decision, you pay the use tax on each payment. If you choose to pay the use tax—or if the lessor's system decides this for you—you will be required to pay any increases in the use tax that may occur during the lease term. If the lessor paid the sales tax initially, it is over, and the only sales tax increase you might pay is on the purchase option.

When you compute the overall cost of a lease, don't forget to factor in sales or use taxes. If the lease under consideration has a sizable purchase option to be exercised and your state levies a large tax, taxes can add significantly to total lease cost. Bear in mind that taxes have a habit of increasing and that most leases run three to seven years—plenty of time for tax increases! If you buy with borrowed monies or on a time-sale contract, you pay only the initial sales tax. Also, guard against the lessor who quotes a lease payment and later adds on the use tax.

### Purchase Option = Balloon Payment

Remember, if you negotiate a loan with a balloon payment at the end, there is no way a state can collect any sales tax on that balloon! With a lease, true lease or not, the fiction must be maintained. The lessor owns the equipment; you are buying it back; voila—another sales tax!

- Assuming that leasing is the easiest or perhaps only way to get a deferred sizable balloon payment, it usually makes good business sense to negotiate the largest option the lessor will permit.
- Pay back with cheaper dollars, as we have said! Just be sure you get the proper lower lease rate, to maintain the same yield, compensating you for the greater option price you finally pay.
- If you negotiate a 20% purchase option, the rate factor should drop from 25.09 to 24.13 per thousand per month.

  Your monthly payment would become $241.30 instead of $250.90. Over the 60-month lease term, you have gradually conserved $576.00 to pay the added $1,000 purchase option (20% of $10,000 = $2,000).

- Once again, don't let the lessor improperly change the lease rate factor if you negotiate a larger purchase option. Refer to our Lease Rate Chart. You know the 24.13 factor gives the lessor the same 20% yield and you the proper proportionate compensation for paying a 20% purchase option five years in the future, rather than 10%.

If your particular lease circumstances are not included in our Lease Rate Charts, you may calculate rate and yield comparisons by using the Lease Yield Calculator (Fig. 7-2).

### Lease, Borrow, or Pay Cash?

Who pays cash anymore—especially for a $100,000 piece of machinery? Well, some companies do pay cash, without realizing that a properly structured lease might have been better. Even though they saved interest costs, cash is gone from their businesses.

Many companies borrow or lease to acquire capital equipment, even though they have ample funds to pay cash. Those who use some type of finance payment plan, rather than depleting cash reserves, are probably using a planned money-management system. Cash flow control is important to all businesses and can be crucial to the survival of a company with tight working capital.

It can be proven, under the right circumstances, that it is less costly to lease than to borrow on time payments or to pay cash. More than theory or mathematical sleight of hand, when you understand the value of cash conserved and employed in other profitable ways, you appreciate the time value of money. When leasing equipment, this concept requires additional knowledge of our tax laws and depreciation allowances. Consideration must also be given to how beneficial tax credits and depreciation might be to the lessor versus the benefits to you or your company as lessee.*

There are certain "right circumstances" which help to indicate that leasing can be the best way to acquire equipment. We emphasize and caution you, we use the words *can be* advisedly. What are the right circumstances? First and foremost, you must enter into a lease that will stand up as a true lease (under pre-ERTA guidelines), a rental-type operating lease, or a lease that qualifies under the new Tax Act's safe harbor rules.

It is also desirable to be able to expense the payments off over a shorter term than is available under depreciation guidelines. However, the Act has decreased the opportunities of this criterion because of liberalized cost recovery allowances. This section of the Act has completely changed the old Asset Depreciation Range (ADR) depreciation system. It is replaced by a new concept, the Accelerated Cost Recovery System (ACRS). (See ERTA summary at the end of this chapter.)

You must be able to arrange longer lease terms than a regular two- or three-year commercial loan. Generally, the term should run at least five years, and seven is preferable. At that time, the circumstances are such that the investment tax credit is not as important to you as the lower payment. In this case, you trade off your ITC for a much lower lease rate. It can still be the right circumstances if the lessor passes the ITC to you and reduces the rate only for taking depreciation.

Your investment tax credit and depreciation are very valuable to your lessor. They reduce the lessor's tax payments, just as they do your own taxes if not passed to a lessor. Because the lessor does not actually use the equipment, the lessor benefits while you operate or

*Figure 7-3 is based on a "true" lease, with payments expensed as rentals. Leasing proves more advantageous than either a loan or a cash purchase in these charts. Note that leasing also results in more accumulated cash conserved than a loan or a cash purchase. For your own calculations, we provide two blank forms, Figures 7-4 and 7-5.

employ people to run it. The same thing applies to the investment tax credit. The lessor makes the investment on your behalf and receives your tax credit. But he then starts receiving your payments, reducing his investment and risk. From the remote position of investor, the lessor takes all the benefits of a user without the tribulations of the user-lessee. On top of that, many lessors are in a higher tax bracket than smaller lessees, further enhancing the value of the tax credits.

Your lease finance costs should be greatly reduced by the lessor in compensation for the ITC and depreciation benefits. It is up to you to make sure the rate reduction covers the benefits exchanged. Leasing can make economic sense when the lower rate aids your cash flow while you earn profits with the equipment. What good are tax credits against nominal profits or a loss carry-forward when there are no profits?

If you are unable to negotiate a true lease, either under the new ERTA safe harbor rules or under the criteria of pre-Act guidelines (which are still legally acceptable under ERTA), then the lease alternative will not be the least costly means of acquiring equipment. Yet, leasing may still prove to be the most acceptable means of financing for other reasons. For instance, you may find the lower cash investment in advance rentals attractive, as opposed to the generally higher down payment required on a time sale contract. Or, expensing the equipment off may be much simpler than setting up depreciation schedules for varying types of equipment.

If you negotiate and structure your lease following our instructions and examples at the end of this chapter, you should be able to calculate the least costly lease possible.

Rather than interrupt absorption of your general understanding of the lease financing alternative, we have placed the more technical data at the end of this chapter. We have included a full explanation of the present value concept, charts you may use to compute your own cash flow analysis, lease-versus-buy comparisons, lease yield calculators, and lease rate charts. The reader is encouraged to choose those applicable to obtain answers pertinent to each individual situation.

## ANATOMY OF A TRUE LEASE

If you want to legally expense off lease rental payments and also know they are acceptable as an expense to the IRS, "using generally accepted accounting procedures," you should negotiate a true lease. The Economic Recovery Tax Act has effectively made it easier for both lessor and lessee to structure an acceptable true lease.

The 1981 Act adds a liberalized safe harbor rule to the Internal Revenue Code, Section 168(F)(8), under which an agreement satisfying certain conditions will be considered a true lease despite the presence of many factors that would have otherwise classified the transaction as a conditional sale.

Lessors will be able to receive cost recovery allowances and investment tax credits on all types of leases, whether they are in the form of single-investor, direct-financing, or leveraged leases.

Although the safe harbor rule is of particular interest and concern to lessors, it is important for lessees to understand its provisions in order to negotiate lease financing from a more informed position. Most significant to potential lessees is that the creation of the simplified concept called the *safe harbor lease election* put an end to years of uncertainty as to what constitutes a true lease.

The primary attractions to enter into a lease have always been (1) cash conservation in the form of reduced monies advanced to have the use of equipment, (2) improved cash flow resulting from lower payments by virtue of longer terms or a large purchase option to become due three or more years hence, and (3) significant reduction of rental charges, also aiding cash flow, achieved through trading off investment tax credit and depreciation allowances with a lessor who could use the tax benefits more advantageously.

The primary deterrents to a potential lease have been twofold: (1) the uncertainty of the true cost of a fair market value purchase option, if exercised at the end of the lease term, and (2) the complexities of structuring a lease transaction that satisfied the IRS in qualifying the lease as true and thus expensable. The new Tax Act has virtually eliminated these deterrents.

It should be noted that a transaction that does not meet the safe harbor criteria will still be characterized as a true lease if it complies with all of the requirements set forth under pre-Act regulations.

## Satisfying the IRS

What happens if the IRS audits your tax returns and checks your expense records? Up jumps equipment rental expense. Your auditor may then decide to examine the lease agreements themselves, to see if you have entered into a true lease or a "conditional sale contract." Now that ERTA has become law, the auditor will make his determination based on a lease that qualifies under the safe harbor rules or the more stringent criteria in existence prior to the Act. For simplicity, we will refer to both of these expensable leases as "true" or "qualified." We shall define how each type of lease may qualify as a deductible rental expense by outlining the pre-Act criteria and the new safe harbor lease election rules.

If the IRS determines that you do not have a true lease, they may disallow the rental expense deduction(s). Your taxes will then be recomputed, after reconstructing the equipment asset account to include the "leased" equipment that was expensed off. The applicable depreciation guidelines or new cost recovery allowances are applied to the questioned equipment and backed into your prior year or years' taxes. They should also calculate the interest and sales or other taxes contained in the rental payments that would normally have been expensed anyway. These expense items will serve to alleviate a portion of the disallowed rental expense backed into prior years' reduced income.

If you paid too little tax because you expensed unqualified rental payments, you will pay the back taxes, plus interest, to satisfy the auditor's redetermination and assessment. You can appeal the auditor's determination, claiming you really had a true lease, not a conditional sale contract. If your lease became effective prior to August 31, 1981, the IRS can make their determination based on the following criteria. Only one of these conditions need be present to turn your lease into a title-acquiring contract:

- Portions of the periodic payments apply specifically to an equity to be acquired by the "lessee."
- "Lessee" will acquire title on payment of a stated amount of "rent" which must be paid in any case.
- Total amount that "lessee" must pay for a relatively short period of use is very large compared to the total amount required to secure transfer of title.
- Periodic payments materially exceed current fair rental value.
- Property may be bought under an option at a price that is (1) nominal in relation to value of property at time option may be exercised, or (2) relatively small compared with total required payments.
- Part of the "rent" is specifically designated as interest or is easily recognizable as the equivalent of interest.
- Total rental payments plus option price approximate the price at which property could have been bought, plus interest and carrying charges.

The fact that the agreement does not provide for transfer of title or specifically bars transfer of title does not prevent the contract from being a sale of an equitable interest in the property.

The lease agreement can be adjudged a sale if (1) total rents over a relatively short period approximate the price at which the property could have been bought, plus interest and carrying charges, and (2) the "lessee" may continue to use the property over its entire useful life for relatively nominal or token payments, even if there is no provision for passage of title.

We prepared the above summary and comments by referring to Internal Revenue Service Procedures 75-21, 75-28, and 76-30. Readers who are particularly interested in leveraged leases should obtain these procedures for direct reference.

## Safe Harbor Lease Guidelines

The new safe harbor rules are easier to understand than the IRS procedures outlined above. The language of the Act removes most, if not all, of the uncertainty in structuring a qualifying true lease. Fair market value purchase options are not a necessary ingredient of a true lease and are destined to become extinct, particularly for leases transacted in the lower equipment cost range of $5,000 to perhaps $500,000. Without doubt, the regulations were written to encourage businesses to acquire new plant and capital equipment. They were devised not so much to encourage acquisition through leasing, but to remove impediments if that proved to be the best financing alternative. In addition, the leasing regulations were simplified to attract money sources not usually involved in leasing. Of course, they were also designed to increase the activities of the conventional money lenders, such as bank lease subsidiaries and finance companies. For the lenders, the liberalized guidelines made structuring tax-beneficial leases safe and their return on investment more predictable.

A lease agreement satisfying the conditions set forth below will be treated as a true lease for federal income tax purposes, and the lessor will be entitled to the tax benefits of ownership if:

1. the property subject to the lease is qualified lease property.
2. all parties to the transaction characterize it as a lease and elect to have the new safe harbor provision apply.
3. the lessor is a corporation; a partnership, all of the partners of which are corporations; or a grantor trust with respect to which the grantor and all beneficiaries are either corporations or partnerships and all partners of which are corporations.
4. the term of the lease, including any extensions, does not exceed the greater of 90% of the property's useful life or 150% of the property's ADR class life.
5. the lessor's "at risk" minimum investment in the leased property is at least 10% of the property's adjusted basis both at the time the property is placed in service and at all times during the lease term.

## Qualified Lease Property Defined

The term "qualified lease property" means new, Section 38 recovery property acquired after December 31, 1980. That is, property eligible for investment tax credit and accelerated cost recovery, provided that it falls within one of the following three categories:

1. New Section 38 property purchased by the lessor that is *leased within three months* after such property was placed in service by the lessee and which, if acquired by the lessee, would have been new Section 38 property in the hands of the lessee.
2. New Section 38 property purchased by the lessee that was *sold to the lessor and leased back within three months* after such property was placed in service by the lessee, provided that the equipment was not sold to the lessor for a price in excess of the cost to the lessee.
3. Property that is a *qualified mass commuting vehicle* and which is financed in whole or in part by tax-exempt bonds.

The use of the equipment by the lessee during the three-month grace period prior to the inception of the lease will not jeopardize the property's qualification as new property for purposes of the investment tax credit. This provision will in many cases eliminate potential problems where the original use of leased property could otherwise be deemed to commence prior to transfer to the lessor. However, no depreciation will be allowed the lessee in respect to its use of the property prior to transfer to the lessor.

IRS IS BOUND BY CONSENSUS OF PARTIES Any determination, for federal income tax purposes, whether a person is a lessor or lessee or the property is leased, must be made on the basis of the characterization of such person or property under the covenants of the lease. If the safe harbor conditions are met, no other factors will be taken into consideration for the determination of a true lease. Although not included in the language of the Act, an explanatory Conference Report specifically lists the following six factors as examples of items that are *irrelevant* if an election under Section 168(F)(8) is made:

1. whether the lessor or the lessee is the nominal owner of the property for state or local law purposes.
2. whether the property may (or must) be bought or sold at the end of the lease term at a fixed or determinable price that is more or less than its fair market value at that time.
3. whether or not the lessee or a related party has provided or guaranteed a portion of the financing for the transaction (other than for the lessor's minimum 10% investment).
4. whether the lessor or the lessee must take projected tax benefits into account in order to realize a profit from the transaction.
5. whether or not the property is useful to the lessee only; for example, whether the property is "limited-use property."
6. whether or not the obligation or any person is subject to any contingency or offset agreement.

PURCHASE OPTIONS Fair market value (FMV) purchase option is no longer a requirement of true leases if the five safe harbor lease conditions are otherwise met.

RENEWAL OPTIONS The lease term test (90% of useful life or 150% of ADR class life) includes extensions through renewals. In order to meet this test, any renewals, whether at bargain or fair market value price, must be limited to a period that does not exceed the above ceiling.

NON-QUALIFYING LESSEES Under the safe harbor rule, property leased must qualify as Section 38 property in the hands of both the lessor and the lessee. Thus, no safe harbor election may be made, but the prior standards will apply to leases to tax-exempt organizations, federal, state, and local governments, and other users to which the investment tax credit is presently not available.

**Safe Harbor Lease Election Benefits**

The safe harbor rules make it easier to choose leasing as a financing alternative for those who prefer to expense equipment acquisitions. Gone is the uncertainty of the fair market value purchase option. No longer need lessees fear that, after several years of making rental payments, inflation or increased equipment resale values will create a nightmare of having to pay perhaps 50% of the original cost to own the equipment.

With the fair market value option fading into history, the so-called side-letter or comfort letter also disappears. These letters, designed by lessors or equipment sellers to reassure concerned lessees that the fair market value would not be unreasonable, were at best uncomfortable subterfuges. Gone also are the verbal assurances from lessors that the fair market value was really window dressing to make a contract appear to be a true lease. Many lessees had to worry and wonder if those "notes to the file" or side-letters would hold water, especially if there were lessor management changes. The new safe harbor rules have put an end to the temptations to lessee and lessor alike to fabricate a sale so as to appear to be a true lease. It is no longer necessary to hide a predetermined purchase option letter or document from the prying eyes of the IRS.

If lessee and lessor say it is a lease and comply with the other simple rules and criteria, the IRS must accept the consensus of the parties to the lease. It is that simple. In the final analysis, the new regulations benefit the lessee more than corporate lessors, because it was the lessee who frequently became the victim of an unexpectedly large fair market valuation when it came time to purchase rented equipment.

**Lessee Safe Harbor Considerations**

Although the Economic Recovery Tax Act and the safe harbor rules clarified some very muddy waters, it is not Utopia Found for neophyte lessees. There are several considerations for lessees to bear in mind.

1. Why did you choose a lease as your best financing alternative? You should have a clear idea of the expected benefits. Did you accept the lease concept simply because some vendor salesman thrust it upon you as a quick means of selling his equipment? Or because a leasing salesman representing a bank or other lender-lessor said it was a good deal and a low-down-payment means of acquiring equipment? Those are not necessarily valid reasons for selecting the lease alternative. Review our comments earlier in this chapter concerning your decision to lease or not to lease and your determination as to whether a lease is your best deal. The ERTA has not altered the validity of our

suggestions one iota. In fact, the Accelerated Cost Recovery System, which completely replaces the old Asset Depreciation Range (ADR) system for any equipment placed in service after December 31, 1980, has made obsolete one touted advantage of leasing: rapid expensing of rental payments versus slower depreciation write-off.

2. In choosing a lease for the lower finance costs because you allowed the lessor to take your tax benefits, did you receive sufficiently reduced rental payments to compensate you adequately for the surrendered benefits? If you are unable to compute your true interest cost inherent in this kind of lease, take all of the equipment cost and rental payment quotations to your accountant, or locate a tax accountant. Let that specialist compute your effective annual percentage rate. Or let competition between two or three lessors bring you to the lowest possible tax-benefit trade-off rate. For leases involving more than $100,000, the competition promises to be fierce. There are an increasing number of lessors seeking tax-beneficial leases to shelter an enormous inventory of unused investment tax credits. The rapid recovery allowances available under ACRS are also very attractive to these same lessors.
3. Are you capable of determining for yourself that all of the safe harbor guidelines were completely met? If not, have your attorney, accountant, or an experienced tax person examine the lease documents you will be signing. Unless the lease is quite large or the overturning of it could cause you serious tax consequences (now of lessened impact because of new recovery allowances), you will probably do just as well simply to trust your lessor to structure a true lease. The lessor is as interested as you are in being assured the lease is true and tax-beneficial to him. The lessor's lease rate quote to you is based almost entirely on his tax-benefit expectations.
4. Did you use the lease alternative with the expectation of retaining your tax benefits? The ERTA did not outlaw entering into lease-purchases which you and the lessor treat as a conditional sale contract. Lease-purchase or "quasi" leases will still be used by lessees and lessors, simply to facilitate financing. But there is an extremely important consideration for the lessee in entering this type of lease: Do the documents make it clear that the lessee retains the investment tax credit and may take the recovery allowances? We recommend that lessees require the lessor to put it in writing that they are treating the lease as a conditional sale contract. Otherwise, it is possible that some lessors will innocently assume that they provided you with a true lease and also assume that they have the tax benefits. If you are unfamiliar with the language of a safe harbor lease, we assure you that when it is printed on lessor documents, much of it will be in fine print. You might sign documents that would substantiate the lessor's claim to your ITC and recovery allowances. Know your lessor for unquestionable

ethics, or have every lease document examined by qualified tax people.

### True Lease Variables

The starting point, from the lessor's viewpoint, before considering the value of tax benefits, is determining the desired yield on the equipment investment.

From this starting point, all lessors make internal judgments to decide how low they will go if the lease is on a competitive-bid basis or if the lessee negotiates. They consider credit risk, collateral values, size of investment, value of prospective lessee as a customer, their expected year-end tax status, and the useful and economic life of the equipment.

LESSOR'S TRUE-LEASE CONSIDERATIONS There are two variables the lessor is concerned about in structuring a true lease. First, will the lessee want the investment tax credit or allow the lessor to retain it? Second, what time of the year is the equipment being purchased by lease expected to go into service?

In connection with the investment tax credit, the lessor would prefer to know in advance that the lessee will retain the equipment for at least three years. In that case, under the new applicable percentages for investment tax credit, a 6% credit will be available. That much of the ITC is calculated into the lessor's yield. If the lease is set up for five or more years, the lessor has the full 10% ITC available to calculate into his yield.

However, under the revised ERTA regulations concerning investment tax credits and recapture rules, the lessor has different considerations than existed under prior tax laws. In addition, lessors will have to factor in or consider a minimum tax under ERTA's new list of tax preference items. (Refer to the ERTA summary at the end of this chapter.)

The in-service date is very important, because the date the equipment is placed in service affects the lessor's earnings. The lessor earns more on his investment if the delivery is in the third or fourth quarter of his tax year, due to the earlier impact of reduced income taxes derived from the ITC. If your equipment will be placed in service late in the lessor's tax year, you might also negotiate a lower rate. The new Act also changes the in-service date in another direction. Equipment may qualify for the investment tax credit up to ninety days after the date it is placed in service. The prior law required that if the lease was not in place at the time the equipment was placed in service, the ITC could only be taken by the lessee and was lost to the lessor forever. Obviously, this provision will allow lessees more time to negotiate or consider other financing alternatives. Lessors will be able to enter into leases on an after-the-fact basis, rather than walking away or becoming involved in playing games with invoices, shipping dates, and similar items that pinned down in-service dates. In addition, this longer period will facilitate consummation of complex lease negotiations and documentation, particularly leveraged lease transactions.

## LEASE BROKERS

There are four basic reasons for dealing with a lease broker:

1. You lack the abilities or are too lazy to prepare your own presentation to a lessor.
2. You are more concerned with obtaining financing than with how much it costs you.
3. You have found a broker who
   a. has a line of credit and can truly get his money "wholesale." (Improbable.)
   b. knows how to package your financial and equipment requirements better than you could do yourself. (Quite possible.)
   c. is so talented, so well-connected, he is worth the additional charges he makes for his services. (Not likely.)
4. You are so busy and successful, you do not wish to mess around with bankers or finance or lease companies. (Nice, if you can afford it.)

Lease brokers—and there are thousands of them—are available to assist business people in putting together lease proposals, advising as to lease structuring, and acquiring financing for them.

The best of these brokers can render valuable services. They act as consultants to major companies, placing their leases with the most suitable lenders. Their expertise enables them to consider all factors of rate, type of equipment, tax situation of lender and lessee—a multiplicity of factors.

Some lease brokers are referred to as independent lessors. Many operate under company or corporate names rather than their own, as consultants do in other fields. There are, of course, financial consultants who act as brokers, packaging all types of financing, including leasing.

Those lease brokers who qualify to be called lessors, be they individual broker-consultants or companies, all will have credit lines with one or more banks. They may also have alliances with other leasing companies and broker your lease to them. It is not uncommon for certain brokers to send a lease package to another broker, who in turn places it with a lender. Sometimes the second broker passes it to still another broker. As you might guess, the rate they offer to the lessee prospect includes a fee for each broker involved. In the industry, this is called "packing the rate." As a potential lessee, you may innocently become involved with such a broker. The net result may be significantly higher lease finance costs. The question is, if it is your lease they are dividing, must you pay the price for lease financing they arrange? Or is there a better way?

They may also have connections to other investor capital, including private investors. Those independent lessors who are well established and adequately funded will have a complete finance or lease organization. They will make their own credit decisions. (In some cases, their bank will require reviewing all decisions before funding.) You will sign their documents. You will pay your lease payments to them. When it comes time to buy the equipment under some type of an option or to surrender the equipment, you deal with them, not an assignee.

These independent lessors are the best of the lease brokers. Some of them are able to arrange financing you could not obtain on your own. Through a combination of connections to money sources and structuring expertise, they accomplish things the banks and regular finance companies would not tackle—or even imagine. This summation will hold true for unusual lease situations where independent lessors fit best. It is much less true in the more usual, straightforward lease financing involving standard types of equipment.

Then there are the other lease brokers we refer to as lease broker leeches, who fasten themselves on unsuspecting business people. Unfortunately, there are quite a few of these people operating today who are simply "arrangers." They like to make everyone feel their services are valuable, even indispensable. In truth, many of them are taking advantage of business people so immersed in business operations that they can't take time for financial management.

Here is what to look out for and how to handle broker leeches if they start attaching themselves to the vicinity of your checkbook:

- Ask them where they obtain funding for the leases.
- Find out if they use their own documents. If they do, ask them who they will assign the lease to. Ask them, "Who will I pay my lease payments to?"
- If the broker says he is going to place the lease, ask him what his sources are. Where is he going to shop your deal?
- Watch out for the hard sell, which may include paying a non-refundable deposit or a deposit refundable only if they fail to place your lease.
- Watch out for the "exclusive agreement," requiring you to deal only with or through them.
- Be aware that many independent lessors or brokers will automatically require you to pay a security deposit. Very often they also ask for the first and last months' rentals in advance. They want to get your money and take you out of the shopping market.
- Many will claim you must pay one advance rental for each year of the lease. Five years, five advance rentals; seven years, seven

advance rentals. They try to obtain these rentals, even though your credit standing would dictate less cash up front.

- What they are doing is building as strong a package as possible and getting cash in hand. Quite often this cash is the fee or commission they earn when the lease is placed with a lender at the normal rate. This is called the lenders' buy rate.

We do not claim that all independent lessors or lease broker-consultants are undesirables. Most are honest, and to earn their commissions or fees, they do work hard, long hours. Without a doubt, many business people need and appreciate the services rendered by these brokers. Some business people feel it is worthwhile having a knowledgeable finance or lease man take over the packaging and presentation of their lease requirements. Many businesses are in isolated areas, and the lease broker who comes to them is worth the fee. Others find their local banks or finance companies incapable of serving their equipment finance needs.

## Why Brokers Succeed

Brokers can reach out for the necessary lease funding, into distant cities, to lenders unknown to the lessee prospect. They can present the lease prospect in the best possible light and get him financed where the businessman might have failed. Like most salesmen, they work hard to sell the lease package. Unlike the bankers (to whom they often take your lease proposal), brokers are often resourceful, imaginative people. They open bankers' eyes and sometimes get them to say yes when that same banker might say no to you!

There are three major reasons why a broker can succeed where you might fail or struggle through several time-consuming attempts:

1. The broker may be an expert at assembling everything the lender needs to make a decision, presenting your company and your requirements in a most comprehensive, understandable format.
2. High-volume brokers place most or all of their lease packages with one lender. This way, they receive more favorable treatment. The lender bends a bit here and there because they like the overall flow from this broker.
3. Conversely, the strength of a broker may be in his connections with a number of lenders. His inside knowledge of what certain lenders like in the way of collateral, dollar amounts, or special terms or which lenders are seeking tax-oriented leases can prove critical to achieving lease placement.

If your credit is marginal or your business is fairly new, a broker may be the perfect answer. Just remember, he isn't a miracle man. Leasing, as it is supposed to be done, calls for nearly 100% financing. Generally speaking, that doesn't include new ventures, undercapitalized businesses, or those with marginal credit standing.

We would like to point out certain drawbacks in using lease brokers or smaller independent lessors. Until it happens to you, these facts may come as a shock:

### Does Your Broker Make a Presentation—or Just a Mailing?

- It can be downright embarrassing and injurious to your business when they take your lease proposal to *your* bank!
- It can be troublesome and a nuisance when a broker shops your proposal all over the place—when your bank, given as a reference, gets numerous inquiries. And, not so incidently, every inquiry is recorded on your computerized TRW (credit) report.
- If your broker strikes out and you try with other lenders, each of them runs a TRW. Then they wonder, "Why should we like this deal? No one else did!"
- Some brokers are no help at all. They take your financial statements, tax returns, and prospectus—if you or they even bothered with one—make ten miserable, illegible copies, and mail them to every lender they know and hope for the best!

You know the story: "Throw enough donkey dung against the wall, and some of it will stick!" These aren't lease brokers, they are copymakers Lousy copies at that. They don't make a presentation, they make a mailing.

For this wonderful service, they want five or more points! (In the leasing business, brokers are usually paid by the lenders on the basis of a percentage of the equipment cost. Five points would equal 5% of cost.)

We have seen leases funded by lenders in which the broker received 8% of the equipment cost! (On a $50,000 lease purchase, that's a $4,000 fee.) We have seen even higher fee requests—but most legitimate lenders refuse to be a party to such gouging. Lenders also wonder if something is wrong with your credit or business sense when they see such high built-in fees. These high-fee artists are the lease leeches you must guard against.

Think about it: If a lender will fund your lease at his regular going rate, what the hell did you need a broker for? Wouldn't you have been time and money ahead to have carefully prepared your own presentation, working with two or three local lessors, banks, or finance companies?

Even a 5% fee on a $50,000 equipment purchase will buy a whole lot of assistance, overtime for an assistant, extra help from your secretary, your accountant, or even your tax attorney. True, not all lease brokers charge 5% to 8%. Many work for 2% or 3%, and even less if the equipment cost is into six figures. Many lenders, especially banks, know it is ultimately bad business to have fee-loaded leases reflecting on them when you wake up later!

## Protect Yourself at All Times

Our best advice is, protect yourself! Know who you are dealing with. Know how much you are paying for a broker's services—even when he is doing you a good job. Our lease rate and yield charts will tell you what a broker's services are really costing you. Then you can make an intelligent business decision.

Recognize that most equipment lenders are very happy to fund acceptable leases with creditworthy lessees and decent collateral for 1½% to 4% over prime rate. If the lease broker deal works out to 5% to 9% over prime or more, that is what you have apparently decided his assistance is worth. Is it?

# SUMMARY OF THE ECONOMIC RECOVERY TAX ACT OF 1981

The Economic Recovery Tax Act of 1981, which became law on August 31, 1981, is far-reaching in scope. It includes across-the-board tax rate reductions, reduced withholding, elimination of the marriage penalty, changes in the interest and dividend exclusion, and liberalized retirement savings provisions.

For businesses, this legislation enacts a new accelerated depreciation system, reduces the corporate tax rates, changes several of the investment tax credit provisions, and provides incentives for research and development.

The unified estate and gift tax credit is raised, over a six-year period, and an unlimited marital deduction is provided. Also included are changes of commodity straddles and changes in Windfall Profits Tax provisions.

*Creative Business Financing* here focuses entirely on the business aspects of ERTA, particularly analyzing and explaining the ramifications of changes that may influence financial decision making.

## Depreciation Provisions

ACCELERATED COST RECOVERY SYSTEM A new system of depreciation, called Accelerated Cost Recovery System (ACRS), replaces the former Asset Depreciation Range (ADR) system for most tangible depreciable property used in a trade or business or held for the production of income and placed in service on or after January 1, 1981. Enacted as Code Section 168, recovery of capital costs under ACRS is determined over statutory periods of time that are shorter than the useful life of the asset or the period for which it is used to produce income.

In lieu of the ADR "life" classes, ACRS "recovery property" may be fully depreciated over a three-, five-, ten-, or fifteen-year period, depending on the type of property.

The cost recovery percentages, methods, and periods are mandatory and are the same for both new and used property. The annual depreciation allowance is determined by applying a statutory percentage to the unadjusted basis—which is generally the acquisition cost—of the property. Salvage value is disregarded. Most of the previously available elections, such as facts and circumstances, modified half-year convention, sum-of-the-years digits, and other declining-balance methods are repealed.

The amount of the *allowable deduction* under ACRS is computed by applying the statutory percentage for the type of property involved to the unadjusted basis of the recovery property. (We provide tables for the determination of allowable deductions on the following pages.)

The *statutory percentage* to be used in computing the deduction depends on the class of property and the number of years since the property was placed in service. (We provide tables for assigning types of property to acceptable depreciable number of years on the following pages.)

COST RECOVERY ALLOWANCE The system will be fully phased in by 1986, in three stages, with the annual recovery depending upon when the property is placed in service. The applicable percentage in the appropriate stage further depends on the class of property and the number of years since the property was placed in service (the recovery year). The first recovery year is the tax year (fiscal or calendar) in which the equipment is placed in service.

The statutory recovery allowances are set forth in recovery percentage tables. Different sets of tables apply to personal property in general (referred to as Section 1245 property) and to real property (Section 1250 property). Section 1250 property is classed as fifteen-year recovery property. (See Classes of Recovery Property, which follows.)

The Section 1245 property annual recovery allowances reflect the 150% declining-balance method with a change to the straight-line method for years 1981 through 1984, the 175% declining-balance method with a change to the sum-of-the-years digits method for 1985, and the 200% declining-balance method with a change to the sum-of-the-years digits method for years after 1985. In effect, the system incorporates the half-year convention method, but generally, no recovery deduction is allowed in the year of early disposition.

For property placed in service in the years 1981 through 1984, the applicable recovery percentages are set forth in ACRS Table 1. For property placed in service in 1985, refer to ACRS Table 2. For property placed in service after December 31, 1985, refer to ACRS Table 3. (See page 252 for Tables 1–3.)

## ACRS TABLE 1. FOR PERSONAL (SEC. 1245) PROPERTY PLACED IN SERVICE IN THE YEARS 1981–84.

| Recovery year | Applicable Percentage for Class of Property | | | |
|---|---|---|---|---|
| | 3-year | 5-year | 10-year | 15-year* public utility |
| 1 | 25 | 15 | 8 | 5 |
| 2 | 38 | 22 | 14 | 10 |
| 3 | 37 | 21 | 12 | 9 |
| 4 | | 21 | 10 | 8 |
| 5 | | 21 | 10 | 7 |
| 6 | | | 10 | 7 |
| 7 | | | 9 | 6 |
| 8 | | | 9 | 6 |
| 9 | | | 9 | 6 |
| 10 | | | 9 | 6 |

*Years 11–15 omitted.

## ACRS TABLE 2. FOR PERSONAL (SEC. 1245) PROPERTY PLACED IN SERVICE IN THE YEAR 1985.

| Recovery year | Applicable Percentage for Class of Property | | | |
|---|---|---|---|---|
| | 3-year | 5-year | 10-year | 15-year* public utility |
| 1 | 29 | 18 | 9 | 6 |
| 2 | 47 | 33 | 19 | 12 |
| 3 | 24 | 25 | 16 | 12 |
| 4 | | 16 | 14 | 11 |
| 5 | | 8 | 12 | 10 |
| 6 | | | 10 | 9 |
| 7 | | | 8 | 8 |
| 8 | | | 6 | 7 |
| 9 | | | 4 | 6 |
| 10 | | | 2 | 5 |

*Years 11–15 omitted.

## ACRS TABLE 3. FOR PERSONAL (SEC. 1245) PROPERTY PLACED IN SERVICE AFTER DECEMBER 31, 1985.

| Recovery year | Applicable Percentage for Class of Property | | | |
|---|---|---|---|---|
| | 3-year | 5-year | 10-year | 15-year public utility |
| 1 | 33 | 20 | 10 | 7 |
| 2 | 45 | 32 | 18 | 12 |
| 3 | 22 | 24 | 16 | 12 |
| 4 | | 16 | 14 | 11 |
| 5 | | 8 | 12 | 10 |
| 6 | | | 10 | 9 |
| 7 | | | 8 | 8 |
| 8 | | | 6 | 7 |
| 9 | | | 4 | 6 |
| 10 | | | 2 | 5 |
| 11 | | | | 4 |
| 12 | | | | 3 |
| 13 | | | | 3 |
| 14 | | | | 2 |
| 15 | | | | 1 |

CLASSES OF RECOVERY PROPERTY For purposes of ACRS deductions, recovery property means depreciable property either used in a trade or business or held for the production of income. Each item of recovery property is assigned to one of the following classes:

*Section 1245 Personal Property*

| | |
|---|---|
| 3 years | Automobiles, light-duty trucks<br>Research and development equipment<br>Equipment having an ADR class life of 4 years or less |
| 5 years | Equipment other than 3-year, 10-year, or 15-year property<br>Single-purpose agricultural structures<br>Storage facilities used for distribution of petroleum and its primary products<br>Public utility equipment with an ADR class life from 5 to 18 years |
| 10 years | Public utility equipment with an ADR class life from 18 to 25 years<br>Railroad tank cars<br>Boilers or burners that are neither 3-year nor 5-year property<br>Real property with an ADR class life of 12½ years or less |
| 15 years | Public utility equipment with an ADR class life of more than 25 years |

*Section 1250 Real Property*

| | |
|---|---|
| 15 years | Real property with an ADR class life of more than 12½ years |

STRAIGHT-LINE ACRS ELECTION (S/L ACRS) In lieu of the statutory accelerated method of recovery provided for personal property in the tables, the taxpayer may decelerate recovery by electing straight-line deductions over the regular recovery period or over the following longer periods:

| *In case of:* | *The taxpayer may elect a recovery period of:* |
|---|---|
| 3-year property | 3, 5, or 12 years |
| 5-year property | 5, 12, or 25 years |
| 10-year property | 10, 25, or 35 years |

If S/L ACRS is elected, it may not be later revoked, and the same recovery period must be used for all personal property of a class for which such an election is made. However, a combination of standard ACRS and different S/L ACRS periods is allowable within the same year for property in other classes or for property of the same class but acquired in different tax years.

Furthermore, half-year deduction must be taken in the year the personal property is placed in service and in the year following the end of the recovery period. For early disposals, no depreciation is allowed in the year of disposition.

SITUATIONS TO WHICH ACRS WILL NOT APPLY In order to prevent taxpayers from transferring pre-1981 property solely to take advantage of accelerated recovery, the following "anti-churning" rules were put into the Act:

1. ACRS will not apply to personal property acquired after December 31, 1980, if:
   a. the property was owned or used at any time during 1980 by the same taxpayer or a person related to the taxpayer; for example, transfer among affiliated companies.
   b. the property is acquired from a person who owned the property at any time during 1980 and the user of the property does not change as part of the transaction; for example, the original lessor assigns the lease to another lessor.
   c. the taxpayer leases the property to a person (or a person related to such person) who owned or used the property at any time during 1980; for example, utilizing a sale and lease-back.
   d. the property is acquired in a transaction as part of which the user of such property does not change and the property is not recovery property in the hands of the person from which the property is acquired by virtue of items (b) or (c) above; for example, acquisition by the last owner in a chain of disqualifying transactions.

   Two qualifications to the above rules apply: The property is not treated as owned until it is actually placed in service; and, in the case of corporations or partnerships, "relation" exists if any one has ownership of the other of at least 10% or if they do business under common control (i.e., 50% ownership).

2. Similar anti-churning rules are to be prescribed by the Treasury Department to prevent taxpayers from claiming the faster depreciation write-offs after 1984 or 1985 for used personal property placed in service before 1985 or 1986. Under such rules the transferee will have to use the same recovery period and method of depreciation as the transferor.
3. Public utility property will not qualify as recovery property unless the utility company uses a normalization method of accounting; that is, the tax benefits of ACRS must be normalized in setting the rates charged by the company.

4. With respect to pre-1981 property acquired in the above non-qualifying transactions, *depreciation is determined under the rules in effect before enactment of the ACRS.*

RECAPTURE OF DEPRECIATION UPON SALE OF RECOVERY PROPERTY Gain is generally recognized on the disposition of recovery property to the extent the selling price of the property exceeds its depreciated book value. Such gain is ordinary income up to the amount that represents recapture of ACRS deductions.

A special mass asset election could save calculation of gain on the disposition of equipment from mass asset accounts. Under this election, gain is recognized to the extent of the proceeds realized from the disposition of the equipment. The unadjusted basis of the property is left in the capital account until fully recovered in future years.

A special recapture rule applies to lessees in situations where the lessor is treated as the owner of property under a "safe harbor lease election" and the lessee-user acquires the equipment either during the lease term or thereafter. If the lessee then disposes of the property, the amount of its gain that will be ordinary recapture income is determined by assuming that the lessee had owned the property during the term of the lease and had taken the recovery deductions in fact claimed by the lessor.

However, the amount of any recovery deduction recaptured on the sale of the property by the lessor need not be recaptured again on the sale by the lessee. This provision is designed to operate in situations in which a lessee exercises a below-market value purchase option and then resells the property. This provision is not necessarily limited to such situations, but they are the most typical.

MINIMUM-TAX TAX-PREFERENCE ITEMS Added to the list of tax preference items is the excess of the ACRS deduction for leased items, other than fifteen-year real property, over the allowable deduction for the taxable year had the property been depreciated using the straight-line method (without regard to salvage value and using a half-year convention) and a recovery period as follows:

| *For:* | *Recovery Period* |
|---|---|
| 3-year property | 5 years |
| 5-year property | 8 years |
| 10-year property | 15 years |
| 15-year public utility property | 22 years |

For fifteen-year real property, the tax preference is the excess of the ACRS deduction over the amount the deduction would have been had the straight-line method been used, disregarding salvage value, over a fifteen-year recovery period.

EARNINGS AND PROFITS The adjustment to earnings and profits of U.S. corporations will now be determined using the straight-line method (generally using a half-year convention and without regard to salvage value) over a recovery period as follows:

| *For:* | *Recovery Period* |
|---|---|
| 3-year property | 5 years |
| 5-year property | 12 years |
| 10-year property | 25 years |
| 15-year property | 35 years |
| 15-year public utility property | 35 years |

EXTENSION OF CARRYOVER PERIODS For net operating losses for tax years ending after 1975, the carryover period is extended from seven to fifteen years for the investment and work incentive program credits for unused credit years ending after 1973, for the new employee credit for unused credit years beginning after 1976, and for the alcohol fuel credit for unused credit years ending after September 30, 1980.

ADDITIONAL FIRST-YEAR DEPRECIATION DEDUCTION REPEALED Prior to the Economic Recovery Tax Act, a taxpayer could elect to take an additional first-year depreciation deduction of up to 20% of the cost of eligible property, to a maximum deduction of $2,000, or $4,000 for a joint return. This deduction has been repealed and replaced by a new deduction for taxpayers, other than estates, trusts, or certain noncorporate lessors, who make an irrevocable election to treat qualifying property as an expense rather than as a capital expenditure. If this method of depreciation is elected, *no investment tax credit* is available for the cost of the property.

The amount of the deduction is the cost of the eligible property, but there is an annual dollar limitation on the aggregate cost that may be deducted in any taxable year, as follows: $0 to 1981, $5,000 for 1982 and 1983, $7,500 for 1984 and 1985, and $10,000 for 1986 and thereafter.

## Investment Tax Credit

APPLICABLE PERCENTAGE Under the Act, the full 10% ITC will be available with respect to Section 38 property which is fifteen-year public utility or ten- or five-year property. A 6% credit will be available for three-year property.

An investment tax credit is generally allowable for qualified investment property in the first year the taxpayer places the property in use. The applicable credit, 6% or 10% as stated above, is a statutory percentage of the basis. Present law limits the credit that may be taken for the taxable year to $25,000 *plus* 70% of the tax over $25,000 (for tax years ending in 1980).

The Act provides for an increased percentage of 10% annually, up to 90%, in 1982. That is, $25,000 *plus* 90% of the tax over $25,000.

For ACRS property placed in service after 1980, the qualified investment is determined on the basis of the ACRS recovery period, rather than useful life. Under prior law, a 10% credit was available only with respect to property which had a useful life for depreciation purposes of seven years or more. A 6-2/3% credit was available for property with a useful life of between five and seven years, and a 3-1/3% credit was available for property with a useful life of between three and five years.

INVESTMENT TAX CREDIT RECAPTURE RULES For property that was eligible for the investment credit and is disposed of before the close of the recapture period (generally the first full year after the property is placed in service and the succeeding four years, except for three-year property in which the period is reduced by two years), the taxpayer's tax liability will be increased. This increase is determined by applying the applicable recapture percentage to the decrease in the investment tax credit which would have resulted if the qualified investment used for such property in computing the investment credit for prior years had been zero.

The amended recapture rules change the ITC recapture period to five years for five-, ten-, and fifteen-year property and to three years for three-year property. Within these periods, ITC will be recaptured in accordance with the following schedule:

| *If the disposition is within:* | *The recapture percentage is:* | |
|---|---|---|
| | *5-, 10, or 15-year property* | *3-year property* |
| 1 year | 100% | 100% |
| 2 years | 80 | 66 |
| 3 years | 60 | 33 |
| 4 years | 40 | 0 |
| 5 years | 20 | 0 |
| 6 years | 0 | 0 |

Note: The above holding periods represent the number of *full years* passed after the property was placed in service.

TAX LIABILITY DUE TO RECAPTURE The amount of ITC recaptured is an additional tax in the year of recapture. However, the Act limits this general rule only to credits which were actually used in prior years to reduce the tax liability in those years. For credits recaptured, but not used, the carrybacks and carryovers are to be adjusted accordingly.

**USED PROPERTY** Used Section 38 property qualifies for the investment credit only to a limited annual amount. This limitation is set upon the aggregate cost of used property purchased by the taxpayer during the tax year; otherwise the percentage calculation (100% or 60% ITC) depends on the ACRS class of the property purchased.

Under the Act, the purchase amount ceiling is increased from $100,000 to $125,000 for tax years beginning in 1981 through 1984 and to $150,000 thereafter. If the cost of used property exceeds the limit, the taxpayer may select the items to be used for the investment credit.

ITC on used property may not be passed on by a lessor to the lessee. That provision prevents lessees from passing the investment credit to a lessor in exchange for a reduced rental charge. Accordingly, lessors in search of investment credits will generally avoid leases involving used equipment.

Furthermore, related persons or corporations are considered for the purpose of limitation as only one taxpayer. For example, for married couples filing separate returns, the limitations are cut in half for each taxpayer.

**ACRS IN SHORT TAX YEARS** Recovery (depreciation) deductions in the first taxable year of a newly formed entity (and/or other short tax year due to the provisions of the code) are subject to certain proration by the number of months in the short year that bears to 12. However, such rule does not apply to a deduction for the first tax year of a lessor whose property is the subject of a safe harbor lease election.

FIGURE 7-1

# PRESENT VALUE CONCEPT

PRESENT VALUE CONCERNS THE TIME VALUE OF MONEY.

A dollar collectable a year hence does not have the same value as a dollar in hand. The PRESENT VALUE factor is used to determine the present-day equivalent of a cash flow due in the future.

The Present Value factor (P.V.) is simply the RECIPROCAL of a COMPOUND INTEREST FACTOR.

For example: If \$1.00 is invested at a 10% annual rate:

End of year 1 - - \$1.00 X 110% = \$1.10

End of year 2 - - \$1.10 X 110% = \$1.21

Present Value of \$1.00, one year in future:

$$\frac{\$1.10}{\$1.00} = \frac{\$1.00}{X}$$

$$X = \frac{(\$1) \times (\$1)}{\$1.10} = 0.91$$

Present Value of \$1.00, two years in future:

$$\frac{\$1.21}{\$1.00} = \frac{\$1.00}{X}$$

$$X = \frac{(\$1) \times (\$1)}{\$1.21} = 0.83$$

The P.V. method makes it possible to compare two dissimilar cash flows to determine which is LESS COSTLY in terms of interest on invested capital.

Company money managers, such as the financial officer, budget chief, controller or whoever is involved in equipment acquisitions and allocation of available funds, are interested in what is the TRUE EFFECT of leasing. They often make their own comparisons in the "LEASE VERSUS BUY" decision process. The analysis is MORE than a simple comparison of apparent costs involving interest, depreciation or the use or passing of the Investment Tax Credit to a lessor or investor. It is necessary, among several considerations, to determine the ANNUAL YIELD they can reasonably expect from CONSERVED CAPITAL. If they have an average Net Profit on WORKING CAPITAL of 10%, they will realize a NET RETURN of 10¢ from EACH conserved dollar.

If the money manager is able to POSTPONE full payment to some FUTURE date, as with payment of a PURCHASE OPTION payable at LEASE MATURITY . . . when LEASING . . . what is the VALUE of that CONSERVED CAPITAL? In addition, how does the lease payment RENTAL STREAM and the payment of the purchase option . . . *compare to other forms of time payment programs?*

FIGURE 7-1 (continued)

# PRESENT VALUE OF $1

| YRS. | 1% | 2% | 4% | 6% | 8% | 10% | 12% | 14% | 15% | 16% | 18% | 20% | 22% | 24% | 25% | 26% | 28% | 30% | 35% | 40% | 45% | 50% |
|---|---|---|---|---|---|---|---|---|---|---|---|---|---|---|---|---|---|---|---|---|---|---|
| 1... | 0.990 | 0.980 | 0.962 | 0.943 | 0.926 | 0.909 | 0.893 | 0.877 | 0.870 | 0.862 | 0.847 | 0.833 | 0.820 | 0.806 | 0.800 | 0.794 | 0.781 | 0.769 | 0.741 | 0.714 | 0.690 | 0.667 |
| 2... | 0.980 | 0.961 | 0.925 | 0.890 | 0.857 | 0.826 | 0.797 | 0.769 | 0.756 | 0.743 | 0.718 | 0.694 | 0.672 | 0.650 | 0.640 | 0.630 | 0.610 | 0.592 | 0.549 | 0.510 | 0.476 | 0.444 |
| 3... | 0.971 | 0.942 | 0.889 | 0.840 | 0.794 | 0.751 | 0.712 | 0.675 | 0.658 | 0.641 | 0.609 | 0.579 | 0.551 | 0.524 | 0.512 | 0.500 | 0.477 | 0.455 | 0.406 | 0.364 | 0.328 | 0.296 |
| 4... | 0.961 | 0.924 | 0.855 | 0.792 | 0.735 | 0.683 | 0.636 | 0.592 | 0.572 | 0.552 | 0.516 | 0.482 | 0.451 | 0.423 | 0.410 | 0.397 | 0.373 | 0.350 | 0.301 | 0.260 | 0.226 | 0.198 |
| 5... | 0.951 | 0.906 | 0.822 | 0.747 | 0.681 | 0.621 | 0.567 | 0.519 | 0.497 | 0.476 | 0.437 | 0.402 | 0.370 | 0.341 | 0.328 | 0.315 | 0.291 | 0.269 | 0.223 | 0.186 | 0.156 | 0.132 |
| 6... | 0.942 | 0.888 | 0.790 | 0.705 | 0.630 | 0.564 | 0.507 | 0.456 | 0.432 | 0.410 | 0.370 | 0.335 | 0.303 | 0.275 | 0.262 | 0.250 | 0.227 | 0.207 | 0.165 | 0.133 | 0.108 | 0.088 |
| 7... | 0.933 | 0.871 | 0.760 | 0.665 | 0.583 | 0.513 | 0.452 | 0.400 | 0.376 | 0.354 | 0.314 | 0.279 | 0.249 | 0.222 | 0.210 | 0.198 | 0.178 | 0.159 | 0.122 | 0.095 | 0.074 | 0.059 |
| 8... | 0.923 | 0.853 | 0.731 | 0.627 | 0.540 | 0.467 | 0.404 | 0.351 | 0.327 | 0.305 | 0.266 | 0.233 | 0.204 | 0.179 | 0.168 | 0.157 | 0.139 | 0.123 | 0.091 | 0.068 | 0.051 | 0.039 |
| 9... | 0.914 | 0.837 | 0.703 | 0.592 | 0.500 | 0.424 | 0.361 | 0.308 | 0.284 | 0.263 | 0.225 | 0.194 | 0.167 | 0.144 | 0.134 | 0.125 | 0.108 | 0.094 | 0.067 | 0.048 | 0.035 | 0.026 |
| 10... | 0.905 | 0.820 | 0.676 | 0.558 | 0.463 | 0.386 | 0.322 | 0.270 | 0.247 | 0.227 | 0.191 | 0.162 | 0.137 | 0.116 | 0.107 | 0.099 | 0.085 | 0.073 | 0.050 | 0.035 | 0.024 | 0.017 |
| 11... | 0.896 | 0.804 | 0.650 | 0.527 | 0.429 | 0.350 | 0.287 | 0.237 | 0.215 | 0.195 | 0.162 | 0.135 | 0.112 | 0.094 | 0.086 | 0.079 | 0.066 | 0.056 | 0.037 | 0.025 | 0.017 | 0.012 |
| 12... | 0.887 | 0.788 | 0.625 | 0.497 | 0.397 | 0.319 | 0.257 | 0.208 | 0.187 | 0.168 | 0.137 | 0.112 | 0.092 | 0.076 | 0.069 | 0.062 | 0.052 | 0.043 | 0.027 | 0.018 | 0.012 | 0.008 |
| 13... | 0.879 | 0.773 | 0.601 | 0.469 | 0.368 | 0.290 | 0.229 | 0.182 | 0.163 | 0.145 | 0.116 | 0.093 | 0.075 | 0.061 | 0.055 | 0.050 | 0.040 | 0.033 | 0.020 | 0.013 | 0.008 | 0.005 |
| 14... | 0.870 | 0.758 | 0.577 | 0.442 | 0.340 | 0.263 | 0.205 | 0.160 | 0.141 | 0.125 | 0.099 | 0.078 | 0.062 | 0.049 | 0.044 | 0.039 | 0.032 | 0.025 | 0.015 | 0.009 | 0.006 | 0.003 |
| 15... | 0.861 | 0.743 | 0.555 | 0.417 | 0.315 | 0.239 | 0.183 | 0.140 | 0.123 | 0.108 | 0.084 | 0.065 | 0.051 | 0.040 | 0.035 | 0.031 | 0.025 | 0.020 | 0.011 | 0.006 | 0.004 | 0.002 |
| 16... | 0.853 | 0.728 | 0.534 | 0.394 | 0.292 | 0.218 | 0.163 | 0.123 | 0.107 | 0.093 | 0.071 | 0.054 | 0.042 | 0.032 | 0.028 | 0.025 | 0.019 | 0.015 | 0.008 | 0.005 | 0.003 | 0.002 |
| 17... | 0.844 | 0.714 | 0.513 | 0.371 | 0.270 | 0.198 | 0.146 | 0.108 | 0.093 | 0.080 | 0.060 | 0.045 | 0.034 | 0.026 | 0.023 | 0.020 | 0.015 | 0.012 | 0.006 | 0.003 | 0.002 | 0.001 |
| 18... | 0.836 | 0.700 | 0.494 | 0.350 | 0.250 | 0.180 | 0.130 | 0.095 | 0.081 | 0.069 | 0.051 | 0.038 | 0.028 | 0.021 | 0.018 | 0.016 | 0.012 | 0.009 | 0.005 | 0.002 | 0.001 | 0.001 |
| 19... | 0.828 | 0.686 | 0.475 | 0.331 | 0.232 | 0.164 | 0.116 | 0.083 | 0.070 | 0.060 | 0.043 | 0.031 | 0.023 | 0.017 | 0.014 | 0.012 | 0.009 | 0.007 | 0.003 | 0.002 | 0.001 | |
| 20... | 0.820 | 0.673 | 0.456 | 0.312 | 0.215 | 0.149 | 0.104 | 0.073 | 0.061 | 0.051 | 0.037 | 0.026 | 0.019 | 0.014 | 0.012 | 0.010 | 0.007 | 0.005 | 0.002 | 0.001 | 0.001 | |
| 21... | 0.811 | 0.660 | 0.439 | 0.294 | 0.199 | 0.135 | 0.093 | 0.064 | 0.053 | 0.044 | 0.031 | 0.022 | 0.015 | 0.011 | 0.009 | 0.008 | 0.006 | 0.004 | 0.002 | 0.001 | | |
| 22... | 0.803 | 0.647 | 0.422 | 0.278 | 0.184 | 0.123 | 0.083 | 0.056 | 0.046 | 0.038 | 0.026 | 0.018 | 0.013 | 0.009 | 0.007 | 0.006 | 0.004 | 0.003 | 0.001 | 0.001 | | |
| 23... | 0.795 | 0.634 | 0.406 | 0.262 | 0.170 | 0.112 | 0.074 | 0.049 | 0.040 | 0.033 | 0.022 | 0.015 | 0.010 | 0.007 | 0.006 | 0.005 | 0.003 | 0.002 | 0.001 | | | |
| 24... | 0.788 | 0.622 | 0.390 | 0.247 | 0.158 | 0.102 | 0.066 | 0.043 | 0.035 | 0.028 | 0.019 | 0.013 | 0.008 | 0.006 | 0.005 | 0.004 | 0.003 | 0.002 | 0.001 | | | |
| 25... | 0.780 | 0.610 | 0.375 | 0.233 | 0.146 | 0.092 | 0.059 | 0.038 | 0.030 | 0.024 | 0.016 | 0.010 | 0.007 | 0.005 | 0.004 | 0.003 | 0.002 | 0.001 | 0.001 | | | |
| 26... | 0.772 | 0.598 | 0.361 | 0.220 | 0.135 | 0.084 | 0.053 | 0.033 | 0.026 | 0.021 | 0.014 | 0.009 | 0.006 | 0.004 | 0.003 | 0.002 | 0.002 | 0.001 | | | | |
| 27... | 0.764 | 0.586 | 0.347 | 0.207 | 0.125 | 0.076 | 0.047 | 0.029 | 0.023 | 0.018 | 0.011 | 0.007 | 0.005 | 0.003 | 0.002 | 0.002 | 0.001 | 0.001 | | | | |
| 28... | 0.757 | 0.574 | 0.333 | 0.196 | 0.116 | 0.069 | 0.042 | 0.026 | 0.020 | 0.016 | 0.010 | 0.006 | 0.004 | 0.002 | 0.002 | 0.002 | 0.001 | 0.001 | | | | |
| 29... | 0.749 | 0.563 | 0.321 | 0.185 | 0.107 | 0.063 | 0.037 | 0.022 | 0.017 | 0.014 | 0.008 | 0.005 | 0.003 | 0.002 | 0.002 | 0.001 | 0.001 | 0.001 | | | | |
| 30... | 0.742 | 0.552 | 0.308 | 0.174 | 0.099 | 0.057 | 0.033 | 0.020 | 0.015 | 0.012 | 0.007 | 0.004 | 0.003 | 0.002 | 0.001 | 0.001 | 0.001 | | | | | |
| 40... | 0.672 | 0.453 | 0.208 | 0.097 | 0.046 | 0.022 | 0.011 | 0.005 | 0.004 | 0.003 | 0.001 | 0.001 | | | | | | | | | | |
| 50... | 0.608 | 0.372 | 0.141 | 0.054 | 0.021 | 0.009 | 0.003 | 0.001 | 0.001 | 0.001 | | | | | | | | | | | | |

"PRESENT WORTH OF ONE DOLLAR -- PAYABLE AT END OF EACH PERIOD": This chart SIMPLIFIES the determination of a DISCOUNTED PRESENT VALUE of an amount to be RECEIVED or DISBURSED at YEAR-END . . . using an ANNUAL INTEREST PERIOD. ACROSS the TOP of the chart are the NOMINAL ANNUAL INTEREST RATES . . . from 1 to 50 Percent. The LEFT-HAND COLUMN, headed-up as "YRS.", numbered 1 through 30, and years 40 and 50, are the "PERIODS UNTIL PAYMENT". These are ANNUAL PERIODS . . . at the END of which a SUM of MONEY is expected to be RECEIVED or DISBURSED . . . such as a Balloon-Payment or a Purchase Option, on a LEASE.

HOW TO USE: Select the ANNUAL RATE OF INTEREST that is to be charged in the LOAN or LEASE, by READING ACROSS THE TOP-COLUMN. Then, READING DOWN the "YRS." Column, locate the number of years that the Loan or Lease will run, before the Balloon-Payment or Purchase Option becomes DUE. READ ACROSS to the selected RATE of INTEREST, locate the three-decimal place discount percentage to be applied to the lump-sum ANTICIPATED as DUE or PAYABLE. MULTIPLY this Present Value Percentage TIMES the ANTICIPATED LUMP-SUM . . . and you have the DOLLAR AMOUNT of the DISCOUNTED PRESENT VALUE of that FUTURE SUM. (For Rates or Periods not shown, use INTERPOLATION, to obtain approximate values).

FIGURE 7-2

# AN EXPLANATION OF OUR LEASE YIELD CALCULATOR

## USES OF THIS CALCULATOR

We have included this "Calculator" to SIMPLIFY the task of determining the Lessor's YIELD, utilizing ANY GIVEN LENGTH OF TERM . . NUMBER of ADVANCE RENTALS . . . ANY SIZE SECURITY DEPOSIT . . . COMBINED WITH . . . ANY PURCHASE OPTION or RESIDUAL AMOUNT BEING REQUIRED or PROJECTED.

You must have the MONTHLY PAYMENT to insert into the formula to "CHECK-OUT" the YIELD for the "Calculator" to WORK-OUT PROPERLY.

In this respect, you have alternatives or sources to begin your calculations:

1) You can insert the payment QUOTED by the LESSOR.

2) You can insert a payment derived from our LEASE RATE CHARTS, directly, or by INTERPOLATION.

3) You can "invent" a payment, such as your BUDGETED or DESIRED monthly rental cost.

   To make the payment as realistic as possible, you should "factor-in" a reasonable Lease Finance Charge by using our ADD-ON FINANCE RATE CHARTS, on the desired TERMS and INTEREST COST.

4) You can utilize your Financial Calculator, following the manufacturer's instructions to obtain at least a "tentative" payment; then insert this payment on our Calculator - Part 2, to "play-with-the-numbers", by inserting different variables.

## WHY BOTHER WITH THIS CALCULATOR IF YOU CAN USE LEASE RATE CHARTS?

There are several reasons this Calculator will come-in handy. Many Lessees DO NOT HAVE ACCESS to complex rate-charts with all the POSSIBLE VARIABLES, which set forth a RATE PER THOUSAND, for easy calculation.

Sométimes there are so many variables, not found on ANY CHART, it is necessary even for the LESSOR to work with LEASE FORMULA CALCULATIONS, which can be quite complex.

FIGURE 7-2 (continued)

The most IMPORTANT USE is probably to be able to QUICKLY CHECK-OUT a LEASE PAYMENT QUOTATION to make sure the LESSOR is not "CONNING-YOU" . . . or, has made an error in calculations. The MOST FREQUENT cases of Lessor "YIELD OVER-CHARGE" occur when they make quotations that requires several advance rentals, a Security Deposit of an ODD-BALL amount . . . or there is an unusual ending Residual or Purchase-Option, not found on most charts.

SECONDARILY, using our "KNOWLEDGE is POWER" thinking, advanced by YOUR BEST DEAL, you "PUT YOURSELF IN THE DRIVER'S SEAT" of NEGOTIATION . . . by TELLING the Lessor what his yield REALLY IS . . . and WHAT you INTEND to ACTUALLY PAY in Payments and Yield!

When some fast-talking Lease Representative gives you the "Song-and-Dance" routine about a SUPER-GOOD RATE with a LOW YIELD "On-The-Stream-of-Payments" . . . (meaning he is omitting talking about the Purchase-Option or Residual Yield, his LESSOR gets), or JUST PLAIN UNDERSTATES the TRUE yield, YOU CAN STRAIGHTEN-HIM OUT-IN-A-HURRY, by running through this CALCULATOR PROCEDURE!

This "LEASE YIELD CALCULATOR" is much EASIER to use than it may at first APPEAR. Everything you need to make the necessary calculations are in YOUR BEST DEAL. Our INSTRUCTIONS will refer you to the PROPER CHARTS, to get your ANSWERS.

In our INSTRUCTIONS, part of the calculations involves the use of PRESENT VALUE DISCOUNT FACTORS. These factors depend upon the SELECTION of an INTEREST RATE. This "missing factor" is not as critical to the calculations as the Monthly Payment, but must be pre-determined to run the calculations.

Our SUGGESTED PROCEDURE is as follows:

1) ASK the LESSOR making the QUOTATION for the YIELD they have included in your PAYMENT CALCULATION. You are ENTITLED to know, but we cannot guarantee you will get the TRUTH. Use what they tell you anyway, because if INCORRECT, it will SHOW-UP in YOUR FINAL YIELD ANSWER.

2) If you have determined your own monthly payment from our charts, some other charts or by using your Financial Calculator, make your PRESENT VALUE CALCULATIONS using the INTEREST RATE stated in the charts or the rate you programmed into your calculator.

3) Or, SELECT an INTEREST RATE you are willing to pay. The BEST way to do THAT is to ADD POINTS to the existing PRIME Rate, that are reasonable under the circumstances . . . or the INTEREST RATE you would pay for a COMMERCIAL LOAN.

FIGURE 7-2 (continued)

## REGARDING PRECISION IN CALCULATIONS:

If you are CAREFUL to use the PRESENT VALUE CHART, as to the NUMBER OF YEARS before paying the Residual or Purchase-Option . . . selection of an improper interest rate, even plus or minus 1%, will not seriously effect your FINAL YIELD ANSWER, because the GRADATIONS are fairly small. However, it is better to work with an EXACT RATE you have pre-selected, to have confidence in your YIELD determination.

Keep in mind your TRUE objectives in making these calculations. The REALLY IMPORTANT factors that give the LESSOR sometime UNCONSCIONABLE YIELDS are the ACTUAL MONTHLY RENTAL PAYMENTS and how MUCH YOU PAY UP FRONT, followed by the SIZE of the "BUY-OUT" at the end-of-the-lease. Get those in the CALCULATOR properly.

Just doing THAT, and coming close on the INTEREST RATE for PRESENT VALUING, your NET YIELD will tell the story as to HOW MUCH PROFIT THE LESSOR is probably making. ASSUMING the LESSOR quoted you a proper MONTHLY RENTAL COST, but fudged on the INTEREST RATE IMPLICIT IN THAT QUOTATION . . . your objective is to FIND OUT HIS TRUE YIELD and whether or not you can TRUST that LESSOR. If the INTEREST RATE he gives you is NOT FACT (and is LOW), it will SHOW-UP glaringly in YOUR YIELD ANSWER.

The PRESENT VALUE CHART in YOUR BEST DEAL is only to three decimal places, which is entirely adequate for any usual YIELD DETERMINATION. When you consider the fact that you are ESTABLISHING A PRESENT-DAY VALUE FOR MONEY TO BE PAID 3 to 10 years in the FUTURE, you can see that INFLATION alone can warp that DOLLAR AMOUNT VALUE considerably. For that reason, there is little necessity to use ten decimal places that are found in Compound Interest and Annuity Tables.

However, if you are seeking maximum PRECISION, because you are dealing in extremely large equipment lease costs, or you are obtaining CLOSE COMPETITIVE BIDS . . . we suggest that you maximize on the insertion of ALL NUMBERS. Begin with a four or five decimal-place LEASE RATE, continue with a ten decimal place PRESENT VALUE percentage and DO NOT DROP DECIMAL PLACES IN THE FINAL CALCULATIONS.

FIGURE 7-2 (continued)

# LEASE YIELD CALCULATOR

## PART 1

### INSTRUCTIONS:

The TOP PART of our LEASE YIELD CALCULATOR - PART 2, is for your own information to keep calculations separated . . . if you are preparing analysis on several items of equipment or the SAME lease with different VARIABLES. Complete the REQUIRED ENTRIES so they are AVAILABLE to be CARRIED-DOWN to the LINE ENTRIES.

The Total Equipment Cost is to indicate your TOTAL EQUIPMENT INVESTMENT, which may be different than your LINE 3 Entry . . . LESSOR CASH ADVANCE, because of DEPOSITS made to the VENDOR, (and NOT REFUNDED by LESSOR at LEASE COMMENCEMENT). In some cases, the LESSOR PAYS ONLY THE PRICE OF THE EQUIPMENT . . . NOT the SALES TAXES, LICENSE FEES, DELIVERY or INSTALLATION COSTS).

### EXPLANATION OF LINE ENTRIES

LINE 1: Enter the FULL TERM from Top of Part 2, subtract ONE MONTH to arrive at NET TERM.

LINE 2: Multiply NET TERM from Line 1, TIMES the MONTHLY RENTAL, to arrive at TOTAL RENTAL RETURN. (Refer to "USES OF THIS CALCULATOR" to complete this line entry).

LINE 3: Enter LESSOR CASH ADVANCE from TOP of Part 2. (This is the amount the LESSOR actually PAYS for your EQUIPMENT).

LINE 4: Enter the DOLLAR AMOUNT of ONE (1) MONTHLY RENTAL, from LINE 2.

LINE 5: Total the amount of ANY other ADVANCE RENTALS or SECURITY DEPOSITS paid to LESSOR, as entered in TOP of PART 2.

LINE 6: Locate the PROPER PRESENT VALUE % in our PRESENT VALUE OF $1 CHART for the NUMBER of YEARS the lease will run prior to termination and the INTEREST RATE used in CALCULATING the MONTHLY RENTAL PAYMENT.

(Refer to "USES OF THIS CALCULATOR", to complete this line entry).

LINE 7: To compute NET VALUE OF ADVANCES, MULTIPLY THE PRESENT VALUE PERCENTAGE TIMES the TOTAL dollar amount of CASH ADVANCES on LINE 5. (You do NOT Present Value the ONE ADVANCE RENTAL PAID). If there are no OTHER ADVANCE RENTALS or SECURITY DEPOSITS paid or to be paid, Lines 5, 6 and 7 may be left-blank; just bring Line 4 down to Line 8.

FIGURE 7-2 (continued)

LINE 8: Complete the ADDITION, as indicated, if there were OTHER advances. Otherwise, simply bring LINE 4 down to LINE 8, and enter.

LINE 9: Complete the SUBTRACTION, as indicated.

LINE 10: From the TOP of PAGE - PART 2, enter the DOLLAR AMOUNT of ANY PURCHASE OPTION or RESIDUAL VALUE to become due upon COMPLETION of the LEASE TERM.

LINE 11: Enter the same PRESENT VALUE FACTOR USED on LINE 7. (If there were no Advance Rentals or Security Deposits, follow the same instructions as indicated in LINE 7, and refer to "USES OF THIS CALCULATOR".

LINE 12: Compute NET VALUE of PURCHASE OPTION or RESIDUAL VALUE the same way as instructed for LINE 7.

LINE 13: Complete the SUBTRACTION, as indicated. The RESULT represents the Lessor's "NET INVESTMENT", used in the YIELD CALCULATION.

YIELD CALCULATION: Complete the calculations, bringing down the APPROPRIATE LINE ENTRIES, as indicated. REFER TO OUR "EXAMPLE" on the PAGE FOLLOWING OUR "LEASE YIELD CALCULATOR - PART 2". Assuming your entries, premises and calculations were properly completed, the FINAL EQUIVALENT YIELD should be ACCURATE, plus or minus "2", in the SECOND DECIMAL PLACE. Thus, an answer of 13.76, could be 13.74 or 13.78. (See, also, our preceding comments concerning PRECISION).

FIGURE 7-2 (continued)

# LEASE YIELD CALCULATOR PART 2

Equipment to be Leased: ______________________
(Brief Description of Equipment for this Calculation)

Total Equipment Cost: $ 69978 Lessor Cash Advance: $ ________

Full Term of Lease : 60 Months. Number of Advance Rentals Payable 1

Security Deposit: $ 0 Purchase Option or Residual: $ 0

---

LINE 1: Full Term 59 (Months) MINUS ONE (1) Advance Rental = NET TERM: 59

LINE 2: Net Term 59 (Mos.) X ________ (Mthly Rental) = TOTAL RENTAL RETURN: $ ________

LINE 3: Enter LESSOR CASH ADVANCE (from Top of Page) . . . . . . $ ________

LINE 4: Enter Amount of ONE (1) Advance Rental . . . . . . . . . $ ________

LINE 5: Enter Total Amount of ALL OTHER ADVANCES or DEPOSITS . . $ ________

LINE 6: Enter PRESENT VALUE % of Advances . . . . . ________ %

LINE 7: Compute NET VALUE of Line 5, Per INSTRUCTIONS, Part 1.
Enter Total $ AMOUNT of Advances, Present Valued . . . . $ ________

LINE 8: ADD Line 4 $ ________ to Line 7 $ ________ Enter TOTAL = $ ________

LINE 9: SUBTRACT Line 8 $ ________ from Line 3 $ ________ = $ ________

LINE 10: Enter Purchase Option or Residual Value (Top of Page) = $ ________

LINE 11: Enter PRESENT VALUE % Factor . . . . . . . . ________ %

LINE 12: Compute NET VALUE of Line 10, Per INSTRUCTIONS, Part 1. $ ________

LINE 13: SUBTRACT Line 12 $ ________ from Line 9 $ ________ $ ________

THE AMOUNT ON LINE 13 REPRESENTS LESSOR'S NET INVESTMENT FOR YIELD CALCULATION:

---

YIELD CALCULATION: (SEE INSTRUCTIONS, Part 1, for explanation of calculations).

Total Rental Return $ ________ (Line 2) MINUS Net Investment $ ________ (Line 13) = ________ NET RETURN

$\frac{\text{Net Return \$}}{\text{Net Investment \$}}$ = ________ (Gross Add-On)

$\frac{\text{Gross Add-On}}{\text{Net Term (From Line 1)}}$ = ________ X 12 = ________ Annual Add-On = ________ YIELD %

FIGURE 7-2 (continued)

# LEASE YIELD CALCULATOR PART 2

Equipment to be Leased: *CNC Lathe*
(Brief Description of Equipment for this Calculation)

Total Equipment Cost: $ *176,748.48* Lessor Cash Advance: $ *176,748.48*

Full Term of Lease : *84* Months. Number of Advance Rentals Payable *One (1)*

Security Deposit: $ *None* Purchase Option or Residual: $ *17,675.00*
*(10% of equipment cost) (Rounded-up)*

---

LINE 1: Full Term *84* (Months) MINUS ONE (1) Advance Rental = NET TERM: *83*

LINE 2: Net Term *83* (Mos.) X *$3,101.23* (Mthly Rental) = TOTAL RENTAL RETURN: $ *257,402.09*

LINE 3: Enter LESSOR CASH ADVANCE (from Top of Page) . . . . . . $ *176,748.48*

LINE 4: Enter Amount of ONE (1) Advance Rental . . . . . . . . . $ *3,101.23*

LINE 5: Enter Total Amount of ALL OTHER ADVANCES or DEPOSITS . . $ *None*

LINE 6: Enter PRESENT VALUE % of Advances . . . . . *0* %

LINE 7: Compute NET VALUE of Line 5, Per INSTRUCTIONS, Part 1.
Enter Total $ AMOUNT of Advances, Present Valued . . . . $ *-0-*

LINE 8: ADD Line 4 $ *3,101.23* to Line 7 $ *-0-* Enter TOTAL = $ *3,101.23*

LINE 9: SUBTRACT Line 8 $ *3,101.23* from Line 3 $ *176,748.48* = $ *173,647.25*

LINE 10: Enter Purchase Option or Residual Value (Top of Page) = $ *17,675.00*

LINE 11: Enter PRESENT VALUE % Factor . . . . . . . . . *.412125* %

LINE 12: Compute NET VALUE of Line 10, Per INSTRUCTIONS, Part 1. $ *7,284.31*

LINE 13: SUBTRACT Line 12 $ *7,284.31* from Line 9 $ *173,647.25* $ *166,362.94*

THE AMOUNT ON LINE 13 REPRESENTS LESSOR'S NET INVESTMENT FOR YIELD CALCULATION:

---

YIELD CALCULATION: (SEE INSTRUCTIONS, Part 1, for explanation of calculations).

Total Rental Return $ *257,402.09* (Line 2) MINUS Net Investment $ *166,362.94* (Line 13) = *$91,039.15* NET RETURN

$$\frac{\text{Net Return } \$\ 91{,}039.15}{\text{Net Investment } \$\ 166{,}362.94} = \frac{.5472321}{\text{(Gross Add-On)}}$$

$$\frac{\text{Gross Add-On } .5472321}{\text{Net Term (From Line 1) } 83 \text{ (Mos.)}} = .0065931 \times 12 = \frac{.07911}{\text{Annual Add-On}} = \frac{13.6 \text{ (Prox.) \%}}{\text{YIELD}}$$

FIGURE 7-3

# HOW A LEASE COMPARES TO A BANK LOAN

**Comparison of Cash Costs**
**LEASING VERSUS BANK LOAN**

| At End Of Year | Annual Payment | Depreciation and Interest | Tax Savings 50% Rental Or Depreciation Plus Interest | Cash Cost | Cumulative Cash Cost | Accumulated Cash Savings With Leasing |
|---|---|---|---|---|---|---|
| LOAN | 38,160 | 27,766 | 13,883 | 24,277 | 24,277 | |
| LEASE | 28,800 | | 14,440 | 14,400 | 14,400 | 9,877 |
| LOAN | 38,160 | 20,914 | 10,457 | 27,703 | 51,980 | |
| LEASE | 28,800 | | 14,400 | 14,400 | 28,800 | 23,180 |
| LOAN | 38,160 | 14,598 | 7,299 | 30,861 | 82,841 | |
| LEASE | 28,800 | | 14,440 | 14,400 | 43,200 | 39,641 |
| LOAN | -- --- | 10,240 | 5,120 | (5,120) | 77,721 | |
| LEASE | 28,800 | | 14,400 | 14,400 | 57,600 | 20,121 |
| LOAN | -- --- | 8,190 | 4,095 | (4,095) | 73,626 | |
| LEASE | 28,900 | | 14,400 | 14,400 | 72,000 | 1,626 |

1. Based on $100,000 equipment cost, 5-year lease and monthly payment of $2,400.
2. Based on 9% conventional 3-year loan on $100,000 equipment. Double declining balance used to calculate depreciation.

**Net Earnings on Conserved Capital**
**LEASING COMPARED AGAINST BANK LOAN**

| CASH SAVED | Cash Saved Plus Accumulated Earnings | Net Earnings Based on 12% Profit on Net Working Capital | Accumulated Net Earnings With Leasing |
|---|---|---|---|
| 9,877 | 9,877 | 1,185 | 1,185 |
| 23,180 | 24,365 | 2,924 | 4,109 |
| 39,641 | 43,750 | 5,250 | 9,359 |
| 20,121 | 29,480 | 3,357 | 12,896 |
| 1,626 | 14,522 | 1,742 | 14,638 |

The accumulated five-year earnings on conserved capital by leasing vs. a bank loan is $14,638.

# HOW A LEASE COMPARES TO OUTRIGHT CASH PURCHASE

**Comparison of Cash Costs**
**LEASING VERSUS OUTRIGHT PURCHASE FOR CASH**

| At End Of Year | Annual Payments | Depreciation | Tax Savings | Cash Cost | Cumulative Cash Cost | Accumulated Cash Savings With Leasing |
|---|---|---|---|---|---|---|
| BUY | 100,000 | 20,000 | 10,000 | 90,000 | 90,000 | |
| LEASE | 28,800 | | 14,400 | 14,400 | 14,400 | 75,600 |
| BUY | -- --- | 16,000 | 8,000 | 8,000 | 82,000 | |
| LEASE | 28,800 | | 14,400 | 14,400 | 28,800 | 53,200 |
| BUY | -- --- | 12,800 | 6,400 | 6,400 | 75,600 | |
| LEASE | 28,800 | | 14,400 | 14,400 | 43,200 | 32,400 |
| BUY | -- --- | 10,240 | 5,120 | 5,120 | 70,480 | |
| LEASE | 28,800 | | 14,400 | 14,400 | 57,600 | 12,880 |
| BUY | -- --- | 8,190 | 4,095 | 4,095 | 66,385 | |
| LEASE | 28,800 | | 14,400 | 14,400 | 72,000 | (5,615) |

3. Based on outright cash purchase of $100,000 equipment and using double-declining balance method to calculate depreciation.

**Net Earnings on Conserved Capital**
**LEASING COMPARED AGAINST CASH PURCHASE**

| CASH SAVED | Cash Saved Plus Accumulated Earnings | Net Earnings Based on 12% Profit on Net Working Capital | Accumulated Net Earnings With Leasing |
|---|---|---|---|
| 75,600 | 75,600 | 9,072 | 9,072 |
| 53,200 | 62,272 | 7,472 | 16,544 |
| 32,400 | 48,944 | 5,873 | 22,544 |
| 12,880 | 35,297 | 4,236 | 26,653 |
| (5,615) | 21,038 | 2,524 | 29,177 |

The accumulated five-year earnings on conserved capital by leasing vs. a cash purchase is $29,177.

**DUN & BRADSTREET analysis indicate the average net profit on net working capital among all businesses is approximately 12% after tax.**

**Since leasing requires less cash outlay than either a bank loan or a cash purchase, you can put your conserved capital to its most productive use.**

FIGURE 7-4

# CASH FLOW ANALYSIS -- LEASE versus LOAN

You can USE this form to make a valid comparison between leasing your equipment . . . or, buying it on a finance or bank loan contract. The main reason for charting the payments, interest costs, depreciation and taxes . . . is to determine if there is a CASH ADVANTAGE to LEASING versus a LOAN.

## HOW TO COMPLETE THE ENTRIES

**LEASE - (COLUMNS 1 through 4):**

COLUMN 1: Annualize the LEASE PAYMENTS that become due in each year of the LEASE. If the payments are made monthly, simply multiply the QUOTED or PROJECTED Lease Payment by 12. ENTER that amount in EACH YEAR the Lease will run, starting with YEAR ONE (1).

You may elect to work with the calendar year, entering in YEAR ONE only those payments to be paid in THAT YEAR. However, for analysis purposes, it is easier to simply spread the lease over the term it will run, considering each year as 12 months.

NOTE: If you are required to pay a SECURITY DEPOSIT, which will be held until the lease is paid, enter this CASH PAID on the YEAR "0" line. (It is the same as a DOWN PAYMENT).

COLUMN 2: Enter your FEDERAL TAX RATE and STATE TAX RATE (if any), as a combined equivalent percentage, at the TOP of the Column. MULTIPLY your-TAX RATE TIMES the RENTAL PAYMENT, to arrive at the YEARLY entries.

COLUMN 3: SUBTRACT Tax Saving from Rental Payment to arrive at NET CASH COST.

COLUMN 4: ADD YEAR "ONE" NET CASH COST, to YEAR "TWO", etc. to obtain the CUMULATIVE NET CASH COST.

**LOAN or FINANCE CONTRACT - (COLUMNS 5 through 10):**

COLUMN 5: Enter on the LINE YEAR "0", any DOWN-PAYMENT made.

COLUMN 6: Determine a DEPRECIABLE LIFE, your DEPRECIATION METHOD . . . such as Double-Declining, Straight-Line, etc. Starting in YEAR ONE, enter the amount of Depreciation applicable to each year of that EQUIPMENT'S LIFE. That means your entries in COLUMNS 6, 8, 9, 10 and 11, will LIKELY continue well-beyond the LOAN CONTRACT.

COLUMN 7: Enter the INTEREST or FINANCE CHARGES applicable to each year of the loan or finance contract. (Follow our instructions at the BOTTOM of the EXAMPLE FORM).

COLUMN 8: Use the same TAX-RATE entered in COLUMN 2.

COLUMNS 9, 10, 11 are self-explanatory. Just be sure to carry your numbers down and across, as INDICATED at TOPS of COLUMNS.

COLUMN 11 will reveal the CASH ADVANTAGE, (if any), of a LEASE when compared to a LOAN or FINANCE CONTRACT.

FIGURE 7-4 (continued)

# CASH FLOW ANALYSIS

## LEASE VERSUS LOAN/TIME-SALE CONTRACT

| | LEASE | | | | LOAN/TIME-SALE CONTRACT | | | | | | Cash Advantage |
|---|---|---|---|---|---|---|---|---|---|---|---|
| | 1 | 2 | 3 | 4 | 5 | 6 | 7 | 8 | 9 | 10 | 11 |
| YRS. | Rental Payment | Tax Savings ______% of (1) | Net Cash Cost (1) - (2) | Cumulative Net Cash Cost | Payments | Depreciation ______at ______yrs. | Interest or Finance Charge | Tax Savings ______% (6) + (7) | Net Cash Cost (5) (8) | Cumulative Net Cash Cost | Cash Available (10) - (4) |
| 0 | | | | | | | | | | | |
| 1 | | | | | | | | | | | |
| 2 | | | | | | | | | | | |
| 3 | | | | | | | | | | | |
| 4 | | | | | | | | | | | |
| 5 | | | | | | | | | | | |
| 6 | | | | | | | | | | | |
| 7 | | | | | | | | | | | |
| 8 | | | | | | | | | | | |
| 9 | | | | | | | | | | | |

NOTE: Column 7 -- If you wish to compare an interest-bearing loan to a lease . . . you will have to compute annual interest on the descending balance and enter total interest costs for each year. For close estimate of finance charges, when the charges were computed on an ADD-ON RATE . . . REFER TO OUR RULE OF 78ths REFUND CHARTS for percentages EARNED EACH YEAR.

FIGURE 7-5

# PROJECTED INCOME FROM CONSERVED CAPITAL

## HOW TO COMPLETE THE ENTRIES

To complete your ANALYSIS, below, you must first complete the CASH FLOW ANALYSIS on the preceding page.

COLUMN "A": CARRY-OVER your entries from COLUMN 11, entering the amounts shown on YEARS "0" through the LAST YEAR of the LEASE TERM. (You may also elect to carry your computations through the EQUIPMENT LIFE).

COLUMN "B": These entries depend upon your AFTER-TAX EARNINGS PERCENTAGE RATE, entered at TOP of COLUMN "C".

MULTIPLY this % EARNINGS RATE times the amount you have entered in COLUMN "A", YEAR "0".

COLUMN "C": Each YEAR-ENTRY is the PRODUCT of your MULTIPLICATION of AFTER-TAX EARNINGS RATE times COLUMN "B", after adding your PRIOR PRODUCT to COLUMN "A".

THUS, the series of calculations becomes: MULTIPLY the amount entered in COLUMN "B", YEAR "0", times the TAX-RATE. Enter PRODUCT in "C" and ADD to YEAR 1 of "A". Enter this SUM in "B" and multiply again by TAX-RATE, adding SUM to COLUMN "A", and continuously CARRY-FORWARD.

("B" X TAX-RATE = PRODUCT + "A" + ACCUMULATED "D").

COLUMN "D": These entries are simply YEAR "0", COLUMN "C", plus YEAR 1, Column "C", plus YEAR 2, etc.

| | A | B | C | D |
|---|---|---|---|---|
| YEAR | Cash Advantage or Conserved Capital | Conserved Capital + Accumulated Earnings | Net Earnings on (B) at ______ % Rate after Tax. | Accumulated Earnings |
| 0 | | | | |
| 1 | | | | |
| 2 | | | | |
| 3 | | | | |
| 4 | | | | |
| 5 | | | | |
| 6 | | | | |
| 7 | | | | |

FIGURE 7-6

# A Glossary of Lease Terms and "Buzz-Words"

We said at the beginning of our leasing chapter, the leasing industry is *replete with misunderstandings. Many people, inside and outside of the business of equipment leasing, misuse leasing terms and phrases.* Many of the words, intended to, are interchangeable -- creating redundancies and confusion.

"Your Best Deal" presents a Glossary Of Lease Terms, to provide the most acceptable definitions. Instead of the usual alphabetical list, dictionary style . . . we have divided leasing into subject matter and areas of interest. To provide additional useful insight, we have made explanatory comments *in italics, following the definitions.*

## PARTIES TO A LEASING TRANSACTION

### LESSOR

The OWNER of EQUIPMENT which is being leased to a lessee or user.

*The LESSOR is also the LENDER and SECURED PARTY in all lease transactions that are not "true leases". In some cases, including "true leases", the Lessor appears as Secured Party on the UCC filing -- even if the filing is for "informational purposes". When a Lessor acquires the lease transaction from another, perhaps from an originating vendor or "lease broker", he is the ASSIGNEE -- or, "Assignee of the Secured Party".*

*In any case, the Lessor holds "title" to the equipment.*

### LESSEE

The USER of the equipment being leased.

*Users say, "The Lessee is me." If the lease is a "nominal" lease or "Lease/Purchase", the Lessee is also the DEBTOR--and you will find yourself so designated on the UCC filing form.*

FIGURE 7-6 (continued)

## VENDOR

Any SUPPLIER of the leased equipment —— manufacturer, distributor, dealer or importer. The Vendor SELLS to the LESSOR.

*In some cases, any of these VENDORS could also have been the LESSOR... ORIGINATING THE LEASE for later assignment to another lender-lessor. These are sometimes called SALE-TYPE LEASES.*

We have listed the usual participants in a lease transaction. For those who are curious or would like to better understand "LEVERAGED LEASES", there are additional *participants* peculiar to that type of lease.

## EQUITY PARTICIPANT

The LESSOR or one of the group of lessors in a LEVERAGED LEASE. Equity participants hold trust certificates evidencing their beneficial interest as owners under the owner trust.

*An EQUITY PARTICIPANT is the SAME AS AN OWNER PARTICIPANT, TRUSTOR OWNER or GRANTOR OWNER.*

## GRANTOR TRUST

A trust used as the owner trust in a LEVERAGED LEASE TRANSACTION, usually with only ONE EQUITY PARTICIPANT.

*The Internal Revenue Code (Sec. 671) refers to such a trust as a grantor trust. With more than one equity participant, the Grantor Trust is usually treated as a partnership (see Subchapter K).*

## INDENTURE TRUSTEE

In a leveraged lease, the Indenture Trustee holds the security interest in the leased equipment for the benefit of the lenders. In the event of default, the Indenture Trustee exercises the rights of a mortgagee.

The Indenture Trustee also is responsible for receiving rent payments from the lessee and using such funds to pay the amounts due the lenders with the balance being paid to the Owner Trustee.

The Indenture Trustee verifies that correct UCC filings are made to protect the Security Interest of the lenders. The "bond register" is maintained by the Indenture Trustee, who also acts as Transfer Agent.

FIGURE 7-6 (continued)

## LOAN PARTICIPANT

A LENDER in a leveraged lease. A holder of debt in a leveraged lease usually evidenced by bonds or loan certificates issued by the Owner Trustee.

## OWNER PARTICIPANT

Same as EQUITY PARTICIPANT.

## OWNER TRUSTEE

In a leveraged lease, the Owner Trustee holds title to the equipment (for the benefit of the Equity Participants). The Owner Trustee issues trust certificates to the Equity Participants, maintains the register and acts as transfer agent for the certificates.

The Owner Trustee issues bonds to the lenders, receives distributions of rent payments from the Indenture Trustee, takes fees due itself and the Indenture Trustee and disburses amounts due the Equity Participants.

This trustee also makes appropriate filings to perfect and protect the lenders' interest in the collateral (equipment). Compliance certificates and other information required from the lessee under the lease are received by the Owner Trustee and distributed to the other parties.

*An Owner Trustee is sometimes called "Grantor Trustee".*

## PACKER

A name given to describe the leasing company, investment banker or broker who arranges a leveraged lease.

*PACKER, another name for "Packager".*

## TRUSTEE

A bank or trust company which holds title to or a security interest in leased property in trust for the benefit of the lessee, lessor, and/or creditors of the lessor. A Leveraged Lease often has two trustees: Owner Trustee and Indenture Trustee.

## TRUSTOR OWNER

Same as EQUITY PARTICIPANT.

# TYPES OF LEASES -- "LEASE CLASSIFICATIONS"

This is an area of leasing where there is the most confusion. Many otherwise knowledgeable bank and finance company managers, vendors and business owners do not know one lease from another . . . or, if they do . . . they are unable to call it by the correct name.

## DIRECT FINANCING LEASE ... VERSUS ... CAPITAL LEASE

These lease "types" are virtually identical, except for "point of view" that is, if you are the Lessee, it's a capital lease. If you are the Lessor, it's a Direct Financing Lease. In either case, the lease is NOT a TRUE LEASE or a LEVERAGED LEASE.

*A Direct Financing Lease is also known as a Direct Lease.*

There are four (4) criteria used to identify a Capital or Direct Financing Lease. The criteria are EXACTLY THE SAME...and the presence of any ONE of them causes the lease to be called "Capital" or "Direct". There are two (2) additional criteria *important only to the lessor.* Here they are --→(numbers 5 and 6 belong to the Direct Financing Lease).

1) The lease transfers ownership to the Lessor at end of the lease term.

2) The lease contains an option to purchase property at a bargain price.

3) The "present value" of minimum lease rental payments is equal to 90% or more of the fair market value of the leased property...less related Investment Tax Credit retained by the Lessor.

4) The lease term is equal to 75% or more of the estimated economic life of the property. (Used property, leased toward the end of its useful life, is an exception).

Items (5) and (6) cause Lessor to call the lease

5) Collectibility of minimum lease payments must be reasonably predictable.

6) There are no uncertainties as to the amount of costs to be incurred by the Lessor under the Lease.

*Let's say this, if it isn't a True Lease, the Lessee should capitalize the asset, just as he would on a Conditional Sale equipment purchase. Thus, a Capital Lease definition seems most appropriate.*

*The next definition is an example of why there is CONFUSION and MISUNDERSTANDINGS in LEASING . . .*

FIGURE 7-6 (continued)

## FINANCE LEASE

This type of lease has been defined as a financing device whereby a user can acquire use of an asset for most of its useful life. Rentals are net to the lessor; and the user is responsible for maintenance, taxes and insurance. Rentals over the life of the lease enable the Lessor to recover the cost of equipment, *plus* a return on its investment. A finance lease may be either a True Lease or a Conditional Sale!

*So, why bother with this definition? As Lessee, your main interests are in three kinds of leases: Capital Lease, True Lease and "Operating Lease".*

## OPERATING LEASE

An Operating Lease is sometimes so defined when the user acquires use of equipment for a fraction of the useful life of the asset.

The Lessor may provide services in connection with the lease such as MAINTENANCE, INSURANCE and PAYMENT OF PERSONAL PROPERTY TAXES.

*This is what the accountants call a lease that isn't a Capital or Direct Financing Lease.*

## NET LEASE

In a Net Lease, the rentals are payable NET to the Lessor. All costs in connection with the use of the equipment are to be paid by the Lessee and are NOT part of the rental. Taxes, insurance and maintenance are paid directly by the Lessee. Most Capital and Direct Financing Leases are Net Leases.

*A "Net - Net" Lease is the same as a Net Lease.*

## TRUE LEASE

A True Lease is a transaction which qualifies as a lease under the Internal Revenue Code, so the Lessee can claim rental payments as tax deductions and the Lessor can claim tax benefits of ownership . . . such as DEPRECIATION and ITC.

FIGURE 7-6 (continued)

## MASTER LEASE

This FORM of lease is generally used in conjunction with a "lease line of credit". The Lessee can add equipment under the same basic terms and conditions, without negotiating a new lease contract. Additions to the lease are made by attaching new schedules to the original agreement.

*The lease rate and terms are subject to individual negotiation, sometimes schedule by schedule, with monthly or quarterly payment dates coincided. If the Master Lease and/or the schedules prescribe a fixed-rate future credit-limit and minimum/maximum terms, renegotiation is unnecessary. YOU SIMPLY SIGN SCHEDULES AND NEW UCC filing forms. A "Prime-Plus" floating lease rate also eliminates renegotiation. Insurance coverage must be extended to protect Lessee/Lessor for add-on equipment.*

## LEVERAGE LEASE

A lease which meets the definition criteria for a Direct Financing Lease or a Capital Lease, *plus each of the following:*

1) At Least three parties are involved; a Lessor, a Lessee and a long-term creditor.

2) The financing provided by the creditor is substantial to the transaction and WITHOUT RECOURSE to the Lessor.

3) The Lessor's net investment typically declines during the early years of the lease and rises during the later years of the lease.

## CONDITIONAL SALE or CONDITIONAL SALE LEASE

A transaction for purchase of an asset in which the user, for federal income tax purposes, is treated as the OWNER of the equipment at the outset of the transaction —— in substance a Conditional Sale —— NOT a lease.

*If the document is called "LEASE" but the words say "PURCHASER", "DEBTOR" or "OWNER", it's a Conditional Sale —— with the name "LEASE" hooked-on for cosmetic purposes. This type of "lease" is sometimes called a Hire-Purchase Agreement.*

FIGURE 7-6 (continued)

**SALE - LEASEBACK**

A transaction which involves the SALE of the property of the OWNER . . and a lease of the property BACK TO THE SELLER (OWNER).

*This definition covers the TRUE MEANING of a Sale and Leaseback. The same words are often MISUSED to describe or define a "regular" lease wherein the Lessor buys equipment for the end-user (Lessee), and then "Leases-it-back" to him —— a totally INCORRECT use of "Sale-Leaseback". Unless the Lessee already owned the equipment, rather than requested the Lessor purchase it for him, it can't be a Sale-Leaseback.*

## OPTIONS AND RENEWALS

Here is another area of leasing full of misunderstandings and words improperly used as if they were interchangeable. There are also a number of variations in options and renewals which are meaningful to Lessees . . . so an understanding becomes IMPORTANT. *There's more to it than the all-inclusive phrase, "What's the BUY-BACK?" —— even though it's a good question.*

**BARGAIN PURCHASE OPTION**

A provision allowing the lessee, AT HIS OPTION, to purchase the leased asset for a price which is sufficiently lower than the expected fair market value (at the date such option becomes exercisable), that exercise of the option appears, at the inception of the lease, to be reasonably assured.

*A "Bargain Option" is about certain to negate a "True" lease, if examined by IRS.*

**BARGAIN RENEWAL OPTION**

A provision allowing the lessee, at his option, to renew the lease for a rental sufficiently lower than the expected fair rental for the property (at the date the option becomes exercisable), that exercise of the option appears, at the inception of the lease, to be reasonably assured.

FIGURE 7-6 (continued)

## BURDENSOME BUYOUT

A provision in a lease allowing the lessee to purchase the leased equipment at a pre-determined value in excess of termination value, or at a value to be determined in some fashion when the buyout is exercised, in the event that payments under the tax or general idemnity clauses are deemed by the lessee to be unduly burdensome.

*Care must be taken if the existence of such a provision is not to invalidate the true lease nature of the transaction and thus, by its existence, make the lessee liable under the tax indemnity clause.*

## CALL

An option to purchase an asset at a set price at some particular time in the future. Care must be used in negotiating a purchase option or call in a lease agreement.

*If this is done improperly, many of the advantages of a true lease - such as tax savings - might be disallowed by the Internal Revenue Service.*

## ESTIMATED RESIDUAL VALUE OF LEASED PROPERTY

The estimated fair value of the property at the end of the leased term.

*This is also a method Lessors use to provide a Lessee with "comfort" and reassurances as to the Fair Market Value he must pay at end of lease.*

## EXTENDED TERM AGREEMENT

An agreement to renew a lease, commonly used to describe a guaranteed renewal of a lease by a third party.

## PURCHASE OPTION

An option to purchase leased property at the end of the lease term. In order to protect the tax characteristics of a true lease, an option to purchase property from a lessor by a lessee cannot be at a price less than its fair market value at the time the right is exercised.

FIGURE 7-6 (continued)

## PUT

A "Put" is an option one person has to sell an asset to another person at a set price at some established point in time in the future. In lease agreements, a lessor sometimes negotiates an option to sell leased equipment to the lessee or to some third party at an established price at the end of the lease term.

*Care must be used in negotiating a "put" to a lessee lest the true lease characteristics of the transaction be destroyed and money-saving advantages lost. A lessor may also negotiate a "put" to a third party as a hedge against future loss on the sale of the residual.*

## RENEWAL OPTION

An option to renew the lease at the end of the initial lease term.

*Here, too, care must be used in granting a renewal option for a fair rental value. If this is not done properly, it may later be ruled that the lease is not a true lease; tax advantages are lost and tax indemnity clauses activated.*

## RESIDUAL OR RESIDUAL VALUE

The value of equipment at the conclusion of the lease term. To qualify the lease as a "True Lease" for tax purposes, the estimated residual value at the end of the lease term must equal at least 20% of the original cost of the equipment.

*The keyword here is "VALUE". The Residual Value MAY be the amount to be paid for the equipment —— but unlike an option expressed in dollars or a percentage of original cost, it does not provide the Lessee with a fixed or assured "buy-back" price.*

## SALVAGE VALUE

The minimum value for a depreciable asset. After sufficient depreciation is taken so that cost less accumulated depreciation equals salvage value, no more depreciation may be taken.

*NOT the same as Residual Value.*

## UNGUARANTEED RESIDUAL VALUE

The portion of residual value "at risk" for a lessor in his yield computation, i.e., for which there is not a party obligated to pay.

FIGURE 7-6 (continued)

There are two additional definitions, directly related to OPTIONS and RENEWALS, which we include below:

### RESIDUAL INSURANCE

An insurance policy guaranteeing a certain residual value at the end of the lease term.

### RESIDUAL SHARING

An agreement between the lessor and another party providing for a division of the *residual value* between them.

*Care must be taken in any such agreement, lest the tax benefits be lost and the lessee become liable under the tax indemnity clause.*

## EQUIPMENT -- DEPRECIATION -- INSURANCE

We have segregated definitions pertinent to the EQUIPMENT and INSURANCE FOR your EASY REFERENCE.

### ADR - ASSET DEPRECIATION RANGE

Refers to regulations under the Internal Revenue Code (Section 167(m)) which permits shorter or longer than usual life to be used for tax depreciation. Under certain circumstances, capital equipment may be depreciated over a period which may be up to 20% more or less than the applicable class life, rounded to the nearest half-year.

### CERTIFICATE OF ACCEPTANCE

A document whereby the lessee acknowledges that the equipment to be leased has been delivered to him, is acceptable to him, and has been manufactured or constructed in accordance with specifications.

*This document is also known as the "D & A"; the Delivery and Acceptance.*

### COLLATERAL

Collateral under a lease is the equipment which is leased.

FIGURE 7-6 (continued)

### ECONOMIC LIFE OF LEASED PROPERTY

The estimated remaining period during which the property is expected to be economically usable by one or more users, with normal repairs and maintenance, for the purpose for which it was intended at the inception of the lease.

### INSURED VALUE

A schedule included in a lease which states the agreed value of equipment at various times during the term of the lease, and establishes the liability of the lessee to the lessor in the event the leased equipment is lost or rendered unusable during the lease term, due to a casualty.

### SPECIAL PURPOSE PROPERTY

Property which is uniquely valuable to the lessee and not valuable to anyone else except as scrap.

### STIPULATED LOSS VALUE

The same as *insured value.*

*Lessors more frequently use Stipulated Loss Value and include a percentage - type schedule in the Master Lease, Lease Agreement or as an Addendum to Lease Contract.*

### USEFUL LIFE

The period of time during which an asset will have economic value and be useable. Useful life of an asset is sometimes called the economic life of the asset.

*To qualify as a true lease, the leased property must have a remaining useful life of 20% of the original property at the end of the lease term, and at least a life of one year.*

## AGREEMENTS AND SPECIAL CLAUSES

There are special agreements and clauses peculiar to leasing. Some are pertinent only to Leveraged Leases.

### BURN-UP CONTRACT

Another name for a nuclear fuel lease.

FIGURE 7-6 (continued)

## FINANCING AGREEMENT

An agreement between the owner trustee, the lenders, the equity participants, the manufacturer, and the lessee, which spells out the obligations of the parties under a Leveraged Lease. Also called *participation agreement.*

## HELL-OR-HIGH WATER CLAUSE

A clause in a lease which reiterates the unconditional obligation of the lessee to pay rent for the entire term of the lease, regardless of any event affecting the equipment or any change in the circumstance of the lessee.

*This clause is also inserted for the benefit of Lessees who SHOW THE SLIGHTEST INDICATION OR THOUGHT THEY'RE ONLY "RENTING" THE EQUIPMENT.*

## INDEMNITY AGREEMENT

An agreement whereby the owner participants and the lessee indemnify the trustees from liability as a result of ownership of the leased equipment, in a Leveraged Lease.

## INDEMNITY CLAUSE

Although lease documentation contains various indemnities, the indemnity clause usually refers to the tax indemnity clause whereby the lessee indemnifies the lessor from loss of tax benefits.

*This clause may be inserted in any lease, but generally appears in Leveraged Leases and a True Lease, where the Lessor quoted a rate dependent upon achieving future tax benefits.*

## INDENTURE OF TRUST

(Used in a Leveraged Lease). An agreement between the owner trustee and the indenture trustee whereby the owner trustee mortgages the equipment and assigns the lease and rental payments under the lease as security for amounts due to the lenders. The same as a security agreement or mortgage.

## LEASE UNDERWRITING

An agreement whereby a packager commits firmly to enter into a lease on certain terms and assumes the risk of arranging any financing.

FIGURE 7-6 (continued)

### LOAN CERTIFICATES

(Used in a Leveraged Lease). Debt certificates or bonds issued by the owner trustee to lenders.

### MORTGAGE

An agreement between the owner trustee and the indenture trustee whereby the owner trustee assigns title to the equipment, the lease, and rental payments under the lease as security for amounts due the lenders. The same as an indenture of trust or security agreement.

### PARTICIPANT AGREEMENT

An agreement between the owner trustee, the lenders, the equity participants, the manufacturer, and the lessee which spells out the obligations of the parties under the leveraged lease.

*Also called a financing agreement. There can also be a Participation Agreement between two "lender" Lessors, such as a bank and a finance company, to offer the Lessee a lower "average" lease rate.*

## RATE, CREDIT AND RENTAL TERMINOLOGY

There are words and phrases found only in the leasing industry . . . sometimes a bit deceptive unless you are familiar with the correct definition. We list below those commonly used, including the phrases (related to term of lease):

### CONTINGENT RENTALS

Rentals in which the amounts are dependent upon some factor other than passage of time.

### FLOATING RENTAL RATE

Rental which is subject to upward or downward adjustments during the lease term. Floating rents sometimes are adjusted in proportion to prime interest rate or commercial paper rate changes during the term of the lease.

*"YOUR BEST DEAL" has called this Prime Rate - "Plus".*

### INCREMENTAL BORROWING RATE

The interest rate which a person would expect to pay for a certain loan at a certain time.

FIGURE 7-6 (continued)

## INTEREST RATE IMPLICIT IN A LEASE

The discount rate which, when applied to *minimum lease payments* (excluding executory costs paid by the lessor) and *unguaranteed residual value,* causes the aggregate present value at the beginning of the lease to be equal to the fair value of the leased property at the inception of the lease, *minus any investment tax credit retained by the lessor and expected to be realized by him.*

## INTERIM RENT

Daily rental accruing from delivery, acceptance and/or funding until a later starting date for a basic lease term. Often used when equipment delivers over a period of time.

## LEASE LINE

A lease line of credit similar to a bank line of credit which allows a lessee to add equipment, as needed, under the same basic terms and conditions without negotiating a new lease contract.

*(Refer also to Master Lease definition).*

## LEASE RATE

The equivalent simple annual interest rate implicit in minimum lease rentals.

*Not the same as Interest Rate Implicit in a Lease.*

## LEASE TERM

The fixed, non-cancellable term of the lease. Includes, for accounting purposes, all periods covered by fixed-rate renewal options which for economic reasons appear likely to be exercised at the inception of the lease, and for tax purposes, all periods covered by fixed-rate renewal options.

## LESSEE'S INCREMENTAL BORROWING RATE

The interest rate which the lessee, at the inception of the lease, would have incurred to borrow over a similar term the funds necessary to purchase the leased assets.

*In a Leveraged Lease the rate on the bonds is normally used.*

FIGURE 7-6 (continued)

## LEVEL PAYMENTS

Equal payments over the term of the lease.

## LEVERAGE

An amount borrowed. A lease is sometimes referred to as 100% leverage for the lessee. In a leveraged lease, the debt portion of the funds used to purchase the asset represents leverage of the equity holder.

## MINIMUM LEASE PAYMENTS FOR THE LESSEE

All payments the lessee is obligated to make or can be required to make in connection with leased property, including residual value guaranteed with lessor and bargain renewal rents or purchase options, but excluding guarantees of lessor's debt (seldom encountered) and executory costs such as insurance, maintenance and taxes.

## MINIMUM LEASE PAYMENTS FOR THE LESSOR

The payments considered minimum lease payments for the lessee plus any guarantee by a third party of the residual value or rental payments beyond the lease term.

## RETURN ON INVESTMENT -- "R.O.I."

The *yield*. The interest rate earned by the lessor in a lease which is measured by the rate at which the excess cash flows not needed for debt service or payment of taxes amortize the investment of the equity participant.

## SINKING FUND

A reserve or a sinking fund established or set aside for the purpose of payment of taxes anticipated to become due at a later date. *(Generally applicable only in Leveraged Leases.)*

## SINKING FUND RATE

The rate of interest allocated to a sinking fund set aside for future payment of taxes. *(Generally applicable only in Leveraged Leases.)*

### YIELD

The interest rate earned by the lessor or equity participant in a lease, which is measured by the rate at which the excess cash flows permit recovery of investment. The rate at which the cash flows not needed for debt service or payment of taxes amortize the investment of the equity participants.

## ACCOUNTING, TAXATION AND OTHER LEASING "BUZZ-WORDS"

In this final section of our GLOSSARY, we have assembled the remaining words and phrases pertaining to Accounting, Taxation and "buzz-words" that just did not fit in our other sections!

### SECURITY AGREEMENT

(Used in a Leveraged Lease). An agreement between the owner trustee and the indenture trustee whereby the owner trustee assigns title to the equipment, the lease, and rental payments under the lease as security for amounts due the lenders. *The same as an indenture of trust or mortgage.*

### SUB-LEASE

A transaction in which leased property is re-leased by the original lessee to a third party, and the lease agreement between the two original parties remains in effect.

### TERMINATION SCHEDULE

Leases sometimes contain provisions permitting a lessee to terminate the lease during the lease term in the event the leased equipment becomes obsolete and surplus to its needs. In such event, the equipment usually must be sold or transferred to some third party unconnected in any way with the lessee. The liability of the lessee in the event of such termination is set forth in a termination schedule which values the equipment at various times during the lease term. If the equipment is sold at a price lower than set forth in the schedule, the lessee pays the difference. In the event the resale is at a price higher than in the termination schedule, such excess amounts belong to the lessor.

*The termination schedule is NOT the same as the casualty value schedule, insured value schedule or stipulated loss value schedule.*

FIGURE 7-6 (continued)

## TRUST CERTIFICATE

(Used in a Leveraged Lease). Document evidencing the beneficial ownership of a trust estate of an equity participant (or owner participant, trustor owner, or grantor owner) in an owner trust.

## DEBT SERVICE

Payments of principal and interest due lenders.

## FOREIGN SOURCE INCOME

Income earned overseas (net of depreciation expense allocable to such income) as reported for United States federal income tax purposes.

## INCEPTION OF A LEASE

The date the lease commitment or lease agreement is signed, provided the property to be leased has been constructed or has been acquired by the lessor; otherwise, the date construction is completed or the property is acquired by the lessor.

## INDEPENDENT LESSOR

Any leasing company investing in leases; also, brokers without funds to invest in leases sometimes prefer to call themselves "independent lessors" rather than "brokers".

## INITIAL DIRECT COSTS

Direct costs incurred by a lessor in negotiating and consummating a lease, such as commissions and legal fees.

## INSTITUTIONAL INVESTORS

Investors such as banks, insurance companies, trusts, pension funds, foundations, and educational, charitable, and religious institutions.

FIGURE 7-6 (continued)

## LOW-BALL BID

A bid to perform a lease transaction purposely priced below market or with terms not acceptable from a tax or accounting standpoint, with a view to renegotiation of a higher price and/or more expensive terms at a later date once the bid is awarded the low-ball bidder and the other interested lessors are no longer available.

*Typically, the low-ball bidder raises the price when it is too late for the lessee to seek other leasing sources.*

## MINIMUM INVESTMENT

For a leveraged lease to be a *true lease*, the lessor must have a minimum "at risk" investment of at least 20% in a lease when the lease begins, ends, and at all times during the lease term.

## "PIC AND RIC"

These are abbreviations leasing people use, sometimes expressed as "PICK" and "RICK". A PIC lease is one structured so that the LESSOR *passes* the Investment Tax Credit ("ITC). A RIC Lease allows the LESSOR to retain the ITC.

## RELATED PARTIES

In leasing transactions under FAS 13: a parent and its subsidiaries; an owner and its joint ventures; an investor and its investees; provided the parent, owner, or investor has the ability to exercise significant influence over the financial and operating policies of the related party.

*Under the Internal Revenue Code, 50 percent ownership is a general test for a related party.*

## REVENUE PROCEDURES

Commonly used in leasing to refer to IRS Revenue Procedures 75-21 and 75-28, which set forth requirements for obtaining a favorable revenue ruling on a leveraged or "True Lease".

FIGURE 7-6 (continued)

**REVENUE RULING**

A written opinion of the Internal Revenue Service requested by parties, which is applicable to assumed facts stated in the opinion. May also refer to published IRS rulings with general applicability.

**STRIP DEBT**

Debt in connection with a leveraged lease, arranged in tiers with different maturities and amortization to improve the Lessor's cash flow and reduce the Lessee's costs.

# 8

# THE INS AND OUTS OF ACCOUNTS RECEIVABLE FINANCING

This financing alternative is often incorrectly referred to as factoring. To call it that isn't a very serious error in terminology, but we feel it is always helpful for business people to sound as knowledgeable as possible. Getting the financing you need starts with gaining the lender's respect. Using the proper terminology helps you gain that respect.

Factoring is related to accounts receivable financing only because it involves obtaining cash for receivables. The mechanics differ drastically. A factoring company will purchase your sales on a nonrecourse basis—the factor assumes the full credit risk. After that, the factor naturally does all the bookkeeping and collections. As the manufacturer, you have sold your future receivables to the factor, who discounts your invoices 1½% to, perhaps, 3%.

Factoring is often used in the textile and carpet industries, where the product is made up well in advance and warehoused for extended periods. Repayment terms may range from three to twelve months. The factor normally notifies the account debtor that the receivable was purchased and payments are to go to the factor.

So much for factoring. Let's talk about accounts receivable financing, a financing alternative you are more likely to become involved with—and itself a somewhat misunderstood source of funds. For many years there was a stigma attached to a company who resorted to financing their accounts receivable. The stigma lingers, but it has lessened as business people have become more sophisticated.

## YESTERDAY'S NEGATIVES

A/R financing's bad name came about for several reasons. In the early days of A/R financing, the lender usually notified the account debtor of the financing arrangement. The lender often stated or strongly implied, "You had better pay. We're not easy, like the manufacturer you've been riding!"

The account debtor, by being notified or hearing about the A/R arrangement, often had two sorts of reactions, both causes for concern:

1. Maybe his supplier was in financial trouble and might go out of business (better find a new supplier?).
2. "If he is involved with those accounts receivable "high binders," he will be paying high interest rates. Was he already packing the price—or will he soon increase his prices?"

Manufacturers who resorted to A/R financing paid extremely high interest costs—one thirtieth to one fortieth of the face value of the accounts pledged for each day they were outstanding! This cost the manufacturer 15% simple interest when he received an advance of only 75% of face value!

Remember, in the early years of which I speak, the prime rate was 5% to 6½%. The manufacturer financing his A/R was paying 9% *over* prime rate. In comparison to the usual 8% to 10% simple interest borrowing costs at the time, A/R financing seemed like the road to bankruptcy.

A/R financing costs, in relation to normal money costs, were so high they could put the borrower out of business. If the A/R debtor could not raise his prices or reduce his costs by utilizing A/R monies, he quickly became noncompetitive and went down the tube. The lender, often secured by the A/R as well as all machinery or other assets, simply took over and bailed out without a loss. Sometimes by quickly auctioning off assets and collecting the A/R, the A/R lender earned a profit!

The negative vibes arising from a manufacturer's financing his A/R have largely disappeared. Although A/R financing is not a permanent answer to a shortage of working capital, properly used, it can assist a well-managed company become self-sufficient. The goal is usually to get out of A/R financing as soon as practicable. There are, however, businesses that use A/R financing for many years, without ill effects.

### Where Did the High Binders Go?

The high binders are still around, charging very high interest rates. There are still some A/R loans being made that are abusive to the unsuspecting, troubled borrower. We will tell you what to look out for, how to negotiate a reasonable A/R program, and how to go into and get out of this costly financing.

A lot has happened in the A/R financing arena since the 1950s. Many banks now offer A/R financing; so do the lower-cost major finance companies. They have helped to legitimatize this form of borrowing, making it another financing alternative rather than a last-ditch effort before going out of business.

## HOW A/R FINANCING WORKS

To aid in making you more knowledgeable about the mechanics and buzzwords of accounts receivable financing, we will outline the beginnings of the typical A/R loan.

The A/R lender you have selected first reviews and analyzes your financial statements, consisting of your last three to five year-end reports. He will examine your A/R aging lists.

The lender compares your business to similar businesses, for industry averages, ratio comparisons, product acceptability, and other performance criteria. His primary objective is to determine the risk of your particular products and receivable customers.

The lender makes some very important preliminary decisions as to the acceptability of your accounts. First, do you create enough receivables each month? The larger banks and major finance companies set up minimums—often $50,000 to as much as $250,000 per month—before they will even consider your A/R financing request. In other words, you must be generating $600,000 per year, in eligible sales, just to qualify. You may not borrow it all, every month, but the potential must be there.

They determine the average invoice amount, per month and per customer. The larger lenders may turn down an A/R request if there are numerous small invoices scattered among many customers. If the A/R are all small, but good, they often raise their quoted interest rate to cover administration.

They consider the nature of the receivables. Are the products perishables? Are they useless until some other company completes them? Is the receivable for services rendered rather than for a product? Although difficult receivables are sometimes financed, the rate charged is derived from the risk taken. The larger lenders (who generally charge lower rates) usually pass these up—forcing you to use the higher-rate lenders.

Service invoices are very difficult to finance. For instance, there may be offsets to the receivable because a service rep damages the customer's equipment or property. Many A/R lenders refuse to consider service-type receivables.

What are the standard invoice terms? Is there long-term dating involved? Lenders generally will not disqualify the receivables based on long-term due dates, but the hazards of collection increase risk, and up goes the rate!

They do a preliminary survey of your A/R, usually right off the aging you will be required to provide. If you have not regularly maintained an accounts receivable aging of some sort, this may be a contributory cause of problems and the need to borrow! An aging is a definite assist to sound receivables management. A useful format for an aging can be found in Figure 8-1 at the end of this chapter. The illustration includes suggestions for effectively using our aging worksheets.

Most lenders will check the individual accounts in Dun & Bradstreet, entering their rating next to each account. If your A/R consists of mostly unrated or unlisted accounts, up goes the rate! Larger A/R lenders will not consider loaning on your numerous small, unknown creditors.

The lender's account executive, perhaps with the credit manager in tow, will usually come to your place of business and make an on-the-spot inspection. They are now primarily concerned with your accounts receivable controls, your manufacturing, shipping, and invoicing procedures—your overall managerial systems.

After your business and your individual accounts have passed all the preliminary tests, the lender gives tentative credit approval. Then the lender has one or more of his auditors come to your place of business.

You have already agreed to open your books, and those auditors do just that—right down to the journal entries. The audit is extensive, often covering all financial statement entries unless they were CPA-audited, but they concentrate on your accounts receivables.

Every receivable is scrutinized as to past performance. All receivables are graded to some degree. Disproportionately large or key receivables are fully credit-investigated. Using their own grading criteria, lenders will declare certain receivables ineligible, meaning that the lender will not advance on them, sometimes even when they are paying as agreed.

The lenders are particularly concerned about how your receivables are turning. They want to know how long your customers take to pay your invoices, on average. You should be equally cognizant of the importance of this measurement. Figured in relation to your sales and normal invoice terms, the lenders use a common formula to determine A/R turnover. Good management practice requires constant watch of receivables performance. Slow turnover is costly. Whether you are borrowing against your receivables or not, it is useful to know the cost of excess days over your normal invoice terms. If you are borrowing on your A/R, every day an invoice remains unpaid costs in interest. Our two-part form (Fig. 8-2) will aid you in making these calculations.

The lender assembles all of the data, and the account executive and the credit manager or committee then decide on the final interest rate and the amount they will advance. The first advance will consist of how much cash they will pay or make available to your for your existing, eligible receivables. In some cases, you may decide not to draw down the full amount approved, keeping it available as future needs occur.

The lender also decides what percentage will be advanced on each invoice presented to them during the course of each succeeding month thereafter. They decide how long you must commit to this A/R borrowing, what the minimum usage should be, and what legal and handling procedures are to be followed.

Typically, the account executive returns to your office with this contract. Most contracts will require you to remain with the lender for six months to a year. The lender can cut you off, but usually you do not have reciprocal cutoff privileges during the contract term.

The term is most frequently for a full year, which is generally fair, because the lender has quite an administrative investment in setup costs. Although the rate may range from 2% to 5% floating over the prime rate, it takes a few months for the lender to earn back his original investment in investigating, auditors, and paperwork.

After the A/R plan is in place, the costs continue to be higher than servicing a loan or contract. Despite computer assistance, there is extensive paperwork in the posting of payments and in controlling advance requests. Most lenders periodically have their auditors come to your business to at least spot-check your books and invoices. In some cases, they require a full audit every three to six months, and this expensive procedure causes A/R interest rates to remain higher than those for regular borrowing.

The major concern of every lender is the possibility of advancing funds on fraudulent invoices. The fraud can consist of pushing the invoicing, which involves borrowing prior to actual product completion and shipment. Total fraud occurs when invoices are created for nonexistent products sent to a fictional customer or straw company. Because the lenders exercise close audit supervision, few A/R borrowers try to play games. Fewer still actually succeed in defrauding the lender for any length of time or at a loss to the lender.

In setting up the A/R financing, the account executive will provide you or your staff with the necessary forms to maintain the records required. There will be schedules to list the invoices and complete instructions for requesting advances and making loan reductions. The first borrowing is usually completed with the lender's assistance. The schedules of eligible invoices are completed. Whatever promissory notes and loan contracts the lender requires are executed. (Sometimes each loan advance is considered a separate borrowing, requiring a signed promissory note.)

## HOW ACCOUNTS RECEIVABLE FINANCING IS STRUCTURED

Accounts receivable financing can be structured in a number of ways, but all generally follow a similar pattern. There are variances in customer notification or nonnotification, in the manner in which payments are made from customer to lender, and the amounts lenders advance. There is also terminology peculiar to A/R financing. We will go through these varying structures, explaining the more common applications and providing insight as to rates and the computation of finance charges.

### To Notify or Not to Notify

A/R financing programs take one of two forms.

NOTIFICATION The lender advises your customer you have assigned your invoices to him under a financing agreement and requests that payment be sent directly to him. As borrower, you remain responsible if your customer does not pay.

The notification method is not used as often today as it was in the early days, from about 1940 to around 1965. There are still cases in which it is used because the borrower prefers it that way in the belief that customers will pay the financer more readily than they will his company. Sometimes lenders will not make the loan unless they can notify and institute direct collection, thus maximizing their control. There are industries or commercial businesses where notification is the accepted, prevailing practice.

NONNOTIFICATION The method most businesses prefer is to borrow on A/R without their customers' being advised or made aware. Most customers never know about the arrangement.

As borrower, you will be making the collections as agent for the lender. You're collecting the lender's money—at least to the extent of the advances. So don't think an accounts receivable loan will relieve you of collection problems. This is still your full responsibility; the lender merely keeps track, along with you.

### Invoice Advances

The original accounts receivable agreement always stipulates the maximum percentage amount the lender will loan on the face value of your invoices. The most lenders will advance is 90% of the face value of the invoices of eligible customers. The average maximum advance is around 80%. The lenders' reasoning is that they do not wish to advance your profits, just your costs.

Sometimes the advance is pushed down to as little as 65%, which could prove too restrictive for the borrower. The borrower's problem with such a low advance is that less than the actual costs are covered, hence, cash problems are not alleviated.

The borrower, working within the established advance maximum, may pledge any A/R that the lender has cleared as eligible. In some cases, you may choose not to pledge certain invoices if the funds are not needed. In other arrangements to reduce borrowing, you can reduce the percentage advance requested.

Under most arrangements, when cash is needed, the borrower simply lists the invoices on the lender's standardized schedule form. The lender deposits the funds to the borrower's account or advances the cash for the borrower's discretionary use. Effectively, the usual A/R plan gives the lender a lien on all receivables generated by the borrower, borrowed against or not.

After a borrower is well established with a lender and has maintained a good record of A/R handling, if a temporary need for additional cash arises, the lender may agree to an overadvance. This usually entails a temporary increase in the agreed percentage advanced.

Lenders will not want to do this too readily, nor too often, because they may become overinvested in the account and later encounter trouble with the borrower should he be unable to pay off his advances as agreed.

Borrowers should avoid an A/R agreement requiring credit clearance on each individual invoice. You want a blanket deal. You want to be able to assign every invoice for shipped product. The only exception is those customers originally declared ineligible, who are still slow-paying.

Lenders may also impose individual account limits—which they will watch. This can be an assist to you in not getting in too deep with one particular customer, especially one who is not financially strong.

## Equity Adjustments

Upon collection of the accounts, the lender generally receives a larger amount than the percentage advanced. However, invoice payments from customers will sometimes be less than the original invoice because of returns, allowances, and discounts. This is not a problem and is worked out in the accounting procedure.

The excess—invoice payments in excess of lender's advance—is known as equity. The equities generated are credited to the A/R borrower's account. There are four usual means of paying the equity to the A/R borrower:

1. Applied on account to reduce the amount of funds advanced to client, especially if the advances exceed the percentage called for by the agreement.
2. Immediately transmitted to the client by check.
3. Accumulated and transmitted periodically.
4. Applied on account to reduce the advance until the client no longer requires financing.

## Computing Charges

There are several methods of computing your interest or finance charges:

1. Straight interest on the amount of funds advanced, expressed as a rate per annum, per month, or per diem.
2. A commission charged on the accounts assigned, plus interest on the funds advanced.

   The logic behind the commission is that the borrower may not fully utilize the approved loan—he may not pledge all the approved eligible accounts. The commission is said to be a more accurate reflection of the costs of setting up and maintaining the account in the lender's system.

3. Charges expressed as a percentage of the average balance of the collateral assigned.
4. A minimum charge, levied up front or charged each month, as assurance the borrower will meet expenses for initiating and servicing the account.
5. Graduated, decreasing rates as borrowings increase. This option is fair and should be negotiated originally, because the lender's operating costs decrease as dollars advance. If you anticipate significantly increased sales, be sure to work out lowered interest rates, based on volume assigned to the lender.

## Rates Charged

A/R financing rates vary widely, but they are consistently somewhat higher than other financing alternatives. Despite heavier reliance on computers, there is still extensive paperwork involved in handling thousands of invoices, pages of schedules, and the inevitable labor-intensive "policing" (auditing of the borrowers). These costs are always reflected in the borrower's rate. Because A/R financing involves soft collateral, the lender has a greater risk than loaning against machinery or real estate, and this is reflected in higher average rates.

Because of the increased risk, many A/R lenders, including banks as well as the high binders, will go after other assets to further secure their advances.

BANK A/R RATE CHARGES To discuss rates charged, it is necessary to talk about averages. But there are banks that like A/R financing and find it profitable. It attracts and keeps checking accounts and other depositary relationships.

You will probably pay lower rates if you can locate a local bank that is already involved in A/R financing. The local bank will usually reduce your float time, because incoming monies spend less time in the mails or other forms of transport and thus less time being applied to your loan balance.

Banks charge from an average "low low" of 1½% over prime rate for heavy volume accounts with strongly eligible customer receivables and which maintain consistently large checking account balances.

Banks are fairly consistent in offering graduated rates based on the monthly flow of invoices pledged, even applying differing rates with fluctuations in advances requested. The A/R agreement may state it thus: $500,000 in advances—2% over prime rate; $300,000 in advances—3%; $100,000—4%; or variations on this theme.

You should definitely negotiate for some type of rate decrease based on increasing volume. The lender's average cost per dollar advanced goes down as volume goes up.

FINANCE COMPANY A/R RATES The major finance companies, including the giants who specialize in factoring and accounts receivable financing, generally charge somewhat more than the banks. However, in some cases, they may meet or get close to the "low low" of the banks when they service a client with subsidiaries or branch operations in widely scattered cities—a service banks usually are unable to offer.

Major finance companies and those specializing in A/R financing charge about 2½% over prime rate for the largest borrowers, up to 6% over prime for others. If the major company is willing to handle small average monthly advances, the rates may go up to 10 points over prime rate.

Sometimes it is worthwhile to pay the higher finance company rate if the company will advance a greater percentage. Accounts receivable financing can be a losing proposition if the advance percentage is very much below your cost of production or wholesale cost.

Sometimes, because of these companies' expertise and computerized posting, the resulting reduced float time and more rapid reduction of your loan balance will cut your net cost below the bank's lower stated rate.

SMALL A/R FINANCE COMPANIES Some of these specialized lenders are definitely in the high-binder rate area, preying on the unfortunate business person who desperately tries to stay afloat in a business that must ultimately go down.

The incidence of A/R lenders' capitalizing on the misfortunes of a failing business person who has pledged all the company's assets only to see the business ultimately seized by the lender and sold at a profit by a cooperating auctioneer appears to have greatly diminished in recent years. Business people have improved somewhat in their caution and sophistication.

Lenders now seem to prefer avoiding time-consuming problems—auctions, repossessions, the courts—and are concentrating their marketing and ultimate credit approvals on borrowers who show probability of successful A/R financing. They look for those borrowers that A/R financing will help, possibly leading to their graduation to less costly sources.

Some borrowers, despite high interest costs, eventually work out of A/R borrowings entirely. There are thousands of businesses in profitable operation today that owe their survival to a workable accounts receivable plan.

Despite their high rates, many of the smaller A/R lenders do render a valuable service to businesses that properly utilize their funding. Those who enter A/R financing must take some very positive steps towards the time they can either graduate to a lower-cost lender or pay off the lender and return to their bank for short-term borrowings only when cash shortages occur. Interest costs up to 30% are a staggering burden for most businesses that are obliged to compete with others in the same industry which do not have those high interest costs.

## What's Good About Small A/R Lenders?

1. When you are confronted with the grim reality of needing them, it may be a signal to take a close look at your complete business operation—especially your pricing policies and your receivables controls.
2. When you turn to A/R financing, it is essential for you to develop and work consistently with a cash forecast and a financial plan. Use a projection of financial statement form as a guide in preparing your forecast. Be sure to determine the interest costs of the A/R financing by projecting your average borrowings at the interest rate quoted by the lender.
3. The smaller A/R financing companies will usually finance lower monthly volume flows. They will also tackle more difficult types of products and lower-rated customer lists.
4. Because they are local, they can work more closely with you. Many times, the managers or owner-operators of these small A/R companies are experienced finance people. They have seen all kinds of business operations and can spot problem areas very quickly. Their timely advice can be very helpful.
5. Although you should watch them like a hawk, small A/R lenders are usually very close by. By exerting careful supervision, you can squeeze the float time to a minimum.

Get those receivables collections posted to your loan advance as fast as possible! Do not agree to any long, prestated minimum float time that these small A/R lenders will try to insert in the loan agreement!

Always remember, no matter who your A/R lender source may be, A/R financing is revolving credit, just like Visa or MasterCard: you pay only for the funds in use. You must pay close attention to the lender's application of incoming funds. Use the available funds wisely, only when needed. Those high interest costs can take a heavy bite out of your profits if you or your staff are lackadaisical in flowing the money.

#### Reduce Your A/R Interest Costs

It is true, borrowing against your receivables generally entails higher interest rates than other methods of secured borrowing. As a rule, nonbank A/R financing is higher in cost than the bank plans. Yet, many banks are not equipped for A/R financing or offer it only to heavy monthly volume customers. If your bank does not offer this specialized financing or restricts its financings to larger borrowings, it is still possible to achieve a lower rate by arranging a bank-participation loan. These arrangements, sometimes called split loans, can be instigated by you or your independent A/R finance company.

- Banks will cooperate rather than lose your checking account or other depository relationships.
- Encourage your A/R lender to approach your bank to work out a participation loan. The A/R financer advises the bank how you have performed—or, if you are just starting, how the analysis looks. The lender handles all daily details and provides 50% to 70% of the needed funds; the bank provides the remaining 30% to 50% of the funds, earning a profit with little involvement. The bank's risk is minimized because of the A/R lender's supervision and management expertise.
- Encourage your bank to meet with the A/R lender to work out a plan. It won't hurt to infer that the bank's cooperation will encourage you to maintain your other banking relationships and not move to another bank. If the bank will put up a portion of the funds, at the usually lower simple interest rates, it will help you to grow out of A/R borrowings or to achieve sufficient monthly volume to qualify for the bank's plan.

The blending of rates to lower net borrowing costs is not uncommon between banks and finance companies in A/R financing or other secured loans. However, it is often up to you to be the instigator and press both the bank and the outside A/R lender to get together. Sometimes the bank and lender are made comfortable by dividing the risk and the investment and will do things neither would do individually. If A/R financing looks too expensive, consider a participation plan before dismissing this financing alternative.

## PROBLEMS AND PITFALLS OF ACCOUNTS RECEIVABLE FINANCING

High finance costs can be a continuing deterrent to using A/R financing. Because there is likely to be wider rate variances in this financial service, it requires more vigilance and negotiating.

We suggest that you pursue the best possible lenders and do a real shopping trip before agreeing to *any* A/R financing. Once you have negotiated the most satisfactory rate and terms, watch out for these other pitfalls:

### The Float

- Be sure the lender is as close to your business as possible, if you are going to first receive your customer's payments and then transmit them to the lender for credit to your loan.
- A lock box at which the lender actually receives your customer's payments may shorten the posting time.
- Several days float time before the payments are posted and your loan balance reduced can add up to big bucks. For whatever reason, if you can find a lender that minimizes the float, you can pay a slightly higher rate and come out ahead. Those two to five extra float days can make A/R financing an impossible burden which cannot be recovered by product price increases.

### UCC Filing

A/R lenders, especially the smaller ones, do everything they can do to secure themselves. Read the UCC form they will present for your signature.

These lenders will really do a "kitchen-sink" filing on you if you let them. They are entitled to filing against your products and the proceeds from those products, along with a blanket filing statement on your A/R. But are they entitled to a security interest in your inventory—"all machinery now owned or hereafter acquired," "all furniture, fixtures, and other personal property"? Not necessarily! And especially not if you did not specifically agree to these as additional security.

If you later try to buy machinery, using your existing equipment as partial or full down payment (collateral pledged in lieu of cash) or borrow money against your machinery or other personal property assets, subsequent lenders will search the UCC filings and discover the priority interest of your A/R lender. They may decide to back off and not lend or finance your new request. Or, they will at least be obliged to request that the A/R lender subordinate his security interest to *their* proposed UCC filing for the specific machinery or other assets they are lending upon.

What if the A/R lender refuses to subordinate, saying he doesn't want you to buy or borrow and jeopardize his loans? Your needed loan or financing may just never happen! And it's very difficult, if not impossible, to locate a lender who will fail to run a search these days, especially when they learn you are borrowing on your A/R!

## REASONS FOR A/R FINANCING

Modern borrowing techniques now include accounts receivable financing as a permanent part of a business's funding. In certain industries, particularly retail businesses, A/R financing, coupled with computerized accounting, is often the only solution to handling million-dollar monthly invoicing or charge sales.

On the other hand, if you are in a business or industry in which very few of your competitors finance their invoiced sales, you must be prepared for reduced profits unless the A/R cash availability aids in your growth or provides you with other savings.

There may be instances when you are sitting there with several hundred thousand dollars in eligible, unfinanced receivables and you locate some modern, labor-saving machinery at bargain-basement prices—provided you can pay cash. Or, perhaps you find some raw materials you will soon be needing, at great savings, if you pay cash.

When you analyze the borrowing situation, compare interest costs and long-term borrowing repayments; you may discover borrowing on your receivables is the best way. It may be quicker and easier, and, in some cases, the only way, because your unencumbered A/R may be your strongest, most liquid collateral.

In such cases, A/R borrowing may make good sense. The high interest costs are mitigated or erased by the cash savings generated by the bargain-priced machinery or raw materials.

Other common reasons for using A/R financing are:

- It avoids dilution of your ownership interests. Why bring in outside capital or sell off your shares or personal business interest when needed money is sitting there in your A/R?
- It avoids long-term debt. Why get strung out on long payment terms, often at high interest rates, when you can handle your needs out of your A/R flow? A/R borrowing can usually be terminated at the end of one year.
- It provides instant operating cash.
- It increases turnover of your working capital.
- It improves return on your invested capital.
- It can improve your credit rating. If you use A/R advances wisely, tailored to your business, you can reestablish your credit standing.
- Good A/R financers can provide you with useful advice and technical assistance. The management personnel who handle receivables financing, analyzing all manner of businesses and the flow of cash through them, are constantly up-to-date on modern management techniques. Use their advice and expertise to your advantage.
- Financing your A/R can lead to other good things. A/R financing often involves frequent personal contact with the lender. You can build up a position of respect and cooperation through these daily or weekly contacts.

If you perform well, manage the receivable program, and squeeze the most out of it, the lender will introduce you to other lenders—or open his own doors—to machinery financing or leasing, long-term loans, a participation plan, any of which could take you to a better bank.

FIGURE 8-1

# ACCOUNTS RECEIVABLE AGING

| ACCT. NO. | ACCOUNT NAME | TOTAL AMT. DUE | AMOUNT CURRENT | AMOUNTS 31-60 DAYS | AMOUNTS 61-90 DAYS | AMOUNTS 91-120 DAYS | AMOUNTS over 120 DAYS |
|---|---|---|---|---|---|---|---|
| | | | | | | | |

YOUR BEST DEAL comments:

This Aging and Worksheet is a suggested format intended for GUIDANCE PURPOSES, to assist you in setting up a form suitable to YOUR BUSINESS.

- If you do not have account numbers, tied to a computer or for bookkeeping purposes, this column can be omitted.

  However, we suggest you establish numbers for FUTURE use when going to a computer . . . or to facilitate posting . . . for ease of customer reference . . . to establish confidentiality . . . to facilitate accounting and/or A/R financing.

- Account or Customer Name. Customer Name or Account Name . . . a matter of preference. When it comes to the actual listing . . . it should be alphabetically arranged. Names can be handwritten, so long as legible to everyone concerned. If dealing with the same accounts over and over . . . it is better to type them . . . make copies . . . adding new ones to the end of the list and later bringing into correct alphabetical order.

- Total Amount Due. This column is the total of all billings made to the account . . . including amounts past due. Businesses put different headings on this column . . ."Total Billings". . . "Total Invoiced" . . . "Full Balance Due" . . . "Amount Invoiced to Date" etc.

- Amount "Current". This column is intended to show invoiced billings that are not PAST DUE when the entries are made . .(such as the end of each month). Businesses generally "head-up" this column simply as "Current".

- Amounts 31-60 Days Past Due. This column assumes your standard terms are Net 30 days. Balances past that date are moved into this or older columns. These columns can be headed simply "31-60", "61-90", etc.

FIGURE 8-1 (continued)

# WORKSHEET FOR ACCOUNTS RECEIVABLE AGING

| CONTACT DATA | SPECIAL TERMS AGREED | 1st Week COLLECTION ACTION | 2nd Week COLLECTION ACTION | 3rd Week COLLECTION ACTION |
|---|---|---|---|---|
| | | | | |

Naturally, if your standard terms are DIFFERENT . . . the headings must be changed. Some businesses have standard terms of 7 days, 10 days, 60 days etc. So the columns after "Current" should be modified to suit your business.

- Contact Data. This column is a suggestion, when using your A/R Aging as a worksheet. Enter here the phone number of the customer and RIGHT person to contact.

- Collection Activity Columns. These columns, shown here in 3 parts . . . are also a suggested format . . . to enter your follow-up calls or letters . . . planned actions or customer promises through time progression. You might wish to eliminate or add columns . . . or post collection activity on an Account Card.

FIGURE 8-2

# AVERAGE COLLECTION PERIOD

## HOW LONG DO YOUR CUSTOMERS TAKE TO PAY?

| | YOUR COMPANY CALCULATIONS | EXAMPLE |
|---|---|---|
| Sales | ______ | $1,825,000. |
| Days in sales period | ______ | 365 |
| Average value of 1 day's sales | ______ | 5,000. |
| Accounts receivable at period's end | ______ | 250,000. |
| Days Sales Outstanding (A/R for period divided by value of 1 day's sales) = | ______ | 50 |
| Selling terms (days) | ______ | 30 |
| Excess days | ______ | 20 |

## WHAT DO THE "EXCESS DAYS" COST YOU?

| | | |
|---|---|---|
| Value of 1 day's sales multiplied by number of excess days | ______ | $ 100,000. |
| Multiplied by assumed interest rate | ______ | 12% |
| Cost of excess | ______ | 12,000. |

*If your business is seasonal, quarterly or monthly figures may be more RELEVANT than annual ones. Simply use a quarter's sales, 90 days, and the receivable balance outstanding at the end of the period to calculate the Days Sales Outstanding.*

# INDEX